W9-AOB-374

RESEARCH IN THE HISTORY OF ECONOMIC THOUGHT AND METHODOLOGY

A Research Annual

RESEARCH IN THE HISTORY OF ECONOMIC THOUGHT AND METHODOLOGY

Series Editors: Warren J. Samuels and Jeff E. Biddle

RESEARCH IN THE HISTORY OF ECONOMIC THOUGHT
AND METHODOLOGY   VOLUME 20-A

RESEARCH IN THE HISTORY OF ECONOMIC THOUGHT AND METHODOLOGY

A Research Annual

EDITED BY

WARREN J. SAMUELS

Department of Economics, Michigan State University,
East Lansing, MI 48824, USA

JEFF E. BIDDLE

Department of Economics, Michigan State University,
East Lansing, MI 48824, USA

2002

JAI
An Imprint of Elsevier Science

Amsterdam – London – New York – Oxford – Paris – Shannon – Tokyo

ELSEVIER SCIENCE Ltd
The Boulevard, Langford Lane
Kidlington, Oxford OX5 1GB, UK

First edition 2002

Library of Congress Cataloging in Publication Data
A catalog record from the Library of Congress has been applied for.

British Library Cataloguing in Publication Data
A catalogue record from the British Library has been applied for.

ISBN: 0-7623-0847-8
ISSN: 0743-4154 (Series)

∞The paper used in this publication meets the requirements of ANSI/NISO Z39.48-1992 (Permanence of Paper).
Printed in The Netherlands.

CONTENTS

v

vi

LIST OF CONTRIBUTORS

David R. Andrews

Department of Economics,
Cazenovia College, New York, USA

Vincent Barnett

Department of Agricultural and Food
Economics, University of Reading, UK

Y. S. Brenner

Faculty of Social Sciences,
University of Utrecht, The Netherlands

Lawrence Busch

Department of Sociology,
Michigan State University, USA

Ken Dennis

Department of Economics,
University of Manitoba, Canada

Véronique Dutraive

Department of Economics,
Lumiére-Lyon 2, France

Geoffrey Gilbert

Department of Economics, Hobart and
William Smith Colleges, New York, USA

William D. Grampp

Law School, University of Chicago, USA

Willie Henderson

School for Professional and Continuing
Education, University of Birmingham, UK

Geoffrey M. Hodgson

Business School, University of
Hertfordshire, UK

J. E. King

Department of Economics and Finance,
La Trobe University, Victoria, Australia

David Laidler

Department of Economics,
University of Western Ontario, Canada

Maria Eugénia Mata   Faculty of Economics,
                             Universidade Nova de Lisbon, Portugal

Thomas Mayer   Department of Economics,
                             University of California-Davis, USA

Anne Mayhew   Department of History,
                             University of Tennessee, USA

F. Taylor Ostrander   Williamstown, Massachusetts, USA

Warren J. Samuels   Department of Economics,
                             Michigan State University, USA

John P. Tiemstra   Department of Economics,
                             Calvin College, Michigan, USA

Rick Tilman   Department of Economics,
                             University of Nevada-Las Vegas, USA

Vivian C. Walsh   Department of Economics,
                             Muhlenberg College, USA

A. M. C. Waterman   Department of Economics,
                             St. John's College, Winnipeg, Canada

Murray Wolfson   Department of Economics,
                             California State University, Fullerton, USA

EDITORIAL BOARD

xi

ACKNOWLEDGMENTS

The editors wish to express their gratitude for assistance in the review process and other consultation to the members of the editorial board and to the following persons:

Stephan Böhm

Jose Cardoso

Richard Dawson

Harald Hagemann

John Tiemstra

Anthony Waterman

'OF WAGES AND PROFIT IN THE DIFFERENT EMPLOYMENTS OF LABOUR AND CAPITAL': PATTERNS OF EXPOSITION AND EXEMPLIFICATION IN ADAM SMITH'S *WEALTH OF NATIONS*

Willie Henderson

In a previous paper, I made an analysis of the first three chapters of the *Wealth of Nations*, looking at Smith's exemplification strategy (Henderson, 2002). In that paper, Smith's strategy was textually explored within the context of overall patterns of his writing, as evidenced in the first three chapters. The study examined the use and type of examples and the structure and language used to develop them. This paper continues to explore Smith's rhetoric. This time a feature that was touched upon in the earlier work – the points of similarity between a modern introductory textbook and the moves made in Smith's writing – is given a more central position. If Smith's text is indeed 'teacherly', how does it compare to a modern introductory textbook?[1]

Superficially there are huge contrasts and at various levels. Smith's text helped establish a discourse community whereas a modern textbook aims to maintain such a community by engaging (young) readers in a deliberate educational process. Smith's text has little in the way of textual inserts that have become such a feature of the modern-day introductory text. Both texts are

Research in the History of Economic Thought and Methodology, Volume 20-A, pages 1–16.
© 2002 Published by Elsevier Science Ltd.
ISBN: 0-7623-0847-8

located in the technological and educated culture of their respective epochs and the *Wealth of Nations* cannot be pressed easily into the textbook mould. It has been seen as a 'monological text' (Brown, 1994) and this may put it into the 18th century genres of lecture and sermon. Textbooks, as such, have evolved from a straightforward reliance on language almost to a dominance of image. The modern-day economics textbook at introductory level is a complex array of language, diagrams, graphs, tables and other visual material.[2] The economics introductory textbook also tends to be encyclopedic and authoritative, features shared by Smith's *Wealth of Nations*. Normally, all Smith has to help sustain his argument is a series of examples constructed and manipulated through language.[3]

Examples are a central buttress to Smith's reasoning. They perform a variety of functions: the illustration and familiarisation of concepts; the illustration and analysis of small-scale problems within case studies (real or imagined); historical case study for analysis ('conjectural' and authentic); the stimulation of the economic imagination and as a source of evidence. But even in a modern-day textbook it is necessary for the reader to enter into the imaginary world of the writer. In a modern text book, it is words such a 'suppose', 'assume', 'consider' and 'take' that help signal hypothetical or partial conditions (Henderson & Hewings, 1987). Smith also uses such language, though in limited ways, and partial and hypothetical situations are present in his writing. Smith makes considerable use of 'suppose' in ways that have parallels in modern-day textbooks. Each of the other verbs is hardly used at all in the modern sense.[4] Furthermore, Smith's text is not organised by headings and sub-headings. So how does Smith signal stages in an argument? What about examining structure and process, or the pattern of argument? The paper will conclude that, although there are many differences, there is, nonetheless, a family resemblance between Smith's writing and that of a modern-day introductory textbook.

Chapter Ten, Book one, of the *Wealth of Nations* is the penultimate chapter in Book One. Its position, from our knowledge of modern textbooks, suggests that it is likely to be more complex than the strategically important opening chapters. Its 'macro' structure is visibly more complex as it consists of two parts proceeded by a two paragraph introduction.[5] Part One consists of an exploration of 'Inequalities arising from the Nature of Employments themselves'. Part Two consists of an exploration of 'Inequalities by the Policy of Europe'. The first part is concerned with the development of principles, and their illustration in the context of particular trades, and the second part is setting out to explore issues of 'policy' concerning apprenticeships. Given this, it may be possible to detect a different pattern in the use and familiarisation of principles and examples when the rhetorical structure of the first part is compared to that of the second part. A close analysis may provide insight relevant to the wider division in the *Wealth of Nations* between the books concerned with principles and those concerned with practice. The structure of the chapter may also allow something to be said about argumentation when Smith is writing on 'theory' and when he is evaluating 'practice'.

THE INTRODUCTION

The introduction is composed of three paragraphs. Only the first of which is subject, here, to close analysis. What is interesting is the tightly constructed nature of the writing. There is a lot going on in a very small piece of text.

> The whole of the advantages and disadvantages of the different employments of labour and stock must, in the same neighbourhood, be either perfectly equal or continually tending to equality. [Sentence 1] If in the same neighbourhood, there was any employment evidently either more or less advantageous than the rest, so many people would crowd into it in the one case, and so many would desert it in the other, that its advantages would soon return to the level of other employments. [Sentence 2] This at least would be the case in a society where things were left to follow their natural course, where there was perfect liberty, and where every man was perfectly free both to choose what occupation he thought proper, and to change it as often as he thought proper. [Sentence 3] Every man's interest would prompt him to seek the advantageous, and to shun the disadvantageous employment. [Sentence 4]

Sentence one: This is a statement of a principle or proposition delivered as a strong, clear statement that the rest of the chapter is going to support and justify. Notice that Smith is concerned with the 'whole of the advantages and dis-advantages' though he does not say what this means. He does not specify any particular neighbourhood: the location is perfectly general.

Sentence two: Notice the if/ 'implied' then structure – the then is not present but would be placed before the so. The construct is used much later: 'If colliers, therefore, commonly earn double and triple the wages of common labour, it ought not to seem unreasonable that coal-heavers should sometimes earn four or five times those wages'. The use of the 'if/ 'implied then' has the same function as it has in modern day economic texts, to illustrate, in the context of a problem developed in relation to a principle, how that problem would be resolved. The 'advantage-disadvantage' pattern of the first sentence is maintained and developed in the second. This is a small-scale textual episode that matches a small-scale 'problem-solution' pattern, already identified in modern-day textbooks.

Sentence three: Notice the strength of 'natural course' and 'perfect liberty'. Notice too that Smith defines what is meant by 'prefect liberty' in terms of choice in employment. This is a condition that must be fulfilled if the resolution is to be possible. The second paragraph starts by looking 'everywhere in Europe' where the condition does not hold, so the 'compare and contrast pattern' i.e. between principles and practice (a variety of the 'advantages and disadvantages pattern) is also suggested.

Sentence four: This is a behavioural implication of the condition and illustrates how the initial proposition would be realised. It is perfectly general: 'every man'.

The introductory passage shares many of the elements expected from an introductory passage in a modern day economic textbook. It pre-organises what is to come, in more abstract language than is found later in the main body of the text. Thus, there is exemplification but it is not spelled out in terms of specifics: the meaning of significant elements such as 'the whole of the advantages . . .' is not fully explained: 'things' are not 'left to follow their natural course'. None of this becomes full apparent until the text is read in detail. It summarises what is to come in terms of the significant principles and prepares the reader for the conceptual elements. It announces the way in which the text is organised: 'The particular consideration of those circumstances and of that policy will divide this chapter into two parts'. This short sentence is an example of Smith's economy as a writer: 'circumstances' refers back to 'certain circumstances in the employments themselves' (stated in the previous paragraph and the focus of the greater part of Part One). Also, 'that policy' refers back to the 'policy of Europe', in the previous paragraph, and suggest the content of Part Two.[6]

'INEQUALITIES ARISING FROM THE NATURE OF EMPLOYMENTS THEMSELVES'

Although there is, initially, a clear signal only for the first part of Part One, it could be argued that the section is divided into two. The first half is an elaboration of five considerations that influence wages whereas the second part looks at the role of expectations and 'the chance of gain'. However, Smith, in effect, divides probability of qualifying from probability of success once so qualified.

The opening paragraph carries forward the pattern of an introduction that is concerned with principles. But in contrast to the overarching principle already given, the introductory paragraph lists a set of circumstances, treated in numerical order in the paragraphs that follow, that influence pecuniary gains.

> The five following are the principal circumstances which, so far as I have been able to observe, make up for a small pecuniary gain in some employments, and counterbalance a great one in others: first, the agreeableness or disagreeableness of the employments themselves; secondly, the easiness and cheapness, or the difficulty and expense of learning

them; thirdly, the constancy and inconstancy of employment in them; fourthly, the small or great trust which must be reposed in those who exercise them; and, fifthly, the probability or improbability of success in them.

The means of signaling what is to follow is a numerical one and Smith sticks to the set of numbers. As the overarching principle deals with 'advantages and disadvantages' so to does each of the five 'principal circumstances'. The list is a central organisational feature not only for the identification of the main sections that follow but also for the internal organisation of each. Only instances from one and two will be analysed in detail.[7]

Two long and one short paragraph contain the elaboration of Smith's first circumstance. Although the circumstance is repeated, it is not repeated word for word for 'agreeableness or disagreeableness' becomes further elaborated: 'the wages of labour vary with the ease or hardship, the cleanliness or dirtiness, the honourableness or dishonourableness of the employment'. Three pairs of considerations are then matched to a hierarchy of examples. Smith is careful to consider a number of examples in a slightly more sophisticated way that might be predicted from the pattern already introduced. The wages of a 'journeyman tailor' are compared with those of a 'journeyman weaver' (the reader is instructed to 'take the year round'). The tailor earns less because his work is easier. 'A journeyman weaver earns less than a journeyman smith. His work is not always easier but it is much cleaner.' 'His' refers backwards at each level to the first element in the comparison, throughout this section. As the move up the linked hierarchy goes, each example becomes progressively more complex that the previous set: 'A journeyman blacksmith, though an artificer, seldom earns so much in twelve hours as a collier, who is only a labourer, does in eight. His work is not quite so dirty, is less dangerous, and is carried on in daylight, and above ground.' Smith's identification of the worker with his work serves to add to the authenticity of the examples. Smith returns to the example of collier later, under 'fourthly' when he combines the 'inconstancy of employment' with 'hardship' and other negative aspects.

The examples here conform to the rule-example pattern found in the opening chapters of the work. They are also tightly written.

'Honour' is hardly dealt with at all in this section – Smith will deal with it 'by and by' – though 'disgrace' is elaborated upon with some detail. To deal with 'disgrace', Smith's examples are the 'butcher' ('a brutal and odious business'), the 'public executioner' and 'fishermen'. In the last example Smith comments on how fishing in an advanced society becomes an 'agreeable amusement', rather than a difficult and disagreeable chore. In the final paragraph of this section Smith extends the notion from wages to 'profit on stock' citing the example of innkeeper ('never master of his own house and who is exposed to the brutality of every drunkard'). Although this intention to treat the links between wages and profits on stock is made in the overall introduction, it is not signaled in the introduction to Part One. Here there is an influence. In circumstances two, three and four, no influence is detected by Smith.

The second circumstance is introduced by a very minor rephrasing of the original heading. What is of greater interest is the second paragraph where a principle not as far as I can see derived from the previous chapter is introduced as a 'known':

> When an expensive machine is erected the extraordinary work to be performed by it before it is worn out, it must be expected, will replace the capital laid out upon it, with at least the ordinary profits. [Sentence 1] A man educated at the expense of much labour and time to any of those employments which require extraordinary dexterity and skill, may be compared to one of those expensive machines. [Sentence 2] The work which he learns to perform, it must be expected, will replace to him the whole expense of his education, with at least the ordinary profits of an equally valuable capital. [Sentence 3] It must do this, too, in a reasonable time, regard being had to the very uncertain duration of human life, in the same manner as to the more certain duration of the machine. [Sentence 4]

What happens here is that a proposition is put forward about machines and then an educated man is compared to 'one of those expensive machines'. Notice the parallelisms:

> When an expensive machine is erected the extraordinary work to be performed, it must be expected, will replace the capital laid out upon it, with at least the ordinary profits. [Sentence 1]
>
> The work which he learns to perform, it must be expected, will replace to him the whole expense of his education, with at least the ordinary profits of an equally valuable capital. [Sentence 3]

Consider also the significance of the phrase 'it must be expected' – By whom?; As a matter of reason?; As a matter of common sense? What is the force of the 'must'? Is Smith asking us to take his word for it? The expression 'must be expected' is rare in the *Wealth of Nations*.

The rhetorical argument leads to a new principle: 'The difference between the wages of skilled labour and those of common labour is founded upon this principle'.

The first section of Part One look as if it ends at the twenty-second paragraph. The second section starts at the twenty-third paragraph. This is a transitional paragraph in that Smith has just dealt with talents and abilities and he is going on to discuss 'chance of gain'. He makes the transition through the self-evaluation people make of their abilities. It is worth quoting the paragraph in full:

The overweening conceit which the greater part of men have in their own abilities is an ancient evil remarked by philosophers of all ages. [Sentence 1] Their absurd presumption in their own good fortunes has been less taken notice of. [Sentence 2] It is, however, if possible, still more universal. [Sentence 3] There is no man living who, when in tolerable health and spirits, has not some share of it. [Sentence 4] The chance of gain is by every man more or less overvalued, and the chance of loss is by most men undervalued, and by scarce any man, who is in tolerable health and spirits, valued more than its worth. [Sentence 5]

The first sentence refers back to the preceding paragraph that is concerned primarily with individual talents. The next sentence, sentence two, introduces the evaluation of 'their own good fortune' making a link of sorts with the notice taken of the 'conceit' by ancient philosophers. The next two sentences (i.e. three and four) elaborate on the 'presumption of their own good fortune'. The paragraph ends (sentence five) with the organising idea for the next section: 'The chance of gain is by every man more or less overvalued, and the chance of loss more or less under-valued, and by scarce any man, who is in tolerable health and spirits, valued more than it is worth'. Smith, then, by a series of awkward manipulations introduces at the end of the paragraph, the new topic that is developed over the next six paragraphs: 'The chance of gain is by every man more or less overvalued . . .'. The problem of such transitions is not one that modern writers need face too often: a new topic can be easily introduced by a new heading.

Smith gathers together the argument:

Of the five circumstances, therefore, which vary the wages of labour, two only affect the profits of stock; the agreeableness or disagreeableness of the business, and the risk or security with which it is attended. In point of agreeableness, there is little or no difference in the far greater part of the different employments of stock; but a great deal in those of labour; and the ordinary profit of stock, though it rises with the risk, does not always seem to rise in proportion to it. It should follow from this, that, in the same society or neighbourhood, the average and ordinary rates of profit should be more nearly upon a level than the pecuniary wages of the different sorts of labour. They are so accordingly. The difference between the earnings of a common labourer and those of a well employed lawyer or physician, is evidently much greater than that between the ordinary profits in any two different branches of trade. The apparent difference, besides, in the profits of different trades, is generally a deception arising from our not always distinguishing what ought to be considered as wages, from what ought to be considered as profit.

So out of five possible influences, only two are relevant to a consideration of 'the profits of stock' and only one is likely to have some influence on 'stock'. Smith then modifies the force of both of these influences on the returns to stock and traces out an implication: 'It should follow from this . . .'. Smith then asserts 'They are so accordingly.' No evidence is supplied for this authoritative claim. His overall conclusion is that in considering returns in various employments it is necessary to distinguish 'what ought to be considered as wages, from what ought to be considered as profit'. The next four paragraphs are spent exemplifying specific contexts in which it is necessary to distinguish 'profit' from 'wages'.

The last long section is introduced at paragraph thirty-six by the following:

> The five circumstances above mentioned, though they occasion considerable inequalities in the wages of labour and profits of stock, occasion none in the whole of the advantages and disadvantages, real or imaginary, of the different employments of either. The nature of those circumstances is such that they make up for a small pecuniary gain in some, and counterbalance a great one in others.

We must remind ourselves that this is, according to the pre-organising section of the chapter, a central proposition. The elements of this paragraph can be found in several places earlier in the chapter: 'the whole of the advantages and disadvantages of the different employments of labour and stock' (initial sentence in the initial paragraph of the chapter as a whole); 'certain circumstances in the employments . . ., make up for a small pecuniary gain in some, and counter-balance a great one in others'(paragraph two in the pre-organising section); 'particular circumstances . . . make up for a small pecuniary gain in some employments and counterbalance a great one in others'. But Smith does not tell us any where in the chapter thus far what he means, precisely, so far as I can see, by 'the whole of their advantages and disadvantages'. In the next paragraph Smith uses the phrase 'the whole of their advantages or disadvantages' though this 'or' may be simply a slip of the pen.

That the phrase implies some long term equilibrium, there is no doubt. This is signaled in the first paragraph of the introduction. From the way in which the 'equality' is set up in language then it is clear that the equilibrium is influenced by factors external to the consideration of the particular circumstances of labour. Smith lists the factors:

> First, the employments must be well known and long established in the neighbourhood; secondly, they must be in their ordinary, or what might be called their natural state; and, thirdly, they must be the sole or principal employments of those who occupy them.

This list becomes the basic organisational pattern for the rest of the chapter, with each proposition repeated at the head of each relevant section, any elaboration in the proposition being restricted to what is necessary to make it a short but free-standing, single sentence paragraph. For example: 'First, this equality can take place only in those employments which are well known, and have been long established in the neighbourhood.' This is repeated immediately after small-scale pre-organising section, exemplified above. A modern-day textbook would have used headings and subheadings.

Thus, 'long established' leads to a discussion, built around competitive conditions and enticements, of the influence of new and old industry on wages. The pattern of wages is influenced by competitive conditions within each industry. Manufacturers of items dictated by 'fashion and fancy' (the implication is the need to keep innovating) are contrasted with those in which demand arises 'from necessity'. Smith refrains from providing a list of contrast examples but cites Birmingham as a place where the demand is based upon 'fancy' and Sheffield where it is based upon 'necessity' (these are illustrations of two contrasting neighbourhoods within each of which conditions are deemed to be the same throughout). The assumption is that target readers would know something of the activities found in each of the two places. New kinds of manufacturing business disrupt 'the whole of the advantages and disadvantages' i.e. the nature of the equilibrium. In the rest of the chapter, Smith elaborates on the other two points using a whole range of examples though these are not, perhaps, as focused as the examples used in the opening parts of the chapter. Part One, perhaps suffers from a structure in which the first half is clear, concrete and limited and the second part, of much greater significance for what is to come is less focused. The concept of 'the whole balance of the advantages and disadvantages' is essential to the development of Part Two.

THE RHETORIC OF PART TWO: INEQUALITIES BY THE POLICY OF EUROPE

Part One establishes the general set of principles from the specific building up to the general whereby inequalities 'in the whole of the advantages and disadvantages of the different employments of labour and stock' can be analysed and understood. Part Two is devoted to a consideration of 'the policy of Europe'. Part Two is comprehensive and authoritative. A detailed analysis will be made of the first section only.

In many ways the division of the two parts and the internal organisation of each reflects the structure of an introductory chapter of a modern day text-book. In such a text book, the simple theoretical equipment is set out; terms are defined and socialised; exemplifications are provided and carried sometimes in very small-scale applications. In the later part of the chapter, more sophisticated applications are made and this is true for the later chapters in the textbook where problems of greater complexity are treated. Part Two is an investigation of policy and its evaluation from the point of view of the theoretical principles and the 'advantages and disadvantages of the different employments'. However its opening paragraph should be examined:

Such are the inequalities in the whole of the advantages and disadvantages of the different employments of labour and stock, which the defect of any of the three requisites above mentioned may occasion, even where there is the most perfect liberty. But the policy of Europe, by not leaving things at perfect liberty, occasions other inequalities of much greater importance.

The first sentence is a summary of the conclusions from Part One. Part One ends without a concluding statement. The subject matter of Part Two is to be found in the second sentence of the opening paragraph and it is this sentence that is expanded upon in the second paragraph.

The 'list' continues to be system of organisation within which material is organised. The list is, of course, a prototype 'heading and subheading' method of textual organisation, especially as used by Smith. There are several lists: the most significant is the first one to which we are introduced as it is under the three headings supplied with in the list that 'policy' and its disturbing effects are considered. There are lists in evidence within some of the component parts of the list and a list is used to round the chapter off. In this respect at the 'macro' level the textual organisation is the same as in Part One. However, the organisation of the whole section is substantially different. This can be illustrated by considering the organisation within each main section, signaled by the numbering system 'first', 'secondly' and 'thirdly'.

Under the 'first' consideration, Smith examines the way that 'policy in Europe' restrains competition: 'The exclusive privileges of corporations are the principal means it makes use of for this purpose'. 'It' refers to the 'policy of Europe'. The opening phrase is then repeated in the lead sentence of the paragraph that follows. Smith then provides a paragraph on the general means that 'incorporated trade' uses to restrict competition: 'directly' by restricting the number of apprentices and 'indirectly' by lengthening the life of apprenticeships. There then follows a paragraph of detailed exemplification: 'In Sheffield' 'In Norfolk and Norwich'; 'in England' and 'in London' with trades such as 'master cutler', 'master weaver', 'master hatter', and 'silk weaver'. The pattern is generalisation-exemplification and the exemplifications serve the same role as they do elsewhere in Smith's text: to support and sustain the generalisation. In other words they follow the rule-example pattern and are in a minority in Part Two.

The next paragraph examines the length of apprenticeships (seven years). The general discussion, that also includes Universities, is followed by a series of specific examples: 'By the 5th of Elizabeth'; 'In France; 'In Scotland'. The set of examples here must be enough to justify Smith's reference to the 'policy of Europe'. His actual examples illustrate confusion with respect to the coverage of policy, and, a progressive amelioration of the length of apprenticeships from one country to another. These are not examples of the 'rule-example' type common in Part One but examples woven into a narrative, a set of cases that require further discussion and analysis. These paragraphs examine the status quo and the confusions that exist in particular instances. The content is generally descriptive and historical. The pattern of the four paragraphs is 'general-specific'. The intention is to set up a description of what exists.

The next section is headed by a statement that could come straight out of Locke: 'That property which every man has in his own labour, as it is the original foundation of all other property, so it is the most sacred and inviolable'. This and the rest of the robust paragraph, a microcosm of Enlightenment thinking encompassing Locke and Hume and no doubt others, signals the commencement of Smith's attack on the status quo.[8] The argument is conducted on justice (founded in Enlightenment thinking on property rights and here used by Smith it its widest possible sense) or as Smith puts it 'just liberty'. The issue is the impediments that the law puts in the way of an individual 'working at what he thinks proper' and an employer 'employing whom he thinks proper'.

The next three paragraphs explore the futility of the regulated apprenticeship system to achieve useful ends. 'Insufficient' workmanship is not avoided by long apprenticeships. Other means are required to prevent 'fraud'. Because of the lack of financial reward within apprenticeships it has a negative impact on motivation: this argument in developed over two paragraphs. It is worthwhile exploring one in detail:

> The institution of long apprenticeships has no tendency to form a young people to industry. [Sentence 1] A journeyman who works by the piece is likely to be industrious, because he derives a benefit from every exertion of his industry. [Sentence 2] An apprentice is likely to be idle, and almost always is so, because he has no immediate interest to be otherwise. [Sentence 3] In the inferior employments, the sweets of labour consist altogether in the recompense of labour. [Sentence 4] They who are soonest in a condition to enjoy the sweets of it are likely soonest to conceive a relish for it, and to acquire the early habit of industry. [Sentence 5] A young man naturally conceives an aversion to labour when for a long time he receives no benefit from it. [Sentence 6] The boys who are put out apprentices from public charities are generally bound for more than the usual number of years, and they generally turn out very idle and worthless. [Sentence 7]

The pattern of argumentation is complex and its status as knowledge is problematic. A generalisation (sentence one) is followed by two contrasting examples (sentences two and three). But compare and contrast is not the only aspect for there is also a 'situation-problem-response-solution' pattern that explores apprenticeship motivation. There is some hedging : 'is likely to be' and 'almost always is so'. A further generalisation is made in sentence four, concerning the link between rewards and effort. The pattern of a double, contrasting exemplifications, found at the start of the paragraph, is then repeated in the two sentences that follow (sentences five and six). The final sentence (sentence seven) is an exemplification of the generalisation made in the preceding sentence. There is some hedging: 'generally'. The whole analysis is rhetorically constructed and manipulated in a highly persuasive way. This is a fairly typical example of a small-scale problem-solution pattern in Smith that although it is signaled differently has many of the same elements that are found in the modern-day text.

Smith argues for a short period of training with constant exposure to cost and market considerations. His overall conclusion that such a market-led style of training would lead to 'the work of all artificers coming this way much cheaper to the market'.

The next section (again a long one) starts with a newly stated argument that in part summarises what has gone before but also serves as an introduction to what is to follow. The first part of the sentence points to what has gone before, the second part to what is to come. This is a different kind of transitional strategy to that described above.

> It is to prevent this reduction in price, and consequently of wages and profit, by restraining that free competition which would most certainly occasion it, that all corporations, and the greater part of corporation laws, have been established.

Smith punches home that it is not the regulation of standards but the regulation of the economic context of trade that the 'corporations' are about. This summary as a signal to a new section is used elsewhere by Smith. As corporations are identified with towns in the remainder of the paragraph, Smith then initiates in the set of paragraphs that follow an extensive series of comparisons between the economic conditions in town and country with respect to the possibilities and practicality of incorporation. This is provided together with an analysis of the terms of trade between town and country. The superiority of industry in the towns is partly due to the manipulation of trade through restrictions in the supply.

The final section of first part of the argument starts with a move to an examination of 'other regulations': 'The superiority which the industry of the towns has everywhere in Europe over that of the country is not altogether owing to corporations or corporation laws. It is supported by many other regulations'. The next six paragraphs exemplify a range of regulations, both formal and informal, designed to restrict trade and raise prices.

The structure of the paragraph in this section that begins 'In Great Britain the superiority ...' is curious. For the first half, Smith maintains his formal relationship with the reader that is standard for the work as a whole. In the second half, the author is formally present in the text: 'if I may say so';

I shall endeavour to show hereafter'; 'I shall endeavour to explain as fully as I can . . .'. This is another awkward moment and one not usually found in the modern day text-book. Smith introduces the notion of excessive accumulation in towns spilling its benefits into the countryside. Whilst this capital and opulence 'spreads itself . . . over the face of the land' the growth path is 'in every respect contrary to the order of nature and reason'. The authorial intrusion is motivated by the need to justify the postponement of this significant topic until later in the work.

The concluding paragraph of the section and the opening paragraph of the next section, illustrate together additional ways in which transitions are manipulated:

> It is in this manner that the policy of Europe, by restraining the competition in some employments to a smaller number than would otherwise be disposed to enter into them, occassions a very important inequality in the whole of the advantages and disadvantages of the different employments of labour and stock.
>
> Secondly, the policy of Europe, by increasing the competition in some employments beyond what it naturally would be, occasions another inequality of the opposite kind in the whole of the advantages and disadvantages of the different employments of labour and stock.

A number of processes are in evidence. The phrase 'in this manner' points to what has been argued above; the phrase 'restraining the competition' provides a convenient label for summarising the whole of a very long argument and the 'whole of the advantages and disadvantages ' is the principle concept that is being considered throughout. In the next paragraph, 'secondly' reminds readers of the original organising list, 'by increasing the competition' focus on the topic for the whole section but points out the operational part of the distinction already signaled by 'secondly'. In both Smith's writing and in the modern text-book, summarization would be used, as recapitulation, to mark an end point and to prepare the reader for moving on to new material or a new stage in the argument. The strategy in a modern-day text is likely to be more formally worked out and consistent.

CONCLUSION

An analysis of the use of examples within the general arguments set out in Chapter ten shows that the general pattern of the chapter resembles that of a modern-day introductory text-book. In to-day's text-book, the introduction pre-organises the material to be read in terms that are more abstract than in the body of the text where the work of familiarisation of concepts take place in detail. Once the concepts have been established and familiarized through examples and very small-scale applications, the rest of the chapter tends to make a larger-scale application of the concept or (say) consider policy implications. The first part of an introductory theoretical chapter, then, sets out the relevant terms and concepts. In chapter ten, book one, of the *Wealth of Nations*, the introduction pre-organises the material. The first part of the first section develops a theoretical analysis based in a number of simple categories, these categories are then placed within the wider set of considerations concerning equilibrium conditions, thought still on a theoretical level.

The second part makes an analysis of policy. The match is not exact but there is a 'family resemblance' between the structure and moves of Smith's argument in Book one chapter ten of the *Wealth of Nations* and the structure and moves of an introductory first-year economics text-book. Although Smith is limited to language (there are no diagrams, no significant mathematical and statistical manipulations) the content, context and sequencing suggests a similar pattern of thought and argumentation. Because of the lack of other textual support, the examples carry much of the work of exemplification and evidence. The problem of what is taken to be 'authentic' and what is 'imaginary' is found in Smith and in the modern day textbook as is exposition of problem-solution patterns on a small-scale and within a few clauses. Because of the lack of headings and sub-headings, Smith is faced with the problem of awkward transitions. Summary and introductory statements in one paragraph or adjacent paragraphs is required. The primary lists and the textual repetitions of the elements to be considered in each section act as 'headings and sub-headings'. Even within the compass of a (long) chapter, Smith illustrates a command of authentic production situations through the provision and manipulation of a huge range of examples, based around given trades. By merging the 'labour' aspects with the 'trade' aspects, Smith gives the impression that he is discussing both returns to work and returns to stock though in fact his text concentrates upon labour.

The 'list' method of organising the text is used in both parts. The list is not uncommon in modern-day textbooks. In Part One the list is fully developed in the opening section that makes a systematic analysis of the influences of work conditions upon the returns to labour. The pattern is generalisation-exemplification, though there are variations. In Part Two, consideration one, generalisation-exemplification is in evidence though the existing situation is looked at within a general-specific textual pattern. Small-scale problem solution patterns are found in the modern text book and are in evidence in Smith's writing. The specific examples in the first section of Part Two are used to outline the basis of the status quo. The examples are historical and historical examples predominate in this section. The examples are not intended to illustrate a concept but to justify a context. This status quo is then subject to further analysis. In a modern-day textbook, printing technology makes for a greater choice in the way in which exposition and illustration can be handled. Smith exercises choice by variation in the pattern of argument and by variation in summarisation techniques. Given the huge differences, there is nonetheless an underlying method of argumentation that marks Smith's approach as 'economic' in the form or argument and it its attempts to organise the learning. It is this and the associated moves that provide the basis for the family resemblance.

NOTES

1. It may seem strange to economists to treat *The Wealth of Nations* as a textbook. Was it not more a stimulus to the creation of textbooks rather than a textbook itself? Is it not more common to treat James Mill or McCulloch as textbook writers? Yes, no doubt, but recognition of the ways in which Smith encodes his economic argument suggests that the treatise is 'teacherly' or 'educative'. The existence of Jeremiah Joyce's abridgment (a work that had a very long life) suggests that the *Wealth of Nations* was a set text. The idea that it is like a textbook is not meant to be exclusive nor to deny the 18th century context of Smith's text. Here, it is to be taken as just another way of exploring Smith's writing.

2. How these textual inserts work and the relationship that they have with the main body of the text pose interesting questions. Does the text or diagram come first? How do the captions relate to the longer exposition? How is the economics student expected to use or able to use the two different but related methods of exposition? These questions are under explored for the economics textbook. Kress and van Leeuwen have explored the issue in educational texts more generally (Kress & van Leeuwen, 1990). Henderson and Hewings (1987) made some analysis of 'non-textual features' in economics textbooks though the exploration must be seen as preliminary.

3. There are tables on the price of wheat, on the herring industry, on sources of revenue, on the price of bullion and coin at the Bank of Amsterdam and detailed statistical material built into the text e.g. when dealing with sources of revenue.

4. 'Take' is only used twice as an instruction to the reader, as far as I can see.

5. The chapter that follows, 'Of the Rent of Land' is even longer and even more complex in its structure.

6. Smith is not consistent in the way he chooses to develop chapters divided into parts. Sometimes there is a formally identified pre-organising section – this may be long or short – sometimes there is none. Books two and four have a formal pre-organising section and so does the work as a whole. Where he has a pre-organising section he does set out how what follows is organised: see for example the final paragraph in the introduction to book one chapter eleven. Whilst there is exemplification in such sections, the general 'tone' is more abstract, less detailed than that of what follows.

7. I set out to produce a paper that can be read independently of the original primary text. I soon realised that where a pattern is carried in a sequence of paragraphs that this objective was not going to be met. Whilst the paper can be read without having immediate access to book one, chapter ten of the *Wealth of Nations*, it will be helpful, at times, to read the commentary in parallel with it.

8. Smith often refers to complex arguments in Enlightenment thinking in short and, sometimes, inexact ways. See the opening moves of Book one chapter two where the phrase 'original principles of human nature' is likely to have come straight from Hume.

ACKNOWLEDGMENTS

Thanks go to Sebastian Mitchell and Sue Hunston for comments on an earlier draft.

REFERENCES

Brown, V. (1994). *Adam Smith's Discourse: canonicity, commerce and conscience* London: Routledge.
Henderson, W. (2002). Exemplification Strategy in Adam Smith's *Wealth of Nations*. In: M. Hewings (Ed.), *Essays in Honour of Tony Dudley-Evans*. Birmingham: University of Birmingham Press (forthcoming).
Henderson, W., & Hewings, A. (1987). Entering the Hypothetical World: Assume, Suppose, consider and Take as signals in Economics Text. Unpublished paper, University of Birmingham.
Henderson, W., & Hewings, A. (1987). *Reading Economics: How text helps or hinders*. British National Bibliography Research Fund Report 28. London: British Library.
Kress, G., & van Leeuwen, T. (1990). *Reading Images*. Victoria: Deakin University Press.

ANTÓNIO HORTA OSÓRIO, PARETO'S PORTUGUESE DISCIPLE

Maria Eugénia Mata

ABSTRACT

This paper analyzes the first attempt to introduce in Portugal economic studies based on a neoclassical approach. In 1910 António Horta Osório wrote a textbook, A Mathematica na economia pura [Mathematics in pure economics], in the context of an attempt to obtain the chair of Political Economy at the Lisbon Polytechnic School. He did not receive the appointment, and although the book was translated into French, under the title Théorie mathématique de l'échange, and praised as a good elementary presentation of the basic framework of the general equilibrium theory of Léon Walras and Vilfredo Pareto, it had almost no effect on the Portuguese intellectual scene. Neoclassical economics would only become a standard paradigm in Portuguese universities in the 1940s.

This paper explains why his name faded from the intellectual scene in Portugal and elsewhere.

We don't study any practical problem and we don't present any solution to concrete questions.

António Horta Osório, Théorie mathématique de l'échange, 1913, p. 1.

Research in the History of Economic Thought and Methodology, Volume 20-A, pages 17–34.
© 2002 Published by Elsevier Science Ltd.
ISBN: 0-7623-0847-8

I. THE MAN: ANTÓNIO HORTA OSÓRIO

António de Sousa Horta Sarmento Osório was born in Lousã to a wealthy family in 1882, and graduated in law from the University of Coimbra in 1903. His interest in economics and mathematics began during his years at Coimbra, where an eclectic perspective based on a diversified bibliography was the rule. Although steeped in the Classical paradigm, the prevailing teaching of Economics was an eclectic vision emerging from a variety of theories – a "plural canon".[1] German universities commanded a great deal of respect, and their message was very well received in Portugal. The stewpot of theory included Classical economics along with the principles of the historical and nationalist schools and elements of the new socialist dialogues, as well.[2] These ingredients were stirred well by leading Portuguese economists such as Marnoco e Sousa, a top figure of the University of Coimbra.[3]

In spite of achieving a fine academic performance, Osório did not follow an academic career at his *Alma Mater*. For reasons which are unknown (and perhaps trivial) the University of Coimbra did not offer him an appointment, and upon completing his studies, he left for Lisbon, to begin a career in law.

As he had read Pareto's work, Osório struck up a correspondence with him. The correspondence blossomed into friendship, and Osório travelled to Céligny to meet Pareto – staying there with him for some months and growing into a close and enthusiastic disciple.[4] Their close relationship is evident in his book, where Osório identifies Walras and Pareto as his two masters in economic themes.

In 1910 the Lisbon Politechnical School announced the intention to fill a vacant chair in Political Economy. According to the rules, candidates for the chair would present a book relating to the field, and this would constitute the principal element in the selection committee's considerations. To this end, he wrote *A Mathematica na economia pura* in that same year, the date of which is confirmed by the fact that he refers to Pareto's *Manuel d'économie politique* as having been published in the previous year (1909).[5]

Three candidates, all lawyers from the University of Coimbra, submitted their works: Osório, politically a monarchist; Afonso Costa, a well known Republican politician and member of the first Republican government in 1910–1911; and António Lino Neto, a Christian-Democrat. Osório presented *A Mathematica na economia pura*, an excellent textbook on Neoclassical general equilibrium. Costa presented a study of applied political economy on emigration, in which he tried to examine Portuguese emigration in the context of European emigration.[6] Neto presented a study about Portuguese municipalities, in which he advocated the revival of mediaeval administrative principles adapted to modern time.[7]

This paper appraises Osório's book as the first attempt to introduce economic studies based on a Neoclassical approach into Portugal and applauds the excellent presentation of the general equilibrium theory. In the end he failed to obtain the Political Economy chair he sought. The position went to Afonso Costa. This paper also offers an explanation for the selection of Costa's work – a contribution which, from today's perspective, was far less impressive than Osório's.

In addition to its failure to secure the author the desired position, Osório's book also had little or no impact on the Portuguese intellectual scene. The entire "Osório episode" can be written off as a false start for Neoclassical economics teaching – something which would not become a standard paradigm in Portuguese universities until the 1940s.[8] The text was translated into French, however, as noted above, and was well praised as good elementary presentation of the basic framework of Walras-Pareto general equilibrium theory. The most important reference, of course, is Schumpeter, but other authors recommended Osório's.[9]

Two papers presented in Portuguese (Nunes, 1988; Farto, 1992), have thoroughly explained Osório's contribution. This paper analyzes why the effort made by António Horta Osório to introduce a Neoclassical approach to economic studies into Portugal failed. Osório's undertaking was a false start, as neoclassical economics did not approach economic development policies. Although his book was translated into French, under the title *Théorie mathématique de l'échange* with an introduction by Pareto, himself, it fell into scientific oblivion in Portugal and elsewhere.

II. THE BOOK: A MATHEMATICA NA ECONOMIA PURA (THÉORIE MATHÉMATIQUE DE L'ECHANGE)

Since the book had failed in the purpose for which it had been written, it is clear that the translation and French edition must have had a new aim – to serve as an instrument of diffusion for the general equilibrium theory of Léon Walras and Vilfredo Pareto.

At the time, French was the major international language, and the Portuguese, in particular, were far more literate in French than in English. José d'Almada, a civil servant in the Portuguese Ministry of Foreign Affairs, translated the Portuguese original. It was published in 1913 under its new title, *Théorie mathématique de l'échange*, and contained an introduction written by Vilfredo Pareto, himself. All quotations below are based upon this edition.

In his introduction, Pareto strongly recommends the book as an excellent treatise on economics to all those who may wish to study scientific economics.

In his opinion, Osório's book possessed all the qualities that an outstanding textbook should: it was clear – he writes – well organized, of an easy formal style and deep in reasoning.

> All we may ask is to have clear manuals, well organized, knowing how to couple the formal simplicity with the deepness of thought. It is of this kind, this treatise; and this is why I believe it will provide a great service to those who wish to study the science (p. xviii).

It is impossible to follow Osório's presentation of general equilibrium here. Following a first chapter devoted to the history of mathematical economics, he presents two more chapters which introduce the reader to the so-called "pure economics". Chapter IV is a pledge to use mathematics in the study of pure economics.[10] Chapters V and VI are devoted to Walras' general economic equilibrium, and the last two chapters, to Pareto's formulation.

Osório's presentation explicitly states that economics had not made much progress in the past. In his opinion, it was still a science in its infancy. Most contributions up to that time, he claimed, could be placed into one of two categories:

- a set of practical discussions having no theoretical basis
- a set of doctrinal systems in "scientific" dress, preaching politics and ideology, (as if scientists were religious priests wishing to influence public beliefs and revolutionize social opinion).

Osório included socialist writings in the second category, for example.

It was his desire to make a wholly different kind of contribution. In a methodological discussion, Osório presents an eclectic concept of economics, remarking upon the need to learn from history and a wider range of human experience, helping reality to generate hypotheses. Although mathematical deductive power should be the key to scientific economics, he claims, inductive methods should be indispensable.[11] Other methods – statistical, historical, etc. – are neither wrong nor useless. On the contrary, the role of human feelings in human action concedes an advantage to interdisciplinary approaches. Economics would be a true science if it applied psychological and sociological knowledge to empirical phenomena in order to explain and formulate a generalized synthesis, which could then be expressed in a mathematical language. This, he reduces to its simplest terms: "We propose nothing other than a pure and abstract science."[12]

Mathematics was, in his opinion, not only a briefer and clearer language, but also a much more comfortable way of reasoning. Deduction based on mathematics is indispensable. Though ordinary logic is able to deal with causality relationships, only mathematics is capable of tackling inter-dependence relationships.[13] He uses the example of successive approaches to the general equilibrium (*tâtonnement*) to illustrate his point. Pure economics is able, he tells us, to determine the influence that different relevant variables have on one another. Stating the problem in the form of an equation affords it the precision that we expect of issues in astronomy or mechanics. Iterative mathematical process describes the real world equilibrium because it is a limit state toward which all markets tend. It is not something that is permanently attained, because the relevant conditions are always changing. Only when it is couched in mathematics, can it be depicted and described as a limit state. It is, in the end, the only way to grasp economic phenomena.

He observes, however, that mathematics scares away many sociologists and even many economists, due to their lack of the necessary knowledge to use it. Acoording to Osório, this was the reason, for example, why Cournot's work had been so poorly received in his lifetime. With this in mind, Osório gives his readers some warning, right from the start:

> The first four chapters are accessible to everybody. The last four require some knowledge
> of algebra, analytical geometry, and infinitesimal calculus (p. 1).

On the evolution of mathematical economics, he briefly mentions the 18th-century Italians, Beccaria, Silio and Ortes, and the works of Canard (French) and Whewell (English), and examines in some detail the works of Cournot, Dupuit and Gossen.[14] He then identifies Stanley Jevons and Léon Walras as the founders of modern mathematical economics. He acknowledges the contributions of Menger, Weiser and Böhm-Bawerk, to whom he adds Pantaleoni, and identifies them as the Austrian school. This may surprise some, but Schumpeter essentially agrees with Osório on the matter, although he deplores their insufficient use of mathematics.[15] He goes on to list Edgeworth, Marshall, Fisher, Lehr and Barone as the most important contemporary mathematical economists, praises the textbook of Auspitz and Lieben, and singles out Pareto as the leading figure in the field of mathematical economics.[16]

III. THE TEACHING OF ECONOMICS IN PORTUGAL

Osório's book was a marked change to the teaching of economics in Portugal. Before the First World War the bibliographies in Portuguese economics textbooks included Neoclassical authors, but the texts glossed over their message. They did not really engage the Neoclassical approach. Despite the fact that the Classical school dominated the scene, economics teaching did not really adhere too strictly to the standards of pure Classical theory. As the 18th century came to a close, an eclectic vision was emerging, drawing upon a variety of theories. This vision – a "plural canon" – was, in fact, something of a reflection of the interventionist realpolitik which prevailed at the time.[17] German universities, which commanded a great deal of respect, were advancing the historical paradigm at this time, and their message was very well received. The message of adapting theoretical dogma to local needs and nationalistic interests struck Portuguese economists as something which they had been doing all the while. Along with the principles of the historical and nationalist schools, into the stewpot of theory went elements of the new socialist dialogues, too. These ingredients were stirred well and allowed to blend – then served up by such leading economists as Frederico Laranjo and Marnoco e Sousa, who were among the top figures of the Portuguese academic (and political) scene.[18] Classical economics teaching favored, and generally deferred to, market mechanisms, suggesting a policy of no public enterprises, no subsidies to private enterprises, and no legal monopolies. But some of these, it was said, were inevitable in the current Portuguese reality. Free-trade theory was taught, but pragmatists acknowledged the need for tariffs to protect some economic sectors and feed the budget. Protectionism, colonial expansion and human capital formation were the main thrusts against the rigors of Classical liberal doctrine.

Osório can be considered as one of the forerunners of Neoclassical teaching, as his treatise was a genuine "package presentation" of general equilibrium.

IV. CRITICISING WALRAS – FOLLOWING PARETO

Osório's enthusiasm for the mathematical approach to economics does not prevent him from criticizing Walras' definition of pure political economy, and he does not follow Walrasian thought without protest.[19] He clearly disagrees with Walras' distinctions between pure science, applied science and moral science, and between natural and human facts. His incomprehension is sincere, and he asks how it is that someone as intelligent as Walras could suggest such things – and rejects Walras' theses in these matters out of hand.

> One is shocked that so clear and lucid a spirit as Walras could conceive the metaphysical muddle that we just explained (. . .) Walras posed the problem wrongly and solved it even more wrongly (p. 41).

In the *Elements d'economie politique* Walras must have abandoned his defini-tions and studied not only economic exchange, but production, capitalization and circulation, as well. Osório deplores Walras' use of such a weak scientific base:

> Walras could be the first to establish the fundamentals of pure economics and to develop its underlying parts scientifically (. . .) [but] [i]t is surprising that a thinker such as Walras has used such a poor scientific base as his departure point (p. 53).

Regarding *rarity*, Osório clearly follows Walras. *Rarity*, a property of useful goods in short supply, is defined as the intensity of the last satisfied need. Moreover, only *rare* goods have an exchange value in the market, only scarce goods can be multiplied by using production methods, and only scarce goods can be appropriated. But value and exchange value are dropped in his book as useless concepts, due to the vast number of interpretations which had been given to those words previously. Discussing prices of goods and the exchange rate between them was deemed to be much more important and useful than discussing the philosophical concept of value and exchange value.

> Walras sometimes employs the expressions *value* and *exchange value*, and at other times the word *price*. However, I cannot understand the utility of the first words [. . .] the price of a good is [. . .] equal to the direct relationship between the exchange values, and also to the inverse relationship of the exchanged quantities, as mentioned before.
>
> The value or exchange value entity, even so defined, does not present any advantage. It is superfluous enough in Walras' theories, that we can abandon it altogether (p. 195).

Price thus stands out as the main concept of exchange theory, according to the standard Neoclassical tradition. Demand curves were obtained by maximizing *ophelimity* to conclude that they are also declining schedule functions, like Cournot and Walrasian demand curves. The main basic assumption is constant prices, otherwise the consumer's budget would be in a permanent state of change. Even the order in which goods were consumed would force changes in price, and again, the consumer's budget would be in a permanent state of change. The definition of the consumer's budget is the same as Walras': expenditures and receipts must be equal, because if a person wants to consume more of a particular good, he must give up something in exchange to obtain it.

An important feature from Walras' general equilibrium is the fundamental proposition of equality between demand and supply of each commodity, and the well-known discussion of the number of equations and unknowns. Osório does the same, but much more succinctly: for each good, demand must be equal to supply. Walras had preferred to say that excess demand curves must be equal to zero and had spent much more time and far more pages to build his framework.[20]

Having arrived at this point, Osório further criticizes Walras for never explaining why the economic system needed the first "m × n" equations.[21] Was it possible to assume that in order to obtain the equilibrium, it would be enough that the demand and supply of each good be equal? Osório tells his readers how consumers make their own budgets, taking their own tastes and prices into consideration. In this way, the first "m × n" equations are respected, leaving to the market the role of solving the last "(m−1) × n" equations (in the market the price of a good will rise if its demand exceeds its supply, and *vice versa*). Osório believes that the solution for the equations of equalizing demand with supply presupposes that other equations were already taken care of.

In this way, the system of equations describes exactly the successive approaches to the general equilibrium. The ups and downs of the market are, of course, the market's real attempts to find the system's solution empirically:

> ... we must see how the successive transformation of prices is achieved in the marketplace, approaching the equilibrium prices that solve the system, step by step (p. 243).

Osório omits the discussion of economic equilibrium with non-continuous demand functions, and forgets the Walrasian examples of goods consumable by units (e.g. clothing and furniture). He always prefers to use continuous demand curves, meaning that, although capturing Walras' contribution, he is selective in building the argument in his own book.

He does stress, however, how unfair it is to consider Walras' mathematical school as a chimera. On the contrary, he says, it is a down-to-earth contribution which describes reality through an experimental method. Repeating Walras' system, and building an original discussion about it for the final equilibrium, Osório assumes that is always obtained through the solution of a set of simultaneous equations, and that the only way to solve them is through the use of algebra.

Osório expresses regret that some economists lack a clear notion of the inter-dependence of economic phenomena and are ignorant of the most-recent theories of political economy. Although rejecting at the outset any discussion based solely upon literary arguments, he also emphasizes that even eminent mathematicians such as Bertrand had made surprising errors because they had not studied Walras' arguments carefully enough. Osório never denies to Walras the scientific relevance of his contribution as the "father of mathematical economics", founder of the Lausanne school and enlightened pioneer in general equilibrium study.

> The mathematical expression of utlity and the exchange theory cannot be attributed to him, but it was he who could find the most important conclusions, it was he who could show the multiplicity of their consequences with an admirable clearness; it was he who conceived the economic equilibrium for the first time [. . .]; it is thus only fair that Walras should be considered as the founder of the mathematical equlibrium, which is also known under the name of Lausanne School (p. 21).

Osório's definition of pure economics follows Pareto's. Like him, he praises the role of abstraction, generalization, and successive approximation for science. Abstraction is the capacity to separate the arguments in a discussion in order to analyze each of them separately. Generalization is the human capacity to compare, to associate, and to connect the arguments. Science uses both of these capacities, he remarks – as does economics, as it is nothing more than an empirical subject or a practical art. Pure economics gives a first approximation to economic phenomena, then, by abstracting the *homo oeconomicus* from the real man. In defining the *homo oeconomicus*, he also uses the distinction made by Pareto between logical and ilogical actions. *Homo oeconomicus* is concerned, of course, only with logical actions, while human actions include religious, political and erotic actions, among others. To develop the concept of logical action, he focuses on the distinction between utility and *ophelimity*, just as desire and appetite are not necessarily logical actions. The fundamentals of the analytical framework of preferences and obstacles are clearly recognized as being psychological. Pleasure and desire are related to utility, but he enumerates good examples to lead his readers into distinguishing between utility and desirability or *ophelimity*. The gun which the suicidal man obtains to kill himself with is desired by him, but is not useful, for example. Morphine is, of course, *ophelime* to the addict, but likewise, is not useful. The bad-tasting medicine to treat the sick child is useful, but not desired by the child.

Ahead of Walras, Osório considers pure economics to be an experimental science, which snatches an abstract theory about human tastes from small empirical facts – a kind of rational mechanics for human desires, useful for practical applications, just as mechanics is useful for engineering and construction. Economics, he says, may also come to be seen in the future as part of psychology, as all of the human actions derive from a personal assessment of desire and pleasure.

> Pure economics may tomorrow be a science of human actions, in general – an immense chapter of psychology, of which the social sciences are only a subdivision (p. 86).

On utility theory he is much more detailed than Pareto. He explains that each consumer regards his *ophemilities* in assessing the agreeable and disagreeable aspects of his decisions. Deciding whether to take a walk depends on the place to go, the weather, and the prospect of companionship, he tells us.

In the market, man looks for the goods he desires most and exchanges one good for another whenever the *ophelimity* he receives outweighs the one he forgoes in the exchange. All goods are exchangable, including capital, productive services, raw materials, fertilizers, plows, seeds, domestic services, and so on. Goods may be used, then, to obtain direct *ophelimities* or to produce other goods – producing wheat, for example, to be exchanged for *ophelimities* such as tobacco, tea, furniture, or anything else.

If someone refuses *ophelimities* to produce wheat and loses more *ophelimities* than those he obtains upon selling it against other goods, he will learn the lesson as a consumer and as a producer: in the next year he will produce less wheat.

His decisions, moreover, will depend on the prices. In the market, prices depend on the collective demand and supply resulting from individual decisions.

Osório was careful not to neglect pointing out the limits for the exchange theory. Many *ophelimities* are not exchangeable, as they cannot be produced. Health, strength, beauty, love, personal character and virility are very important factors in human happiness, but cannot be considered in the exchange theory, as they are gifts of Nature, and non-produceable. By addressing these topis Osório reveals his humanity and compassion, as well as an accurate capacity for understanding life, joy and happiness.

In its study of the equilibrium, economics is generalizing on the individual *ophelimities* and the obstacles to fulfilling them. These obstacles are essentially other men's tastes and *ophelimities* (as Pareto had explained).

Contrary to Walras, and following Pareto, Osório accepts that *ophelimities* for a good depend not only on the amount of that good already consumed, but also on the amount already consumed of all other goods. The *ophelimity* was understood as a partial derivative of the utility function.[22] Recall that for Walras the intensity of the last satisfied necessity, or "rarity" (*rareté*), depended on the amount of the good already consumed. But Osório explains the empirical evidence on this issue clearly. Pareto had stated it briefly: "In short, a consumption's *ophelimity* depends on all of the circumstances surrounding consumption".[23] Osório illustrates the Paretian concept by explaining that the enjoyment which a person experiences from having a painting hanging on the wall depends also in part upon being well fed, well dressed, and comfortably seated in a warm room.

In his opinion, Edgeworth was the source for this important correction to Walras' theories. The difference is significant, indeed. Summing up the *rarities*, one can obtain total utility, but one cannot obtain it by integrating the elementary *ophelimities*. This is also empirically evident, as Osório explains, as it is important to consider the consumption of other goods – even the order of consuming them is relevant.

If in the Walrasian system utility was maximized when the price ratio was equal to the ratio between the *rarities*, in the Paretian equilibrium, utility is maximized when the price ratio is equal to the ratio between the *ophelimities*.[24]

Ahead of Pareto, Osório explains that these equations are similar to the Lagrangean equilibrium defined for mechanics. He goes on to explain that there are also two forces (prices and quantities, in this case) which are applied on two points with virtual velocities dp and dq. One of them assures that man desires the goods which are *ophelime* to him and which he does not have. The other assures that man at the same time desires to preserve those *ophelimities* which he already has. The mechanical Lagrangean equilibrium is similar to the Paretian economic equilibrium, he concludes.

V. THE SELECTION COMMITTEE'S APPRAISAL

From today's perspective, the committee's decision to award the chair to Afonso Costa is more than a little bewildering – and some might claim that it was an out-and-out error. According to Nunes, 1985, it was an error. First, because Osório used a sound theoretical approach

> Horta Osório's work (. . .) represented, in the epoch in which it was written, the most up-to-date thinking regarding the theories of the new methodology as represented by mathematical economics.[25]

Second, because his teaching would have been based on mathematical reasoning for economics.[26] Pareto's introduction praised the work for its quality, and several other authors acknowledged that the treatise was a fine alternative to the study of elementary mathematical economics. The book progresses from the easier to the more complex, and each subject is approached in three stages – or three languages (the current language, the graphical language and the mathematical formulae). Marshall, Walras and Pareto, too, used all three approaches, but not in as clear a format as did Osório (Pareto's *Manuel* left most of the mathematics to the appendices; Walras relegated the graphs to the final pages (in the 1900 edition, on); Osório included all three in the main text). Osório begins the explanation of each matter with a discussion of real life examples, using clear speech and an easy style. Sometimes he repeats this stage using alternative examples – always striving to elucidate the issue as much as possible. Following these (often lengthy) explanations, he employs figures to pose the questions from a geometric point of view, and explains each variable with great care in order to reinforce the earlier "straight language" exposition. Finally, he repeats all of the reasoning and results employing exhaustive mathematical presentations.

> Excessive concision in some fundamental deduction is one of the great difficulties we must overcome in the work of the two masters (p. 7).

Nunes (1988) discusses the composition of the selection committee, observing that it was made up of aged, monarchist, conservative professors. He goes on to suggest that they perhaps had a dislike for both Costa and Osório, who were the two most qualified of the three candidates, and in the end, were able to overcome their political distaste for at least one of them (Costa).

The only explanation advanced by Almodôvar and Cardoso for the failure of Neoclassicism to take hold in Portugal was in its reliance on mathematics.[27] Those who could not grasp a system of two equations in two variables could not fathom the new school, and they suggest that the school's elaborate mathematical character simply did not appeal to the economists of the day. This notion simply follows from Osório's own complaint in which he points out that asking someone who cannot manage a system of equations to appreciate the general equilibrium would be like asking a person who has been blind from birth to comment on the colors of the world.

I argue that another cause for rejection of Neoclassical doctrine must be underscored, and is perhaps the most important of all. The committee decided that Osório's approach to economics was not only different, but also inapplicable to the economic problems, which prevailed in Portugal at the time. Neoclassical economics promotes a liberal perspective, which utterly lacks any explicit social concern about economic development. The book has no message for a small, struggling nation striving to industrialize and modernize – trying to keep abreast of its European neighbors. This, in my opinion, was the main problem with Osório's application. Portugal was obsessed with its comparison to other more-developed countries. Professors of economics dealt with economic development and government policies as overriding social concerns. An illiterate labor force, little savings and low private investment were brakes on the economic growth in Portugal. Government deficits and borrowing, the abandonment of the gold standard (1891) and a partial bankruptcy (1892) earned the Portuguese economy little credibility in foreign capital markets. Underdevelopment was the watchword of the day.

The Republican political blueprint at the time urged education, economic development and a prosperous and profitable colonial empire. Osório advocated the virtues of market mechanisms. Political criticism of the Monarchy's inefficient policies for promoting industrial development were main concerns, and Neoclassical reasoning seemed to hold out little encouragement to a hard pressed social system. Although Osório appreciates Pareto's conceptual framework of economics as a social and global science in the *Manuel d'économie politique*, his proposal for the chair of Political Economy was one of pure economics "pure science", in his words:

> ... in consequence, this book is only a study in pure science (p. 7).

He aimed very strictly to teach the evolution of the available theories on economic equilibrium, and did not adopt an empirical or sociological style. Here, he is following Walras' and Pareto's enthusiastic lead.[28] The interest of the theoretical analysis lay not in working out the general equilibrium equations, but in understanding the principles underlying their existence. The market, itself, solves the equations of economic relationships, without any need for calculus.

> [it is] the political economy that will come to the aid of mathematics. The only way which is humanly possible to solve [all the equations] is to observe the practical solution provided in the marketplace.[29]

Market mechanisms, he says, would best satisfy human needs, under the conditions of a single price for each good in the market, and a marvelous respect for the equilibrium between demand and supply. What hope did this textbook hold out for the issues that plagued economic development in Portugal? "Efficiency", perhaps, but Portugal was a backward country by international comparisons, and these comparisons were at the fore in the days leading up to the First World War (Portugal, for example, was the least literate of all Mediterranean countries, which were the less literate of European countries at this time).[30]

Most Portuguese economists of the day repeated the nagging belief that the Portuguese economy was somehow intransigently laggard. Others touted a number of blueprints for recovery. In spite of the perceived advantages of the market virtues and the Smithian "invisible hand", concessions were made to government intervention. The history of economics is the history of worries about economic growth and development. Neoclassical economics marks the exception to that, and Osório was far from recommending any type of inter-ventionist policy. In fact, he even goes so far as to say that in the past, the traditional praise for the principle of *laisser-faire* had been nought but lip service and a philosophical conclusion emerging from metaphysics, but that *now*, with the general equilibrium theory, it had achieved the status of scientific principle. Although he did not repeat the Classical and Walrasian hope that the knowledge of neoclassical economics would be a way to build an organized economic world in order to attain the universal economic equilibrium in a society full of hapiness, harmony and peace for all nations, he says that with the Neoclassical framework, individual freedom is respected and the maximization of utility is achieved. Briefly stated, this was the ultimate goal of Walrasian scientific works – that economic equilibrium would drive the nations to happiness and harmony. Walras had written:

> When my teaching is [someday] diffused ... and when the political economy [someday] replaces the current doctrine of *lassez-faire*, one will recognize the chaos [of the situation] where agriculture and industry are now, as they cannot balance the supply and demand of their goods at [their] selling prices. This disorder must give way to an economic order organized on the Lagrangean equations which already regulate the work of our machines, and which could also take us, someday, into the era of peace.[31]

This message did not sit well with the Portuguese society's urgent needs, and the framework of the model was just beyond the grasp of traditional economists.

It is of little surprise, then, that Walras and Osório encountered similar friction in spreading the teaching of general equilibrium theories. Walras could teach them at Lausanne, but never in France (as he wished to). France, like Portugal, was a country with a long tradition of government economic policy, and Walras wrote in his memoirs:

> [. . .] I never [bothered] to pause and long for the reknown of my efforts in my country [France]. I tried with no success to send three papers on the exchange equations, production and capiatization to the Academy of Moral and Political Sciences. I thereafter made renewed attempts to make my ideas known in France, but was never able to realize any of my hopes, as my efforts were always met with deaf ears or fierce hostility from certain hereditary mandarins who thwarted the progress of science.[32]

Likewise, Osório expected neither immediate personal gratification nor social praise from the publication of his book in 1911.

> If [even] one of the few readers we will have in Portugal shall deem the issues to be clearly exposed, we will feel compensated (p. 10).

Osório was writing theoretical reasoning.

The neglect of Neoclassical Economics, which lasted for so many years in Portugal, illustrates just how selective and socially driven the spread of theoretical systems may be. Science, it seems, is required to produce useful applications for practical purposes.

In the introduction to Osório's treatise, Pareto actually questions the role of economics. He presents a critique of the Classical definitions (e.g. Smith) and the Classical illusions regarding the effects that the spread of knowledge of political economy would have on practical affairs and political decisions (e.g. Say). He also reveals his recognition that pure economics had only a very indirect usefulness. Economic policy could not spring directly from pure economics or even applied economics.

> What place is it that is occupied by economics among the social sciences? What is it for? (p. v)

> Anyone seeking a solution for a practical problem exclusively in the theories of pure economics, or even in those of applied economics, will usually be wrong (p. xvii).

From the point of view of Osório's personal life, it is pointless to bemoan the selection committee's decision. He continued in his carreer as a successful lawyer into the 1930s. His second book deals with his most famous case as an attorney, which also happened to be the most famous case of fraud in Portuguese history. It has even earned a place in the Guiness Book of World Records.[33] Osório represented the Bank of Portugal (in Portuguese courts) against the men who obtained duplicates of the notes of the Bank of Portugal from Waterlow & Sons, in London, in 1925. He also prepared the case brought by the Bank of Portugal against Waterlow & Sons in the English courts. Following this, he retired, dedicating his time to the study of fine arts.[34] Like Pareto, he was widowed and took a younger wife. He died in Lisbon in 1960.

Curiously, António Lino Neto was the only one of the three candidates to become a full career professor, as he obtained the chair of Political Economy at the Technical University of Lisbon. He would become one of the few teachers of political economy in Portugal – and where they could be found, they were often ill-prepared or ill-equiped for the Neoclassical economics perspective. Afonso Costa still taught at the University of Lisbon, but was primarily a politician, and served several terms as minister and Prime Minister in later years.

Osório's rejection for the post in Political Economy at the Politechnic School of Lisbon meant a forgone opportunity for the introduction of Neoclassical economics teaching in Portugal. His treatise had almost no effect on the Portuguese intellectual scene, and the episode was a false start for Neoclassical diffusion. In the 1940s, when sustained modern economic growth was achieved in Portugal, the teaching of Neoclassical economics would become a standard paradigm in Portuguese universities.

NOTES

1. Almodôvar; Cardoso, 1998, p. 90.
2. Bastien, 1993. Cardoso; Almodôvar, 1992.
3. On the teaching of economics at the University of Coimbra, see Pedrosa, Alcino, *A Faculdade de Direito de Coimbra e o ensino da economia politica em Portugal*, in Cardoso; Almodôvar, 1992, p. 434.
4. The letters between the two men are lost. Joaquim Feio's attempts to find them have failed.
5. Osório, 1911; Pareto, 1909.
6. Costa, 1911.
7. Neto, 1911.
8. This occurred first in the Technical University of Lisbon, thanks to the enthusiasm of a few young economists, namely António Manuel Pinto Barbosa, Francisco Pereira de Moura, Manuel Jacinto Nunes and Luís Teixeira Pinto. Even then there was some resistance to the new programs from older professors. On this issue, see Nunes, 1989.
9. Schumpeter, 1954, p. 957. The main references to Osório's book are: Brodsky, 1949; Kuene, 1963; Patinkin, 1955; Roll, 1945; Schumpeter, 1954; and Zumalacarregui, 1951.
10. Chapter IV (*De la nécessité de la méthode mathématique*).
11. See p. 118.
12. p. 1.
13. In proving this, he resorts to some fairly complicated discussions about philosophy and psychology, which were examined in Farto, 1989.
14. He devotes Chapter I to this issue.
15. Schumpeter, 1954, p. 857.

16. Osório's references are: Auspitz; Lieben, 1889, *Untersuchungen über die Theorie des Preises;* Beccaria, 1765, *Tentativo analitico sui contrabbandi;* Cournot, 1838, *Recherches sur les principes mathématiques de la théory des richesses;* Dupuit, 1844, *De la mesure de l'utilité des travaux publiques;* Dupuit, 1849, *De l'influence des péages sur l'utilité des voies de communication;* Edgeworth, 1881, *Mathematical psychics;* Fisher, 1892 *Mathematical investigation in the theory of value and prices,* (unavailable); Jevons, 1871, 2nd edition, 1879, *Theory of political economy;* Lehr, J., 1893, *Grundbegriffe and Grundlagen der Volkswirtschaft;* Marshall, 1890, *Principles of economics;* Menger, 1872, *Grundsätze der Volkswirtschaftlehre;* Pantaleoni, 1889, *Principi di economia pura;* Pareto, 1896, *Cours d'économie politique;* Pareto, 1902, *Les systèmes socialistes;* Silio, 1792, *Saggio su l'influenza d'ell analisi nelle scienze pilitiche ed economiche applicata ai contrabbandi;* Walras, 1874, *"Principe d'une théorie mathématique de l'échange";* Walras, 1874–1877, 1889, 1896, 1900, *Éléments d'économie politique pure.*

17. Almodôvar; Cardoso, 1998, p. 90.

18. Bastien, 1993. Cardoso, Almodôvar, 1992.

19. Chapter II (*L'économie pure selon Walras*), which is also a critique of Classical definitions of political economy (see Quesnay, Smith, Say).

20. Compare Osório, 1913, pp. 197–253 and Walras, 1952, pp. 54–163.

21. m commodities, n individuals.

22. Pareto said: *"Les accroissements différentiels de l'utilité ou les accroissements du plaisir, qui adviennent de la consommation d'une nouvelle petite quantité d'une marchandise quelconque, ne dépendent seulement de la plus ou moins grande quantité de cette même marchandise consommée antérieurement; ils dépendent aussi de plusieurs quantités plus ou moins grandes d'autres marchandises, consommées auparavant."*

23. *Manuel*, p. 259.

24. Osório, 1913, p. 279.

25. Schumpeter's *History of Economic Analysis* refers to the book in exactly this context, p. 957.

26. As he announces at pp. 7–8.

27. Almodôvar; Cardoso, 1998.

28. Compare Osório, 1913, p. 213; Walras, 1952, p. 65; and Pareto, 1927, p. 234. Pareto stresses that for a human community composed of 100 individuals and 700 goods, there will be 70,000 plus 6,999 equations to be solved – more for a community made up of 40 million individuals!

29. *Manuel*, p. 234.

30. Reis, 1988.

31. Quoted by Amzalak, 1934, p. 45.

32. Quoted by Amzalak, 1934, p. 29.

33. Osório, 1928. He published also a few brochures about his case as a lawyer.

34. His third book is a study about art, written in 1946, after he had retired from his law career.

ACKNOWLEDGMENTS

I express my gratitude for the support of the Portuguese *Fundação de Ciência e Tecnologia* (and the *PRAXIS* program) and the Luso-American Foundation to visit the Departments of Portuguese and Brazilian Studies and Economics at Brown University. I thank my colleague Joaquim Feio and Osório's family for information on the subject of this paper. I also thank professors Carlos Bastien, Jorge Braga de Macedo, Luís Cunha, Manuel Farto, Manuel Jacinto Nunes and Nuno Valério for discussions about the same issue and John Huffstot for correcting my English. Any errors or omissions are, of course, my own.

REFERENCES

Amzalak, M. (1934). *Léon Walras e a economia pura.* Lisbon: Oficinas Graficas do Museu Comercial.

Bastien, C. (1989). Para a história das ideias económicas no Portugal contemporâneo – a crise dos anos 1945–1954. Ph.D. thesis presented at the Technical University of Lisbon.

Brodsky, M. (1949). *"Le développement historique de l'économie mathématique." L'économie politique mathématique.* Paris: Librairie Générale de Droit et Jurisprudence.

Cardoso, J. L., & Almôdvar, A. (1992). *Actas do Encontro Ibérico sobre História do Pensamento Económico.* Lisbon: CISEP.

Costa, A. (1911). *O problema da emigração.* Lisbon: Imprensa Nacional.

Cournot, A. (1838). *Recherches sur les principes mathématiques de la théory des richesses.* Paris: Librairie Hachette & Cie. Modern edition, Paris: Calmann-Lévy, 1974.

Dupuit, J. (1844). De la mesure de l'utilité des travaux publiques. In: R. H. Back (Tr.), *International Economic Papers,* No. 2: On the measurement of the utility of public works (1952). London: Macmillan.

Dupuit, J. (1849). De l'influence des péages sur l'utilité des voies de communication. In: E. Henderson (Tr.), *International Economic Papers,* No. 11: On tolls and transport charges (1962). London: Macmillan.

Edgeworth, F. (1881). *Mathematical psychics.* London: Kegan.

Farto, M. (1992). *"António Osório e a teoria do equilíbrio geral", Actas do Encontro Ibérico sobre a história do pensamento económico.* Lisbon: CISEP.

Farto, M. (1906). *The nature of capital and income.* New York: Macmillan.

Jevons, S. (1871). *Theory of political economy (1970).* Harmondsworth: Penguin.

Kuene, R. (1963). *The theory of general equilibrium.* Princeton: Princeton University Press.

Lehr, J. (1893). *Grundbegriffe and Grundlagen der Volkswirtschaft.*

Marshall, A. (1890). *Principles of economics (1982).* London: Macmillan.

Menger, C. (1872). *Grundsätze der Volkswirtschaftlehre (1952).* Glencoe: The Free Press.

Neto, A. L. (1911). *A questão administrativa – o municipalismo em Portugal.* Lisbon: Tipographia José Bastos.

Nunes, M. J., & Moura, F. P. (1954). Sobre a teoria da procura. *Anais do Instituto de Ciências Económicas e Financeiras.* Lisbon.

Nunes, M. J. (1988). *Subsídios para a história do equilíbrio geral.* Lisbon: Memórias da Academia das Ciências de Lisboa – tomos XXVI e XXVII.

Osório, A. H. (1911). A mathematica na economia pura. Lisbon: Centro Tipografico Colonial, Translation into French: Théorie mathématique de l'échange – Paris: M. Giard & E. Brière, 1913.

Osório, A. H. (1928). O caso do Banco Angola e Metrópole. *História do crime.* Lisbon: Banco de Portugal.

Osório, A. H. (1946). *Psychologie de l'art*. Lisbon: Radio Renascença.

Patinkin, D. (1955). *Money, interest and prices*. New York: Peterson and Company.

Pareto, V. (1896). *Cours d'économie politique* (1963). Geneve: Buzino.

Pareto, V. (1906). *Manuel d'économie politique*. Paris: Bibliothèque Internationale d'économie politique, A. Bonnet.

Pareto, V. (1902). *Les systèmes socialistes*. Paris: Bibliothèque Internationale d'économie politique, A. Bonnet.

Pedrosa, A. (1992). *"A Faculdade de Direito de Coimbra e o ensino da economia política em Portugal."* Cardoso; Almodôvar.

Reis, J. (1988). 'O analfabetismo em Portugal no século XIX: uma interpretação'. *Nova Economia em Portugal, Estudos em homenagem a António Manuel Pinto Barbosa*. Lisbon: Universidade Nova de Lisboa.

Roll, E. (1945). *History of economic thought*. London: Faber and Faber.

Schumpeter, J. (1954). *History of economic analysis*. London-Boston-Sydney: George Allen & Unwin.

Stigller, G. J. (1965). The development of utility theory. *The Journal of Political Economy, LVIII*, Aug-Oct (1950), reprinted in *Essays in the History of Economics*. Chicago and London: University of Chicago Press.

Walras, L. (1874). Principe d'une théorie mathématique de l'échange. *Journal des Economistes*, avril.

Walras, L. (1874–1877, 1889, 1896, 1900, 1926). *Éléments d'économie politique pure*. Lausanne: F. Rouge.

Zumalacarregui, J. M. (1951). *Vilfredo Pareto 1848–1923*. Madrid: Instituto Superior Sancho Moncada, 8, serie A.

MR SMITH GOES TO MOSCOW: RUSSIAN EDITIONS OF *THE WEALTH OF NATIONS*

Vincent Barnett

ABSTRACT

Adam Smith never travelled to Russia but his published works certainly did. This short research note chronicles some pertinent facts on this topic, tracing the publication of editions of Smith's The Wealth of Nations in Russia in the nineteenth century and early part of the twentieth century; in particular it highlights a remarkable edition of this work published in the USSR in 1935. It also sketches some interpretations of Smith's ideas as given in Russian encyclopaedias and journals, and briefly chronicles the influence of some of Smith's ideas on policy-makers and economists in Russia in the nineteenth century. This account does not claim to be definitive, only to provide an introductory description of the propagation of some aspects of Smith's teachings in Russia from the end of the eighteenth century to World War Two. Smith himself was at least a little interested in Russia, as the three volumes on various aspects of Russia in his personal library indicate (Bonar, pp. 51, 111, 161), although unlike John Milton he never wrote a history of Moscovy.

Research in the History of Economic Thought and Methodology, Volume 20-A, pages 35–42.
Copyright © 2002 by Elsevier Science Ltd.
All rights of reproduction in any form reserved.
ISBN: 0-7623-0847-8

SMITH IN RUSSIA BEFORE 1917

Smith's ideas first reached Russia through two of his students, S. E. Desnitskii and I. A. Tret'yakov, who spent six years in Glasgow from 1761. On returning to Russia they were appointed as Professors at Moscow University, teaching law in line with Smith's ideas. Ian Ross suggested how Desnitskii managed to sway the Empress Catherine the Great with some of Smith's views on taxation and monopolies (Ross, 1995, pp. 131–132). Smith was thus influential in Russia eight years before *The Wealth of Nations* was first published in English in 1776, this influence reaching the highest possible level.

The leading Soviet historian of economic thought I. G. Blyumin declared categorically that the influence of Smith on Russian economic literature in the first two decades of the nineteenth century was very strong indeed (Blyumin, 1940, p. 50). This influence was accompanied by (or perhaps achieved in part by means of) the production of various Russian editions of Smith's works. For example the first complete Russian translation of Smith's *The Wealth of Nations* was published in St Petersburg in four parts between 1802 and 1806. The Emperor Alexander I, who according to J. F. Normano was for a time 'completely under the influence' of Smith and Bentham, ordered the translation, which was undertaken by N. R. Politkovskii for a fee of 5000 rubles (Normano, 1945, pp. 17–18). As one source explained:

> Though it was not remarkable for exactness, especially in the definition of the terms employed, it had a great influence on Russian students, who very quickly accepted the economic ideas of the great Scotchman (Miklachewsky, 1908, Vol. 3, p. 338).

Russian was sequentially the eighth language that *The Wealth of Nations* was translated into, German being the very first (Lai, 2000, p. xvii). Currents in nineteenth century Russian thought affected by Smith include the Decembrists, active in the 1820s and 1830s, and H. F. Storch, employed in the Russian service for much of his life. For example the Decembrist Pavel Pestel argued in favour of large-scale capitalist ownership of the land, such arguments being heavily influenced by Smith's thinking (Walicki, 1988, p. 63). Storch had studied philosophy and law first in Germany before travelling to St Petersburg in 1787 and becoming a (critical) disciple of Smith.

In addition, according to the well-known Russian/Ukrainian economist M. I. Tugan-Baranovsky, from the time of Alexander I the Russian government had desired an end to serfdom, this wish being in part inspired by Smith's idea of the unprofitability of this institution. Smith had referred to bondmen as a species of slavery and thought that the work done by slaves was 'the dearest of all' (Smith, 1976, p. 387). However, whether it was Smith's ideas that actually first inspired the drive against serfdom, or whether Smith just provided useful ideological ammunition for an already-selected policy, is an intricate point that cannot be resolved here. With regards to the reception of *The Wealth of Nations* in Britain, one historian has argued that 'there is no sign that the popularity of liberal economic policy in the 1780s was inspired by any reading of the *Wealth of Nations*; in fact, the relationship here appears to have worked the other way around' (Teichgraeber, 1987, p. 364). This may very well have been the case in Russia with respect to the abolition of serfdom.

Smith's teachings were also expounded in the official Russian government publication *The St Petersburg Journal* in the first decade of the nineteenth century, where it was suggested that the obligations of the government with respect to manufacture were limited to 'protecting the natural freedom of industry' (Tugan-Baranovsky, 1970, p. 216). Smith's ideas were so popular in government circles that in 1803 the Russian Minister of Internal Affairs had spoken of the tasks of government in purely Smithian language, for example referring to the need for 'removing all constraints' from industry and trade (Blyumin, 1940, p. 50). However that the propagation of this interpretation of Smith was not fully successful can be seen in the fact that by the end of the nineteenth century, what came to be known as 'the Witte system' included significant government support for certain strategic branches of industry such as the railways. It also encompassed a favourable view of some types of protectionism, Sergei Witte explicitly acknowledging his intellectual debt to Friedrich List. This suggests that in practice (as opposed to in official ideology) the enthusiasm of the Russian government for *laissez faire* in the nineteenth century was rather limited.

Another edition of Smith's *The Wealth of Nations* was published in three volumes in St Petersburg in 1866 (Fal'kner, 1925, p. 330). It was this edition which V. I. Lenin had consulted for his influential 1899 work *The Development of Capitalism in Russia*. Lenin had criticised Smith for dividing the price of a commodity into only two parts – variable capital (wages) and surplus value (profit and rent) – thus ignoring what Marx had christened constant capital (Lenin, 1899, pp. 47–49). More importantly Lenin failed to mention that four years before *The Development of Capitalism in Russia* was first published – in 1895 – a Russian edition of *The Theory of Moral Sentiments* (*Teoriya nravstvennykh chuvstv*) was published in St Petersburg. Lenin did not explain that this work opened with an acknowledgement of human motivations higher than self-interest, something that Marxist critics of Smith were sometimes reluctant to recognise. Lai suggested that in the nineteenth century Russian Marxists defended Smith against Populist critics, who had suggested that Smith's ideas were inapplicable to Russia and its communal traditions (Lai,

2000, p. xxx). In fact Marx himself had undergone something of a change of heart on the question of the importance of the Russian peasant commune, a shift which (in consequence) pitted him against the universal applicability of Smith's view of the significance of capitalist development.

Entries on Smith in Russian encyclopaedias written before 1917 give accounts of his life and character that throw some light onto the approach of the authors of the entries in question. For example in the entry on Smith in the multi-volume Brokgauz and Efron *Entsiklopedicheskii slovar'*, Tugan-Baranovsky highlighted Smith's alleged 'deficiency of moral courage' as shown in his refusal to publish David Hume's anti-religious works after Hume's death. Tugan-Baranovsky was at the time attempting to ground political economy in neo-Kantian moral philosophy. Tugan-Baranovsky was also concerned to point out that in *The Wealth of Nations* and *The Theory of Moral Sentiments* Smith had proceeded from feelings both of sympathy and egoism, egoistic behaviour being grounded in direct and involuntary sympathies created by human judge-ments (Tugan-Baranovsky, 1900, pp. 536–537). Regarding the ideological significance of Smith's work Tugan-Baranovsky's evaluation was that:

> Smith was completely free from a conscious defence of the interests of the upper classes, the bourgeoisie or land owners, which characterised the social position of his pupils of recent times. On the contrary, in all cases when the interests of the workers and the capitalists come into conflict Smith energetically comes down on the side of the workers. Nevertheless the ideas of Smith were put to use in service of the bourgeoisie. In the irony of history is written the transitional character of Smith's epoch (Tugan-Baranovsky, 1900, p. 539).

Tugan-Baranovsky thus distinguished between the original approach of an author and how their work was used by later generations. For Tugan-Baranovsky's most famous pupil, N. D. Kondratiev, Smith's contradictory account of the origin of value had provided the basis for two profoundly different conceptions of the labour theory of value (Kondratiev, 1991, p. 122). These involved seeing labour either as simply a scale of exchange value or more fundamentally as the essence of true value, a duality which enabled both Marxists and non-Marxists to claim Smith as a predecessor.

Smith's works were not always received positively by government officials in pre-revolutionary Russia. On 5 January 1884 *The Wealth of Nations* and *The Theory of Moral Sentiments* could be seen in a list of translated books which were to be banned from all reading-rooms and public libraries in Russia (Brown, 1975, pp. 268–269, fn. 59). This ban was probably short-lived and less than vigorously enforced, but it suggests that some uneasiness about Smith's ideas existed in Russia even before 1917. Smith was also the subject of various Russian biographical portraits, such as V. I. Yakovenko's *Adam Smit. Ego zhizn' i nauchnaya deyatel'nost'* published in St Petersburg in 1894. In general *The*

Wealth of Nations was reasonably well disseminated in Russia in the nineteenth century – a final one-volume edition being issued in 1895 – although opinion about its ultimate validity was split along predictable political lines.

SMITH IN RUSSIA AFTER 1917

While many perceived the October revolution as a revolution against *The Wealth of Nations*, in some ways it was also a revolution against *Capital*, given that Marx had predicted that advanced Western countries would be first to achieve socialism. Even so the Bolshevik *coup* generated changes in official attitudes towards Smith's works. After October 1917 Smith was treated in official Soviet ideology as one of the founding fathers of what was called 'classical bourgeois economics'. In particular he was characterised as the economist of the manufactory period of capitalism. This meant he was identified as the ideologue of the movement away from capitalism's initial implantation as justified by mercantilism, to promoting its further development through free trade (Rubin, 1979, p. 161). This followed a rather dour version of Marx's theory of historical materialism, which suggested that the ideological superstructure of any society simply reflected the requirements of the economic base. This interpretation of Smith was echoed in part by the Chairman of the U.S. Federal Reserve between 1970 and 1978, Arthur F. Burns. According to Burns, Smith's advocacy of 'the principle of free enterprise' was in direct countenance to the mercantalist system of government regulations which had been stifling economic growth in Europe between the sixteenth and eighteenth centuries (Burns, 1978, p. 24).

The first Soviet one-volume edition of *The Wealth of Nations* was issued in Petrograd in 1924 under the direction of P. I. Lyashchenko, a colleague of Kondratiev's (Lai, 2000, Table A15). A more extensive two-volume edition followed in 1931. However, perhaps one of the most extraordinary editions of *The Wealth of Nations* ever to be published was the 1935 Moscow-Leningrad edition, under the title *Issledovanie o prirode i prichinakh bogatstva narodov* (Smit, 1935). At a time when a series of political show-trials were being organised on Stalin's orders and when economists and many others were being accused of 'bourgeois sabotage' and shot, a Soviet edition of what was regarded by some as the 'founding text of free trade liberalism' was being prepared. The three people listed in the edition as responsible were I. Udal'tsov, R. Shapiro and V. Antonov. A print-run of 20,000 copies was indicated, with volume one costing 8 rubles 25 kopeks and volume two ten rubles. The edition included a 14-page foreword and the title page was printed in both Russian and English. It is unlikely that top government officials had not sanctioned this edition.

1935 had been a rather eventful year in Soviet history. In December 1934 one of the candidate members of the Politburo, Sergei Kirov, was assassinated, which resulted in a special decree on terrorist offences that gave the NKVD (the People's Commissariat of Internal Affairs) increased powers of trial and execution. A new 'Stalin constitution' was issued in 1936, while the first great show trials of leading Bolsheviks such as G. E. Zinoviev also began in 1936 (Ward, 1993, pp. 111–114). Internationally renowned Russian economists such as Kondratiev and L. N. Yurovsky, who had been arrested in 1930 for their pro-market and pro-peasant policies, were finally executed in 1938 (see Barnett, 1998, pp. 189–201). Yet amidst this heady atmosphere of fear and paranoia the Soviet State Social-Economic Press issued a two-volume octavo edition of *The Wealth of Nations* in Russian. This edition included a rather caricatured portrait of Smith opposite page vii and was bound (as was the fashion) in drab cloth with brown wrappers.

The foreword to the 1935 edition emphasised that Smith's work was firstly a theoretical tool in the struggle of the British bourgeoisie against the old feudal order. However as classical political economy was one of the three component sources of Marxism, study of it was still a useful activity. The analysis presented in the foreword stressed how Smith conceived of everything in terms of the natural order and natural rights. Egoism was posited as the basic motivation of human beings and individualism the natural consequence of this. Smith was thus accused of naturalising and making absolute a historically specific economic order. While this was all standard Soviet Marxist reductionism, the author of the introduction did admit that this approach allowed Smith to 'free himself of feudal appearances' and suggested that Smith's book played a positive role in the development of economics at the time of its first appearance. That Smith might have been concerned with issues such as distributive justice was however not discussed (Verburg, 2000). Nor was there any suggestion that Smith might have provided some pointers for an alternative to Ricardo's theory of international trade, one based on increasing returns rather than comparative advantage (Krugman, 1990, p. 4). According to Roger Backhouse the idea that Smith's economics was linked to the interests of the rising industrial class at the time of the industrial revolution was '*extremely* misleading' (Backhouse, 1985, p. 15).

Speculating a little, various possibilities suggest themselves in relation to the intentions of the originators of the 1935 edition. It is possible that by (at least tacitly) authorising the publication of an edition of *The Wealth of Nations* in 1935, Stalin was trying to drive home a point about Soviet industrialisation strategy. The industrial revolution in Britain had begun after free trade ideas had triumphed over protectionism, at least according to the leading authority on the Russian factory Tugan-Baranovsky (Deutscher, 1988, p. 339). Perhaps Stalin was making the point that Soviet industrialisation was now taking place in direct opposition to the principles of free trade liberalism that Smith represented to Soviet Marxists. The USSR had thus 'tamed' Smith's individualism and had provided an alternative to egoistic economics, and the 1935 edition of *The Wealth of Nations* was designed to triumphantly parade this fact before the world.

Another possible overtone of the 1935 edition could be connected to Smith's critique of mercantilism. This was noted by the canonical Soviet history of Russian economic thought, where the national character of the mercantilist system was emphasised (Pashkov, 1955, vol. 1, p. 309). Smith's internationalism contrasted starkly with Stalin's conception of developing socialism and promoting industrialisation within the bounds of one country, something that many Russian Marxists had thought impossible before 1917. It is also worth noting that 1935 was the mid-point of what are regarded as the 'three good years' of 1934–1936: 'good' in the sense of Soviet industry experiencing rapid expansion in line with the second five-year plan, not necessarily good for the individuals involved in generating this rapid growth (Davies, 1994, p. 154). That the West was in the midst of a 'great depression' whilst Soviet industry was 'thriving' was another point possibly being suggested by this edition.

Today of course the position is reversed, and the West is perceived by many to have won the battle of 'central planning' (Karl Marx) versus 'the market' (Adam Smith), although the reality is infinitely more complex than a simplistic understanding of these categories would suggest. Whether an American publisher might decide to issue a new English-language edition of Marx's *Capital* in response to this victory is an interesting point to ponder. If so the author of the introduction might want to consider Irving Fisher's remark that:

> ... each system has been compelled to borrow from each other. The capitalistic system, for instance, is not wholly capitalistic ... On the other hand, Russia ... has, in ten years, drifted as far toward capitalism as we, in a thousand years, have drifted toward socialism (Fisher, 1933, pp. 156–157).

An institutional economist might want to suggest that, during the period of the cold war at least, both the USSR and the USA had economic structures and mechanisms that could (in darker moments) be mistaken by the uninitiated for systems of power, despite the dramatically differing attitudes of high government to *The Wealth of Nations*.

REFERENCES

Backhouse, R. (1985). *A History of Modern Economic Analysis*. Oxford: Blackwell.

Barnett, V. (1998). *Kondratiev and the Dynamics of Economic Development: Long Cycles and Industrial Growth in Historical Context*. London: Macmillan.

Blyumin, I. G. (1940). *Ocherki ekonomicheskoi mysli v Rossii v pervoi polovine XIX veka*. Moscow-Leningrad: AN SSSR.

Bonar, J. (1932). *A Catalogue of the Library of Adam Smith*. New York: Kelley, 1966.

Brown, A. H. (1975). Adam Smith's First Russian Followers. In: A. Skinner & T. Wilson (Eds), *Essays on Adam Smith*. Oxford: Clarendon Press.

Burns, A. F. (1978). *Reflections of an Economic Policy Maker*. Washington: American Enterprise Institute.

Davies, R. W., Harrison, M., & Wheatcroft, S. G. (1994). *The Economic Transformation of the Soviet Union, 1913–45*. Cambridge: CUP.

Deutscher, I. (1988). *Stalin*. London: Penguin.

Fal'kner, S. A. (1925). *Proiskhozhdenie zheleznogo zakona zarabotnoi platy*. Moscow: Voprosy truda.

Fisher, I. (1933). *Booms and Depressions*. London. Allen and Unwin.

Kondratiev, N. D. (1991). *Osnovye problemy ekonomicheskoi statiki i dinamiki*. Moscow: Nauka.

Krugman, P. R. (1990). *Rethinking International Trade*. Cambridge, MA: MIT.

Lai, C. (2000). *Adam Smith Across Nations*. Oxford: OUP.

Lenin, V. I. (1899). The Development of Capitalism in Russia. In: *Collected Works, 3*. London: Lawrence & Wishart (1977).

Miklachewsky, I. (1908). Russian School of Political Economy. In: R. H. I. Palgrave, *Dictionary of Political Economy*. London: Macmillan.

Normano, J. F. (1945). *The Spirit of Russian Economics*. New York: John Day.

Pashkov, A. I. (1955). *Istoriya Russkoi ekonomicheskoi mysli*. Moscow: GosIzdat. Vol. 1.

Ross, I. S. (1995). *The Life of Adam Smith*. Oxford: Clarendon Press.

Rubin, I. I. (1929). *A History of Economic Thought*. London: Ink Links (1979).

Smit, A. (1935). *Issledovanie o prirode i prichinakh bogatstva narodov*. Moscow-Leningrad: GosSotsEkon.

Smith, A. (1776). *An Inquiry into the Nature and Causes of the Wealth of Nations*. Oxford: OUP (1976).

Teichgraeber, R. F. (1987). 'Less Abused that I had Reason to Expect': The Reception of *The Wealth of Nations* in Britain, 1776–90. *Historical Journal, 30*(2): 337–366.

Tugan-Baranovsky, M. I. (1900). Smit, Adam. In: F. A. Brokgauz & I. A. Efron (Eds), *Entsiklopedicheskii slovar'*. St Petersburg, Vol. 30.

Tugan-Baranovsky, M. I. (1970). *The Russian Factory in the Nineteenth Century*. Illinois: Irwin.

Verburg, R. (2000). Adam Smith's concern on the issue of distributive justice. *European Journal of the History of Economic Thought, 7* (Spring), 23–44.

Walicki, A. (1988). *A History of Russian Thought*. Oxford: Clarendon Press.

Ward, C. (1993). *Stalin's Russia*. London: Arnold.

RECOLLECTIONS OF A DINNER FOR JOHN MAYNARD KEYNES, WASHINGTON, D.C., 1941

F. Taylor Ostrander

ABSTRACT

This paper recounts my personal recollection of the small dinner meeting for Keynes during his first wartime visit to Washington, D.C. I recall the occasion well as it was a memorable one, and I have often told this story to students and friends. Despite the passage of time, I write about it now to get my story on the record as a part of my memoirs.

The paper also includes my comments on Roy Harrod's references to that dinner in his 1951 biography of Keynes, and a review of Keynes' correspondence following the dinner with some of the economists who were there.

BACKGROUND

On April 11, 1941, President Roosevelt had created a new independent agency, the Office of Price Control and Civilian Supply, OPACS, and named Leon Henderson its Administrator. On May 1, Henderson named Kenneth Galbraith Deputy Administrator for Price Control; Joseph Wiener became Deputy for Civilian Supply.

Research in the History of Economic Thought and Methodology, Volume 20-A, pages 43–50.

OPACS took over the earlier work and staff of Henderson's Price Stabilization Division, one of seven Divisions of the National Defense Advisory Commission, NDAC, which had been established on May 29, 1940 just before the fall of France in mid-June. NDAC was the first new agency to deal with the impact on USA of the war in Europe, though we were still a neutral.[1]

I had joined Henderson's Price Stabilization Division at NDAC in mid August 1940 as co-director of a newly formed unit, the Defense Finance Section. That is why I was one of those invited to attend Henderson's dinner for Keynes. This was to be the only time I would ever meet in person that eminent economist whose writings I had been studying since 1930 in college days.

THE DINNER MEETING

Leon Henderson arranged and was host of the dinner for Keynes. It was held on Tuesday June 10, 1941 in a private dining room at the National Press Club.

Present were Keynes, Henderson and his two deputies Ken Galbraith and Joe Wiener and his guests: Sumner Pike, a member of the Securities and Exchange Commission; Isador Lubin, one of the six assistants to the President; Professor Jacob Viner, economic consultant to Secretary Morgenthau; and John Cassels.

Also present were two senior advisors to Henderson, Columbia Professor J. M. Clark and Duke Professor Calvin B. Hoover.

From Henderson's staff were: Richard Gilbert, director of the Defense Economics Section, Walter Salant and Don Humphrey of that section; Raymond Goldsmith and I, co-directors of the Defense Finance Section; and David Ginsburg, general counsel of OPACS. I believe Homer Jones, senior advisor of our section, and Donald E. Wallace, economist at OPACS, may also have been there.

Someone from the British Embassy may have been with Keynes, but it was not the Embassy's economic advisor, Redvers Opie.

Everyone present knew Keynes' famous brochure published in early 1940, *How to Pay for the War*, in which he advocated very strong fiscal restraint on civilian consumption including "compulsory saving." Most were also aware of the National Income White Paper issued at the time of the Budget speech in March 1941, just three months before the dinner, in which its authors, James Meade and Richard Stone, working in collaboration with Keynes, had buttressed his view of the need for strong anti-inflationary wartime fiscal policy in Britain.

Predictably, in his after-dinner talk Keynes repeated those views he had set out before and applied them to the American scene. Although the U.S. was not yet at war, Keynes urged increased fiscal restraint in the U.S. in order to be better prepared to prevent inflation resulting from our defense build-up and Allied purchases of war materials.

A general discussion followed Keynes' long and detailed talk. Walter Salant and Don Humphrey, who sat opposite Keynes at the inside of the U-shaped table, argued strongly that increased fiscal restraint was not then needed in America as it would inhibit further progress in reducing unemployment. Challenging Keynes, they argued that Keynesian principles required that all resources be fully employed before applying fiscal restraint.

Keynes responded to their argument, gently but without giving any ground. The two young American economists continued to argue with the famous man until some of us felt it almost embarrassing to watch. Finally Keynes, obviously somewhat displeased, pushed his chair back from the table and brought the debate to an end as he said, rather sharply, "On this point you are more Keynesian than I." It was an electrifying moment, never to be forgotten!

HARROD'S ACCOUNT OF THAT DINNER

Ten years later Roy Harrod, noted economist at Oxford, published his insightful and charming biography, *The Life of John Maynard Keynes* (1951). It is a classic memoir, and I thought it revealed almost as much about the author as about his subject.

Harrod's biography made two references to the dinner for Keynes. Together, they accord with much of what I recall.

In his Chapter XII, "Into the Second World War," Harrod mentions a small dinner party for Keynes given by Leon Henderson at the National Press Club with about a dozen from Henderson's staff who were "responsible for policy." Harrod briefly summarized the main points of Keynes' after-dinner talk:

> Keynes urged that a more repressive fiscal policy was needed to prevent the American economy falling victim to inflation (p. 508).

However, Harrod did not refer here to the discussion that followed Keynes' talk, or to Keynes' sharp response to those who had differed with him, or to his now famous statement that they were "more Keynesian than he was himself." Thus Harrod's account missed the drama of the evening.

Instead, Harrod's next sentence – in the same paragraph – referred to *correspondence* that had taken place *after the dinner* when Walter Salant had written Keynes to repeat the position he had taken at the dinner, providing figures and Keynesian analysis to justify his view that no change in U.S. policy was then needed. Continuing on the next page (p. 509) Harrod quoted a paragraph from this correspondence: in his letter to Salant of July 27, 1941,

Keynes wrote of his admiration for the forward-looking views of some younger American economists; he felt such men were more numerous in Washington than in London.

Harrod's second reference to the Henderson dinner in Washington in the spring of 1941 comes on the first page (p. 525) of Chapter XIII, "Bretton Woods," where Harrod wrote:

> He [Keynes] certainly had supporters in the United States. Indeed he is remembered to have chaffed a group of experts assembled to meet him on his first war visit for being more Keynesian than he was himself.

That was not at all what Keynes had meant when he used that phrase at the Henderson dinner earlier that year. Harrod has *reversed* its meaning from negative to positive. At the Henderson dinner, those who were "more Keynesian than he" had gone *too far*, and had differed with Keynes, they were protagonists, not on his side. In Harrod's new formulation, those "more Keynesian than he" are shown as no longer *protagonists*, they are *supporters*, even further committed internationalists than Keynes.

Not only was the story of Keynes' classic phrase misplaced in context. The subject matter was entirely different in the two cases. Salant and Humphrey, as good internationalists, could be counted on to be supporters on international postwar policy, but that was not at issue at the dinner. What was at issue was American fiscal policy in relation to Keynesian principles.

Having not been at the dinner, Harrod had not himself witnessed the scene; he no doubt worked from notes made by Keynes or perhaps by a British official who accompanied Keynes to the dinner. Harrod certainly knew of the contretemps at the end of the dinner for he put the classic phrase together with Keynes having "chaffed" some of Henderson's staff.

Why would Harrod have so mixed up his reporting of this event in his 1951 biography of Keynes? I have no answer, but as a surmise, I offer one possible explanation.

Could it have been possible that Harrod had *deliberately* split his account of the dinner into two parts *in order to* soften any implied criticism of Walter Salant as one of the participants in the argument at the dinner?

I attended Harrod's lectures on Money at Oxford in 1932–1933, and knew him slightly. I recall him as a very gentle man, a true gentleman. This quality stands out in other parts of Harrod's biography of Keynes, as when he tries to explain Harry Dexter White's Anglophobia!

I believe it would have been quite in character for Harrod *deliberately* to have arranged his account of the dinner in the way he did. In his *Preface* in 1951 Harrod acknowledged receiving help from Walter Salant, and he may have known Salant personally by that time. Salant was such a nice person, one can easily understand why Harrod would have wanted to avoid identifying him as one of those whom Keynes had "chaffed."

In the 1960s I met Sir Roy Harrod at a conference reception in New York City. I had an opportunity to mention to him my questions about why he had described the Henderson dinner as he did in his biography of Keynes. Harrod seemed quickly to recall the facts I mentioned and took my point at once. He told me he would make a correction if he revised his book. (No revision, but only *reprints* of the original text have been published.)

KEYNES' CORRESPONDENCE FOLLOWING THE DINNER

I began to draft this paper during 1996 and up to this point in its revisions my recollections of the 1941 dinner for Keynes were my own oft-recounted memories of the event. My reactions to Harrod's 1951 account of the dinner were formed many years ago, before I spoke about them to Harrod in the 1960s.

I referred above to Harrod's mentioning that Keynes corresponded with Walter Salant after the Washington dinner, and that Harrod had quoted some sentences from a letter Keynes wrote to Salant on July 27, several weeks after the dinner. Those quoted sentences, however, had not mentioned the dinner or the discussion afterward.

That brought to mind two questions that nagged my curiosity: what else did Keynes say in that letter to Salant, and did Keynes himself leave any record of the Washington dinner?

In February 2001 I found the answer to both these questions. There are indeed a number of Keynes' own writings about his meetings and correspondence with Salant and other American economists who were at the Henderson dinner in June 1941. They provide valuable information that Harrod did not use.

This material was first published more than twenty years ago, but I did not know of it until now when I have just seen it for the first time. It confirms my earlier recollections of the dinner and adds new perspective to round out this paper.

These letters and other related materials were published in Volume 23, one of the later volumes in the set of 30 volumes of Keynes' *Collected Writings*.[2] They are in Chapter 5 of volume 23 entitled "Washington 1941: Discussions with Economists."[3]

In a letter dated May 23 to his friend Abba Lerner (who was teaching at London School of Economics), Keynes described his first encounter with a group of "youngish" American economists at Lauchlin Currie's home the evening before. Gilbert, Salant and Humphrey were among those present but were not mentioned in this letter. Keynes had expressed his concern about the danger of inflation from America's mobilization of resources in its defense program. The American group argued against imposing any fiscal restraint in a defense economy before full utilization of resources was reached. Keynes wrote Lerner that he had not accepted their argument.

This letter may also confirm the central role that Currie is known to have played in espousing this position at that time. (Sandilands, *The Life and Work of Lauchlin Currie*, 1997, pp 104–105.)

There is no account by Keynes himself of the Henderson dinner, about three weeks later. However, the Editor of *Collected Writings* has included an extensive summary of Keynes' after-dinner talk at the Henderson dinner and the discussion that followed, written the day after the dinner by Salant and Humphrey for their director, Richard Gilbert.

As well as naming those present, the Salant/Humphrey account of the dinner shows that Keynes' after-dinner talk was long and very detailed. Their account also shows that there was a long and emphatic debate between the two disciples and their master.

Keynes referred to and carried forward the discussion that had begun earlier at Lauchlin Currie's home. Essentially, Keynes argued the position as Harrod described it (quoted above): Keynes urged more and early fiscal restraint in America.

Apart from a few minor points, my story of the dinner and my commentary on Harrod as presented here are confirmed. However, my memories of the details of both the Keynes and the Salant/Humphrey points of view have been considerably enhanced.

I suppose it would have been too much to expect that Salant and Humphrey would report Keynes' "chaffing" them, or his classic remark, "You are more Keynesian than I" when he terminated their argument – and apparently the dinner as well! The Salant/Humphrey summary does indicate that they carried their argument right up to the very moment when the meeting ended in a "general melee," as their account puts it:

> At about this time the meeting broke up and the few remarks which we were able to get in along these lines were probably lost in the general melee.

Two days after the dinner, on June 12, Salant wrote Keynes a very polite, long and detailed restatement of the position he and Humphrey had argued at the dinner, and provided tables of figures. Later, he and Humphrey called on Keynes a couple of times, and Gilbert also had a meeting with him. Keynes wrote to

Salant on July 9 and July 24, and wrote him a "farewell letter" on July 27 – the one quoted in part by Harrod (above).

Illuminating as it might be to the theorist, I will not go into the intricacies of the debate between the two sides as revealed in this correspondence. The three disciples had constructed in Keynesian notation a detailed statistical model using all the new Keynesian concepts – the multiplier, accelerators, propensities, the savings/investment gap, degree of utilization of industrial capacity, labor and other kinds of resources, etc.

These indicated both their familiarity with Keynes' new *General Theory* approach and the policy result that they hoped to achieve – to reduce stubbornly high unemployment by continuing deficit financing, so as not to inhibit any growth of GNP.

Essentially, in the continuation of the argument in these letters, Keynes did not deviate from what I described earlier in this paper: Keynes felt they were over-optimistic and were stretching their figures to reach a conclusion he did not accept.

Nevertheless, Keynes came to know and appreciate his former protagonists. In his letters to Walter Salant there is none of the sharpness that lay behind Keynes' classic retort that ended the Henderson dinner. In the "farewell" letter to Salant on July 27, Keynes expressed his admiration for their skills and earnestness. It seems to me that Keynes was clearly trying to offset his earlier sharp response.

At the Henderson dinner Keynes had met John Maurice Clark the noted American economist and Henderson advisor. They met again at a conference in late July. They were of the same generation, Clark at 56 only one year younger. Clark wrote Keynes on July 24, expressing his admiration for the "coherent logical theoretical system" Keynes had constructed which, Clark wrote, furnishes

> a key for working out definite answers in terms of policy . . . All that has tremendous power; and is also exposed to the dangers of too-undiscriminating application . . . of which I think the Gilbert-Humphrey attitude is one illustration.

I quote the full text of the reply that Keynes sent to Clark on July 26:

> Dear Professor Clark,
>
> I have much appreciated getting your letter. . . . As you will have gathered the other evening, I agree with what you say about the danger of a 'school', even when it is one's own.
>
> There is great danger in quantitative forecasts which are based exclusively on statistics relating to conditions by no means parallel. I have tried to persuade Gilbert and Humphrey and Salant that they should be more cautious. I have also tried to persuade them that they have tended to neglect certain theoretical considerations which are important in the interests

of simplifying their statistical task. I am afraid I have only partially succeeded, though I expect the results of the argument will sink in.

I am very sorry to have differed from them in opinion, because I have a high appreciation of their gifts and of the work they are doing. I like Gilbert's persistence and indomitableness. They are so much on the right side of things and thinking so well and clearly that one need not be afraid perhaps of criticising them.

I felt in our discussion the other day that underlying the superficial differences of opinion there really was a wide measure of general agreement, and nearly all of us would have found ourselves united in any contest with the outside world. And that is as it should be between colleagues and economists.

Yours,

J. M. KEYNES

With his agreement on ". . . the danger of a 'school', even when it is one's own" Keynes adds another classic phrase of particular relevance here. His perceptive letter provides a fitting conclusion for this paper.

NOTES

1. On August 28, 1941 OPACS became the Office of Price Administration, OPA, after the civilian supply function was split off to the Office of Production Management, OPM, which later was renamed the War Production Board, WPB.

2. *The Collected Writings of John Maynard Keynes*, edited by Donald Moggridge, 30 volumes, 1971–1983 (Index in volume 30); Cambridge University Press and Macmillan, New York.

3. Chapter 5, "Washington, 1941: Discussions with Economists" pp. 181–193; Volume XXIII, *Activities 1940–1943, External Finance*, 1979, *Collected Writings*.

ACKNOWLEDGMENTS

I am indebted to Professor D. E. Moggridge, University of Toronto, for his helpful suggestions on an earlier draft of this paper.

GHANA: A WORLD APART

Y. S. Brenner

INTRODUCTION

Heinrich Heine once wrote: *"Denk ich an Deutschland in der Nacht, dann bin ich um den schlaf gebracht . . ."* (When at night my thoughts turn to Germany I can no longer sleep . . .). Lately the same is happening to me when I think of Africa. In spite of the foreign aid which has perceptively increased to the poorest countries their GDP fell between 1980 and 1998 from about 400 dollars to 300 dollars, and their foreign debts rose from about 150 dollars to 300 dollars per head of the population.

Friends ask me why I decided to publish my collection of stories at this time and not earlier. The reasons are many, but the most important was that I did not wish to furnish ammunition to people who would grasp at any thing that might help them to make people believe that foreign aid is money wasted. I did not want my recollections misconstrued to serve such purpose. I firmly believe that help for the economically backward countries is imperative, but I strongly object to the manner in which it was given. The risk that my stories will be misconstrued persists but this risk is overshadowed these days by the need to warn the genuine friends of the peoples of the underdeveloped countries against repeating the errors which blighted their earlier efforts. The point is that a new situation has arisen. The old political coalitions in the rich countries which sustained the misapplication of the aid flowing to the Third World is falling apart; and the introduction of genetically manipulated crops, which cannot be reproduced in the poor countries, and therefore deprives farmers in Africa of the chance to supply their growing domestic urban markets, does not

Research in the History of Economic Thought and Methodology, Volume 20-A, pages 51–147.
Copyright © 2002 by Elsevier Science Ltd.
All rights of reproduction in any form reserved.
ISBN: 0-7623-0847-8

allow me to remain silent now that the search for a new approach to development is on.

In June 2000, at the special session of the General Assembly in Geneva the Secretary General of the United Nations, Kofi Annan, himself a Ghanaian, called upon the rich countries to open their markets to exports from the Third World, to cancel the poor countries' foreign debts, and to provide *better directed* development aid. It is the last mentioned – the need to think again about the manner in which aid ought to be given and distributed, which decided me to publish my recollections at this time.

Almost forty years ago, like many others from England, France, Russia, and the USA, I went to Ghana hoping to play a part in the economic development of this first African country liberated from the colonial yoke. Naive as most of us were, we believed that it was mainly lack of capital and technological know-how which separated the developed from the undeveloped countries. Those of us who came from western Europe had seen the success of the Marshall Plan and thought that with massive foreign financial support and with our scientific and technological knowledge it was only a matter of a few decades before Ghana caught up with the developed world. We all knew that economic growth requires investment, and that investment requires savings. We also knew that the people of Ghana were too poor to save. What we did not know was that development involves much more than investment and technology. When some of us finally realized this, it was too late. Too many vested interests in both the rich and the poor countries had become so firmly entrenched that it made a new start with a more sophisticated development doctrine almost impossible in Africa. Politically powerful coalitions of variously motivated partners had formed which, each partner for reasons of his own, resisted the abandonment of old misconceptions. In the rich countries this coalition combined Christians, humanists, socialists, social democrats, industrialists, bankers, politicians and generals. In the poor countries it united bureaucrats with greedy and power hungry political parvenus.

The Christians and humanists were unaccustomed to concern themselves with the manner in which their money was used and distributed. Socialists and Social Democrats were scared of being branded neo-colonialists if they attached the necessary conditions for the proper allocation and distribution of resources in the former colonies. Industrial enterprises and banks were more keen to secure raw materials and markets and making profits in the Third World than interested in development. Politicians wanted to make sure that the new nations would be on their side in their global designs and tow their line at the United Nations even if this meant financing despotic and corrupt rulers. The industrial military complex and its generals supported foreign aid for profit and to serve their Cold War strategies. Thus, while those motivated by compassion and humanity were unwilling or unable to ask questions about how the money was spent, those motivated by different reasons saw no cause for interfering in "the internal affairs" of the newly independent states unless the money received by them was expended where it did not jibe with their particular interests, and as long as the country did not change its allegiance in the struggle between the eastern and the western blocs.

The result of this partnership was that East and West courted whatever government ruled the developing countries and allowed it to spend aid in any way it wished. For the large companies in the donor countries which were doing business in the Third World foreign aid was a boon. It not only made sure the flow of raw materials, but created an effective demand for goods where previously people had been too poor to buy. For them it made little difference whether this demand was helping the long-term development of the country or was squandered on building economically unnecessary prestige constructions, for military hardware or for luxury consumption goods to gratify the wants of a small unproductive elite. If they wanted a moral justification, they could always fall back upon mainstream economics professing that distribution does not matter. "All ships rise with the rising tide" – if some Africans were becoming rich by appropriating the aid for themselves, their ill gotten wealth would "trickle down" and eventually everyone will benefit.

In the poor countries the attainment of independence exacerbated tribal and social conflicts. In Ghana, it intensified the rivalry for power and prestige between the urban literate elite and the traditional leadership of village elders and chiefs. Economically the former rulers bequeathed to the new state a typically colonial structure. Most Ghanaians lived in small villages and eked out a scanty almost self-sufficient livelihood from farming. The country's main foreign-currency earnings came from cacao, its most important export crop, and from gold, hardwoods, manganese and bauxite. Cacao was produced next to their subsistence crops by a fairly large number of relatively affluent farmers in the costal forests and sold through a reasonably well functioning marketing organization. Gold extraction and the timber trade were foreign-run and technologically advanced. Rail tracks and roads connected the three major towns to serve the needs of the extraction and timber trades but had few if any links to rural communities. The approximately 30,000 African wage workers in mining and extraction came from various tribes and were loyal to their traditional chiefs and institutions.

The people who spearheaded the struggle for independence in Ghana belonged mainly to the intellectual elite. The Convention People's Party, which was in the front of the struggle, was led by Dr. Kwame Nkrumah. Like many

African pioneers of independence he was foreign educated. Having first been to Achimota College, he then went to the United States, where he studied at Lincoln University in Pennsylvania, and later to the London School of Economics in the United Kingdom. After his return to the Gold Coast he became Prime Minister in 1954 when his party won the general elections. The country, which he renamed Ghana, achieved dominion status in 1957, and in 1960 he became the independent state's President. His followers were mainly members of the old locally recruited colonial bureaucracy and employees of foreign trading companies who were hoping for personal advancement once the foreigners were gone and they inherited their positions. He received active popular support from teachers, urban unemployed, the relatively well organized Accra market women and women's church organizations.

Thus, having no economically productive strata of society behind him, and in need of funds to meet the increasing demand on the country's resources for infrastructural development, and to satisfy his bureaucratic supporters, the not inconsiderable reserves from the colonial era soon dwindled away. Before long the only alternative open to him was to squeeze more money out of the rural population, particularly from the cacao farmers, which alienated him further and further from the majority of his people and made his rule increasingly dictatorial. Labour unrest in 1961, especially in Accra, obliged him to spend even more than before on public works to provide employment for the urban unemployed and assuage their dissatisfaction. Failing to obtain more help from the West, because of his neutralist stand on international affairs, he strengthened his links with the Soviet bloc, and in 1964 established in Ghana a one-party state. A severe slump in world cacao prices exacerbated the economic decline and led to inflation and chaos, and in 1966 Dr. Nkrumah's government was overthrown by a military coup.

Naturally, given the economic and social structure of the country, the new leaders could do little to change the causes which precipitated Nkrumah's downfall. The one thing they could do was to sever the link with the Soviet bloc and receive Western economic aid. Before long, many previously scarce imported consumer goods became available again and gave to those able to afford them the feeling that things were looking up. For the majority of people not much changed but many welcomed the relief from the oppressive atmosphere Nkrumah and his party had imposed on Ghanaian institutions and society.

I arrived in Ghana in the Fall of 1962. At this time the population was estimated at 7,500,000 and the labour force at 2,700,000. Population accretion was reckoned at $2^1/_2\%$ annually. More than three-quarters of the people lived in rural habitations and less than one-quarter in localities with more than 5,000 inhabitants and only 8% in towns with more than 100,000 inhabitants. Approximately 60% of the working population were engaged in farming of which about 1,000,000 produced field crops and foodstuffs, and 600,000 cacao and other export crops next to their food. Together with forestry, lumbering and fishing, agriculture produced half the country's Gross Domestic Product. Cacao accounted for 70% of all exports. Of the remaining labour-force, 24% was engaged in commerce and services and 14% in manufacturing, mining and construction. Since independence there had been a small increase in the number of people employed in services, particularly in teaching and administration, and a somewhat greater increase in people engaged in construction. Population accretion was not matched by increasing employment and productivity in agriculture and consequently food imports rose. On average Ghanaians spent about 60% of their income on food, drink and tobacco, and the augmentation of supplies from abroad became quite formidable, while a slump in world cacao prices was seriously reducing export earnings.

Efforts made since the attainment of independence to build up an industrial sector were largely unsuccessful. Altogether, wage-workers in manufacture and construction totaled less than 150,000 out of close to 300,000 people engaged in these sectors. The rest were home-makers engaged in traditional trades such as home-brewing and weaving. Excluding farmers, workers directly engaged in production totalled approximately 50,000, most of whom were engaged in mining and lumbering. Here too the proportion of wage-earners was about one in two. In short, about 14% of the entire working population, that is less than half of the country's non-agricultural labour force, was directly engaged in production, and half of these did not receive money wages.

Ghana covers an area of about 92,100 square miles of relatively poor soil. The North is typical savannah land where even the top soil is very poor. In the Southern forest region the situation is better. The humus is protected by the overgrowth by which it is produced, but the land is constantly threatened by exhaustion. The farmers in this region developed a particular method of cultivation consistent with their lack of capital but relative abundance of land. This method, known as *shifting* or *rotative* cultivation, consists of using only a small portion of the available land at one time and then moving to another portion and leaving the first used fallow until it regains the fertility that makes it again worth cultivating. In this way at any time no more than 10 or 11% of the total area of Ghana was cultivated.

In the Northwest and Northeast of the country, where population pressure was severe, the land was cultivated continuously. The people kept cattle which provided some manure, but land yields were very scanty indeed. Further South, in most of the savannah, the population was thinly spread and land was often left fallow for as many as ten years before it was planted again. In the southern forests shifting cultivation was broken by tree crops such as cacao, plantains, oil palms and lime. There, too, land not planted with trees, was only inter-mittently exploited but at shorter intervals. Partly this was due to the humus, but often because of the increasing population and the encroachment of the tree crops on the available land. Probably of the 10% of the country's entire cultivated land in any one year no less than 6% was planted with cacao, and 4% with food crops. In the north yam was the staple food. Other crops included millet, groundnuts, guinea corn, and in smaller quantities maize, rice and tomatoes. Cattle was kept for meat and for bride-price. Most of the south of the country is not suitable for yams and the staple food was cassava. The main crop there was cacao and as young cacao trees require plantains and cocoyams for their protection, these were also grown there in some abundance. In smaller quantities, bananas, citrus fruit, coffee, copra, maize, oil palms, rice and tobacco were also grown in the forest region.

Everywhere farms were too small and dispersed to make mechanical equip-ment, even if it had been available, economically viable. During my stay in Ghana several attempts were made to introduce "tractor stations" where farmers could hire mechanical equipment for the number of hours they required it, but the undertaking was unsuccessful because of the earlier mentioned and a variety of other reasons, including the high cost of maintaining machinery in hot and humid climate and without easily accessible repair facilities.

Population accretion in the farming villages compelled farmers to exploit their land at shorter intervals. With more family members seeking work and having to be fed, the length of the period for which land was left fallow to regain fertility became shorter and shorter and its per acre yield decreased. Many farmers who had earlier divided their land into seven portions and exploited one at a time, found it necessary to divide their land into only four portions to find employment for their families. Total output increased but per capita produce diminished. This is the phenomenon known to development economists as *underemployment*.

From the colonial era, Ghana inherited an education system which was good in comparison with that of many other African countries. There were several sound middle schools, most of them established and run by missionaries, and there was a university with a special relationship to the University of London. It provided the country with well educated and able Ghanaian scholars. The problem was that in general the education system produced mainly low-level civil servants and clerks and very few technologically schooled persons. In other words, the system was not geared to serve a nascent industrial state but a colonial administration and foreign trading companies. It spread literacy and provided an administrative personnel capable of replacing the colonial administration but was not suitable for raising the country's economic efficiency. It produced a kind of literate elite which looked down on the rural population and regarded any directly productive work as demeaning. For a long time before independence education gave men prestige and the opportunity to get an office job with an income well above that earned by people doing other work. Frequently, particularly in government service, it also gave the holder of the office the opportunity to help other members of his extended family. As employment opportunities for the educated were almost entirely restricted to the civil service and the expatriate trading firms, the students developed a bias in favor of studying the humanities and law to the exclusion of other disciplines. Education therefore became reduced to the training of low level office personnel. The ability to read and write English established a claim to white-collar employment. In this way the colonial education bequeathed to Ghanaian society a social stratum of people who felt apart and above the rest of the population and who, after independence, aped the attitude and tone of the former colonial rulers in their dealings with the illiterate. Even junior administrative office-workers received an initial salary of 20s. per day while a fully qualified mechanic earned only 15s. and a locomotive driver, a tug master, or a riveters' foreman, seldom received more than 12s.2d. These were the daily rates of pay determined in Article 10 of the collective work agreement (CAO) dated October 1960 which remained in force until 1967 when they were upgraded in line with the rising cost of living index.

There were reasons why the standard of living of the productive labour-force in the towns did not improve. The diminishing per capita output in farming compelled more and more people to seek alternative employment in the towns and the supply constantly exceeded the demand for labour. Then, unlike the European urban working-force before certain social security arrangements were introduced there, the Ghanaian urban worker usually remained part of his extended family in the village and able to return to it or receive its assistance when things were at their worst. Finally, the traditional culture of obedience to authority impeded the workers' aptitude to stand up to their employers. This became even more so after Nkrumah's regime practically imposed his party bosses upon such trade unions as existed and used his political power to repress dissension and protests.

In short, the character of the education system, the legacy of the colonial economic structure, the traditionally authoritarian culture, and the obligation of individuals to share their income with their extended family, drained agriculture and the other productive sectors of the Ghanaian economy of its most ambitious and able manpower and drove many young able Ghanaians out of the country.

Like everywhere else in a dictatorship, so in Ghana, it was mainly the un-imaginative careerists, and persons who will obey orders without questioning their ethical implications, who found their way into responsible positions.

The colonial legacy of appointing rather than electing officials continued after independence and prevented the evolution of a leadership which felt responsible to its constituency. Moreover, the administrators who took over political power from the withdrawn colonial administration were constantly under pressure to create employment for the members of their clans. Thus the number of office workers paid out of state funds steadily increased and the number of people flocking to the towns in search of work, who had to be assuaged by the state finding employment for them, imposed a constantly rising burden on government resources.

Turning to the Soviet Union for assistance and adopting the Leninist-Stalinist prescription for accelerated economic growth, Nkrumah strengthened his political grip on the country and squeezed more and more money out of the agricultural sector to meet the rising costs of his attempt to improve Ghana's infrastructure and industrial base. The result was not very different from that experienced by the Russians.

In a sense, the leadership in Ghana became the prisoner of its own admin-istrative organs. In the absence of another equally well-organized pressure group and of a tradition to organize political power from below on a national or even only regional scale, the civil service, the army and the police remained almost the sole factors in Ghanaian politics. Hence, in spite of much lip-service to socialism and development, the government became increasingly *of, by, and for* the civil servants. There was however one more element that though not organized needed to be watched and taken into account, namely the citizens of Accra. Their proximity to the centers of administration and their propensity to riot made them dangerous unless they were placated by employment and food prices they could afford. The labour unrest in 1961 made this very clear. The government was therefore obliged to create employment for the continually growing number of people flocking to the town. With no industry to absorb this labour supply, Nkrumah's government created work which was often, from an economic point of view, at least in the short run entirely unprofitable.

Paradoxically the growing urban population did not increase but reduced farmers' incentives to produce food for marketing. In part this was due to the earlier mentioned decreasing per capita output in agriculture, but it was also the result of the government's effort to prevent food prices from rising by imposing price controls. In its endeavor to restrict the wage-cost of the growing urban labour-force, victual prices had to remain low, and having neither the wish, nor at this time even any longer the ability, to invest in raising productivity in agriculture, the price controls discouraged farmers from producing for markets. Nkrumah tried to overcome the food shortage by inviting Russian, American and Israeli experts to set up state farms and tractor stations to "industrialize" agriculture in more or less the manner the Soviet Union had organized its *Sovchos*. But the final say about the running of these farms was left in the hands of the Ghanaian bureaucracy which was neither competent nor interested in making the scheme serve the public interest or simply profitable. Thus while from 1954 to 1960 the country experienced a general average annual rise in prices of approximately 3%, prices rose by about 5% in each of the following years, with the exception of 1961, the year in which import controls were introduced, and prices rose by 10%. The farmers did not benefit from this. Inflation, the relatively steeper rise of imported goods, and more taxes, deprived them of their potential advantage from the rising food prices. After the fall of the Nkrumah government the farmers' fate was hardly better.

The strange thing about Nkrumah was that although he claimed to be a Marxian materialist his efforts to solve problems were surprisingly idealistic. He called upon the people to exert themselves for the glory of Ghana and socialism. It is true that such an approach was not entirely alien to Ghana. The mission schools had been trying to do the same though with a different object of veneration. But God or gods had much deeper roots in West African society than nationalism or socialism. Ghana as a *nation-state* was far too new to replace traditional familial and tribal loyalties, and *socialism* was the product of an urban working-class which in Europe accompanied the process of industrialization which had not even started in Ghana. In Europe the socialist ethos developed in opposition to the hardship industrialization imposed upon the working class, and within a cultural framework which was different from Ghana's. The attempt to transplant this ethos was therefore meaningless.

In practice university students were exhorted in the name of Ghana's national aspirations to study science and technology, but no arrangements were made to create or find for them employment in their fields of study, or to adjust the salary structure to encourage students to choose these subjects. Workers were urged in the name of socialism not to claim wage increases, while administrators' salaries were periodically reviewed and party officials made public display of their increasing wealth. By deceptive progressivity the education system was damaged by an ill conceived attempt to spread literacy without paying the cost and to use it for disseminating political ideas. In great haste and with little consideration for details the government introduced universal schooling. In doing so it ignored the insufficient number of competent teachers. In colonial times, and into the early years of independence, teachers were rightly held in high esteem in Ghana for the education they received and for their work. The public's respect for them induced in teachers a code of conduct which was a most valuable asset for the promotion of social and economic improvement particularly in the villages. But this potential was thrown overboard in favor of an ill-phased literacy campaign. To augment the supply of teachers entrance requirements to universities and Training Colleges were lowered; and to reduce the financial burden, teachers' real incomes were reduced by not correcting their salaries in line with inflation. Not surprisingly the profession soon lost many of its best and experienced members and much of its prestige. Within a few years many teachers left the profession and among those who remained many became irresponsible and corrupt. By 1965 malpractice in the teaching profession was so widespread that the dailies were admonishing teachers not to misuse their position to seduce female students, not to steal the money they received from the state for their pupils' books, and not to absent themselves from their schools without good reason. The position in higher education was not much better. Political appointments and the structurally corrupt machinations of international organizations like UNESCO deprived the Ghanaian institutions of higher learning of their previously high academic standard.

Nkrumah's "Leninist" obsession with accelerated industrialization was also as idealistic as most of his other socialist ideas. Just as the educational system confused obtaining a diploma with acquiring true knowledge, so did the construction of factories take the place of real industrial development. More often than not, Nkrumah's government built factories and established costly state enterprises against the counsel of its economic advisors. It created a semblance of but not real development. This was one among several reasons why so many well-equipped state enterprises persistently made losses and became a new source of underemployment. With no real cost-benefit accounting, factories were established in unsuitable locations and without regard for raw materials, power supply, and markets. The concept of planning was turned from a rational instrument for economic development into a disguise for an inefficient utilization of national assets exploited for private gain by corrupt foreign enterprises and Ghanaian civil servants and party officials. Cost accounting and profitability studies were passed off as irrelevant. Each enterprise was presented as part of an overall development plan in which the losses of individual enterprises were said to be made good by their contribution to the general scheme. Many employees in these enterprises held their posts thanks to family connections or bribery and were almost totally immune to dismissal for inefficiency. All this created an atmosphere which can be summarized by the local expression: "government money, nobody's money."

The military Junta that in February 1966 ousted Nkrumah and his government from power called itself the *National Liberation Council*. Naturally, it could not change the social and economic structure it inherited. The country's foreign currency reserves were depleted and world cacao prices continued to be low. The almost bloodless *coup* (only Nkrumah's Russian bodyguard put up an armed resistance) took place when Nkrumah himself was out of the country. The public welcomed the change. The spark which set off the powder keg that blew Nkrumah out of office was his attempt to establish a second military force recruited from his party members. Whether the *coup* was directly assisted by the CIA or not is irrelevant. At the time I doubted the rumors that the CIA had a hand in it. I saw no need for its intervention. Like anyone else, and certainly every army officer, I knew that any successful attempt to remove a pro-Soviet government from power could count on American support. (Years later, when documents were released in the USA, I learned that the CIA claimed to have played a role in this affair). By the time of the *coup* Nkrumah's government had become so unpopular that even his armed men at the party's Winneba Ideological Institute did not try to put up a resistance against the military coup.

The *National Liberation Council* abandoned the pro-Soviet orientation of the previous government, expelled the advisors and teachers from the Eastern Bloc, and having almost no foreign currency reserves appealed to the West for help. The West rewarded the new rulers for breaking with the Russians by providing the country with free and cheap food supplies. By 1966 cereal imports reduced food prices below production cost in Ghana and forced more of the farmers who were still producing for domestic urban consumption out of the market.

In two respects the new rulers were fairly successful. Their negotiations about rescheduling Ghana's foreign debts, and for cacao price support, went reasonably well. With solving the country's internal problems they were less successful. Their efforts to reduce government spending and diminish nepotism and corruption did not produce perceptible results. A number of inquiries into the maladministration of public institutions and probes into the assets of former government and party officials did not deter others from abusing their position. The publicity given to the inquiries and probes only generated an unjustified climate of disbelief in Ghanaians' ability to run their country's affairs efficiently and honestly. In this atmosphere the *National Liberation Council* sold national assets to foreigners in the belief that foreign ownership would free the public enterprises from nepotism, and that profit-minded private enterprise would weed out economically inviable investments and that this would increase productive efficiency, replenish the country's exhausted Treasury, and attract foreign capital. The thought that foreign investments and private enterprise go where it is most profitable, and not where it is most advantageous for the development of the country, never entered the new rulers' mind. It fact, in as far as the economy was concerned, the new economic policy was a return to colonialism.

To be profitable industrial investment requires an array of subsidiary trades, transport facilities, the proximity of raw materials or markets, a skilled labour-force, and political stability. Almost nothing of all this was present in Ghana. Private investors were almost exclusively attracted to the former colonial exports sectors and to ventures with a short term turnover. Moreover, the slump in world cacao prices encouraged other cacao producing countries to extend production to compensate for the low prices by increasing their volume of sales. It takes between five and seven years for cacao trees to mature, but it was easy to foresee that in time the increasing competition was bound to prevent income from cacao to regain the pre-slump level. At this time the prices of exports from many developing countries were falling and efforts were made to reach some international agreement to reverse this trend. Several rich countries introduced tariff cuts for a number of tropical products. The International Bank for Reconstruction and Development studied the possibility of shifting resources away from certain export crops (mainly coffee) to other crops and consultations were held about a similar policy with regard to cacao and sugar. Inter-governmental consultations on commodity exports to obtain regional agreements and supported prices were in progress in various UNCTAD bodies. But the one alternative that might have provided a solution, namely crop diversification, was not on the agenda.

Essentially the *National Liberation Council* was faced with the same problems which Nkrumah had been facing. Soon its methods of suppressing dissent also became no different from those of the preceding government. The one short term advantage the new rulers had was that they could count on foreign aid to appease the urban population and please the better situated. But in the long run the increasing need to feed a growing urban population was bound to come to an end. No western government could be expected, or even able, to foot the bill to sustain the military juntas permanently. Political instability became permanent. A democratic constitution, followed by elections in 1969 brought a predominantly civilian government to power. Yet in 1972, another military *coup* withdrew the constitution and ruled the country by decree. In 1978, it too was deposed by Frederick Akuffo, but this government was also replaced (in the same year) by a second *coup* led by Flight Lt. Jerry Rawlings. In 1979 Rawlings returned the country to civilian rule, but in 1982 he seized power again accusing the civilian leaders of incompetence.

In fact what any of the governments should have done, but did not do, was to select investment targets with long-term development perspectives and invite both Ghanaian and foreign investors to contribute to their realization. In the meantime it should have tackled the short-term problems by trying to eliminate bottlenecks, provide easy credit for farmers and manufacturers, construct storage facilities and feeder roads to promote the economic performance of small farms, and allow the traditional social institutions (the extended family and the local chiefs) to run the agricultural and manufacturing "co-operatives", as the cacao marketing board had successfully done it before Nkrumah. Instead of this, every succeeding governments tried to impose on society institutions which were alien to Ghanaian culture, and pay its way with foreign aid.

Except for helping people in national emergencies, after an earthquake or a catastrophic harvest failure, the value of foreign aid depends on who uses it and for what purpose. Like a syringe, which in the hands of a qualified physician can be put to very good use and in the hands of a heroin-addict can only cause temporary pleasure and later misery and death, so it is with foreign aid. The usefulness of foreign aid can only be assessed in the context of specific circumstances. There was a time when those in charge of distributing aid really believed that injecting capital into an underdeveloped country was the key to its economic progress. When this proved not to be the case the next idea was education. When investment in education also failed to create the technologically trained labour force which was expected to industrialize the poorer countries, "the demonstration effect" was seen as the panacea. Show the people what wonderful things can be obtained if they work hard and save, and all be well. Again it did not work. The rulers and their minions who administered the country became greedier but those who had to work to earn their income could neither work harder than they were doing already or save more than they did before. The fact of the matter is that wealth and income *distribution* matters. Real decolonization and real development can only begin when the political leadership is in the hands of people who represent, and have the power to represent, the material interests of the productive population. Only then can foreign assistance play a truly constructive role. In the past, time after time, the people of Ghana demonstrated their ability to organize in the pursuit of their objectives. The cacao farmers established a marketing organization which functioned well until the government became involved in it. Construction workers organized trade unions who protected workers' rights until the government deprived them of their independence. Even Nkrumah's rise to power was precipitated by the organized pressure on the colonial rulers to grant Ghana self-rule and national sovereignty. The people of Ghana are neither better nor worse, neither more intelligent nor less intelligent, than people in the economically most advanced countries, but their colonial past imposed upon them an elite and leadership which they do not deserve. Jean-Paul Sartre in his preface to Frantz Fanon's book *The Wretched of the Earth* described this greedy ilk as "promising adolescents picked out by the European elite, who branded them . . . with the principles of western culture; . . . stuffed their mouths full with high-sounding phrases, grand glutinous words that stuck to the teeth, and after a short stay in the mother country sent them home, white-washed, walking lies who had nothing to say to their brothers." Sartre exaggerated, but it was such an elite, courted by Eastern and Western governments, that determined Ghana's fate while I was there.

Nowadays, people from Ghana tell me that things are very much improved. I wish to believe them. The end of the Cold War put an end to the rich countries' politicians and generals justification for supporting corrupt rulers in the under-developed countries. Their claims that one had to bribe them to keep them on "our" side has lost its plausibility. The Churches have indicated that the large debts incurred by these rulers, debts which were as much to blame on the donors' policies as on the mismanagement of funds by those who received them, ought to be cancelled. Events in Seattle and Geneva have shown that there is a growing number of people who recognize that the trade arrangements supported by the IMF and similar institutions, and by national governments, are detrimental to the poor countries. However, one thing has not been made clear, namely that what goes as economic dogma in the developed parts of the world is out of place in many of the poorer countries. The western economic behavioral assumptions about individual's and social conduct do simply not apply. This is important and I hope my stories will make this plain.

The last time I visited the country many old friends, mainly from the Ewe tribe, received me ceremoniously at the airport. How they knew that I was coming, and the day and time of my arrival, is still a mystery for me. I had not written to any of them. Perhaps somebody working for the West African Examination Council which invited me had recognized my name on a list and told them? Perhaps it was someone working for the airline who phoned the Chiefs? But perhaps if all is said and done the African belief is true that one needs just to want a person to come and think about it hard enough and he will appear. In any event it made me feel good to see that I was not forgotten by my Ghanaian friends and former students. Here was the real Ghana, not the "white-washed, walking lies" Sartre wrote about. The next day I went to Cape Coast university where I worked for five years before I returned to Europe. Each evening during my sojourn there I enjoyed the traditional Ghanaian hospitality. All former colleagues insisted upon my taking dinner at their house, and my old friend and servant Atinga was given time off from work to make sure that I was well looked after.

When my family and I were still living in Ghana I planted near our bungalow a thick dead tree trunk to make a place for our monkey to sit on. After the monkey was gone it was an eyesore, but I somehow never got around to taking it down. It was still there. But in my absence the trunk struck roots and, symbolically for Ghana, became a beautiful mango tree. Its fruit was delicious though a little stringy.

Y. S. Brenner
Bilthoven, June 2000

Arriving in Another World

My wife, our two little children, and I, arrived at Accra airport. It was a hot mid-afternoon and the short walk across the tarmac from the plane to the wooden shed which served as the arrivals building made us sweat. Inside it was even hotter. Porters brought boxes and suitcases from the plane and placed them on a long table. On one side of the table stood the passengers and on the other side the customs officers. One by one people indicated their belongings for inspection. Some were made to open their suitcases but most were just told to take them and go.

Someone behind me touched my shoulder and said my name. I turned and saw a huge fat sweating African.

"Show me your cases and your passports," he said in a voice which made me think that he was some sort of security man in mufti.

I gave him our travelling documents and indicated our suitcases. He went to the table and picked them up and made a sign to the customs officers that it was all right. Then he signalled a man who was waiting at the exit door to come, and they carried our things to a new black Mercedes waiting in front of the building. They loaded our cases into the boot, and the fat man went back to the arrivals hall.

Curious what he was going to do next I followed. From the door I saw him go to the passport check post and pick up a stamp and stamp our passports. Nobody seemed to take any notice. Then he returned and handed me our documents, wished me a good journey to Cape Coast, and went off. I turned and saw my family seated in the back seats of the Mercedes. The front door of the car was open and the driver was frantically signalling me to come and sit next to him. As soon as I was seated he started the car and we were on our way.

Soon after we left the airport the bush closed in on us from both sides of the road. I was a little disappointed. Having not been to Africa before, I expected to see high trees and the kind of forest I remembered from the picture books I had seen in my childhood. There were a few tall trees, but most of the "forest" was dense impenetrable bush.

The driver, an elderly African wore a row of British combat ribbons on his faded khaki shirt. He spoke English with an unfamiliar pronunciation.

"How long will it take us to reach Cape Coast?" I asked.

"Maybe two, maybe three hours."

"It's far," I said trying to start some kind of conversation.

"Yes Sir." He sounded like a soldier addressing an officer.

I pointed to his ribbons. "You have been in the army?"

"In the war, with the West Africa Rifles."

"Seen much combat?"

"Yea. I was in Burma."

"And now?" I asked not able to think of anything else to say to keep the conversation going.

"I am a driver for the university car pool," he answered with pride.

"Do you like your job?"

"Sure."

"You like driving cars?"

"I am a driver! I like to drive Mercedes. They are very reliable."

I agreed.

"Many people drive Peugeot 404," he said, sounding denigrating. Peugeot also good, but Mercedes is the best."

"The Peugeot is cheaper," I commented.

He smiled.

After an hour it became night and we were still on the road. To the left was the Atlantic ocean. It was too dark now to see it but I could hear the breakers crash onto the shore, and I smelled the salty water. Suddenly the bush receded and I saw dim lights to the right of the road.

The driver pointed in their direction. "This be Cape Coast. Our town. Soon we'll arrive at your house."

A few minutes later we left the road we were following and drove up a narrow driveway. At the end of it I saw a large building silhouetted against the dark sky on a small elevated clearing in the bush. When we reached it the driver stopped the car, asked us to wait, and he got out to look for someone. He returned almost immediately accompanied by a thin dark man dressed only in shorts and carrying a long bow and arrows. "This be your watchman," the driver said, and went to get our cases out of the car's luggage compartment.

Following the driver and the watchman we mounted a few stairs leading to the front door of the house. There we were told to wait until they turn on the lights inside. As we entered the watchman hastily closed all windows.

It was warm in the house and I asked why he was closing them?

"Must close the windows when lights on," the driver explained. "No mosquito nets. Much Malaria here. Nets will come tomorrow. Principal will bring from Accra. Now I go come tomorrow to take you to the university and your wife for shopping in Cape Coast." And he left the room followed by the watchman. After a minute he was back. "Don't let the children go into the garage under the house. The watchman says many snakes there. He killed two but there may be more."

My wife and I inspected the house. It was large, the rooms looked very spacious and had high ceilings. Next to a spacious sitting room, furnished in old colonial style, there were several bedrooms. In one beds had been made for my wife and me; next to it, in another beds were made ready for the children. Someone had certainly made an effort to make us comfortable. There was even some food for us in the larder by the kitchen – mainly tins.

Tired from the long flight from Europe, and from the three hours car journey, my wife and I put the children to bed immediately and prepared to go to sleep as well. After turning off the lights, I opened a window and looked out. In the moonlight I could see the watchman drowsing on the front porch, his bow and arrows at his side. For the rest all I saw was the bush closing in on us from all directions.

I went to bed and fell instantly into deep sleep. I do not know how long I slept but it was still dark when I woke up. The bush around us seemed to be alive. I recognized the chirping of beetles and the croaking of frogs, but there were hundreds of other sounds I never heard before. The night was full of strange and unfamiliar sounds.

For a while I lay in bed listening. Then I went to look out of the window again. The watchman hadn't stirred since I last saw him. He was dozing in the same position as before. But a dense mist had settled on the bush, and there was darkness all around us. I returned to my bed and tried to asleep but couldn't. More and more the enormity of what I imposed on my family alarmed me. Malaria, snakes, almost naked watchmen with bows and arrows to protect us. I must have been out of my mind to take my wife and children to this place. How could I have done this? What if a snake bit our little son or daughter? What if she got an attack of any kind of sickness in the middle of this jungle? Where would I find a doctor? How would I get anywhere? I had no means of transport. I had arranged for my car to be shipped to Ghana but when will it arrive? And even if I had it, where would I go for help? Where would I find people? I could not even find my way to the nearest town in this pitch darkness? Why did I come here? Was it really to help the first independent African state to improve its people's living conditions, as I told myself and anyone who asked me, or was it just because I had no alternative – no other job to earn the money to support my family? I must have fallen asleep, because when I opened my eyes again it was bright daylight.

We had breakfast. There was no bread but we found tea, powdered milk, cereals and tins of cornedbeef. Having eaten, we went for a short walk to explore our surroundings. Next to the door our watchman greeted us with a broad smile. I tried to ask him when the driver would be back with the car, but he did not understand me. He smiled, but only said: "Yes Sir, master." Actually he said "masser" and not "master" but I understood that this was what he meant to say. It was all the English he knew.

In daylight the house and the bush around it looked less strange and menacing. On the contrary, everything seemed interesting and beautiful. There was no other passage through the bush, and we walked along the driveway, As we were walking I asked myself what it was that during the night had so much worried me. We would soon meet the people from the university, and once our car arrives we would explore this new strange and wonderful world.

We did not go far lest the driver or someone else came for us. When we reached the place where on the previous night the car that brought us left the main road and turned into the driveway, we began to make our way back to the house. When we were just in sight of it the skies suddenly darkened. Heavy clouds raced overhead from behind us, the heat became humid and oppressive and made it difficult to breathe. A strong gush of wind pushed us on, and a deep gurgling sound, and a hissing sound of water falling on the leaves in the bush became louder and louder with each moment.

We turned a bend in the driveway and the house came into sight. We saw the watchman running from one window to another hastily closing all the shutters. When we were only a short distance, perhaps fifty yards, from the entrance it began to rain. It was none of the rain we knew but water pouring down as from an open hydrant. The wind had not abated and it pushed us on. In seconds we were at the house wet to the bones.

Inside the watchman was still struggling with the wind trying to close the wooden shutters. Near the windows which he had not yet managed to shut the wind drove in the deluge, and large puddles were forming on the floor. I helped to close the last shutter, and my wife went to get a rag to sweep away the water.

We went to the bathroom to dry ourselves and change our clothes. Even the underwear was soaked. But no sooner we had changed and returned to the sitting room, lines of bright light came through the gaps in the shutters. I opened one and looked out. Outside the sun was shining. As quickly as the rainstorm had come, it had gone again. The only evidence to remind us of the downpour was the steaming driveway.

Close to lunchtime the driver finally arrived to collect us. First he wanted us to leave the children behind – "the watchman can look after them" – but we did not agree. So we all got into the car and were driven to the university campus. For a while the road went along the sea shore. On one side of the road was the ocean and on the other side we first drove along two lagoons with hundreds of flamingoes, and then along a ridge running parallel to the sea, with here and there houses scattered on it. The driver turned off the coastal road and turned into a smaller one leading up the ridge toward a cluster of buildings. "The university campus," he proclaimed. We had arrived.

The registrar showed us around. At one end of the ridge stood several long buildings with many doors on one side and as many windows facing the sea on the other. These, the registrar explained, were the students' "cubicles." Each student had his own small room with a bed, a chair and table, and a place to hang his or her clothes. There were shower rooms at the end of each building. Not far from the "cubicles" was a larger building – the kitchen and dining hall. Further off, at the other end of the ridge, were bungalows and two story buildings, many still under construction. These were to accommodate the staff. In the middle, between the dining hall and the houses for the staff were the buildings in which the lessons were to be given and the administration. The entire ridge was about a mile long and about 50 meters above the sea. In the middle of it all stood a high water tower. Beyond the ridge as far as the eye could see was bush.

While we were driven along the staff accommodations, I noticed a bungalow which I immediately desired for to be our home. It was located on the crest of the ridge at the far end where the road stopped and the bush began. On one side one saw from it the large expanse of the ocean, and on the other side a sea of green – bush stretching as far as the horizon. The bungalow was still under construction, but nonetheless I told the registrar that this was the house we wanted.

He told me what I could see for myself. The house was not yet ready.

I said that we don't mind waiting for it.

The registrar tried to make me change my mind. "You are entitled to a two story house. The two story houses are bigger – they have an extra room."

"The bungalow has a large sitting room and three bed rooms. That is sufficient for us," I told him.

He thought this over before he told us that it would be difficult to arrange for us to get this house. "Senior staff get the two story houses. You are head of department, and we planned to give you one of the large houses."

I tried again to explain that it doesn't matter to me, but I could see that I was causing him a problem. My wife came to my assistance. She said that she saw the stairs in the two story houses and thought it unsafe for our children, particularly for our small daughter, to live in a house with stairs. This apparently convinced him, and he agreed to speak to Dr Ackah, "The Principal", about it. He would see what can be done.

It took several weeks before the bungalow was finally ready and we moved into it on the campus. Until that day we continued to occupy the house we first arrived at. Our daughter contracted malaria and recovered from it; our car arrived but we couldn't put it in the garage because of the snakes. They seemed to become more with everyone we killed; and a new tenant came to share the house with us – Wally.

The Meaning of Civilization

After we moved to the new bungalow on the ridge, every first Wednesday of the month came Kwao to the house to read "the metre." It was his job to see how much electricity had been consumed by the tenants and to report it to the university's accounts office. Later the cost would be deducted from the salary. Kwao always managed to arrange his round of inspection so that he arrived at our bungalow for tea. We knew this and on Wednesdays we waited with our afternoon tea until he showed up.

Kwao was an Ashanti in his late thirties. Before he was employed by the university, he had been a farmer. Four years of school enabled him to read and write and to have a fairly good command of English. He spoke slowly and ponderously the way peasants, not only in Africa, often do. We liked him and enjoyed our talks with him. One could learn more from him about Ghana than from the educated townspeople who usually told us only what they thought we expected them to say. Sometimes the way Kwao looked at you or moved his hands gave one a better answer to a question than the lengthy elaborations we heard from colleagues, and from the politicians and journalists we met.

When we once asked him what he thought of President Nkrumah's "Seven Year Development Plan," and particularly about the part of the plan which dealt with agriculture, Kwao just pulled up his shoulders, and I knew that he thought that nothing will really come of it. When we asked his opinion about one of the Ministers, he just looked at the floor in front of him with an embarrassed smile which said more than all the hundreds of words my colleagues and students used to intimate the same.

Kwao had a farm somewhere in the bush about 30 miles north of the university campus. Every Friday evening he went on a motorbike to his farm and each Monday morning he returned to the campus in time for work. The motorbike belonged to the university's electricity department. It was given to him to do his job.

One day I asked him how things were with his farm. He told me that the weekend before he had harvested his plantains and left them near the track leading to town. Plantains are a sort of bananas which African like to fry. Sometimes they are also offered coated with sugar as desert in European restaurants.

In my mind I saw a truckload of plantains stacked up unattended in the jungle. "When will they be collected and taken to the market?" I inquired.

Kwao thought about it for a while before he answered. "My nephew will take them in his lorry when he comes next Friday."

I asked if he thought that by the end of the week there would be any plantains left there.

"Oh yes. They will be there."

"And nobody will have pilfered them?"

"Oh yes. Some children and poor old women will take some."

With all the stealing that was going on at the university compound I was not convinced. I could not help visualizing the pile of plantains getting smaller with each passing day. "Will half your crop remain for the market?"

"It will all go to the market."

"And the children and poor old women?"

"It's nothing. The few plantains they take make no difference." And making one of his depreciating gestures he added the term Ghanaians use to indicate that something is of no importance: "it be small."

I began to tire of his boundless confidence and tried another approach: "Is it not possible that some driver who passes by your plantains with an empty lorry will simply load them and sell them for himself?"

He slowly shook his head: "No. Not possible."

There was a short lull in our conversation before he spoke again. "The drivers who come this way are from the neighboring villages."

I saw that this explanation seemed to him sufficient to alleviate my doubts.

"Do you really believe that no one who sees an unguarded heap of plantains by the road for an entire week will steal them?"

He looked at me in surprise: "No, this does not happen. They don't steal, they are simple peasants in our region – they are not civilized."

I finally learned the meaning of civilization.

Rash Conclusions

Someone appointed me to the School Committee. I was not asked; I was simply told of my appointment by a circular from the university administration.

The school was established for the children of the employees of the university. Only their children were admitted. Primary education in Ghana was free. The restriction was necessary because otherwise all families in Cape Coast and the neighboring villages would send their kids to this school and make it much too expensive for the university. The rules for accepting pupils were therefore very strict.

One of my tasks as committee member was to examine the applications for admission and weed out those which were not in conformity with the rules. I did not like the job. Except for the cases where the applicant's claims were obviously false, it always gave me an uncomfortable feeling to reject a request for a child to be admitted. The university's school was superior to most, perhaps to all, other schools in the vicinity and who was I to decide which child does and which does not deserve a better education.

On a day a bricklayer from one of the university's construction sites came to register four children for the school. It made no difference whether you were a manual worker, chauffeur, waiter or dishwasher, or a member of the teaching academic staff, as long as you received your pay from the university your children were entitled to acceptance at the school. The bricklayer brought an orderly completed registration form. But when I looked at the dates of birth of his children I noticed that all four were born within eight months of one and the same year. Having had phoney applications before from university employees who were bribed by parents who did not work for the university, to pass off their children as the employees' to get them into the school, I became suspicious. I asked the man to wait and went to the Head of Personnel to find out for how many children this bricklayer received the *Children Allowance* to which all workers were entitled. To my surprise he received an allowance for the four children named on the application form and recently applied to receive it for three additional children of similar ages.

I decided to consult the Registrar. As a Ghanaian I thought he was better able than I to sort this matter out. He too was puzzled and sent someone to bring the worker to his office. At first the bricklayer, who did not understand English, seemed tense. But as soon as the Registrar translated my questions he relaxed. I asked how many children he had, and even before his answer was translated I knew from the man's demeanor that he did not know. The Registrar translated that he said it must be about nine, but he wasn't sure there may be more. When I wanted to know if he did not find it strange that all these children were born in the course of a single year, my question did not disturb the man's composure. He said that the children were from different women, and I could see that this answer seemed for him to settle the matter. So I asked why if he had nine children he had first only applied for a Children Allowance for four? Again my question did not bother him. He says, the Registrar translated, that he simply did not know before that there were more children than the four he knew of.

The bricklayer's answers apparently annoyed the Registrar, and there followed an angry argument between the two men in Fanti – the local language

– which I couldn't understand. Then, all at once the Registrar's anger abated. He told the man to go back to his work, and said to me that all was in good order.

"How come?" I asked, and he explained it to me. Before the man found work with the university he had been unemployed. At that time the women simply did not bother to tell him of his children. But once he found steady employment they became aware of the advantage the children had from the fact he was their father and they came to inform him of his fatherhood.

This I understood, but it still did not explain to me why all his children were born in one and the same year and none before that year or later. So I asked the Registrar and he enlightened me. "In that year the man was made Chief, and a Chief must have a wife in every village. It is an ancient tradition. Probably it was to make sure that the Chief cannot escape his obligations to the village and that the villagers cannot rise up against him. Children in the Fanti matriarchal society belong to the mother and her family and there is therefore no need to tell the father about them if there was nothing he could do for them."

Beliefs

From time to time in the evenings Yao called on us. Yao was from the western part of Ghana and spoke fairly good English. It was always enjoyable to chat with him and to listen to his stories. This time he came in the company of Kofi. I had seen Kofi before, but hardly ever spoken with him outside classes. I knew that, like Yao, he had been a primary school teacher before he came as student to our university. I also knew that his father was a respected Anglican priest somewhere near dunkwa.

It was not the first time that Yao brought some other student along with him when he came to see us. But this time I immediately recognized that his friend had something bothering him and that they came to tell me about it. So, after we gossiped for a while and had some beer, Kofi told me what it was about. It was before the beginning of the final university examinations and Kofi had spent some time studying at his father's home. Things had gone reasonably well and he was almost through all the books and articles he had to read. Then one day his father, the Christian clergyman, took him into the mountains to see a fetish priest who was to tell them if he would pass his examinations. There was the usual ceremony with libation and the rest. In the end the fetish priest predicted that he would fail.

For the rest of the evening Yao and I tried to allay Kofi's anxiety. I told him that as he read all the assigned literature there was no cause for worry;

and Yao said that it was really not so important to pass the examinations because there was always a second chance to sit for them again a few months later. I even looked at my records to see what marks Kofi received when he had followed one of my courses. They were well above average.

Whether it was the beer, the friendly atmosphere, or Yao's efforts and mine to reassure him, Kofi left the our bungalow a little less anxious. As they were leaving Yao whispered to me at the door: "You will see, fetish priest or no fetish priest, Kofi will pass his examinations well."

Everyone went home for the summer holidays as soon as the examinations were over and I did not see either of them again for several weeks. I had almost forgotten the entire affair when I met Yao in Accra. We went into a place to have some cold drinks and remembering our last meeting I asked about Kofi.

Yao smiled his typically embarrassed smile and hesitantly told me that as he expected Kofi had done well."He passed all examinations with good marks."

Having noticed his embarrassment I made no comment. But then he himself told me the rest of the story. After Kofi received his results he returned home triumphantly to tell his father how wrong his fetish priest had been. He would have liked to add something about his father's Christianity but of course he didn't. Yao thought that he should have told his father that it was hardly the thing for a Christian, and a priest at that, to ask for the advise of a witch doctor. But we both knew that he could never have done this.

"And did his father not mention it himself?" I asked.

Yao laughed. "He did! He told Kofi that of course the fetish priest knew what he was saying and was right. Had it not been for this warning, he would certainly have failed his exams. But being forewarned. Kofi's father gave the priest two bottles of Gordon Gin and entreated him to help avoid the calamity. Then he went to pray to the greatest of all gods, to Jesus Christ, to undo the evil spell which the minor African gods had imposed upon his son's examination."

"So you see," I muttered not knowing what else I could say.

Yao grinned: "I am sure it was the Gordon Gin that did the trick. It always does."

Reincarnation

Souls are immortal. No deceased can rest before all the money he owed is refunded and all his promises fulfilled.

Krobo, a Ghanaians working for the agricultural extension service, confirmed it. Ten days after his brother died – he used the word "expired" – Krobo had gone to the north of the country to refund hundred cedis his brother borrowed from somebody and had not paid back before his death. Krobo told me that when he came to settle the debt the man to whom it was owed was very much surprised. He said: "Why? Your brother was here only yesterday and paid it all in full."

For a moment I was tempted to object and tell Krobo that the deceased do not come back to life and do not walk about amongst the living. But I thought better of it and kept quiet. After all it was to him, and not me, to whom it happened. Krobo must have sensed that I was not convinced and told me of other cases when the dead returned among the living to settle their unfinished businesses. When I remarked that it was never he himself, but always someone else, who told him that he came face to face with a deceased, Krobo admitted that this was true but that all the people who told him were absolutely trustworthy.

One of the events he recounted was about an old woman who was afraid that, after her death, some other woman would take for herself the trinkets she wanted a particular granddaughter to have. So, to avoid the risk that the other women take away everything as soon as she was dead, as was the custom in the villages, she buried the trinkets where nobody would find them.

Years went by and people kept on asking themselves where her treasure was buried. They searched but to no avail. Then one of the woman's daughters gave birth to a girl which in so many ways resembled the deceased that everyone was sure she was her reincarnation, that she returned as this girl to settle her unfinished business. When the little girl was about seven years old and by chance overheard people talking of the hidden trinkets, and that they were never found, she announced that she knew where they were. She led the village elders to the place and showed them.

When I mentioned Krobo's tale to some students they told me a story of their own. One day three of them missed the last bus to Kumasi. Kumasi is the main town of the Ashanti region about three hundred kilometers north of our university. For some reason they had to be there before morning. Obviously there were also no mummy-lorries – the trucks which take market women from the villages to town – at that time of night. Eventually they managed to persuade a taxi driver to take them. Having too little money for the taxi fare they kept very quiet throughout the entire ride. When they came close to Kumasi and the driver asked where they wished to get off, they directed him to the entrance of the graveyard. There, as soon as the car stopped they jumped out and rushed strait into the burial ground. Seeing where they went the driver became very frightened. He thought that his passengers were incarnated dead who left their graves to settle some unfinished affairs. Instantly he raced off without waiting for their fares.

"And you? Do you believe in reincarnation?" I asked the students.

They smiled.

I knew this smile. It meant they did but were embarrassed to admit it to a foreigner.

Then there was the time General Kotoka was killed. It happened in Accra near Flagstaff House or on the road to the airport during the fighting with the Russian guards, when President Nkrumah's government was ousted by the military. That afternoon in Cape Coast on my way from work I heard drumming and saw workers streaming from the construction sites in the direction where the sound was coming from. I followed them and joined the crowd next to the drummers. People were singing and performing ritual dances. I watched them for a while, noticed that they were of the Ewe tribe, but could not understanding what it was about. Eventually I recognized one of my students and asked him. He explained that what I was witnessing was an Ewe ritual for the dead. The dancing was part of the ritual and what they were singing were the promises Kotoka had made that he was still obliged to fulfill.

Personal Responsibility

Amatevi was a policeman. He was arrested trying to assassinate the President. Atinga, our *steward-boy*, as servants were called in Ghana, was very much upset. He was certain that Amatevi's arrest and imprisonment was totally unjustified.

"Do you really believe that he would have shot at the President had he not been told to do it by his betters?" he asked my wife. "Why else should he have tried to shoot the President? Who is he that he should want to do a thing like that? His masters must have ordered him and they not he must go to prison!"

My wife tried to convince him that after all it was he, Amatevi, who had pulled the trigger.

Atinga wouldn't hear of it.

My wife tried again. "If my husband told you to go and beat up our neighbour, would you then do it?"

Atinga was not perturbed. "Of course! He be the master. What he tell me I must do."

Listening to this conversation I remembered a lawyer once telling me that a British soldier is always free to choose if he prefers to be hanged or shot. How come? In 1901 or 1902, during the Boer War, the war between the British and the descendants of the Dutch settlers in southern Africa, a platoon of British soldiers lost their way and had no water. They had a prisoner, one of Kruger's guerrilla fighters, who was able to tell them where the next waterhole was, but he wouldn't. The officer in command of the British unit ordered him to lead the platoon to the location. The stubborn Dutchman, or descendant of a dutchman, refused. He said that if they wanted him to lead them to the water their roles should be reversed. Instead of him being their prisoner, they should become his prisoners. The British officer did not like the answer and ordered a sergeant to take the man behind the nearest hill, give him three minutes to consider, and then shoot him if he did not tell them the way to the waterhole. Under military law it was an offence punishable by the firing squad to disobey an officer's command in the presence of the enemy. Consequently, the sergeant did as he was told. The prisoner refused to speak and the sergeant shot him. But this was not the end of the matter. Years later the incident became known in England and someone took the sergeant to court accusing him of murder. The judge decided that murder was murder. The penalty for murder at this time was hanging. The judge recognized that in the sergeant's case there were mitigating circumstances, and therefore only fined him, but he upheld the principle that there were orders which nobody should carry out even under the threat of being shot for disobeying them. Thus, my lawyer friend concluded his tale, henceforth every British soldier can choose if he wants to be condemned by a military court and shot or convicted by a civilian court and hanged.

I asked myself if personal responsibility was really so self-evident as my wife and I were brought up to believe. Atinga obviously thought that it was not. In the Bible Job's wife and children perished because God wanted to test Job – not them. After World War II, the Nazi criminals claimed that they had just been carrying out orders. Some of them really believed that this exonerated them. Why then were my wife and I so surprised to find Atinga infuriated because of Amatevi's punishment? To tell the truth, it amused me to learn that he would beat up my neighbours if I told him. It confirmed to me that Atinga accepted me as a member of African society – that I was integrated.

Ceremonial and Functional Chores

Atinga was not our first servant in Ghana. Before him we had a Nigerian steward boy called Mark.

Coming back from our annual holidays we were astonished to find that Mark was gone and another man was waiting for us at our bungalow's door informing us that he has taken his place. We were astonished but not very much. We were already long enough in Africa to know that all kinds of things happen to which we were unaccustomed. During our absence the new man, Atinga, bought the job from Mark for a week or two weeks wages. But this we learned only much later.

All in all we were not very sad that Mark had left. True enough he was industrious and tried to do his work well, but he seemed to have difficulties accepting what my wife was telling him. After breakfast each morning before I went to work I saw him scrubbing the floors and using buckets full detergents.

Once, when for one reason or another I had to remain in the house, I overheard him arguing with my wife and then grumbling angrily for me to hear: "Madam is never satisfied!"

I was curious to know what happened and went to ask my wife. It appeared that he had shaken out the crumbs from the breakfast table cloth on the floor he had just painstakingly scrubbed only a few minutes before. My wife told him that this was not the right way to do things. He was offended. He had scrubbed the floor well and she had nothing to complain about. Well, they simply did not understand each other. My wife did not see how someone with an ounce of intelligence (and Mark was hardly stupid) could shake out the crumbles from a table cloth on the freshly scrubbed floor, and Mark did not grasp what she was complaining about.

I would have forgotten the incident had it not been that a few days later we had European visitors and while we were talking Mark came from time to time to serve us food and drink. It was hot and the guests frequently asked for cold water. At a certain moment I wondered where all the water he offered them came from. In Cape Coast all drinking water had first to be boiled and filtered for fear of water born diseases, and I remembered that when the guests arrived there were only two or three bottles of clean water in the fridge. But I took it for granted that Mark went to the neighbours and asked them to "lend" us some of their boiled water. We and others did this sometimes. But gradually, as it seemed to me that Mark's supply of water was inexhaustible I became suspicious and went to the kitchen to ask.

He happily explained that he knew that white people like boiled and filtered water. But in the fridge were only two bottles, so to be fair to everyone he filled each glass with a little water from the fridge and topped it up with water from the tap."

As far as I know none of our guests became ill, and years later I learned that my children also often drank water from the tap when they were in the houses of their African friends and we did not see it. But the incident made me understand why my wife's reprimand about the table cloth seemed so unreasonable. For Mark the daily scrubbing of floors with detergents, and the consumption of boiled and filtered water, were some of the Europeans ceremonial obligations, just like their going to Church on Sunday. What other reason could there be for it if not to please their gods? After all, tap water looks just the same as boiled water and a floor brushed with a broom looks just as good as one washed with a detergent.

Why I Had to Have a Telephone

As Head of Department I was entitled to a telephone in my bungalow. There was one in the office, and there were few other people who had phones in their houses. I didn't need one. Yet, a phone was installed in our bungalow.

As phones do from time to time it rang and usually late in the evening and woke us up. In the beginning it was frequently somebody dialling the wrong number or women wanting to speak to a certain Mr. Shama who apparently had my telephone number before I got it. Later it was also students who called at all times of day and night to ask questions such as if a particular scheduled lecture of mine would be given the next day or not although there was no reason why it shouldn't be given. In all my years of teaching at Cape Coast University I never missed a class. The one time I might have missed classes was when I had malaria, but this was in the summer holidays when all students were away. Only our steward boy Atinga made and received frequent calls. All steward boys who worked for staff in whose houses or offices were telephones seemed fascinated by the device and called each another at every opportunity.

As said, I had no use for the telephone and did not want it. I went to the people in charge, I was never able to reach them by phone, and asked them to take it away. I saw them perhaps ten times with this request but it was to no avail. So I wrote them a letter and received a reply. It said that they sent someone to my bungalow to take the phone away but were prevented by somebody who told the technicians that my social and academic position required for it to remain in the house.

I didn't believe this tale and asked my wife if she had seen someone coming to collect the gadget. She had not; but suggested that I should ask Atinga. Yes, Atinga met the men who came for the phone. The first time they came he told them that I was an important person, "a big man", who is entitled to a telephone, and sent them away. The second time they came he called all the steward boys from the neighbouring houses and chased the technicians off by the threat of force. He told me this with much satisfaction and I could see that he felt that he had done the right thing.

I tried to explain to him that I really did not need or want the phone and asked him not to hinder the men again who came to disconnect it. But after their experience with the amassed steward boys the technicians never dared to come near the house and probably told their boss that they had been to the place several times and always found it locked.

As for me, I became used to the voices of the nice ladies who woke me up at night wishing to speak with Mr. Shama and the telephone remained in the house to the last day I was in Ghana.

Heavenly Jerusalem

I tried to work but Atinga's wife made such a racket that I soon gave up. She had positioned herself under the window of my study and kept on banging pots and pans all morning to chase away the monkeys. Her husband had planted maize in the clearing behind our bungalow and now that they were almost ready for harvesting the monkeys came to pick them. Not that her efforts were of much use. Whenever she left for a few minutes to attend to her baby or for another reason, the monkeys swooped into the maize field and picked as many cobs as they could carry. From my window I could see the horde waiting at the edge of the bush. There were at lest twenty of them and probably more. As long as the woman was there they kept their distance, but the moment she left they rushed into the maize plot like Joshua's army upon the Canaanite. Each time the poor woman returned her maize crop was diminished. It was quite funny to observe, but rather sad if one thought about the effort she and her husband invested in the maize plot.

As the din prevented me from working I went outside to see what my daughter was doing. She was playing on the front porch. A short distance away stood some workmen talking. I thought they were talking about her. I wished them a good morning, and saw that their conversation became agitated. Hesitating two came closer. They seemed to want to know something but did not really dare to ask. I tried to encourage them but they appeared unable to find the right words to formulate their question.

Finally one overcame the indecision and asked: "Is it true you came here from Jerusalem?"

The question took me by surprise but I told him that indeed I did.

The man went back to his mates and their argument became even more animated than before.

After a while the questioner returned. "You came from Jerusalem? *The* Jerusalem? The Jerusalem of Jesus Christ?"

"*The* Jerusalem. From the Holy Land," I truthfully replied.

Again the man went back to discuss this with the other workers.

Next time he returned together with another man. "But we were told that Jerusalem was in the Kingdom of Heaven."

I looked at them for a moment and trying to sound as seriously as I could answered: "Why? Don't I look like an angel?"

They chuckled and again went back to discuss the matter with their mates.

By this time Atinga's wife had stopped clanging with her pots and pans and I went to see what was happening. The monkeys were in the maize plot. They saw me coming and all but two ran off. I picked up a piece of wood and threw it at them but it did not make much of an impression. They retreated a little and waited for me to go away.

I returned to the front porch. My daughter was still playing peacefully. I watched her for a while, but when I turned to go back into the house, the worker who had asked about Jerusalem was standing right behind me. He was obviously struggling with a problem. Finally he came out with it: "They cheated us. There is no Kingdom of Heaven. Jerusalem does not lie behind the river Jordan but on earth." He held up for me to see an issue of the local newspaper and pointed at the banner headline. It read "Israel forces Jordanians to surrender Jerusalem." It was June in the year 1967.

I was glad that he found it out from the paper. It bothered me that I had acquitted myself with a quip instead of having given the worried workers a proper answer to their question about Jerusalem.

Competent Technicians

My wife had ordered the latest Bosch washing machine. For two years it served us well. Then it broke down. Try as we may, it wouldn't work. There were several English and Czech technicians at the university and we asked their help. They looked at the machine and the electric wiring scheme which my wife managed to get from the producers, tried one thing and another and in the end gave up.

Wally heard of our problem and told us to ask Quist.

"Quist? Who is Quist?" I never heard of him.

Wally grinned "You don't remember him but you remember his wife, I'm sure. They were at my party. You spoke to her while he was dancing with Mrs. Kwampong."

I remembered her. She was the most beautiful black woman on the campus. I also remembered the party. Wally had ordered a barrel of rum from Jamaica. He got it through customs without paying any duties. He said that it was alcohol for his lab and that there was nothing to be paid for goods imported for "scientific" purposes.

On the day of the party he filled half a pail with rum and took it to his bungalow. There he "diluted" it by adding several bottles of red wine, cutting into the brew pineapples, oranges, and other fruit, and finally topped it up with tap-water.

"This will make a good drink," he told my wife who was looking on while he was preparing this concoction.

"But you poured in a lot of tap-water. We'll all get ill."

Wally who was biologist laughed. "With this amount of alcohol?"

"So, what about this Quist?" I asked. "Is he also a technician?"

Wally nodded his head in affirmation. "He spent some years in England. I don't know if he got a formal training, but he worked there for an electrical engineering firm. If anyone can repair your machine it is him."

After the dismal failure of the university's European technicians I was not convinced. But there was no harm in trying and I went to look for Quist at the workshop.

The people there told me that he was away repairing the electricity generator which Mr. Hooper again forgot to oil. If it was not repaired by evening the entire campus would once more be without electricity that night. We all knew Mr. Hooper. He was in charge of the generator and always forgot to oil it. But he couldn't be sacked – he was a relative of some local Fanti dignitary.

I inquired where Quist lived and waited till late afternoon. Most Africans who were not members of the teaching and administrative staff were not living on the campus but in town, and I was surprised to learn that he resided on the campus. It made me curious and I asked Atinga for the reason.

"Yes, master, he be on the campus. He no live in Town. He be Ga from Accra and not a Fanti." Atinga's reply sounded as if not being a Fanti or Frafra like Atinga himself made the man a member of an inferior race.

Next morning Quist came and my wife showed him to the machine in the by-kitchen. All the bungalows on the campus were built in the old colonial style with a kitchen for the cook and a by-kitchen for the lady of the house to prepare some small things by herself.

He unscrewed the back cover and pocked the wiring with his screwdriver. Then he pulled up a chair in front of it and remained seated just looking.

"Shall I set coffee now or when you finish?" my wife asked.

"You can set it now."

When the coffee was ready we called him to the sitting room and talked for a while. Finally he got up and said that he was going home.

My wife asked: "Are you not finishing the repairs?"

"Oh, it is finished. I repaired it right away. It only took a minute."

"What then kept you looking at the machine so long before I came to call you?"

"That? It was too fascinating to learn how it all works. Not every day I have an opportunity to see how such an intricate machine is wired."

We waited until he was gone before we went to the by-kitchen to try it out. The machine functioned as well as it did when we just got it from the factory.

All Whites Look Alike

We were sitting in the living room discussing the black and white members of staff residing on our ridge. The whites usually went home to Europe or America in the summer and we were wondering what Mr. Amarty Kwaku and his family, who were black, were doing in their summer holidays. Our daughter, who had just turned four, was playing next to us on the floor. Suddenly she intervened in the conversation: "Mr Amarty Kwaku is not black."

"But Mr. Amarty is black," my wife said, as indeed he was.

Our daughter insisted: "No! He is not!"

My wife mentioned the names of Mr. Amarty's children with whom she used to play, and asked her if they were black or not.

She persisted. "No, they are not black."

I asked her if Wally was black?

She thought this over for a while and replied that Wally was copper – not black.

I had to laugh. A few days earlier, Wally had come to us practically foaming with anger. An official who filled in some form for him wrote in answer to the question colour that his was copper. Wally, who had given up his job with Imperial College in London, and came to Ghana because he was black and wished to help his African brethren to develop their first independent state, was deeply offended by having his African origins denied.

My wife continued asking our daughter about our neighbours. Who was black and who was white? She could not tell. She maintained that some blacks were white and some whites were black. Apparently, the distinction between black and white people is something learned and does not come naturally.

I would have forgotten this had it not been that a few days later our daughter came home crying bitterly that the materials my wife gave her for the embroidery time at the kindergarten was given to another child that day.

My wife was angry and went to see the kindergarten teacher. The woman was embarrassed. Indeed, she had mistakenly given our daughter's work to Sharon, the only other white girl in the play group. "You know," she explained apologetically, "all the white children look so much alike that I cannot easily distinguish between them."

Our daughter has black hair, and Sharon's hair is very blond. But we understood. Did we ourselves during our first days in Ghana not feel that all blacks looked alike?

In the Bush

Once a week I drove to a small village in the bush. The fist time I went there it was curiosity. A student asked me to come with him to see his "home town." He said that there was no real road leading there and that I better take the jeep. He was right. There was not even a proper track. It took almost two hours driving the 35 kilometres through the thick forest before we reached the place.

Somehow the news of our coming had preceded us. When we arrived the entire village population was assembled in front of the chief's house. Except for this house, and another larger building that I later learned was the school, there were some twenty wood and mud houses roofed with corrugated iron sheets. There were several chairs and makeshift benches lined up by the chief's house. I was invited to sit in the middle, next to the chief and his ocheame, facing the assembled community. An ocheame is a spokesman for the chief whose task is to speak for him and explain his decisions to the people.

As soon as I was seated a coconut shell filled to the brim with palm wine was handed around. The ocheame made a speech which I could not understand. From his demeanor I gathered that he was welcoming me and explaining who I was and where I came from. After this ceremonial reception everyone but the children went away. Followed by a horde of small children, the chief took me around to show me the village. He spoke English fairly well. We had no difficulty communicating. He told me that the school was built recently by the government, and that he was very grateful to the President Dr. Nkrumah for having given it to his village. Near the school we were joined by the teacher. He told me that he was not a local but an Ashanti from Kumasi. He complained that he was "exiled to this place to educate the peasants" leaving his family behind in town. At one point on our walk, the chief asked me if I was willing to help the village. The women, he said, had to go very far to fetch water and it wasted a lot of their time. Could I not "speak for them" to the government to do something about the water supply?

I told him that I had no influence with the government but he pretended not to believe me. He said that being a professor and a white man the government would listen to me. I knew that he was wrong, but I was left with no alternative but to promise that I shall try. Later, on the drive home, when I told my student about this conversation, the student laughed. "He knows that you will get nowhere with the government."

"Why then does he tell me to try?"

"He wants *you*, not the government, to do something about the water."

"Me? How can I?"

"He wants you to come and help him to make a well."

"Me? A well? So why didn't he say so?"

"It is not our way. He knows that now you have promised to do something, you'll have to think about it. In the end you'll find a way to solve our problem."

"But I don't know anything about wells. Doesn't he know that?"

"He knows. But you have become part of our village and you will ask your friends at the university to help you."

I was a little annoyed. "You knew about all this when you suggested that I come with you to your village. You set me up."

The student smiled.

It took me two weeks to find someone from the geology department and an engineer who were ready to come with me to the village and see what could be done. It soon became clear that it was not difficult to dig a well there. The villagers could do it themselves. The engineer thought it best to install a small oil powered water pump, and he knew a Lebanese shop in Accra where one could be bought. I explained all this to the chief and the next time I came the work on the well had started. On my next visit the chief asked me to tell his people that each of them must contribute some money for the pump. With the interpreter's help I did this wondering why he didn't do it himself.

When I asked my student he was amused. "He is a clever old Fanti. He knows that the people will trust you, an outsider, with their money but none of their own people. He also expects you to contribute your own money if the village cannot collect enough to pay for the pump."

This time I had to laugh. "They cannot trust each other, but they will trust a foreigner. And they expect me to pay for a pump I do not need?"

The student grinned: "Teacher, you are learning fast."

I do not know how they always knew the day and time of my arrival, but when I came to organize the money collection the entire village was already assembled. One by one all men and some women came to hand me bills. There was no registration how much each of them paid and nobody wanted a receipt. One old man proudly handed me two pound notes from colonial times which had long since gone out of circulation and were worthless, and said something which my student later told me meant that he was giving me *real* money and not Dr. Nkrumah's cedis. To my surprise the money collected was almost enough to pay for the pump, and I did not have to delve deep into my pocket to make up the missing difference.

Eventually the pump was installed, but by this time the chief already convinced me to help them also build a pigsty and a cowshed with netting to protect the animals from tzetze flies. I brought Wally to teach them to graft fruit trees in the bush and to grow the vegetables which fetched a good price in town. Without being aware of it I gradually became part of the village, and went there every Thursday afternoon to see how things were getting on.

From time to time I also had embarrassing moments. The most humiliating of these was when I tried to clean my pipe. One of the villagers grew tobacco. He did not know how to cure it and sold it raw to a Nigerian salesman. At that time I was smoking a pipe and when the tobacco was burned out I knocked my pipe against some hard object to get rid of the remaining ash. I was sitting with some of the villagers and as I did it a hush fell over the gathering and the man with the tobacco plot rushed off. For a few minutes nobody else stirred. All were sitting silently – waiting. Then the man returned holding a sheaf of tobacco leaves. He handed them to me and returned to his seat and the conversation was resumed as if nothing had happened. Later, when I told this to my student he explained that my knocking out my pipe indicated that I had no tobacco and was angry that nobody had offered me any.

Naturally, I could not smoke the uncured tobacco leaves, but I put some into my pipe. Had I not done so, my student told me, I would have offended the entire village. The people would have taken it as a gesture that I thought that they did not show me the customary hospitality. It was then that I fist learned the "body language" of the region. If you stretched out both arms to your sides when someone came to your home it meant "*Akwaba*" – you are welcome, but if you did not, your visitor could not know if he was welcome or not.

My visits to the village became regular. I went there every Thursday afternoon to see how the projects were progressing. Normally I stayed an hour or two but occasionally I remained longer and it was already dark when I drove back to the campus. There was no real path and from time to time I explored different tracks through the bush. Sometimes I took one and other times another. One night, half-way to the main road, I suddenly saw a figure in front of me waving a lantern. As I got closer the headlights of my car fell on two other figures crouched by the wayside in the bush. The man with the lantern stood in the middle of the track and made me stop.

He came to my side of the car and pointed to the two figures: "Master, you take these women to Cape Coast."

The man must have thought that I was hesitating and added: "the one woman she be with baby. She need go Cape Coast hospital quick."

By this time the two women were approaching the jeep and I could see them. One was an old woman and the other young and very pregnant and obviously in great pain.

"Step in," I said.

The man turned off his lantern and helped the pregnant woman into the back seat of the vehicle. The other woman followed and set beside her. The man came to the front and seated himself next to me. From time to time the pregnant woman moaned. As the moaning became more frequent and turned into screams I became increasingly anxious that she would have her baby in the car. I wanted to drive faster but on this path it was impossible. I had no idea what I should do if the baby started to come. My children were both born in hospital and I was only allowed to see my wife after they were born. All I knew about birth was from a short story by Maxim Gorki. The story was called "How a Human Being was Born." It told of a young student of the *Narodnaya Volya* movement who helped a Ukrainian peasant woman to deliver her child in a field. I remembered that he had pressed her shoulders against the ground while the boy or girl was born – that was all.

I asked the man beside me what would happen if she gets the child before we reach Cape Coast?

"No. That is the trouble. Her time has come and the child cannot get out. The old woman she be midwife. She say other woman very sick. Must go hospital quick quick or expire." He sounded sombre.

"What would you have done if I did not come this way? How would you have gotten to the hospital?"

"We know you come. You every Thursday in village."

"But I do not always take the same path home."

"We know you come this way this time."

"How?"

"We think strong and make you come this way."

"All right. You made me choose this route, but how could you be sure I'll stop? I may be afraid of robbers or of ghosts?"

My question seemed to surprise the man. "You no stop because afraid? All people know you. You go by night. You not afraid of robbers. You not afraid of ghosts. You be great hunter."

His words flattered me. Somehow they made me less apprehensive about the moaning woman. When we reached the asphalt road I pressed down the accelerator to the floor, and ignoring the risk of running into trucks parked on the road without light, I raced to the hospital. Once there, the man and the midwife helped the pregnant woman out of the car. By this time she was hardly able to move. I followed them into the hospital to make sure by my presence, the people knew me there, that she would directly be taken to the doctor. The journey had somehow made me feel responsible for her.

I never learned if she or her baby survived. In the hospital nobody could tell me, and elsewhere there was no one I could ask. I did not know her name, nor did I know what village she came from. I could not even remember which particular path I had taken through the bush that night or the place where the man with the lantern had stopped me. But for days Gorki's "How a Human Being was Born" kept preying on my mind.

Tropical Rain

It rained all night but in the morning it cleared up and I drove my wife to Accra where she wanted to stay for two or three days. By noon, on my way back home, it began to rain again. The closer I came to Cape Coast the harder it poured down. The road went along the ocean and usually I drove the 150 kilometres leisurely stopping from time to time to look at the ruins of the slavers' castles which were scattered along the shore. This time I was in a hurry. In the morning, before I left Cape Coast I arranged with the neighbours to collect our children from kindergarten and school and take them to their house. I was sure to be back in time to give them their dinner in the evening.

Suddenly, near Biriwa, about 20 kilometres from my destination, I came upon a long line of trucks and cars parked by the roadside. Carefully I drove to the head of the column to see why they all stopped. Water was streaming across the road carrying in its current scrubs and large logs of wood and even trees. A river perhaps 150 metres wide, that had not been there before. It was a magnificent sight but I wondered what was going to happen with our children when it became dark, the neighbours sent them home, and there was nobody in the house. Looking at the "river" I knew that I wouldn't make it in time to be there to receive them. From where I was the only alternative way to reach Cape Coast was to go back to a road inland to Kumasi and from there come back by way of Takoradi – a detour of about 600 kilometres. But even if I tried to take this route, I would never be able to make it home before morning; and how was I to know if there were no similar obstacles on this road as well.

Among the vehicles by the roadside were several high timber trucks, and I wondered if I could not convince one of their drivers to try to cross the stream and take me with him. But I soon saw that it was impossible. Someone had already unsuccessfully tried it. Half submerged in water a huge trucks was stuck the middle of the flood.

The place was two or three kilometres from a village next to which was the beach were we often went to swim in summer and a small shed were one could get a drink. To get out of the pouring rain, have a drink, and think what I could do, I drove back the short distance and went there. For some time I just sat nursing my drink, looking at the waves, and worrying. Then I had an idea. Perhaps the fishermen from the nearby village could help me. I asked the man running the place where I had my drink if he would take me and a canoe on his truck to the place where the road was flooded. He agreed. I went to the village and looked for a friend – a fisherman I knew. I found him with some other fishermen. I told them what I wanted and they looked at me as if I was out of my mind. I tried to explain that with their outboard-motor it was a small matter to rush across the stream. They knew better. It was far too dangerous with the logs and trees carried by the current. I made another effort and suggested that we go out to sea and land again behind the "stream." But that too was out of the question. In this weather, they said, their canoe would never make it through the breakers. I offered them all the money I had on me and this finally did the trick. They agreed to try by my first method.

It was hard work and took much time to get the canoe onto the truck and required the help of twenty men. The men who helped came with us to unload the canoe. Meanwhile it had become evening and we arrived in pitch darkness. Two policemen stood with lanterns in the road to warn off the oncoming traffic. As soon as we began to unload the canoe a police sergeant appeared out of the dark, and realizing what we were planning warned us not to try. He reminded us that in the dark we could not even see what came floating down the stream, and that even with the outboard at top speed the risk of the canoe to collide with something and overturn was too dangerous to attempt the crossing. "You will drown and my officer will blame me for allowing you to try."

The man was right and I knew it. But the thought of the children alone at home on such a dismal night made me unreasonable. It even made me forget Atinga who was certainly there and looking after them. I told the police sergeant that if he prevented me from taking the canoe across I would try to swim which would be much more dangerous. I believe that at the time I was desperate enough to do it. The sergeant insisted that he was under orders not allow anyone pass. I maintained that nobody had the right to stop me. In the end he gave in and I got ready to attempt the crossing.

Meanwhile the fishermen had been arguing among themselves and came to the conclusion that it could not be done. Only my friend was ready to come with me. Somehow he had confidence. He trusted that I knew what I was doing. I gave my car papers and car keys to one of the fishermen and told them that if something happened to their canoe and I drowned the car was theirs in compensation. The one who was prepared to go with me told his mates that he would watch the canoe at the other side until water abated and the truck could fetch it back to their village.

Just before we started the outboard motor another African jumped into the canoe who also wanted to get to the other side in a hurry. My friend tried to make him go back and argued with him in a language I did not understand (I later learned that it was Ewe). But the man remained in the canoe.

How we actually got across I don't remember. All I recall is that I held on to the handle of the motor which steered the canoe as if my life depended on it, as it may indeed have done, and tried to steer the canoe against the current. Suddenly I heard a scratching sound coming from below and I knew that the canoe was scraping the road on the other side of the torrent. We jumped off and helped by some people who had seen us coming hauled the canoe out of the water.

On this side of the stream things looked very much the same as on the other side. A long line of vehicles was waiting by the roadside. The rain hadn't stopped and I was hoping to find a car to take me on the last leg of my way. There was none, and I began to walk. Soon I realized that the old man who came with me on the canoe was following. I slowed down a little to allow him to catch up with me. After some minutes I saw the lights of an African bar by the wayside and heard the sound of music coming from within. For a brief moment I thought to go inside and ask for a drink but I changed my mind and walked on. There was no point getting out of the rain. I was wet to the bone already, and as soon as I got out of the bar again I would immediately be as wet as before. I had only done a few more steps and I heard people running after me calling my name.

I waited and two men caught up with me. They were students who recognized me near the bar and brought me an umbrella. I thanked them but did not take it. There was no point. Suddenly the old man next to me said in perfect German that it was kind of me to have permitted him to come along on the canoe and that he wished to thank me for it. He had an urgent court case in Takoradi in the morning and would never have been able to make it in time had it not been for my "kindness." Seeing how wet he was I invited him to stay the night in my house when we reached Cape Coast. He could then take the first available transport to Takoradi early next morning. I asked how it was that he spoke good German and he told me that as a child he went to school in Togo before the first World War when the country still was a German colony.

A little later we managed to stop a car going in our direction. The driver was on his way to Accra when the "river" prevented him from going on. He became fed up waiting at the stream and turned back. He took us Cape Coast. It was about ten o'clock in the evening when we arrived at my bungalow. Atinga was sitting in the living room waiting for me. The children were sleeping peacefully. Next day I learned that when I did not arrive on time the neighbours gave them dinner, put them to bed, and told Atinga to call them if anything should happen.

Next morning I woke up with the sun shining in my face. The rain had stopped and the ocean was as calm as on a summer day. I asked for one of the university cars and a driver to take me to the place where I experienced all the trouble on the previous night. I also took some more money for the fishermen who helped me and hoped that the water on the road had gone down sufficiently to get to them and to my car. All the vehicles which had been waiting by the "river" on the previous night were gone, and I could not even recognize the place where they had stopped. The "river" vanished as quickly as it appeared. We drove to Biriwa without seeing any sign of it.

Having given the money to the fishermen and collected my car papers and keys I drove back looking for the location of the previous night's adventure. It took me some time to find it. When I did I stepped out of my car and inspected the road. There was hardly any damage. Only the sand covering part of the road and some cracks at the edges was evidence of what had gone before.

Suddenly the sergeant who tried to stop me crossing the water appeared out from nowhere in the bush. He was smiling. "You see? White men always too much in a hurry."

Medicare

Doctor J. was the only white physician in town. His bungalow stood at the edge of the bush not far from the government hospital which served the 60,000 inhabitants of Cape Coast. The colonial administration built it in the late 1930s and little was done since then to renovate it. It was the only hospital in the region. Day and night people were sitting on the ground in front of its entrance waiting their turn to be admitted.

Dr. J. was enthralled by his work; but when he took a few hours off he sat on the veranda behind his bungalow reading or talking with friends about the books they were reading. I liked Dr. J. He was one of that other breed of Englishmen one occasionally met in the colonies who were not posturing as if they were a superior race. He had studied medicine and became a surgeon because he wanted to help people. After he had practised his profession for some years in England he decided that his services were more needed in Africa than in Exeter and he took his wife and children to Ghana. It was there where we first met. Like many educated Europeans of his generation he loved to read the classics as well as modern novels and to discuss them with his friends.

It was during one of these conversations, when we were sitting on the veranda behind his bungalow, that a man appeared out of the bush and was approaching us. It was a small man. He had an old-fashioned shotgun loosely slung over his back. He took a few steps in our direction, hesitated, stopped and waited for us to call him to come closer. His right arm hung limply from his shoulder and was plainly causing him considerable pain.

The doctor whispered: "They are not supposed to come to my home. They ought to go to the hospital."

A little annoyed that our conversation was interrupted I said: "Why don't you tell him to go there."

He gave me a surprised look that made me feel uncomfortable. "No. This man knows that he ought to have gone to the hospital. See how embarrassed he looks. Can't you recognize how it humiliates him that he needs to come here?"

The man noticed that we were talking about him and came nearer. When he was close to us he stopped and waited to be spoken to.

"So, what's wrong?" The doctor's voice was calming – friendly.

The man said that he was a hunter and that during the hunt another hunter's gun went off and some pellets of buckshot hit him in the arm.

The doctor told him to make a fist but the man couldn't do it. I saw that the very effort to move his fingers made him wince from the pain.

"OK. First thing tomorrow morning you come to the hospital and tell the nurse on duty that I want to see you right away."

The man didn't move.

"Anything else?" the doctor asked.

The hunter looked at the ground in front of him. "Master, I am a poor man."

My friend thought for a moment and then went into the house. He came back holding a piece of paper. He scribbled something on it and handed it to the hunter who immediately looked very much relieved. The man folded the paper carefully, deposited it in his pocket and thanked the doctor. Then he took a few steps walking backward, turned, and disappeared in the bush.

"And what was this all about?" I asked, hinting at the pen which my friend still held in his hand.

For a moment Dr. J. looked at me as if he did not understand my question. Then, cheerlessly he answered that no one can come to see him in the hospital unless one bribes the receptionist and the nurses. "Try as I may, I cannot get rid of this corruption. I've been struggling against it for months but is all to no avail. The one thing I managed to achieve is that they do not dare to stop someone who has a written note from me. I think that when somebody has a note they believe that he is family of an important person with whom one better does not tangle."

The following day Dr. J. phoned me. Would I like to join him on a trip in the bush. He wants to take the hunter to a medicine-man. If I feel like it, I can come along.

Riding in the jeep with the hunter in the back seat, the doctor told me that he made some roentgen pictures. There were several pellets of gun-shot in the

man's arm which in a few days would cause him no more pain or other incon-
venience. It was much safer to let them remain where they were than to operate.

"Did you tell him?" I asked.

"He doesn't trust me. One of the nurses said that he told her in Fanti that if
he were white or rich I would operate and relieve him of his pain. But being
black and poor I do not care about him."

I had the urge to ask him if the hunter wasn't right. But I managed to restrain
myself. Perhaps he wouldn't immediately see that I was joking.

The doctor went on. "The nurse also told me that he said that if he had the
money for the fare, and for paying for it, he would go to some fetish priest or
medicine man for help."

"So, you felt offended," I mumbled.

He looked surprised. "Offended? Why? He doesn't know me from Adam.
Why should he think that I am different from all the rest here? No, no, I am
not offended but I am very curious what his witchdoctor can do."

"And so you offered to take him there and pay the medicine man's fee. But
don't forget to tell the witchdoctor that you belong to the same profession. You
may be entitled to a price reduction."

My friend smiled. "You see, that's one of the problems here with the
free health-care. Since President Nkrumah made it a law that people can be
treated without having to pay for it we are no longer trusted. They think
that anything you get free of charge cannot be good. Our hunter here told
me that his medicine man will want 15 cedis for the treatment. This is a lot of
money for him. Therefore he is certain that this quack's help must be very
solid."

The hunter behind us in the jeep had been following our discussion. Obviously
his English was sufficiently good to grasp what we were saying because he
intervened in our conversation to remind the doctor that it was not 15 cedis
but also two chicken which were to be paid to the medicine man. He lifted up
a sack from the floor of the jeep for us to see it. "This be two chicken inside."

After a long journey through thick bush we finally arrived in the village, and
people showed us to the medicine man's hut. He received us with much ado
and offered us palm-wine and apatashi. There was no doubt. He enjoyed our
coming for his help. The customary welcome over, the hunter handed him the
money and the chicken. Then the medicine man left the hut and made a small
fire outside. He slaughtered one of the birds, cut it into four portions, and threw
them into the flames. Busying himself with this he explained to us that it was
of the utmost importance to put pepper on the chicken before it was burned.
"Pepper no salt," he emphasized, add salt and the potion will not work." After
this he wrapped a rag like a bandage around the hunter's arm, and told us to

go for a walk and look at the village. "Go for the time it takes to smoke five cigarettes and then return."

We did as we were told. When we came back several old women and men were gathered by the hut. The medicine man muttered some words which none of us, and probably nobody else, could understand. Whenever there was a pause in this incantation the men mumbled some words and the women swayed to and fro. Then, all at once, the man stopped muttering and called the hunter to approach him. He slowly peeled off the "bandage" from the hunter's arm and turning to us showed us several pebbles of shot he had in his hand. "Here they are. Now his arm is fine again," he said triumphantly, and ordered the hunter to move his fingers one by one.

One by one the hunter tried to move his fingers and then made a fist and opened it. Then he swung his arm, tried his fist again, and laughed. His pain was gone. He could do again all the movements he could not do before.

I saw the amazement on my friend's face. Dr. J. was certainly impressed. All the ride back to Cape Coast he did not say a word. Only when we arrived he suddenly turned around to tell the hunter to accompany him into the hospital. It was clear to me that he simply had to make another roentgen picture of the hunter's arm and compare it with the one he had taken before.

It had become much later than I expected when we left and I had to leave them. But later that evening I phoned Dr. J. to hear what the comparison had shown.

"Oh. The hunter? He is well." I heard the doctor at the other end of the line, "It is as if he never had any trouble with his arm before. He can do everything he wants with it. He is very happy."

"Yes. But what about the roentgen?" I asked.

For a moment there was silence. Then he asked: "And what do *you* think?" And he put the phone back into its cradle.

Evil Spirits

Asafuagey was the university's paymaster. The salaries of the academic staff went through the bank, the other workers wages were paid in cash at Asafuagey's office. Every payday after work more than 300 labourers waited in front of the office to be paid. There were always women, many of them with small children on their backs, waiting with the workmen. Most of them were market-women making sure to get the money they advanced the workers or credited them for victuals during the previous week. The rest were members of the workers' families who came to take the money home to their villages.

They all knew that if they were not on the spot when the workers received their pay the money would be gone.

Asafuagey wanted to spend Christmas with his family in Kumasi and wishing to arrive there before dark he left in his Mercedes immediately after lunch. So, when at the end of the workday the workers came to his office there was nobody there to pay them. At first they just stood around waiting. They were used to be made to wait for "big men." But then they became worried and someone went to look for the cashier. The news he brought was that Asafuagey had gone for several days to his family in Kumasi and taken the safe keys with him. Not to worry, a cashier told the man who went to ask, next week everyone will get his money.

Slowly the crowd in front of the office dispersed. Only a few of the 400 or 500 people who were there before remained and complained to an administrator who, attracted by the commotion, had come to find out what was going on.

A few days later I met Neyamey. Neyamey was one of the workers who did not receive his pay that day. He too had planned to spend Christmas with his family and counted on his wages to pay the fare to his village and to buy some presents.

"So you couldn't go. Why didn't you come to me? I would have lent you the fare."

"No. I go, but not to my village. Me and some others borrow small small money from market-momma and go to *Juju-man* to put curse on Asafuagey."

I heard of such curses so often that I had almost forgotten it when I met Neyamey again and he told me that Asafuagey's Mercedes was involved in a road accident on his way back from Kumasi and that the crash had been fatal for his wife. Neyamey was older than I, and always felt obliged to teach me something. "You see," he said, "our spell worked. Asafuagey lost his wife."

My objection that it was not his wife but Asafuagey who had wronged the workers, and that it was not her but him they cursed, did not impress Neyamey. With the forgiving smile adults reserve for little children when they do not understand the obvious, he explained to me that it is not a person but a family which takes the blame for its members misdeeds. First one of the family is afflicted as a warning. Then another and another. And if all these warnings go unheeded and the culprit still does not show remorse then he is lost himself.

I did not answer.

"You no see? Even the Holy Bible tells us this be right. You no read book of Job? First the oxen were taken, then the sheep were burned, then the camels were carried away and the servants were slain, then a wind smote the four corners of Job's house and it fell upon his sons and daughters and killed them all, and then he even lost his wife Bildad the Shuhite."

Asafuagey did not mend his ways and in the months that followed gave more cause for workers to complain about him. Neyamey was certain that his end was nigh. Each time I saw him he was more convinced that Asafuagey's end was imminent. I gave up arguing with him about it.

Then one day Asafuagey was suddenly taken ill and admitted to the hospital. The next morning he was dead. All the labourers on the university campus "knew" with certainty that he died exactly one year to the day after he was cursed. The curse had done its work.

I asked Dr. J. who had dissected the body in the hospital about the cause of death. His reply was clear. He knew the man. He was a heavy drinker and his liver had for a long time given the doctor reason for concern.

I looked at the calendar. It was not exactly a year but one year and six weeks after the car accident in which Asafuagey lost his wife. None of the Africans to whom I told this believed me. Asafuagey was killed by evil spirits. He "expired" precisely one year after he received his warning.

It is Not the Money But the Principle

The Dutch Embassy asked me to go to the port in Takoradi to release two new vehicles from customs and have them driven to Accra. The vehicles were specially equipped land rovers, donated by the Netherlands government (DTH) to the Ghanaian Ministry of Agriculture, Fisheries and Mining, for agricultural extension work – a present from the Dutch to the Ghanaian government. I asked two drivers from the university car pool, and my friend and student Mensa, to come with me. The former to drive the vehicles to Accra, and the latter to serve as an interpreter in the event that an interpreter was needed. I did not expect any difficulties.

We arrived in Takoradi shortly before noon and went directly with our customs release papers to the director of the customs service. The official inspected the papers and asked us in perfect English if we brought the customs money.

I tried to explain that the vehicles were a gift to his government and that diplomatic imports were in any case free from import duties.

It was to no avail. The man was adamant. If we want the vehicles we have to pay. The longer we argued the more I realized that he was not going to change his mind. Mensa never said a word until in exasperation I got up to leave. Then he said something in Ewe to the man. I did not understand Ewe and had no idea what he told him.

Once we were outside the office, Mensa suggested to me that I should phone the Dutch Embassy for new instructions.

At first I was reluctant to do so. I was angry. "Why should I? When we get back, I shall tell the Ambassador what happened, and advise that the vehicles be returned to Holland."

Mensa was surprised by my anger. "All the man wants is a small *dash*."

Dash is the word for bribe in Ghana. The very idea of bribing an official on behalf of the Dutch government, and in order to give a present to the Ghanaian state, appalled me.

Mensa noticed my resentment and laughed: "You will never understand this country. Why don't you phone the Embassy now? Ask them what to do."

I phoned the Embassy. The man at the other end of the line did not interrupt me. Only when I finished he asked in a matter of fact voice how much the official wanted?

My first reaction was to put down the receiver and wash my hands of the entire affair. But on second thought I decided that after all it was none of my business what the Dutch government does. I turned to Mensa who was standing next to the phone and asked him.

"Twenty will do."

"Twenty what?" I asked.

"Twenty Cedis."

"Twenty Cedis? Less than US$50, –," I said incredulously. "Is this what the fuss is all about?"

Mensa smiled. "I told you that you do not understand."

I picked up the phone again and told the man at the Embassy what Mensa thought we ought to pay.

He did not seem surprised and asked: "Can you book the money as expenses?"

"How? What expenses?" I said unable to conceal my annoyance.

"Book it as travelling expenses, as pay for your interpreter, as extra lunch money for your drivers. What does it matter? As long as it is formally booked its all right."

"Why not book it as a bribe for the privilege to give the Ghanaian government a present?"

The man at the other end of the telephone line giggled. "You better not do that. Our accountants in the Hague have no sense of humour."

I hung up and told Mensa what I was told.

Mensa seemed happy. He apparently expected this answer because he took an envelope out of his pocket and gave it to me to put the twenty cedis inside. Then he sealed the envelope, and told me to follow him back into the customs office.

Again we were invited to sit. Mensa and the official conversed for a while in Ewe, and then he handed over the envelop, with a gesture indicating that it came from me. The man smiled and put it into his desk without opening it. Then he shouted something to someone in the next room. Another official entered with a sheaf of papers which our director of customs signed and gave me one by one.

"These are the release papers. Give them to the drivers so that they can take the land rovers out of the harbour. You can send them off to Accra. Also give them some money to buy petrol near the port entrance. You don't want to find them later waiting for you without petrol near the roadside when you go home." He laughed.

I wanted to leave the office and send the drivers off. But Mensa stopped me and asked me to wait for him in the office while he gave the papers and the petrol money to the drivers.

While he was away our customs man told me that both he and Mensa came from the Volta region and had been to school together. After school Mensa joined the police force and he went into the Civil Service. The man's attitude to me was completely changed. The earlier stiffness was gone and he was talking to me like an old friend. When Mensa returned to the office, he asked us to follow him. He locked the office and led us to his car.

"Now we go to the hotel to take our four o'clock tea," he said laughing, imitating the English upper class pronunciation of four o'clock tea.

Our negotiations about the release of the vehicles had taken several hours, and I realized that it had become late afternoon. I turned to Mensa and asked if it wouldn't be better to go back to Cape Coast immediately. The man did not give him a chance to reply. "No, no, no. You have not eaten since morning, and had no beer all day," he laughed again. "Now you must be my guests. We go to the hotel and have some food and lots and lots of beer."

There was no point in arguing. Mensa was already seated in the man's car and waiting for me to join him.

We went to the modern tourist hotel which had only recently been built in Takoradi by the Ghanaian government. We got a good meal and had many bottles of beer. I offered to pay but our custom's official wouldn't hear of it. He insisted that he was our host and that it was up to him to see us happy in "his" town.

During our ride back to Cape Coast much later in the evening, I couldn't resist asking Mensa what this day's strange experience was about. I failed to understand how a person could argue with us about a puny bribe, and then spend four times the sum to treat us to a meal in the town's most expensive hotel?

"It is not the money, it is the principle,.." Mensa explained.

"What principle? The principle of taking bribes?" I said unable to suppress my irritation.

"You do not understand. I told you this before – you do not understand! When our people go to see a chief, what do they do? They bring a present. If they are rich cocoa-farmers they bring a bottle of Gordon Gin for libation. If they are poor they bring some fruit. It is to show respect. The price does not matter. The important thing is that they show respect, that they make it clear that the chief is the 'boss' and that they respect him. Later the chief must show that he is important – that he is rich and generous. So you see, the money we gave this man was not a bribe, it was a token of respect. He wished to show you that he was important – that he was "a big man." Mensa laughed.

His laughter angered me. "What is there to laugh about? The man is not a tribal chief but a government official. How can you run a country like this?"

Mensa continued to laugh. "You'll never understand. I told you, it's a matter of principle. Why does it worry you? You did not pay a bribe. You showed the man some respect. What's wrong with that?"

Justice and the Legal System

For days the expatriate staff on the university campus had no other topic of conversation than the Adamafio court case. Adamafio was Minister of Information in the Nkrumah government and apparently tried to oust Nkrumah from power and take his place as Ghana's head of state. He failed, was detained and brought before the court. The British trained judge Aku Korsa heard his case, found the evidence insufficient to declare him guilty, and ordered his release. But as soon as he left the courthouse he was picked up by the police and again incarcerated under some regulation by which suspects could be held for an indeterminate period.

The expatriates were in uproar. This was a blatant breach of the rule of law. Nobody brought up in the belief that people are considered innocent unless proven guilty was able to accept what happened. There were very few who liked Adamafio. His dictatorial tendencies were well demonstrated by the manner in which he had handled the workers' strike in Takoradi. All were however agreed that this was a matter of principle. It made no difference if there was sympathy or dislike for the man – the law had to be respected.

The African colleagues said nothing but seemed not to share the expatriates' indignation. For this reason, one evening when some students came for a visit to my bungalow, I brought up the topic. To begin with everyone seemed to agree that the rule of law must under all circumstances be upheld. But I sensed that this agreement was due to the Ghanaian custom that one does not contradict the host. So I decided to ask Kodzo directly what he thought about the rearrest of Adamafio. I knew that if I wanted a true answer it was Kodzo I must ask. He was not only my senior in age and a respected leader in his tribe but a good friend, with sufficient authority to speak his mind without much inhibition.

Looking at the other students, as if he wanted their consent for what he was going to say, he replied that in the villages people had their own conceptions about justice.

When I kept quiet he went on: "If we suspect somebody we have him interrogated by the village elders. If they cannot come to a clear conclusion they ask the people and the gods for guidance." Having said this he looked at the floor as if he had told me all there was to say, but after a short pause he added: "Dr. Nkrumah was right and our people know it."

I was so surprised that I only mumbled something about principles of justice and accepted rules of law.

Mensa, who was sitting next to Kodzo and until then had not taken part in the conversation, suddenly asked me what I myself thought about the Adamafio case. "Do *you* think he is innocent or guilty?"

I answered that what I thought was of no consequence. The point was that a court of law found Adamafio's case not proven and that this was sufficient reason for him to be given the benefit of doubt and released.

They all looked at me and I could feel that they were thinking that I gave more weight to the formal aspect of the case than to its substance.

Without saying as much, which would have been bad manners in Ghanaian society, Kodzo maintained that the people know what is right and what is wrong. The people knew that Adamafio tried to overthrow the government and accepted the President's decision.

I asked: "Why then the ceremony, with prosecutors, solicitors, attorneys?"

My guests smiled, and Mensa said a little embarrassed: "That's for the whites. We must look civilized, mustn't we?"

His words were greeted by loud laughter.

"So the entire legal system you inherited from the British is a farce."

"No. Not a farce," said Kodzo. "It is important, only the ceremonial must not thwart real justice."

"Why then do you not say this to my colleagues at the university? Why do you avoid telling them that by justice as you see it Dr. Nkrumah has done the right thing?" The moment I said it I knew that it was a silly. My expatriate colleagues were no less estranged from the Ghanaians than the Ghanaian people in the villages from Aku Korsa's court.

Violence, Love and Respect

The one thing that had puzzled me a little when Atinga first came to work for us was that when I signed his work-book (a booklet all Ghanaians seeking employment need to have) I noticed that for the last four years he had not been employed. It puzzled me, but I was not particularly bothered by it. He probably had gone back to his farm. Only employees required registration, self-employed did not.

Atinga could neither write or read and his English was poor by the other steward boys' standard. But we soon noticed that he had an unusually high natural intelligence, and his English was also rapidly improving. He got on well with our children, did his work, and was altogether a likeable person. We got used to him and my wife was happy to have found someone to whom she could explain what she wanted and why who understood her.

After some time that he had been working for us, he asked if he could bring his wife and child from the north to stay with him. My wife had no objections. Next to each bungalow, on a patio just outside our kitchen, there was a "servants flat." A very small room and a shower.

After being with us for several months, my wife suggested to him to learn to read and write and he registered for classes. By the time we left Ghana he was able to write us letters. The one thing I found difficult to understand was that Africans who learned that Atinga was working for us were usually surprised. I asked several Ghanaians about it but their answers were evasive. "Me surprised? Why? I didn't say that I was surprised." Eventually one colleague told me that it was because Atinga was known as a very violent man. Atinga violent? It seemed ridiculous. But when I prodded my colleague to show some evidence for this assertion, he told me that he had been four years in prison for beating up people and even a policeman.

Although I remembered that there was no work record for four years in his work book, the story seemed to me improbable. By this time he had been in our house for several months and I never saw him showing the slightest inclination to be violent. But when I told the story to my wife she knew. He had told her himself that he had been in prison for causing a furor at a wedding in Accra and that he had severely beaten the policemen who were trying to stop him. My wife also knew the cause of this commotion. He was in love with some Ga women and wanted to marry her. Her family decided that he was not good enough, and worse, that he was a Frafra and not a Ga. The girl was married off to another man. By coincidence he came to see her on the wedding day. In his anger he smashed all he could in the bride's parents house and was so wild that nobody could stop him until the police arrived. Before he was overpowered he struck one of the policemen so hard that he required medical treatment. It earned him four years prison and as soon as he was released his tribe obliged him to get married with the woman he brought to us.

One day a policeman came to our bungalow asking for Atinga. My wife wanted to know why but did not receive a proper answer. The man wanted

Atinga to come with him to the police station. That was all he was prepared to say.

By this time my wife already knew that it was not customary to speak to a member of a family without first talking to its head. Atinga was working for us and living by our house and we were considered his "family."

My wife asked the constable if he had spoken with the "master" – meaning me.

The policeman who had not expected a white woman to know the African conventions was surprised but had to admit that he had not spoken to me.

"So, you cannot take him," my wife told him.

"I am a policeman," the man insisted. His tone was threatening.

"If you are a policeman than show me your arrest warrant." My wife does not like to be threatened.

The man did not have a warrant, and my wife told him to go away.

When she told Atinga of the incident he was pleased with what she did. He knew that the policeman did not have a warrant. "He came in a personal matter. He thinks that he can intimidate me because he be policeman."

"And are you scared of him?" my wife asked, although she knew Atinga well enough to know that he was not easily intimidated.

Atinga laughed.

"So what is this all about? What does he want from you?"

He told her. His father having died some years earlier and he, being the oldest son, was now the head of the family and therefore responsible for his brother. His brother, who was also working as a steward-boy with some people on the campus, had fallen in love with a local woman and they wanted to get married. But the woman's relatives did not approve of the alliance. She had been four years to school and was literate, and Atinga's brother was not; she was a Fanti and he a Frafra; her family was fairly rich and he was poor. Now for agreeing to the marriage they demanded from Atinga as the head of his brother's family to compensate them for the cost of the woman's education and the loss of the income she would have brought in for her family had she not been to school. Unless he paid the money there would be no wedding. Atinga was prepared to pay the customary bride-price which he thought enough to compensate them for their loss of income, but he was not prepared to pay for her schooling. His argument was clear and convincing, school in Ghana was free and no one had to pay for it. For the school books he may be ready to pay something but not for school.

"But the school books are also provided by the state," my wife objected.

Atinga laughed. "The books are provided free by the state, but the teachers get them. When they distribute them to the pupils many teachers demand a small *dash* for them which they take for themselves."

"How can they do this?" my wife said furiously. It was not a question. Atinga smiled.

His smile increased her anger. "And you are ready to pay for this corruption?"

For a brief moment Atinga remained silent, then he explained. "Before independence teachers got good salaries and were highly respected. After independence the government wanted everyone to learn and made the literacy campaign. But government had not enough money. Prices went up and up but teachers pay remained the same. They became poorer and poorer, so how can they live? They must take *dash* for books, and sometimes for good grades." He laughed.

"But why should the government not adjust the teachers pay to the rising prices, it did this with all other state employees?"

"If the government pays teachers like it does with other employees it has not enough money to pay for the extra teachers needed for the literacy campaign."

"Are you trying to tell me that if the teachers income is reduced by half because of the rising prices, the government can employ twice as many teachers?"

Atinga nodded his head in agreement.

"And you don't mind that they become corrupt?"

Atinga nodded his head again.

"And that the prestige of the teaching profession is destroyed?"

Atinga remained unimpressed. "Now everyone is taking *dash*," he declared in a matter of fact tone, and went back to do the work he was busy with before the conversation.

The one time I saw Atinga really scared was when it became dark one evening and his little son, Alobda, was not home. At first he and some of his friends went to look for him on the campus and in the nearby bush, but when they did not find him, Atinga came to me for help. He wanted me to take my gun and come with him to the Ewe village near the sea.

I was prepared to accompany him to the village, but wondered why I had to take the gun.

Reluctantly he explained that it may be dangerous to go there. He feared that the Ewe's had taken his son to sacrifice him to the sea. He said that if we came unarmed they might refuse to let us look for his son in their village or even kill us if we found him there. I tried to convince him that it was nonsense, that Ewe's do not sacrifice children to the sea, and that nobody will prevent us coming to the village, but he did not relent. I took the gun and we drove to the village. No one stopped us. Atinga went from hut to hut looking for his child. I saw that he was afraid, and his fear was contagious. Before long I too felt insecure and held the gun ready to fire. Atinga did not find his child and we returned to the campus, wondering where else we could go. But when we arrived at the house my wife was standing at the door holding Alobda by the hand. What happened was that the child wanted to go to town and Atinga's brother had taken him there. Thinking to be back soon he had not told anyone that he was taking the child, but then he met friends and stayed longer than he originally expected.

Atinga was so glad to see the child that he did not even scold his brother or thank me for searching with him. He just lifted up the small boy and hugged and hugged him.

On a day Atinga asked my wife if he could get an advance on his salary. There was no reason not to give it to him, but my wife was a little surprised by the request. It was only two days after he had received his wages.

"Have you already spent your entire money?"

"No madam. I need some more money because my uncle is going to the north, and I want him to buy some sheets of corrugated iron plates for a good roof to cover my mother's home."

We gave him the money.

A few months later he came again asking for an advance. Once more he said that it was for the roof on his mother's home.

"But you already sent her the money for the roof," my wife said.

"Yes madam. But I need it again."

"Why, was it not enough?"

"Was enough. But my uncle did not buy the corrugated iron plates."

"So why don't you ask him to buy them now?"

"No money."

"No money? How? You said that you gave it to him."

"I did, but he did not buy the iron."

"So what did he do with your money?"

"He met some friends on the way and they spent it on drinks."

"How could he? It was your money for your mother's roof. Tell him to pay you back."

"Not possible. He be my uncle and he is older than me. I cannot tell him. It would be disrespectful."

"So he can simply take your money and spend it on drinks and you cannot complain because he is older and your uncle?"

"Yes. I must give him money for the roof again."

My wife said angrily: "And he will again not buy the corrugated iron."

"What else can I do? He be my uncle and he says that this time he will certainly buy the plates."

My wife was doubtful, but we were long enough in Africa to know that there were things we did not understand. We also knew that Atinga does not lie. She gave him the money. A few weeks later the uncle came again and brought with him some eggs for us. They were from Atinga's mother. It was a sign that this time she received the corrugated iron.

Reflections on a Paradox

I went to see Kofi in Accra. We had been studying together at London University. Now he was back in Ghana and he wrote that I must come and see him in his house. I knew that on his return he was given an important post in Dr. Nkrumah's administration. I was happy for him. He was a good man.

He looked unhappy and asked me if I knew of some vacancy at an English or American university for which he could apply.

The question surprised me. "What's wrong?" I asked.

"You know."

"I know what?"

He said again: "You know."

I did not know and asked him the first thing that came into my mind. "Are you in difficulties with the government?"

"No. Not with the government; with life in general."

"Man," I said, "You have an excellent post, a beautiful house, a loving family, so why do you want to leave?"

For a few moments he remained silent. Then the words came like a stream rushing down a waterfall. "My family ignores me, the entire village accuses me of being unfaithful, at work my colleagues hate me, and you know why? Because I refuse to abuse my position and take bribes. I give most of my salary to the village but this is not enough. They want me to use my office to employ all the young men who come to town and to provide the village with electricity and God knows what else. How can I do this? I can not! I do not want to be corrupt but even if I was corrupt I could never give them all the things they want."

I understood. What he said reminded me of a book I just finished reading by the Nigerian writer Chinua Achebe. The gist of Achebe's story is more or less the following.

In a desperately poor Nigerian village the elders decided that there is no other way out of their poverty except getting one of their young men into a government office in the hope that he would see to it that the village is connected to the main water supply and linked by a road to the region's communication network.

They selected a bright youngster, collected whatever little money the villagers had, and sent him to be educated. The boy did not disappoint them. He did well in school, even better at the university, and finally, while the entire village was slowly starving to pay for it, he went to the London School of Economics in England to obtain a diploma in Public Administration which assured him of a good job with the Nigerian Civil Service.

Back in Africa he soon became Head of the Planning Department for his region and all seemed to go the way the village elders had been hoping for. But then nothing. In vain the village waited and waited for their water and their road. So one day the elders went to town to see their boy. Now that he was a "big man" in government they tarried patiently to be received by him and did not speak before he spoke to them.

He treated them with due respect. He offered the elders Fanta and apologized for having no Gordon Gin in the office, told them about England and the English, but said nothing about the things they wished to know. Finally the *Ocheameh* – the one who speaks for the Chief, could not stand it any longer and asked directly. "What are you doing about our water and our road?"

The young man produced a large map of the region and spread it out in front of them. Pointing at various points on the map he said: "here and there are the two large cities with several thousand inhabitants in each of them, and here way off is our village. Surely you see that first we have to link these two cities to the water supply and to the main road leading to *Lagos* and the sea before our village can be helped." To him it seemed obvious that two towns with thousands of citizens have priority over a small village with less than two hundred inhabitants. He was sure that for the development of the country this was the right thing to do, otherwise would be corrupt. This was what they had taught him at the London School of Economics.

The elders left disappointed. They had misjudged the morals of the boy. Sadly they realized that their protégée has been corrupted by the British. The entire village had starved to get him into his high and well remunerated position, and now that he obtained it, and was able to repay them by bringing water and a road to the village, he had become corrupt and ignored the debt he owed them.

Well, I promised Kofi to write to some friends in Europe and America if they knew of any suitable vacancies. Eventually I received a positive reply from someone and sent the letter on to Kofi. The post returned it. He no longer lived at the address. It was only a year later that I heard of him again. He left Ghana, was appointed to some high position with the United Nations and was living in New York.

Things Ain't What they Seem to Be

Some miles down the coast from our campus was Biriwa beach. It was about the only place along the coast where one could swim. The small bay, with its palm covered sandy beach, looked like a picture from a tourist office's advertising brochure. In the middle stood a wooden building which served as a bar where one could buy a bottle of beer and mineral water. Even on a Sunday there were seldom more than twenty persons on the beach, teachers from the schools in Cape Coast and from our university, mostly the same people almost all whites. Biriwa was too far from Accra or Takoradi for town people to come there. All year round the water was about 24 centigrade. On the face of it, Biriwa was the perfect place for a large tourist hotel. But there was one major drawback. If one wanted to swim one either had to remain close to the beach where the water was too shallow for a good swim, or be a very good swimmer and familiar with the string of partly submerged rocks under the water which protected the bay from the ocean's breakers. To reach the deep calm waters beyond the rocks one had to know the exact location of the two gaps in the rock barrier, and to be a good swimmer not to be taken by the currents and crashed against it on the way back. This was probably the reason why neither the government nor private entrepreneurs tried to exploit the place to attract tourists.

One of the "old timers" had shown me the gaps, and sometimes, when I felt adventurous, I ventured out into the sea. But when I did I always felt a little scared. I therefore became very worried one afternoon when I saw a man, whom I thought I never saw on the beach before, swimming way out beyond the rocks. I was still vacillating making up my mind whether I should swim out to guide him safely back, when he rode a wave elegantly precisely through the gap in the rocks into the shallow water. He wore red swimming trunks and as he walked by the place were my wife and I were sitting he greeted us like old acquaintances.

I asked my wife if she knew him? She said that she didn't. There were few whites in the region whom we did not know at least by sight, but this man was a total stranger.

He must have noticed our puzzlement, because, after he picked up his towel from where he left it before his swim, he returned to us.

"Well? You still don't know me?" he asked my wife, obviously amused by our baffled looks.

We didn't answer.

"Perhaps this will help. A line is an area and not the shortest distance between two points."

My wife laughed. "Yes, now I recognize you."

"Never judge a person by his habit." He smiled and went away.

I could still not place him, and as soon as he was out of earshot I asked my wife who he was.

"My boss. The headmaster of St. Augustine college."

"The Franciscan friar?"

My wife laughed. "Yes, that's him. I was so used to see him in his white gown that in the red swimming trunks I couldn't recognize him.

"And what did he mean with a line being an area?"

My wife, who at this time was teaching mathematics at St. Augustine College, told me that she once asked him why her students found it so difficult to grasp the concept of area? Why it was that most of her Ghanaian students were much better than their European equivalents in algebra but clearly far behind them in geometry?

He explained that line with them meant area.

I remembered that Atinga also always spoke of his land as his line, but I still could not understand how one could confuse a line with an area.

My wife tried to enlighten me. She said that many Africans measured the land by the length of a furrow before they turned the plough. As land outside the cities was never private property but was regarded the tribe's, there was indeed no need to measure area. With the tribal chief's consent, which was just a formality, every member of the tribe was always free to clear part of the bush and plant and reap his crop. The one thing he was not permitted was to plant trees which would allow him to hold on to the land for longer than a year.

Still wondering about the monk, and how he knew the precise spot where one could swim between the rocks, I asked my wife how long the man has been in Ghana? She did not know exactly, but she was sure that he was living there for no less than thirty years.

The problem of explaining the difference between a line and an area remained on my mind for a long time. It showed me how little I really knew of what Ghanaians' understood of what I said to them, and how little I really understood of what they meant when they were speaking to me. I was still pondering this question when a few days after our meeting with the monk, my wife returning from the market, where she went with Mrs. Amaati-Kwaku, one of our Ghanaian neighbours, told me the following story.

Mrs. Amaati-Kwaku, a very large Ashanti woman, who despite her size, was one of the best limbo dancers, spoke English and Fanti, the language spoken in our region which is not very different from her native Ashanti. At one of the stands there was a roll of beautiful printed cloth. My wife wanted it for a dress and asked Mrs. Amaati to inquire about its price.

Mrs. Amaati hesitated, and then said curtly: "No. Not for you."

Assuming she thought that the cloth was not nice, or does not fit her for some reason, my wife asked her again to ask the price.

Again Mrs. Amaati said: "Not for you."

A little exasperated my wife took out some money from her purse and tried herself to make the market-woman understand what she wanted to know.

The market-woman shook her head, said something in Fanti to Mrs. Amaati, and they both laughed.

For a moment my wife thought that she had offered too little money and that this was the reason for the women's great amusement. To let the market-woman see that she was ready to pay a good price she took out of her purse all the money she had with her.

By this time several market-women, who sold their wares next to the one who had the cloth, were coming nearer and looked at my wife with great amusement; and Mrs. Amaati was dragging her away.

My wife replaced the money in her purse, and having allowed herself to be pulled a few steps, asked her companion what had been the cause of the hilarity, and why she couldn't buy the cloth?

"Not good for you," Mrs. Amaati said as she had said before.

"Why not good for me?" my wife asked irritably. "I like it and it would make a very nice dress."

Mrs. Amaati smiled. "Not make a very nice dress," and after a short pause she added: "Not now. Not yet. Would make a very nice dress much later," and she burst out laughing.

"But why?"

Mrs. Amaati's voice became sombre. "It is a shroud cloth, the cloth in which we bury our dead.

A Famous Hunter

Before we left Switzerland we were given a list of the things we ought to take with us to Ghana. The list included several peculiar items such as an evening dress, mosquito boots, and a hunting gun. Much later we learned that the list we and others coming from Europe received was one from the time when the British colonial civil servants had administered what was then still called the Gold Coast. But having received the list from an official source, and not having been to Africa before, we went to look for the earlier mentioned items. It was not difficult to find an evening dress in Zürich and a gun, but not mosquito boots.

When I told the man in the gun-shop that I wanted a rifle to take with me to Africa he said that a Winchester 3.75 was the rifle everyone going to Africa found best. As the gun was similar to the one I had in the army I bought it.

Little did I know that I had purchased an elephant gun. But Wally and others knew. And so, when Wally got it into his head that he wanted to mount an elephant skeleton near the entrance to his department, like the dinosaurs in the foyer of the natural science museum in London, it was on account of my gun that he selected me to hunt an elephant. It was true that on the frontier of Ghana and the ivory coast there were wild elephants who now and then did damage to the farmers, but I had no intention of shooting any animals and elephants least of all. Yet, having, because of my gun, obtained the name of a great hunter it was difficult for me to stand up against the general enthusiasm with which Wally's plan was received by one and all.

Having allowed everybody to believe that I was an "acclaimed hunter" my vanity prevented me from refusing to take part in Wally's plan. The only hope left for me was that no elephant would cross our way. But the African gods were on my side. There was a law that for shooting elephants one had to obtain government permission and the local chief's consent. Wally thought that he could overcome these hurdles. The law protecting elephants had some exemptions. One of these was that when the animals put people's lives at risk, and this was actually the case in the village where he expected me to hunt, they could be shot. However, what Wally was not aware of was that the ivory tusks of all dead elephants had to be handed to the government, and all the meat to the local chief. But with no tusks, and without the flesh burned off the skeleton by acid to keep it whole, it could not serve Wally's purpose. He managed to sway the chief by offering him and his village some money in lieu of the meat, but the government could not be persuaded. So in the end I was spared doing the job I did not want to do and without loss of face.

But my name as "a great hunter" stuck with me, and when some children claimed that they were unable to swim in Brimsu for fear of crocodiles, I was again called to go hunting. There were many crocodiles in Ghana, but I had only seen them on the Volta river close to the great Akasombu dam which then was still under construction. I never saw any in lake Brimsu. In addition, I felt quite happy that the children were afraid to swim at Brimsu because the lake was infested with bilharzia. In fact the lake was no lake at all. It was a water reservoir located at the end of a river where a dam had been raised to regulate the water supply for Cape Coast. Next to the dam was an installation to purify the water and a small waterfall to generate the electricity to keep it running. All this was in the middle of the bush, no more than ten miles from our university.

On the appointed day, very early in the morning, an African hunter, a German colleague, and I drove to a place some distance up the river about a mile before it entered into the lake. There the African had placed a canoe for our use. The reason for going there early when it was still dark was that we were told that crocodiles move into deeper water during the night and return to rest in the rushes near the edge of the river or lake when it got warmer. This, then, was the time they were moving and therefore the best time to see and hunt them.

We got into the canoe, I with my rifle ready in the front, and the German and the African hunter behind me. We let the canoe drift slowly with the stream down the river and into the lake. The African hunter told us that this stealthy progress was necessary not to warn the crocodiles of our approach. Well, the canoe drifted very slowly and when we reached the lake it was already light. With every passing hour it became hotter and the metal parts of the gun were burning in my sweating hands. By about ten o'clock we reached the dam at the end of the lake, gave up, and went home. We never saw a crocodile.

And yet, there was a crocodile. It was not in Brimsu but at the university. Someone had given it to Wally when it was very small and he had made a pond for it in the middle of the campus. As crocodiles are apt to do, it grew, and one day got out of the pond and found its way into one of the adjacent buildings. A cleaner who arrived that morning at a lecturer's office was suddenly confronted by a crocodile looking at him from below the desk. The cleaner was very scared and rushed to the lecturer's house to warn him not to enter his office. The lecturer did not believe what he was told and suspected that someone was playing a prank on him. "What nonsense? Crocodiles in offices? This cannot be true." But it was true. Later, when he went to work, he saw it and was no less shocked than the cleaner had been.

In the end Wally was called and with the help of some African workers he managed to get the beast back into its pool. The next day there was a fence around the pond.

Snakes

The one thing which really scared me were the snakes. There were many Constrictors, some Spitting Cobras, but the most frightening were Vipers. Step on one of these slow moving reptiles and within minutes you are dead. Fortunately there were only very few vipers in our immediate vicinity. In fact, except for the one which Wally kept in a cage in his department, we only saw one once. Constrictors there were many. After every rainfall they came onto the tarred roads to dry on the warm asphalt. Many of them were two or even three metres long, but they are not poisonous. There were not many Spitting Cobras. They lived in trees and for one reason or another loved to get into garages. They are truly scary because they spit their very painful and blinding venom from a distance into people's eyes. I never saw one but I met a man who, even though he was wearing spectacles when the poison hit him, could not see for days and suffered much pain.

Wally was driving a Volkswagen of the type where the engine is in the back and the luggage compartment in front. He collected constrictors for a colleague working at Accra university in Legon. When Wally saw one of these snakes he would step out of his car, open the luggage compartment of the car, take the serpent by the tail and chuck it in. Immediately the snakes would curl up and look like a spare tire. Like me, many Africans, the women in particular, were frightened of snakes. On a day when my wife was with Wally in his car and he saw a large constrictor by the roadside and stopped to catch it, he asked her to hold the cover of the car's luggage compartment open for him to deposit the snake. She did what he asked her and Wally threw the snake inside. My wife closed the cover and they drove on.

Some women saw this and from that day on my wife was regarded by them with apprehension. Was she a "snake women"? Had she no fear of snakes? Couldn't the snake wriggle into the front seat of the car? In fact my wife was not afraid. She had seen Wally catch snakes before, and trusted that he knew what he was doing. He told her that constrictors were not venomous and that was good enough for her.

Then there was the attempt on the life of President Nkrumah and the police were searching for weapons in all cars entering Accra. It was at such a police checkpoint that, on the way to Legon, Wally's car was stopped.

"Where are you going?" a policeman mounting the roadblock asked.

"To the university in Legon."

The policeman ordered him to get out of the Volkswagen and searched it. Having completed the inspection of the passenger compartment he asked what he had in the trunk.

"Snakes," Wally answered truthfully.

"Don't make fun of me," the policeman said angrily.

"No fun," Wally replied, and repeated that he was carrying snakes.

The angry policeman ordered him to open the trunk.

While Wally went to the front of the car to follow the instruction, three other policemen who were attracted by the angry tone of their colleague, came to see what went on.

"Do you really want me to open it?" Wally asked.

"Open!" the policeman ordered.

A second later four snakes were raising their heads out of the trunk. Wally, still holding the lid ready to close it again before the reptiles escaped, looked around. He was alone. The police had disappeared. He let the lid down, locked the trunk, and waited.

Slowly, uncertainly, the policemen came back, and from a safe distance signalled him to drive on.

After this, when I had occasion to travel with Wally to Accra, we were never stopped at any checkpoint. Apparently the tale of the crazy black man driving a Volkswagen full of snakes had spread and no one wanted to get involved with him again.

But there were also more frightening events with snakes. Our children had a tricycle and one day my wife saw our little daughter sitting on the tricycle while our seven year old son was playing next to her. Suddenly she heard him order his sister not to stir. My wife looked and saw a snake under the tricycle. Before she could think what to do, our son carefully approached the tricycle and with a strong sudden push moved it to safety and jumped away.

Another time, getting out of bed in the morning, I picked up my shoes and saw a small snake under one of them. I killed it and my wife and I spent several hours looking to see if more snakes were in the house. We found several. Unawares the children had brought them into the house the previous day lodged in a bamboo stick. We then learned that bamboo sticks were a favourite place for snakes to keep their young.

Altogether, our children got much more quickly adjusted to their African environment then we did. Most amazing for us was how our son did in an instant change from his proper English in which he spoke to us and with other Europeans, into the tonal pronunciation of the local patois in which he spoke with his African playmates. After school our children would run around with their African playmates along trails through the bush unperturbed by snakes and other animals. Often, when they knew that we could not see them, they took off their shoes and went barefoot, and drank tap water, like the African children did. When we learned of this, and told one of our African friends about our worry, he seemed unimpressed. "The African gods love children and protect them," he said, there was no reason for concern. Aware of the frightening infant mortality statistics of our region our friend's confidence could hardly put our mind at rest. But we survived.

Monkey Business

A family returning to England asked us to look after their monkey. They were going to live in a flat in London and could not take the animal with them. With the female baboon, which standing on her hind legs was about the size of our three year old daughter, they brought us a kind of dog hut and a chain. The hut was to be placed on a tree trunk for the monkey. Our servant dug a hole by our kitchen window, found some log, secured it in the ground, and fastened the hut on it. The monkey got soon accustomed to its new abode. Occasionally it got loose from the chain but never strayed far, and returned to its hut. When we were having breakfast, it often jumped onto the window frame and looked into our room, which always made me think of the people watching the chimpanzee's tea party at the London Zoo. Now it was the monkey watching the people having their tea and not the people watching the monkeys.

In time we found that it was unnecessary to restrict the animal's freedom of movement. We put away the chain and allowed it to roam about. For a while all went well. Then our neighbour complained. The monkey was eating all the bananas and much of the other fruit he was growing near his house. So we had to restrain our monkey again. I cut part of an old belt to fit around the baboon's waist and attached it to a rope just short enough not to reach the neighbour's fruits. For a few days the monkey had some difficulties to free the rope when it became entangled, but by the end of a week it learned to do it. Alas, by the end of another week, it also learned to undo the belt, and when we solved this problem, it learned to untie the knot by which the rope was fastened to the belt. Time after time we tried new ways to prevent the monkey from getting loose but she always managed to get free. The neighbours who had fruit trees did certainly not love us.

Having become "famous" or "infamous" as the people with a monkey, some African children turned up one day with another small monkey. They had found it wounded and abandoned in the bush and wanted us to look after it. We tied it on a short rope on our veranda and called for our friend from the zoology department. He looked at it and said that it had probably caught it's leg in a hunters' trap. The monkey showed no resistance when he examined its injured leg and put some ointment on the wound and bandaged it. We gave it some bananas, but on the first day it wouldn't eat them. The following days our friend came every morning to examine the monkey's leg and gradually it began to eat and getting better. Finally our friend told us that it was almost recovered and would soon no longer need the bandages.

The next morning our children told us that the monkey was gone. We went out on the veranda and saw the rope and the bandage on the floor, but the animal was gone. Obviously it no longer needed our help and returned to the bush. My wife complained that it forgot to leave a note to thank us.

There was another family on the campus which also had a monkey. It was a small monkey of the kind the people called a putty-nose. Just before Christmas, when they had painstakingly decorated their house with garlands and colourful paper chains, someone forgot to close the monkey's cage door and the little putty-nose got out and made straight for their sitting room. In the five minutes it took to catch, it was swinging from one paper chain to another causing havoc with their Christmas decorations.

When we told this story to our friend from the Zoology department he said that a patty-nose is not a pet; that it is very destructive; and that people should know what animals to keep and what animals should best be left in the bush. He said this in a tone which made me think that far from commiserating with the people, he was thinking that what happened to them was no more than they deserved – it served them right.

On our son's birthday we invited the children from the neighbourhood. After they had eaten all the "goodies" and the customary birthday songs were sung, the children went to play outside. Our monkey was free again and watching them from the top of his hut. Some children thought it fun to try to catch her. A wild and noisy chase ensued until she was too far away to follow and the children gave up the chase.

She did not return. For some time people told us that they had seen her one place or another, and some said that they had given her bananas, which we did not like at all because it only made her stay away longer. But try as we may we could not find her. In fact we never saw her again, and before we left West Africa we took the monkey hut off the wooden log, and gave it to someone.

Years later I was back in Ghana for a few days to complete some unfinished business. Having breakfast on the university campus I remembered how our baboon used to look through our window watching us eating. So I went to the place where its hut had been. The old "dead" log which our servant fastened in the ground to put the monkey's hut on, had sprouted branches and turned into a beautiful mango tree.

Somebody once told me that Africa always wins in the end – that Africa was indestructible.

Spring Tides and White Demons

We went for the weekend to Akazi. Akazi is in the East of Ghana, close to Togo. An Israeli friend invited us to see the state farm he was managing there. When some of my students learned that we were planning to go to this region, one of them asked if he could come to Akazi on Sunday morning to collect us, show us Anloga and meet his family in Keta. Other students from the Volta region insisted that we should also visit their families on the way.

Keta and Anloga were towns on a narrow peninsula hemmed in between the Atlantic ocean and a large lagoon at the mouth of the Volta river. The peninsula was about fifteen kilometres long and one or two kilometres wide. On the west side the Volta separated the peninsula from the mainland. To reach it one had to go all the way east to the end of the lagoon where a narrow strip of land connected it to Ghana. For years the waters from the lagoon nibbled away at the northern part of the peninsula, and one row of houses after another was gradually collapsing and swallowed by the lagoon. A year or two before our visit, someone had the "brilliant" idea of stopping this by opening an outlet for the water in the lagoon into the sea. To those unfamiliar with the sea this seemed an obvious solution – land is higher than the sea and water is always flowing downward. The government invited a Dutch enterprise to undertake the digging of the canal, but the Dutch firm refused the offer. It claimed that due to the elaborate construction work which would have to be done to take account of the ocean tides the project was too costly to be viable. They said something about the rise and fall of the sea level due to the gravitational forces of the moon and sun which the Ghanaian authorities thought a ploy to ask for more money, and that the figure the Dutch mentioned for doing the small job was exorbitant. So they asked the Russians to carry out the project.

The Russian advisers looked at the lagoon, wondered what the moon had got to do with digging an outlet to the sea, found a spot where the peninsula was just a few hundred metres across, said "no problem", brought a large tractor with a scraper, and without much ado opened a narrow gap from the lagoon to the ocean. The entire job took no more than a few hours. But when the scraper reached the Atlantic things suddenly went very wrong. Instead of the lagoon's waters streaming out into the sea, the ocean gushed in. A flood of water drowned the tractor, the Russians next to it and all the other people looking on. Within a day the narrow gap widened into a stream almost half a mile across. The Russians had hoped to build a small wooden bridge over the gap. This was no longer feasible; the peninsula had turned into an island. Keta and Anloga were no longer accessible by road, to reach them one had to cross the water by canoe.

The morning the student came to collect me from Akazi my eight year old son wanted to come along with us. I saw no reason why he shouldn't. My wife wanted to stay with our friends, and so only my son the student and myself got into the car and drove off in the direction of the "Russian gap." The student told me that there I would have to leave the car behind and cross the gap by canoe. But not to worry, on the other side there were many cars to take us to his town. The news that I was in the region had gone before me. The drive to where we had to leave the car turned out to be quite an experience. There were families of students I taught in practically every second village we passed. Time and again we had to stop in villages where local elders and dignitaries were waiting by the roadside to receive us and take us to their houses. In every house we were offered beer and each time my glass was half empty it was immediately topped up. At that time I did not yet know that it was customary for the host always to keep a guest's glass filled to the brim and so my effort not to drink too much by never emptying the glass became counterproductive. By the time

I understood that to show that one had had enough was to leave one's glass full, I was already in a happy daze.

When we finally reached the Russian gap it was noon and the sea was coming in. We stepped into one of the canoes moored by the roadside and I noticed that the oarsmen were using all their might to row straight out into the ocean. But the current drove the canoe back so that eventually we landed on the other side precisely where the road continued. Back on firm land we found ourselves surrounded by a crowd of women who were all looking at my son. At first they glanced at him shyly from a distance, but soon their curiosity got the better of them and they came closer, laughed, touched him, and run off. Obviously they had never seen a white child before. Next I noticed a very old woman, surrounded by an amused group of men, singing and dancing and happily pointing from time to time in my direction. Feeling that I was the cause of the onlookers hilarity, I asked my student what she said. He pretended not to have heard my question, but when I repeated it, he told me that she was singing and dancing to thank and praise the gods.

"Why? And why does she point at us?" I wondered.

My student laughed. "She thanks the gods for bringing you here – for bringing back the whites, the true owners of the land."

His explanation made me smile. This was precisely at a time President Nkrumah conducted one of his periodic press campaigns against "the white's colonialism."

At my student's home there was more beer and while we were talking my son was bored and left the room to join some children who he saw playing near a well outside. A few seconds later we heard terrible screams and rushed to the door to see what happened. My son was standing alone half way to the well looking puzzled after the children who were running away from him in panic. My student asked someone who saw it what the commotion was about and laughed. He later told me that the children who had never seen a white child thought he was a goblin or small white devil and got frightened.

How we got back to Akazi that evening I do not remember. I know that my feet got wet when I stepped out of the canoe, and that I had to concentrate very much to keep the car on the road, but nothing else. After all, how much beer can a man consume in one day and still remember anything?

Women are Worthless

All at once everyone was scared. As soon as it became dark the servants did not dare to leave their rooms, the students only ventured out in groups of five or six, and even the watchmen kept close to the houses.

Walking back to the campus from the club where I had spent the early part of the evening I came across a policeman. He must have heard me coming down the road because, when I was close enough to recognize him, I saw that he had his finger on the trigger of his gun. Even after he also recognized me he did not relax. The man was scared, and so was I. He was so tense that out of sheer nervousness he could inadvertently pull the trigger.

The cause of all this anxiety was a rumour. It was one of those recurring rumours that every three or four years put everyone on edge. Headhunters were on the prowl. The rumour about the headhunters began in the 1930s when four men were executed for murdering and decapitating several people for what the British judges at the trial had called demonic beliefs. I was told that there had indeed once been a custom to bury four human skulls when a chief built a new home for himself – one skull at each corner of the house. But the person who told me said that this custom had long ago been abolished.

My wife and I could simply not believe that educated people on a university campus would lend an ear to such nonsense – but they did. So on an evening when a group of students came to visit us I asked them. To get the conversation on the topic started I made some joke about headhunters. Nobody laughed. The students were all Ewes and so had been the four men whom the British Court had sentenced. I knew that many Ghanaians believed that the Ewe's were still beheading people for "religious purposes", but so were many people in the Ukraine still believing that Jews were killing Christian babies to use their blood for backing Matzos for their Passover feast. But every Jew knows that this is nonsense. So I took it for granted that like the Jews in the Ukraine the Ewes being a minority in our region were subjected to similar absurd slur. I did in fact suspect that the entire story about headhunters was concocted to justify the expulsion of the Ewe fishing village from the land where the university was planning to expand the campus.

After the joke I made, my guests remained silent for a while looking at the floor in front of them. Then the oldest just said: "No smoke without fire."

I was surprised. "Do you really kill people to appease the gods? Do you really bury human skulls under the chiefs' new houses?" I asked in disbelief.

"No. We do not bury skulls. That's an Ashanti custom and not ours."

They began arguing among themselves in Ewe which I could not understand. Only later they told me that they could not agree whether skulls were not also buried at the chiefs houses by their own tribe in some places and whether it was not still practised by some Ewes in Togo and Dahomey. On one point my guests, who all came from fishing villages, were in agreement. In the distant past it had been customary for fishermen to make human sacrifices to the sea to keep it calm and yield them plenty of fish to catch. But none of them was sure if this custom was still practised.

The longer our conversation lasted the more it became morose and difficult for me to follow. Suddenly it occurred to me that if these stories had, after all, some substance my wife could be in serious danger. She was in the habit of taking a long walk by herself each evening when it became a little cooler than during the day. Thus, trying to make it sound like a joke, I asked the students if my wife was not in jeopardy when she made her nightly excursions on the campus?

My question caused so much hilarity that magically all that evening's gloom was gone. My guests could simply not stop giggling. "A woman," they laughed, "and a white woman in particular, how could her head be of use to the gods or to the tribal chiefs? – Women are worthless."

Civil Disobedience

Except for the shops owned by Lebanese, practically all domestic trade in Ghana is in the hands of the market women. The Ghanaians are essentially a matriarchal society and market-women hold a powerful position in the country's economic and political structure. They also control much of the country's transport. A Ghanaian wishing to travel from Accra to Kumasi or Takoradi will usually go by what is called a "*mummy lorry.*" This is a truck equipped with wooden benches to take passengers. Most "*mummy lorries*" belong to market women and are driven by members of their owners' family or hired drivers. Often the trucks are decorated with slogans which have a meaning only for the initiated. Sometimes the slogans are in English, but having been painted on the vehicles by persons who did not know the language or did not know how to write at all, and just copied the characters from somewhere, the words did not always follow in their appropriate order. In this way Dr. Nkrumah's slogan "Forward ever, backward never", became on one of the *mummy lorries* I saw, "forward backward, never ever." On other lorries I saw "fear women!"; "Sea never dry."; "God is my shepherd, I don't know why."; "God will provide" – "*Nyame bechere!*".

Usually these trucks were overcrowded and badly maintained. But the market women from the villages who brought their wares to the towns did not mind. I saw them by the roadside with their baskets near broken down vehicles waiting patiently for the next lorry to take them further. It came therefore as no surprise to me when one day on the way to Takoradi I saw a large gathering of women next to a line of *mummy lorries* as I was approaching the bridge over the river Pra.

I liked the river Pra. Every time I crossed it, it reminded me of "Sanders of the River", a film I had seen as a child. In the film, with Paul Robeson in the leading role, many canoes with tribal warriors were racing down the river carried

by its torrent. At the helm of the first canoe stood Robeson brandishing a long
spear and roaring what was meant to be an African war song:

"On, on, on to battle.

Mow them down like cattle . . .

High-oh-go,

high igedé . . ."

The film, and particularly Robeson's deep voice, had made a lasting impression on me. Several of the old men I met on my strolls along the river bank
still remembered the making of the film. They told me how they brought the
canoes from the fishing villages on the seafront to the one short stretch of the
river Pra where it was navigable. They even remembered how much they were
paid for it, and how difficult it was to act the part of the warriors.

Years later I learned that after World War II, Robeson did all in his power
to have the film withdrawn from circulation. It portrayed him as a colonial
stooge serving the white masters.

Once, when I showed some gramophone records with music from the film,
which had on its cover Paul Robeson's picture dressed as a warrior, to a Zulu
student from East Africa, he told me angrily that there never were Zulus
anywhere near the Pra or in west Africa, and that no Zulu Chief would ever
dress up like Robeson in this film.

Well, I saw the *mummy lorries* and market women with their wares on my
side of the bridge, and a similar congregation on the other side. Unaware of
the reason for these gatherings on both sides of the river I drove past the women
until I was stopped by a policeman who said something to me which I did not
understand. At first I thought that there was something wrong with the bridge,
but it looked all right and I tried to go on. Another policeman barred my way.
I finally realized that they wanted me to pay for crossing. I refused and the
women who had assembled around me broke out in happy cheers and motioned
me to go back. I reversed the car to the end of the line of the waiting vehicles, and walked to the bridge to find out what was going on. I saw women
crossing the bridge carrying their goods to the other side on foot without being
stopped. The toll was only for vehicles.

I found someone who spoke some English and asked her to explain to me
what was happening.

"We make strike."

"What?"

"We make strike," the woman repeated.

"What strike? Why?"

"We make strike. Government made law all cars have to pay to cross the
Pra-bridge. We no pay. Our bridge, not government bridge."

At that moment several women came with their loads from the other side of the river. They mounted one of the trucks and it turned and drove off.

"You see," the woman indicated the departing vehicle. "Walk over bridge, no pay. Drive over bridge, two cedis."

I understood. The government had imposed a toll for all vehicles going across the bridge and the women refused to pay. They simply came in one truck to one side of the bridge, unloaded their goods, and walked to the other side from where they continued their journey in another lorry. To make their objection to the toll effective they stopped all drivers, even those who were prepared to pay the toll, from taking their vehicles across.

I had no urgent business in Takoradi and so I turned my car and drove back to Cape Coast. Two days later I read in the newspaper that the government's decision to impose a toll on the Pra bridge has been abolished. There was no mention of a "strike." The government had simply changed its mind – "fear women!"

Lawful and Customary Wives

Parliament was discussing a motion to make the fathers of illegitimate children responsible for their upkeep. The women on the university campus were furious.

I could not understand their anger. Why should women object to a law that obliged men to pay for their extramarital adventures? I could have asked one of the irate women but it would have been embarrassing. It was not the kind of question a man asked. The woman would giggle and make off without giving an answer. But my wife could ask. She asked Mrs. Aggrey who was not only one of the most vocal opponents of the proposed legislation but had a philandering husband who, as everyone knew, had illegitimate children all over the region.

Mrs. Aggrey, who studied law before she got married, explained to my wife why she thought that the proposed legislation was good for men and bad for women. Under the new law mothers of illegitimate children would be entitled to demand maintenance money for their offsprings from the father. If he had no money the child would be assigned to the man's household. His family would be oblige to feed, clothe, and send the child to school. As Mrs. Aggrey saw it, the law would allow husbands to seek their little pleasures even when there was not enough money in the house to provide for their legitimate families, and oblige their wives to care for all their little bastards. In Mrs. Aggrey's own words: "The proposed law licenses men to enjoy themselves, while their legally wedded wives must pay for it."

I asked some Ghanaian friends if the women outside the campus were sharing Mrs. Aggrey's anger? Their reply was unanimous. Only educated Christian women who were married in church were interested in the law. Traditionally a child belonged to the mother's family and not to the father. For most Ghanaians the proposed law was therefore entirely irrelevant. Alas, Mr. and Mrs. Aggrey had a christian upbringing and were married in church.

Now I finally understood why on the questionnaire I filled in on my appointment with the university I was asked to state the number of my legal and of my customary wives. I was entitled to claim family allowance for all of them.

Everyday Life in a Dictatorship

Kwapong's new car finally arrived. Now he had to find a buyer for his four year old Ford which was still in fairly good condition. A party official from a nearby village wanted it, and after many bottles of beer a price was agreed upon and the sale finalized. Half the price was to be paid at the time the Ford was handed over and the other half on the next pay day – by the end of the following month. My role in the matter was to witness the signing of the agreement.

During the next four weeks Kwapong drove proudly and happily in his new car, and the party official in the old Ford. But then, a few days after the end of the month, Kwapong came to ask me for a loan. He needed the money urgently to pay the bank the remaining debt for the purchase of his new automobile. The sum he owed the bank was exactly the amount of money he was still to receive from the sale of his old car. I asked what he did with the money from the second instalment he received from the party official? He answered that the man told him that something unexpectedly went wrong in his hometown and that he had been obliged to send his entire salary to his family. He asked him to wait another month. Next pay-day he would certainly receive his money.

Four months later I met Kwapong again. The party official had still not paid and Kwapong was considering taking him to court. Then another two month elapsed before we met again. Kwapong looked very worried. That he had not repaid the bank loan I knew. Since I signed a guarantee for him to obtain the loan, the bank had written to me that the debt was still outstanding. I also knew that after I received this letter Kwapong's family had cleared the loan. Why then was he so tense?

It took some time before he told me. When he was about to go to court, the party official came to his house accompanied by two other men and threatened him that unless he stopped complaining about the money, he and his two "witnesses" would go to the police and say that he had spoken ill of the Party and the President.

In fact Kwapong was one of the first organizers of the party when the British were still ruling the country and never in his life said anything derogatory about President Nkrumah, but all this was irrelevant. He knew as well as I did that in the Ghanaian democratic system of 1964 there was no way to prove your innocence if you were accused of dissent. It made me think of the fate of Kamenev, Zinoviev and Bukharin. After all, half the price of a second hand car is a small price to pay for one's freedom.

Democracy and Free Elections

Elections. For days the newspapers were preparing the public for the big event. On the central square in front of the church in Cape Coast a great *Durbar* was organized. All citizens were invited to attend this ceremonial gathering of chiefs. A podium for the speakers was built facing the benches borrowed from the church. On the day before the elections the front rows were occupied by the traditional chiefs and elders; further back several hundred citizens were seated. Those who did not find vacant seats stood in the shadow of the trees surrounding the fringes of the square. The chiefs and party representatives were shaded from sun by vibrant colourful large parasols. Since the days of Queen Victoria these parasols had become a regular feature of any Durbar. Next to the podium stood policemen in ceremonial uniforms and local dignitaries dressed in their traditional tribal finery.

At one corner of the square, close to the park, were the drummers announcing with their drumbeat the arrival of "important men." Later they also accompanied with their beat each new speaker coming the podium. From time to time their drumming was followed by sudden roars of laughter from the audience. But it was almost only the old people who laughed. The younger no longer understood the "language of the drums." As I was later told, often the drummers' comments were not very flattering. The drummers belonged to the older generation who respected the traditional dignitaries but had little appreciation for the party bosses who now ruled the country. They paid lip-service to the government and its officials, but thought that the newfangled arrangements were all nonsense.

The Durbar was scheduled to begin at three o'clock. At four the people were still waiting for the speakers to arrive. Except for me, it did not seem to bother many people. But then, I did not really belong there. Still, when the speakers finally arrived the last benches were already empty. Also, at the far end of the square, where I had previously seen many people, now only a few remained and children were playing oblivious to what was going on. Halfway through the first speeches the benches next to me were also getting empty. As they departed the people chatted with each other without consideration for those who were trying to listen to the speakers.

The party boss read his speech from a paper entirely unperturbed by the thankless conduct of his audience. When he finished his address, I looked around me. Only a few foreigners and the old people on the front benches had remained in their seats, the rest had gone. At this point I decided to leave as well and do not know how the Durbar ended.

The next day one of the offices in town was declared election hall. Several sealed ballot boxes were brought and stored inside. Until the elections, the room remained locked and the boxes were well guarded. On election day loudspeakers mounted on taxies drove through the streets calling the citizens to vote for The Party. By noon long lines of happy people formed in front of the election hall waiting to vote. The voting procedure was simple. There were only two alternatives and the voters could place their ballot paper in one of two boxes. One box was for the ruling party, and the other for the opposition. Both boxes stood out of sight. In this respect the elections were free and secret. When I said this to one of my Ghanaian colleagues he smiled and told me that in many villages the elders had simply seen to it that the box for the opposition remained sealed so that no one could cast his vote for the wrong party.

I asked why the elders should do this?

"They know if too many people vote for the opposition the government will not help the village. It will not get the road they want or the connection to the water or electricity supply, they were promised if they show support for our President."

I looked at both ballot boxes in our place. They were open and in perfect order.

When I arrived at my bungalow, I saw our servant Atinga sitting on the front porch surrounded by several of his northern tribesmen. They too, like me, were in a way "foreigners" in this region and I inquired if they were not entitled to vote? The answer was that as they were registered as residence of Cape Coast they were entitled. So I asked Atinga if he had already voted.

"No Sir. I no vote!"

"Will you not go?" I asked.

Indicating that he was speaking for all those with him he answered: "No. We all no vote here."

Knowing that he was a staunch supporter of Dr. Nkrumah and his ruling party this surprised me and I said something to the effect that it was his civic duty to take part in the elections.

He looked at me as one looks at a small child.

"Are you scared to vote? I asked. You are in favour of the ruling party. You have no reason to be scared?"

Again he gave me that strange look. "Master, we all no vote. With the secret ballot if some people in this town vote against the party we cannot prove that it was not us. We want no trouble with the Fanti, so we no vote."

A Suspect

We were having our dinner when Kodzo came to tell us that Carr has been arrested. Carr was one of my students and chairman of the Students Union.

Kodzo said that two CID men came to the registrar and told him to call Carr to his house. When he arrived they hurled him into their limousine and drove off in the direction of Accra.

The following days I tried to find out where Carr was held and what he was accused of having done. All I learned was that several other student leaders at Legon and Kumasi had also been arrested the same night and taken to secret locations. Our university Principal went to Accra to talk to the Minister but returned no wiser from the meeting. Carr and the other student leaders simply vanished.

The staff and the students talked about it, but when I asked if there was nothing they could do for Carr, I received no answer. I suggested to call for a strike or demonstration to draw attention to the disappearance of the students but nothing came of it. Eventually I was so frustrated with the equanimity with which the students accepted what had happened to their leaders that I said in one of my lectures that I was bothered by the fact that nobody, not even the Principal of the university, was able to discover where Carr and the other student leaders were held.

After the lecture my friend Mensa took me aside and told me that it was unwise to make remarks about the secret services in public. Then he asked if I was really serious about finding the location of Carr's internment.

I admitted that it has been rash of me to say what I did in public, but that as a teacher I felt responsible for Carr and what happened to him.

Mensa asked me for my car keys and said that he will bring them back next day when he hoped to be able to tell me where I could find my student. Sitting at the wheel of my automobile, he said that if the CID or the police should come and ask me why I made such a fuss about the arrest of Carr, I must tell them that as his teacher I am obliged to do so. I must tell them that as his teacher I am legally *in loco parentis*.

"What's that?" I asked.

"It is a legal term. Ghanaian law and custom recognizes that if a child is in a boarding school his teacher has full responsibility for him. The teacher takes the place of his parents."

"But Carr is hardly a child, and the university campus is hardly a boarding school."

Mensa laughed. "You know this, and I know this, but do the policemen know it?"

Next morning Mensa brought back my car. "I'll take you to visit him."

We drove about two hundred kilometres to a military airfield. Next to it was the police station where Carr was held. I asked Mensa how he managed to find him and he told me. Before Ghana became independent he had been a police sergeant. Since then almost all former corporals and sergeants he knew had risen in rank and become officers. Very few had quit the service and so everyone who saw him in civilian clothes assumed that he was a CID officer. "I just asked and they told me." He laughed and I had to laugh as well. All formal requests and procedures failed and Mensa just asked and got the answer.

The commander of the police station and his officers invited us to the canteen to have some beer. It took some time before they remembered the cause of our visit. When they did someone was sent to bring Carr from his cell and join us. He too was given beer and then Mensa indicated that we would like to have a word with Carr in private. There followed a short discussion in a language I did not understand, and then Mensa signalled me and Carr to follow him. Once outside, Mensa told me to hurry because he promised to take Carr back to his prison before nightfall. After this the three of us drove to the Ambassador Hotel in Accra.

Over dinner I asked Carr if there was anything I could do for him? I could. On my next visit I should bring him several books so that he could read the material he missed being unable to attend lectures.

I asked if he didn't want to escape? I had a motor boat and could take him by sea to Togo. I knew that he had family there. His uncle was head of the police in Lome.

He wanted to think it over and tell me on my next visit. After dinner we took him back to the police station and Mensa and I drove home to Cape Coast.

A few days later Kofi Baku, the Minister of Defence, finally agreed to receive me in his office. Before going to the meeting I discussed the matter with some students. They suggested that I should invite Kofi Baku to come to a feast at our university. It was at the feast that they would ask him to free their colleague. I raised the possibility of asking the Minister about the charges levelled against Carr but the students were not very taken with the idea.

The Minister received me as if I was an old friend. The conversation was amicable but led to no results. He accepted the students' invitation to the feast, but was unwilling to tell me anything concerning Carr. All he was prepared to say was that Carr was an agent of the CIA. When I persisted questioning him, declaring that as his teacher I was entitled to know more, I saw that he had been prepared for my questions. He produced a report from a drawer in his desk and read to me that Carr had been to Rio de Janeiro in Brazil and that the CIA had paid his fares.

The next time I visited Carr in his prison, I told him what the Minister had said. Carr did not deny having been to Rio de Janeiro, but protested that his journey was not paid for by the Americans. On the University campus, he said, if I looked in the box under his bed I would find evidence that he travelled to Brazil at the expense of the Soviet Russian youth organization KOMSOMOL and that he went there as the official representative of Dr. Nkrumah's Ghanaian People's Party.

I looked in his box and saw that he told me the truth. Now that it was clear that his incarceration was unjustified, on my following visit to the prison I asked him again if he does not want me to get him across the border.

"No Sir. I better stay in prison. To escape will later ruin my political career."

Minister Baku came to the students' feast and it almost ended in disaster. At the height of the merrymaking some students carried him shoulder high through the hall and his neck came so close to the large ventilator suspended from the ceiling that one of the blades would probably have cut off his head had not someone pushed the student who carried him aside in the very last moment. Except for this nothing happened and Carr remained in his cell.

Several months later Carr was suddenly back at the university. I asked him what happened that led to his release? He did not know. All he could tell me was how he was released. One day several policemen in mufti came to take him from his cell, pushed him into a van where some of the other student leaders, who had been arrested at the same time as he was, were already waiting. For a short while they were all scared of being taken to some secret place and executed, but instead they were driven to the home of the Minister in a village some 50 kilometres from Accra. There they were invited to join the Minister and several other high officials for an auspicious meal with plenty of Heineken beer. At the end of the meal Kofi Baku told them that they were all forgiven for their sins, and that henceforth they should consider themselves good friends of his. By midnight they were told to go home to their families. As no transport was provided they had to wait by the roadside till morning when they stopped passing cars to ask the drivers to take them to Accra. Nobody told them why they had been arrested and why they were suddenly released.

Years later, after Nkrumah had been ousted from power, I met Carr again at an international conference were he represented his country. It was then that I finally learned the true reason for his and the other student leaders arrest. They had signed a letter to the authorities asking why Aku Korsa was dismissed from his post as chief justice when the court found Adamafio not guilty. They had written that it was after all not the judges fault that the prosecutor had made such a poor showing at the hearings.

Never Trust an Honest Politician

One day Vitor introduced us to his wife. We knew that she was a member of Parliament and a strong supporter of Dr. Nkrumah's government, but we had not met her before. My wife and I liked her immediately. She was an intelligent and friendly woman. We showed her around the university campus and over tea answered her questions about the university and what we thought needed improvement. We did not hide our dislike for Dr. Nkrumah's style of government. She listened attentively and from time to time made notes on a small writing pad.

For a long time after this we did not hear from her. Then came the military coup which removed Dr. Nkrumah from power and put most of his parliamentarians in prison. We found her in the newspaper among the detained parliamentarians. From Vitor we learned that in the first hours after the coup she tried to organize resistance to the military in the Volta region. When she failed to find support she fled across the border to Togo. This was not difficult. The Ewe tribe to which she belonged resides astride the frontier between Ghana and Togo. However, after some days in exile she returned to Ghana and gave herself up to the authorities. In the following weeks the former ministers and most other detainees were one by one released. We expected the same would happen with her.

Months went by and she was still in prison. I asked Vitor when he thought she would be freed but he did not know. I inquired what she was charged with and Vitor said that, like all other former ministers and parliamentarians, she was accused of corruption.

I asked if they had evidence against her?

Vitor laughed: "Of course not. She wasn't corrupt. She is as poor as a dormouse. How could she have been corrupt?"

As I also thought it unlikely. She did not look to me like the kind of person who would be corrupt. So I went to see a member of the military junta I knew and asked him why she was not released. In spite of being a foreigner I felt quite safe to speak to him about it. When Nkrumah was still in power Mensa once brought him and general Kotoka to our house and we got on well together. I would have preferred to speak to Kotoka but he was the only officer killed in the coup when Nkrumah's Russian body-guards defended Flagstaff House, the government residence, on the way to Accra airport. I remembered how, on the evening they visited us, we were talking about Ghanaian customs and traditions, the colonel, I was planning to see, taught me some terms of abuse which Ghanaians were using in English. The two terms which particularly amused me were: "You uncircumcised baboon," and "You item of no commercial value." At one time during that evening he suddenly changed the topic of our conversation and asked me if it was true that one could set off a bomb by remote control. I wanted to know why he asked, and he answered that to protect the President it was important to know these things. I told him that it could easily be done and explained how. Little did I suspect at the time that my two guests were in fact preparing a coup to get rid of Nkrumah and his government. Had I suspected, I would not have answered the question.

When I went to see the colonel I was prepared to be told that as a foreigner I had no business to interfere in the country's politics. After all, it was none of my business whom they detained and whom they released. But I counted on the fact that it was not the Ghanaian way to be unfriendly to a person in whose house you had been and with whom you had shared food and beer.

He received me very cordially, and grinned when I mentioned why I came.

"We must hold her. She was corrupt," he said in a tone which allowed no contradiction.

His smile annoyed me and made me go on. "But you released all the former ministers. Where none of them corrupt?"

His grin turned to laughter. "They were all thieves. Some built themselves fine houses, others whisked their ill gotten money to Switzerland. So we held them until they were ready to bring the money back to Ghana so that we could confiscate it."

"But you released them. She has no money. Why don't you let her go?"

He became gloomy. "They, the others, do not matter. But she is dangerous. She is not after money but for Nkruhmah. She is political."

"And that is why you do not let her go?" I felt like saying, so you hold her because she is honest? But I thought better of it and left it at that.

"Have more beer and let us talk about other things," he said in a voice that made it quite clear that he had no wish to continue the conversation.

Only when I was on my way out I mentioned the topic once more, asking him to see what he could do for her release – "she is the wife of a good friend of mine."

He pretended not to have heard me.

I never learned whether it had anything to do with my intervention, but a few days later Vitor's wife was free.

Peasants Know Better

Maize, or corn as the Americans call it, is a staple food in many poor countries. Next to casava, yam and rice, it is probably the most important food crop in west Africa. So Wally, my colleague from the biology department, took me to see how maize was grown and stored. We visited a maize plot and he said that it was a shame that the farmers did not use a better variety of seed. He told me that in America they had assortments of maize that yielded four times as many corncobs as the one we saw. "They have two seasons, a major and a minor season each year and if they planted a better variety they would harvest three times more maize with the same amount of land and labour." Wally was very angry.

So I asked: "Why don't you tell them?"

"I'll do better. Next time I go abroad I'll bring them seed and demonstrate the difference."

Then we went to see how the maize is treated to reduce its moisture before it is shelled and sold. Some farmers placed the crop in clearings in the bush for the sun to dry it and others kept it in a hut below some metal construction with fire to expedite the process.

Smoked maize. It made me think of smoked bacon and smoked salmon.

When Wally returned from his Summer holidays he proudly showed me a bag of kernels he brought from Louisiana, and asked me to come with him to convince a farmer to try it. The farmers were weary of seed given to them by foreign experts. They did not really trust them. Once before they had been provided with high-yield hybrid seed. It was good for one time use. But then they were obliged to buy new seed for the next year because the hybrid did not reproduce itself.

One of the farmers told us that he would rather have a poorer crop and use his own seed than be at the mercy of the merchants or government officials who do not supply the seed on time and often charge exorbitant prices for it.

Wally explained that his seed was no hybrid but a natural variety, which can be used exactly the way they used their local variety. Eventually we found one farmer who was willing to try it out on a small part of his land. Wally was sure that as soon as the others see the result it will cause an "agricultural revolution" in our region.

It seemed to be a big success. When we visited the farm again in the harvesting season the result was plain to see. The patch sown with Wally's kernels produced three or four times more cobs than any other land around it.

The next time we came the maize cobs were spread out to dry along the road. Wally was happy.

However several days later the farmer came to the university campus and asked us to come to his farm and see what has happened to his corn.

The farm was five miles from the university and we rode all the way in silence. When we arrived we saw women shelling the maize-cobs and putting the grains into jute sacks. The farmer directed us to the heap of maize drying near "our" patch, picked up a cob, and tore off the leaves. Then he showed it to us. The grains were empty. Weevils had eaten all the protein.

Wally was devastated. He went to a pile of native maize and examined it. There too the cobs were nibbled by the weevils but far less than our corn. He felt the leaves covering the cobs and then came back to our heap and did the same. He gave the farmer some money to compensate him for his loss and we drove home.

On the way he explained to me the cause of the catastrophe. The domestic strain of maize has firmer leaves than the one he brought. Consequently, with the local method of drying the cobs the weevils found it easier to penetrate the core.

"So how do the Americans solve this problems, have they no weevils there?" I asked.

He answered that they had silos in America and were using pesticides.

"Can't they build silos here?"

Wally laughed. It was the first time he laughed since we saw what happened to his maize. "Who will build them? The government? It is hell bent on industrialization and will not spend a penny for the peasants. They villagers themselves? They have not got the money." He paused and added as an afterthought: "Even if the government would build some silos the peasants wouldn't use them. First the officials would want a bribe to let them use 'em, and then they wouldn't trust the ones who are in charge to pay them for their corn or give it back to them without a bribe when they want it."

"Is there no other way to save the crop?"

"There is. When the Americans want to store small quantities of grain they use some small capsules with pesticide which they put into plastic-lined sacks. The stuff has no smell or taste and evaporates in the course of the three or four months of storage."

I asked if it was not harmful for consumption?

"No. But the sacks have to be well sealed so that the fume does not evaporate before the time the grain is sold."

"Capsules, plastic-lined sacks, sealing equipment, is this not far too expensive for our farmers?" I said more to myself than to Wally.

"It is not. The capsules are a very cheap by-product of refining oil; the sacks cost just a fraction more than the ones they have; and the sealing equipment, which they can use for years and years, costs no more than $5 in America."

When I saw Wally next he told me that he had been to see one of the representatives of a large multinational to inquire about the capsules. The capsules were available and he could get 100,000 for a reasonable price. All they wanted in return was an open import licence for a particular local trading company which would then distribute the product. So, he went to speak to the trading company. They were prepared to supply everything, the lined sacks, the sealing equipment, the capsules, provided he got them the "open import licence."

"So what's the problem?" I asked, seeing the unhappy expression on Wally's face.

He gave me a sidelong look but didn't answer.

"Well?" I prompted him, not understanding what it was that bothered him.

"Don't tell me that you don't know what this means," he said.

"What does it mean?"

"An open import licence means that next to the things I want, they can dump all the rubbish, the things they cannot sell in Europe or America, on Ghana, and then be paid for it in advance and in hard foreign currency. No Minister can be foolish enough to give them an open licence."

"Can't you appeal to the conscience of the producers or the traders? Did you not tell them that this is real development aid?"

"What do you think I tried to do?"

"And how did they react?"

"They told me to offer the Minister in charge a bribe. They were prepared to give me the money for it."

Fishermen and Coca Cola

When I was young, long before I came to Ghana, I earned my upkeep working on a trawler. This gave me a special affinity to the Elmina fisherman. Elmina, a small village in the shadow of what was once a slavers' fortress, lies in a small bay not far from Cape Coast. It is one of the few places on the west African Atlantic coast where the surf is not so violent and fishermen, though with some difficulty, can row their canoes from the shore to calmer waters.

Shortly before my arrival in Ghana the government provided the Elmina fishermen with twenty outboard motors to make it easier for them to get their canoes across the surf. This made not only fishing safer for them but reduced the time they previously wasted in efforts to reach the deeper and calmer waters. It gave them more time for fishing.

Every afternoon when the canoes returned to the shore to land the catch, people came from all over the region to Elmina to buy fish. Women from the village were then busy on the waterfront to sort, clean and sell the fish. Catching fish was the men's task, cleaning and selling them the women's.

Having witnessed all this, and smelling the stench from the decomposing fish which usually lay in the canoes for many hours under the blazing hot sun before they were landed, I decided to find a way to keep the catch more cool on the canoes. There was no ice in Elmina, and little chance of getting the government to build an ice-factory. But even if ice were available it would have melted much too soon on the canoes to make a difference.

One day when I was driving to Accra and stopped on the way in some small town where they served cold drinks from a Coca or Pepsi Cola vending machine, I had an idea. Why not ask Coca Cola or the other company to provide such a machine for Elmina? I could ask one of the technicians working at the university to install it on a canoe and see if this experiment would work and the fish could better be preserved.

I asked the technician if one could use a car-battery or gas cylinder or a belt-link to the crankshaft of an outboard motor to power the machine? The technician thought that it could be done.

So the next time I was in Accra I went to the Coca Cola (or was it Fanta or another) soft drink company's office, and told the manager that there were many potential customers in Elmina and that it was a good move for him to place one of his machines there. I told him about the many people who came there every afternoon to purchase fish, and that while they were waiting in the heat would certainly buy his product.

The manager agreed and a few days later the vending machine arrived and was placed in one of the halls near the fishermen's landing place.

I waited a few days to see how the sales went, but there were few customers. The fishermen were too poor, and most people who came to buy fish preferred star and club beer. Then we took the machine to the university's technical workshop and one of our technicians made it suitable for my real purpose. I convinced a team of fishermen to place it on their canoe and it worked.

The next days every afternoon a woman from Elmina came to our house and brought us wonderful fresh fish. But at the end of the week she came accompanied by the entire crew of the canoe on which we had installed the cooling system. At first none of them spoke. But after I treated them to drinks the eldest hesitantly asked me if I would be offended if they would take the machine off the boat?

Surprised I asked them why?

Looking a little embarrassed at the floor in front of him the old fisherman answered: "We are poor people. We cannot afford it."

Disappointed, I asked why again.

The man who had spoken did not raise his eyes: "The party bosses come early and take all the good fish."

"So?" I asked, still not understanding what this was all about.

The man explained: "The machine takes up much room on the canoe and we have only half the space for fish."

"But you must ask a better price for the fresh fish," I replied. "You can demand twice the old price and people will still buy it."

A younger man intervened: "No we cannot. The government has fixed the price of fish and it makes no difference whether the fish are fresh or not. The party bosses and the government officials always come first, and we do not dare to ask them more than the officially prescribed price."

I began to understand their problem. "Can't you ask the government to change the law?" I asked uncertainly.

The men smiled.

I promised to send someone next morning to take the machine off the canoe. They looked much happier.

They must have been aware of my disappointment, because when I led them to the door, the old man turned to me and said: "We are poor men. We cannot afford to have half our boat taken up by the machine. Your way, the fish are much better, but we must live."

The Lime Juice Factory

Not far from the university campus, deep in the bush, stood a Rose Lime factory. Lime is a sort of wild lemon which the British favour in their Gin. The wild lemon trees must be grafted to obtain lime and the Ghanaians learned to graft them early in the century. In the colonial days the British established lime plantations, but not in our region. In our region the lemon trees grew wild in the bush and the locals grafted them. In the season, the women collected the lime and brought it to the factory in baskets which they carried on their head. At the factory they received six pence for each basket. The factory was a small building with a long table to cut the fruit. Next to the table was a large barrel, equipped with a press which squeezed the juice out of the fruit. At the bottom of the barrel was a wire-mash to filter the fluid and a pipe through which the clear lime juice flowed into another barrel outside the building. Once this barrel was full it was sealed and placed next to others waiting for the truck that took them to the harbour from where the lime extract was shipped to England. On one side of the building was an ever growing heap of lime-shells which attracted an endless amount of insects. Now and then the manager hired workers to dig a deep hole in the ground to bury the rotting mass. But most of the time it just rotted and stank.

My colleague Ken, who taught management, was a huge black West Indian with a voice like Paul Robeson's. He took me to see the factory. Actually he wanted to buy some lime extract for his personal use, but as he was going there, and I also liked the drink he made by mixing lime-extract with water, I went with him to buy some for myself as well.

We got our lime juice and drove back to the university. On the way Ken was very silent. Something was bothering him. All at once he shouted at me as if I was responsible for it: "These bloody morons. They run their bloody factory like idiots."

"What's wrong with the factory?" I asked. It annoyed me that he was constantly denigrating the Ghanaians.

"I'll tell you what is wrong," he hollered. "Look what they are doing, look at it! Instead of having the shells collect flies, and spending money burying them, they should be used. The cretins should instal a dryer and stamp the dry shells into a powder. Then they should fill the powder into small bags and sell them to the farmers as an organic fertilizer. That is profitable for the factory and helps the farmers."

I did not answer and he probably thought that I did not understand him.

"Now the peasants use only one quarter of the land each season. They burn the bush to clear it. The next season they move to another quarter and allow the bush to grow over the one they used in the hope that the soil will regain its fertility in the three years until they return to it. With the population increasing the way it does, and with the tradition that all who eat must work, they soon will have to divide the land into only three parts and come back to the first plot a year earlier. Before long it will be every second year, and then year after year. Fertility will lessen and the people will become poorer and hungrier with each passing season. Already they grow cassava where they used to grow yam."

"What's wrong with cassava?" I asked.

"Yam is nutritious, cassava just fills your stomach. It only makes you feel less hungry."

"They should use fertilizer. Artificial fertilizer is not very expensive," I commented.

"Shit man!" he screamed at me. "Artificial fertilizer must be bought abroad. Where do you think the government will get the foreign currency to pay for it, even if it wanted to help farming which it does not. Chemical fertilizer without water-control and the right strain of plants is just a waste of money."

"So what is it that you want?" I asked.

"Man, it doesn't matter what I want! It is what they want or should want!
They should install a dryer; then pulverize the dry lime shells, sell it to the
farmers, and tell them to spread it on their cleared land before it rains. Once
it soaks in the rain, the powder will become a good fertilizer and they will be
able to use the same plot for several consecutive seasons."

"Ok. You convinced me!" I said. "Now you must only also convince the
factory's director and the peasants."

"Damn you, man," Ken screamed at me again. "That's only the beginning.
They should install some glass container above the place where they cut the
fruit to protect the eyes of the cutters, and to collect the spirit so that it can be
sold as a fuel. They should not throw away the white mash they get when they
clean the filter at the end of the press before the juice flows into the barrel
outside, but mix it with water and spirit and fill it into small bottles. The stuff
has a wonderful fragrance and can be sold as perfume."

I laughed: "Anything else they should do?"

"Shit man, they can cut the best peels into slices, sugar them, let them dry
for a while, and then put them nicely into small boxes and sell them as some
kind of sweets. The Belgians do it, why shouldn't they do the same?"

"Ok! Ok! I get your drift. You want them to produce lime-juice, spirit,
confectionery, and perfume, and God knows what else, in this establishment."

"You got it!"

"Have you also thought of a brand name for the perfume?"

He laughed. "Let's call it *Paris Nights*. If you translate it into French it will
sell even better."

The next time I saw Ken was in town. He was sitting in a bar next to Stanley,
another black lecturer from our university. Stanley was born in the West Indies
but grew up in Canada where he taught for many years before he came to
Ghana. When I entered the place, Stanley was drunk and stared sullenly into
the empty glass in front of him. Suddenly he turned in the direction of the
Ghanaians behind him and bitterly complained with drunken tears in his eyes:
"Your forefathers sold my forefather into slavery."

A hush fell over the room. Everyone was looking at him.

Then, Ken's voice thundered: "And thank God for that!"

The people in the bar laughed. It was an embarrassed laugh.

Then one day Ken disappeared. They found his car near Accra airport with
the keys in the ignition. He had gone back to America without saying goodbye
to anyone except to Wally.

I asked Wally what made him leave Ghana without picking up his pay check
and without selling his car before he left?

"He couldn't stomach it here any longer," Wally replied. He hated inefficiency, but worst he hated the way the Ghanaians treated him. Like all of us blacks, he came to this country full of hope. He wanted to help our black brothers, but the locals treated him like muck."

I wanted to object, but Wally stopped me and continued. "You, the whites, are still treated with respect, but us, the black foreigners, they treat worse than the whites are treating us in America. And this is happening here, in Ghana, the first country in Africa to have cast off the colonial yoke and gained independence."

"So what did they actually do to him?" I asked.

"An English professor arrived. They had no vacant bungalow ready for this white man. So, without even asking Ken, they took his belongings out of his bungalow and put them in a house in town to make room for the Englishman in the bungalow he had inhabited."

State Farms in the Volta Region

There were several state farms and a tractor station in the Volta Region. Two of these farms were managed by Israelis, one by Russians and one by an American. One Israeli managed farm produced vegetables and fruit, and the other raised cattle. The Russians grew rice. An American was in charge of the tractor station.

From time to time my wife and our children went with me to spend some days in Akazi, the Israeli managed state farm. Like me, the manager had his family in Ghana. His children were about our children's age and they liked playing together. A further reason for our visits to Akazi was an experiment which I conducted together with the manager. We wanted to find the most economically rewarding method for growing maize. We wanted to know whether to use advanced farm technology, tractors and the like, or cheap local labour, or any particular combination of both, was most profitable. We selected three plots of similar soil and area to compare results. Given the high rate of depreciation of mechanical equipment in tropical climates, the difficulty and extra cost of getting spare parts in Ghana, and the problem of finding competent and responsible workers to use the advanced technology, the experiment seemed worthwhile to us. We wanted an empirically tested answer to our question.

On one of our visits to the farm we arrived in the middle of a meeting of the Israeli and the Russian state farm managers with a group of FAO experts who came to study the progress of the foreign aid assisted agricultural enterprises. The meeting was held in our friend's home and my wife and I were allowed to sit in on the discussions.

The FAO experts asked questions and took notes and for a while I was tempted to tell them about the Russian tractors which arrived in Ghana equipped with snow ploughs, and much too heavy for the soil, and stood unused rusting away near our university campus. But I restrained myself and kept quiet.

When it was the turn of Grisha, the jovial Russian farm manager, to answer questions it went more or less like this.

The FAO team leader asked what percentage of his heavy equipment, tractors and rice harvesters, were operating?

"Well," the Russian replied, scratching his head as if he was pondering the precise percentage, "If 85% of your equipment is in good working order this is very good."

The FAO team leader looked satisfied: "85%. That's fine."

I saw the members of his team write in their notebooks 85%.

"How about spare parts?" the FAO leader continued.

"We order them from Russia when we need them."

"Does this incur any large extra costs?"

"No extra cost," Grisha answered emphatically.

Again the team wrote it down.

The questioning continued for some time and the longer it lasted the more I sensed our host's amusement.

After everyone was gone I asked our friend how he liked the "inquisition"?

He smiled. "Grisha was great! Of all his equipment only two rice harvesters are still in working order. None of his tractors work. He had to borrow one of mine and two from the American to get at least some of his work done. When they asked him how much of his equipment was in working order, he told them that *if* 85% is working this was fine. He did not say that 85% of *his* equipment was in working order. He only declared that 85% was a good show. I could hardly stop myself from laughing aloud. Eighty-five per cent is excellent indeed. But Grisha never told a lie. He just did not tell them how much of *his* equipment works. And what did the FAO experts do? They wrote down that practically all his equipment is in good working order."

There was no rancour in my friend's voice. He obviously enjoyed the way the Russian led the FAO around the bush.

"But why is none of his equipment working? Most of your equipment works?"

My friend explained that the Russian's could ask for spare parts from the Soviet Union but the spares never arrived. He laughed again. "You heard our Grisha say that he orders spare parts with no extra cost? He orders, and as they never come, there is indeed no extra cost. His problem is that he is not even allowed to *cannibalize* his derelict equipment."

"Cannibalize?" I asked.

He saw that I was not familiar with this term, and told me that it meant taking good parts from machines which cannot be repaired and use them to fix other machines which can be made to work again. He explained that the Russian government was so much in fear of parts being stolen that it strictly prohibited this practice. "Every time some small replacement is necessary, Grisha's machines go out of service, even though ten written off machines stand around on his farm from which the required part could easily be taken with no cost."

"But *you*? You can cannibalize your broken down equipment?" I asked.

My friend told me that he could and did, and took me to see a shed in which all the parts he "cannibalized" from equipment which could not be repaired were orderly stored on shelves.

On another visit to our friend's farm we met the other Israeli who was in charge of the cattle raising experiment. He invited us to see his place, and we did. His "ranch" looked beautiful. There were two large cow sheds with mosquito netting on all windows and double doors to keep out tzetze flies. A lot of provisions were stacked next to the sheds. His cows looked as good as any I had seen in Switzerland and Holland.

"It's crazy," he said unhappily.

"Crazy?" I asked, wondering why he felt depressed.

"These cows are for meat. If cows are raised the way the locals do, if they are left to graze outside, it costs almost nothing to fatten them. One small boy who is paid a few cedis per year looks after them, that's all. But what I am doing here is awfully expensive. It isn't just the cost of the sheds and all that, but I have to grow the feed for the animals or buy it, and then have to have it carried to the cows. You cannot even half imagine how much all this adds to the costs."

I objected reminding him that in the field, under the burning sun, it takes at least three or four years to fatten a cow for meat, while with him it took less than 16 months.

He agreed with me that in the summer the intense heat outside burns off the animals' fat, and that it did indeed take much longer for the animals to gain the desired weight. But he added that it was uneconomical all the same to do what he was doing.

"Why then don't you teach the Africans to build some shelters near the water where the cows congregate? They can build them from palm leaves. It will protect the cattle from the heat."

He answered that this wouldn't do at all. "Once the cows stop moving, and crowd in the shadow, they will be beset by swarms of tzetze flies."

I made a last effort to defend the modern type of dairy farming: "But your meat is so much better. It is not dry and tough like the meat sold in the markets. Certainly it will fetch a better price and make good the difference in cost."

He laughed. "What do you think the Africans want cows for? Meat? Forget it! They want cows for bride-price and for this the number of animals matters not their weight."

He was right and I knew it. It made me think of the child from the village near our campus, who when asked where milk came from, answered that it came from Kingsway. Kingsway was the name of the large shop in Cape Coast where people bought tins of imported Corned beef and evaporated powder milk.

Another day we met the American who was in charge of the tractor station. A well educated friendly black man who came to Ghana motivated by the wish to help. His tractors and bulldozers were mainly used for bush clearing, and to be "hired" free of charge to farmers for their heavy work. Village elders from the region, or government officials, could come to his station and ask him to send them his equipment. After the work was done the machines were taken back to his station for maintenance and when necessary for repairs. He had no problem with obtaining spare parts. With his short-wave radio transmitter he had only to send a message to America and within a few days the required part was flown in. A competent mechanic, and able to supervise the work of his Ghanaian trainees, all his machines were usually in good working order. And yet, he too was unhappy. Ghanaian society disappointed him. He felt that because he was black the Ghanaians did not accord him the same respect they gave to white experts, and that because he was an American they did not accept him as one of their own.

I tried to cheer him up by saying that not being accepted by the Ewe's in this region was not his fault. Ewe's did not even accept other Ghanaians unless they were of their tribe. He knew this, but nonetheless he felt frustrated. What I did not tell him was that it was partly his own fault. Like many foreign experts, and especially Americans, he could not help telling the Ghanaians incessantly how much better and more efficient everything was in America.

The person who impressed us most on our visits to Akazi was the Ghanaian foreman Kofi. He was a Ga from Accra, who had studied agriculture in Ghana, and was a born farm manager. The farm was his great love – his life. We used to joke with him: "Kofi you work like a white man." And he would answer: "only better." Always keen to learn new things and to teach his workers, it seemed obvious that he was the best man to succeed our friend as the farm's manager when he went back to Israel. He gained the necessary experience to do the job, and the workers liked him. The only people who did not get on with him were the government officials. When they wanted him to grow water melons he refused. Water melons, he said, are best grown by traditional farmers. Melons do not need irrigation and take up a lot of land which on the state farm could better be utilized for other more expensive crops. They wanted him to take on more workers, and he refused. There was no need to employ more workers than were necessary. They wanted him not to send trucks with vegetables to Accra unless there was freight in Accra to take back to the Volta region and he resisted. He just could not agree to let his vegetables rot because there was no transport. Things between him an officialdom came to a head when there was trouble between Nigeria and Ghana. Onions were normally imported from Nigeria and when the Ghanaian government stopped all Nigerian imports there followed a great onion shortage. Our friend brought a very fast growing strain of onions and within a short time had more than was needed for the markets. But then, someone in a high position in Accra, whose relative owned a truck, insisted that the onions be transported only by his relative. As the truck could only make one return journey a day, this was not fast enough to transport the large quantity of onions to the markets and they began to rot and sprout. Kofi was furious and hired other transport. It resulted in a terrible quarrel between him and the ministry of agriculture.

Our Israeli friend tried to convince him to be more flexible in his dealings with officialdom but it was to no avail. I was present when he once told him that it was after all not his money that was being wasted by following government orders, and that he had done all he could to prevent the waste, but Kofi wouldn't listen. He gave us an angry look and said that in a year or two we would be going home, but he was a Ghanaians and will remain and cannot allow "the fools to destroy our hopes for a prosperous Ghana."

There was nothing we could say to that. But later my Israeli friend told me that he was certain that as soon as he himself goes home, the officials would see to it that Kofi was not going to succeed him as the farm's manager. "They will sack him and appoint some crony of theirs who will stay in Accra and only visit the farm when he wants some vegetables and fruit for his own household. Before long the farm will be no more."

A few years later, when I had occasion to come back to Ghana, I went to see what happened to the state farm. I could not find it. Some former student from the region showed me the place where it had been. The bush had taken over. I made inquiries about Kofi and learned that soon after our Israeli friend went home, the officials decided that Ewe's must manage farms in Ewe regions and he was dismissed. As our friend predicted, the new manager stayed most of his time in Accra and the farm deteriorated and became economically unviable and finally abandoned to the bush. The only thing that remained to remind me of the farm was the article in a theoretical economic journal in which my friend and I described the various methods we tried for growing maize to determine if mechanization was preferable to the labour-intensive traditional mode of production.

Flight to Lagos

I had to go to Nigeria and was told to take the regular Nigerian Airways flight from Accra by way of Lomé in Togo and Cotonou in Dahomey to Lagos. Boarding the old DC3 made me remember the Spitfires, Hawker Hurricanes, Avro Lancasters and Flying Fortresses of World War II. From my seat I saw the pilot and co-pilot in the cockpit. The pilot looked a typical Englishman and the co-pilot Polish or Ukrainian. Most seats on the plane were vacant. Except for a few British diplomats, myself, five Nigerians and a goat, the plane was empty. The goat stood in the middle of the gangway next to the seat of its Nigerian owner.

After take-off I looked out of the window. We first flew over the lagoons bordering the ocean shore and I enjoyed the view. But soon the plane lost height and a few minutes later we landed in Lomé. The pilot and his mate got out of the cockpit and exchanged some words with the British diplomats. Then the pilot came over to me and asked me if I had been to Lomé before. I answered that I had been to Lomé.

His face brighten. "So you know the hotel, and the wonderful French kitchen."

I answered that I did.

"Then you are coming with us." It was not a question but a statement of fact.

I did as I was told.

Three taxis were waiting on the tarmac. Two were already taken by the diplomats and I was ushered into the third where the co-pilot was already waiting for us to join him.

It was a short ride to the hotel where we had a wonderful French meal, with wines found nowhere else in West Africa except, perhaps, in the Ivory coast.

Two hours later we returned to the plane to continue our journey. The next stop was in Cotonou. This time the pilot did not bother to ask the diplomats and me if we wanted to get off the plane. He just signalled us to follow him. Walking across the airfield I was again reminded of the war. An old four engine Flying Fortress or Liberator was standing on the tarmac.

I pointed it out to the co-pilot who was walking next to me.

He smiled. "Not many of them still around these days. I used to fly one of them in the 1940s. I was with the Polish forces in England."

The pilot, who judging by his age and by the way his mustache was trimmed, made me fairly certain that he had been a spitfire pilot in the war, added that the plane was always standing there ready for take off.

"Ready for take off?" I asked. My impression had been that it stood there as a decoration – as a museum piece.

"Sure thing. Ready for take off," the pilot repeated. "How else can the government escape when the next military coup takes place?"

Little did I foresee at that time that five days later, when I flew back to Ghana, the old plane would no longer be on the tarmac, and a new government would control the country.

There was nothing else to order except beer at the canteen to which the pilot shepherded us. Only the number of empty bottles on the table told me that it was getting late. When we left it had become dark outside and about five hours late. How I got back on the plane I cannot exactly remember. I recollect washing my face with cold water and falling asleep as soon as I was seated. When I woke up the plane had landed in Lagos. My small bag and the carton of cigarettes I bought from the tax-free shop at Accra airport were still on the vacant seat beside me. I glanced at my watch. We were five hours late.

One of the British diplomats asked me something about transportation from the airport to town and I realized that the car which was to collect me was probably no longer waiting.

We got off the plane and the diplomats went to the VIP lounge and left me standing alone in the middle of the arrivals hall. At the far end people were queuing for passport control and customs inspection. I was just about to join the queue when a large Nigerian policeman with a broad smile on his face came up to me.

"You come from Ghana?"

"Yes, from Ghana."

"You brought me something? No?"

At once the alcohol fumes were gone from my head. I handed him the carton of cigarettes: "My friend, I brought you fine cigarettes from Ghana."

The policeman grabbed my bag, asked for my passport, and told me to follow. Without stopping for passport control and customs he guided me straight out of the arrivals hall into the street in front of the building. On the way I saw the puzzled looks on the diplomats' faces who were still waiting to have their travelling documents inspected. Outside my policeman returned my passport and bag; broke open the carton of cigarettes and gave me back two packets;

wished me a good stay in "beautiful Nigeria; and left me standing wondering how I can get to where I needed to go.

Somebody touched my shoulder. I turned and saw a young Nigerian standing behind me.

"You from the University of Ghana?" he asked.

I nodded.

"I be here waiting for you Sir. I be your driver."

I do not know how he recognized me. Perhaps I was the only white man he saw coming from the building, but I was happy that there was someone to take me to my destination without me having to worry how to get there.

"You waited a long time," I said to show my appreciation.

"No problem. Accra air plane always late."

A Minor Battle

Several lecturers including myself came to Nigeria at the invitation of the West African Examinations Council. We were billeted on the campus of Lagos University. On arrival we were told that breakfast would be served at nine o'clock in the students' dining hall. When we entered the dining hall, which seated about 200 persons, the students had already had their breakfast and the stewards had placed the chairs on the tables to let the cleaners wash the floor. Only one table was still laid for us at the far end of the hall.

With my back to the wall I saw near the kitchen door at the other end of the hall, two large samovar like vessels one labelled coffee and the other tea. They stood on a small table or shelf and next to them were trays with cups, saucers and spoons. While I had my second cup of tea I saw a student coming through the door. He looked at us, and then walked up to our waiter. The two began to argue but they were too far from me to hear what they were saying. Even if I had been closer it would have made no difference. They were speaking Yoruba or Ibo and I did not understand their language. Their gestures did however make it obvious that the student wanted to eat and the waiter told him that he was too late for breakfast. The student pointed to us, and I assume that he asked why we were still getting breakfast and he was not? The waiter's reply did apparently not satisfy him, and he went to the shelf, picked up a cup and served himself.

The waiter was infuriated and knocked the cup out of the student's hand. From where I was I noticed that he was careful not to knock the cup so that the hot liquid would spill over the student's hands or clothes.

The next thing I saw was the student brushing the cups and saucers from the shelve sending them crushing to the floor.

The waiter chased the student around the tables and the student pulled down chairs to bar his way. Then the cook and his mate came through the kitchen door and joined in the chase.

A minute later more students entered the dining hall, and waiters and kitchen staff also appeared from nowhere. Soon a veritable battle ensued and cups and saucers were hurling through the air. It was easy to distinguish between the sides because the waiters were clad in white jackets which as the battle lasted lost more and more buttons.

Suddenly, in the middle of all this rumpus, the waiter who was serving us came over to our table. Holding his by now button less jacket together he asked: "Is there anything else you want, gentlemen?"

I felt as if I had been transported into one of Chaplin's old comedies. With difficulty I managed not to laugh when I thanked the man and told him that we had all we wanted. The waiter turned and the next moment he was back in the melee.

Some of the guests at our table began to leave the dining hall. They moved carefully along the wall to avoid being inadvertently hit by "flying saucers." I decided to remain and see out the "show." I was seated with my back to the wall and could easily dodge oncoming objects.

The sound of a car coming to a halt in front of the building made me look out of the window. It was a jeep with four policemen. The driver remained at the wheel and the other three walked confidently to the dining hall. The moment they got through the door and saw what went on their self-confidence was gone. The sergeant shouted something trying to be heard over the din but nobody took any notice. The policemen retreated to their jeep. Outside the building they regained their former self-confidence. Then they spoke into the radio, presumably to ask for reinforcements.

By looking at what the policemen were doing, I missed what happened inside the dining hall. When I looked again I saw that the two combatant sides were slowly withdrawing to the opposite sides of the hall, exchanging verbal abuse. Then the students left the hall and the waiters began to clear up the mess.

Eventually the police reinforcements arrived and ten came into the hall. They looked at the ravage, took a cup of tea, and departed again.

Important and Unimportant Persons

Driving an automobile in Lagos is always hell but worse in the afternoon between five and six o'clock. There are too many cars on the roads and nobody observing the highway code. When I said something about it to the taxi driver who was taking me to the airport he laughed – he was used to the chaos.

I had heard that there was trouble with Colonel Ojukwo, but the war in Biafra had not yet begun. Yet driving through the Ibo populated suburbs on the way, I could feel the tension. On one side of the road Ibos were preparing to protect themselves, and on the other side armed soldiers from the north of Nigeria were nervously fumbling their weapons. Sweat came running down my face, but I felt cold. The threat of impending bloodshed was too obvious to be ignored.

Once we had passed the Ibo dwellings the world fell back into its hinges. There was less traffic on the road and my taxi driver was soon accelerating faster than the permitted speed limit of fifty miles per hour. We arrived at the airport and he stopped in front of the departures hall. I went to the check-in desk and he followed me. The young Nigerian behind the desk was dressed in European clothes. He was probably trained for his job in America, or by Americans, because he asked me for my ticket in precisely the same tone the clerk used who checked me in a week before at LaGuardia airport in New York. I handed him my ticket, which was for a flight four days later, and explained that having finished my business in Lagos I would rather leave by the first available flight.

The young man looked at his flight schedule and another sheaf of passenger lists.

"Sorry Sir, all flights are booked. You'll have to come back in four days."

"Then put me on the waiting list so that if some passenger fails to turn up I can take his place."

"No use Sir. It seldom happens." He showed me the list in front of him. I could see that all seats were booked.

"But I have to get back to Ghana," I said in desperation.

"Go to your hotel and give me the phone number. If there is a vacancy I'll call you."

I had already given up my room and asked the taxi driver, who was still standing next to me, if he knew a hotel by the airport where I could wait. I had no wish to go back along the nervous suburbs we had passed.

The driver said that nearby was an airport hotel where he could take me. He even knew the hotel's telephone number and gave it to the clerk although we could not know if there was a vacant room in the hotel, and returned to the taxi. But before he drove off the driver asked if I was really wishing to go back to Ghana on this very evening.

I thought that this was obvious and nodded my head in affirmation.

"Give me ten dollar. I'll see to it."

I did not have dollars and gave him the equivalent in English money.

He told me to wait and went again into the departures hall.

A few minutes later I saw him coming out and signalling me from the door to come.

I stood in front of the same clerk I had spoken with before. He had the flight schedule and the list of bookings for the Accra flights in front of him. "Why did you not say that you don't mind flying in a Russian plane? There is one departing in two hours."

He sounded as if it was my fault that he could not book me for this flight before. Not willing to risk missing this chance to leave Nigeria by the first plane I kept quiet.

With his pen he crossed out one of the names on the passenger list and wrote mine instead.

"And what if the owner of the seat turns up and claims his place?" I asked.

The clerk gave me a sidelong look. "He does not matter. He is not important."

During the flight I asked myself if somebody who booked my seat had really been left behind or if the entire list was fictitious to allow the clerk to line his pockets by providing seats for people in my situation. I decided that the latter was the case. It made me feel more comfortable.

REVIEW ESSAYS

Multiple Reviews of Louçã and Perlman's IS ECONOMICS AN EVOLUTIONARY SCIENCE? THE LEGACY OF THORSTEIN VEBLEN

Rick Tilman

A review of Francisco Louçã and Mark Perlman (Eds.) (2000) *Is Economics an Evolutionary Science? The Legacy of Thorstein Veblen* (Cheltenham, U.K. and Northampton, MA: Edward Elgar), 234 pp., Hardback ISBN 1-84064 195-9, $90.00.

Four centennial celebrations of Thorstein Veblen (1857–1929) have now appeared. The most recent is the volume under review by Francisco Louçã and Mark Perlman, editors, *Is Economics an Evolutionary Science? The Legacy of Thorstein Veblen* (Louçã & Pearlman, 2000) which consists of thirteen papers originally given at the 1998 meeting of the European Association for Evolutionary Political Economy held in Lisbon, Portugal. However, before I review it, mention must be made of the three other centennial volumes which focus not on Veblen's essay "Why Economics is not an Evolutionary Science" (Veblen, 1898) but on *The Theory of the Leisure Class*. Institutional economist Doug Brown has edited a set of essays, *Thorstein Veblen in the Twenty-First Century: A Commemoration of the Theory of the Leisure Class, 1899–1999* (Brown, 1998) which is aimed at a wider and more popular audience than the other three centennial celebrations. Warren Samuels, editor, casts his nets upon

Research in the History of Economic Thought and Methodology, Volume 20-A, pages 151–163.
Copyright © 2002 by Elsevier Science Ltd.
All rights of reproduction in any form reserved.
ISBN: 0-7623-0847-8

the centennial of both Veblen's classic work and John R. Commons, *A Sociological View of Sovereignty* (Samuels, 1998) while Luca Fiorito has edited an issue of the Italian-based journal *History of Economic Ideas* which focuses on *The Theory of the Leisure Class* (Fiorita, 1999). These three studies all provide important retrospection on the meaning and relevance of Veblen's best known work and are worthy of attention from Veblen scholars.

The essays in the Perlman-Louçã volume were selected as representative from a much larger number of papers presented at the Lisbon Conference. The book is divided into an introduction by the editors and three parts. The eight essays in part one mostly deal with Veblen's challenge to the conventional economics of his day. The four pieces in part two reevaluate that challenge in the face of work done by other seminal writers including Tjalling Koopmans, Karl Polanyi and J. M. Keynes. Part three consists of one longer essay by J. S. Metcalfe and provides a perspective on the dynamic interaction of institutions, technology, markets and competition.

The doctrinal biases prevalent in the other three centennial celebrations are that Veblen is a powerful and penetrating critic of modern capitalism and, perhaps, its most prophetic analyst. Such claims will not impress all Marxists, Weberians or Hayekians, but many of them concede the power and cogency of his ideas. But the contributors to the Louçã-Perlman book do not all share this view; indeed, several raise interesting, if not persuasive, questions about the value and relevance of his work. Still others do not even mention Veblen or attempt to link their main theses directly with his perspective. Indeed, the strength of the collection lies less in the evaluation of his work and its relevance than in analysis of important specific areas, such as rationality, the firm, the diversity of economic institutions, the role and limits of knowledge, the relation of institutions to technical processes, nonlinear relationships, capitalism as a system and the nature of evolutionary economics. It is fair to say that Veblen and his ideas are only one source of interest to the authors and not always the preeminent one.

As far as Veblen's life is concerned, the authors are not very interested in it and they appear to rely on Joseph Dorfman's *Thorstein Veblen and His America* (1934). This study which has been subjected to critical scrutiny since the mid-1980s has often been found wanting both in factual accuracy, conceptual adequacy and interpretive objectivity. Since Dorfman's papers were opened to scholars in the early 1990s and new materials deposited in other collections, the factual errors, conceptual frailties and doctrinal biases of Dorfman's massive study are exposed particularly since 1994 in the *International Journal of Politics, Culture and Society*. Not surprisingly, many of the contributors to this anthology are unaware of the serious inadequacies of Dorfman's study of

Veblen. However, although this would be a serious flaw in the other centennial celebrations, it does not seriously mar the Perlman-Loucã book since biography plays an insignificant role in it and Veblen, himself, is only mentioned in passing, if at all, in several of the essays. In fact, in the only focused comments on Veblen's life Perlman writes (in a footnote) that: "Dorfman had a bottom-less well of stories about what Veblen's loneliness did not only to his manners but also to his spirit." (p. 23). This statement is apparently based on lectures Perlman heard when he was a student of Dorfman. In view of the revisionist scholarship on Veblen which has been underway for the last fifteen years or so, it must be asked, whether or not these lectures carry the weight Perlman assigns to them in understanding Veblen the man.

However, it is the duty of reviewers to explain, however briefly, the nature of each contribution to anthologies rather than focusing on what the contributors did not intend to do. Each of the contributions is now described for the edification of the reader. But more obiter dicta follow at the conclusion of the review.

Perhaps the leading Australian institutional economist Phillip O'Hara argues in "How Can Economics be an Institutional-Evolutionary Science?" that Veblen's important contributions to political economy that are most relevant for the 21st century can be listed under five headings. To paraphrase O'Hara, these are holistic institutional economics, evolutionary circular and cumulative economics, social, technological and ecological capital, an economic surplus approach to business and industry, and an analysis of race, class, gender, nation and species. O'Hara believes that if economics is to become an institutional-evolutionary science, the path implicitly outlined by Veblen, "much work lies ahead in the developing such a perspective" (p. 38). But clearly Veblen's intellectual leadership must be preeminent in such a venture and O'Hara proves an apt, if critical, disciple here and elsewhere.

Mark Perlman, co-editor of the anthology and former editor of the *Journal of Economic Literature*, argues in "Mind-sets and Why Veblen was Ineffectual" that "Veblen failed not because there were inherent flaws in the body of his ideas, but because ... his rhetoric, like Jonathan Swifts', was designed to shock rather than to teach" (p. 14). He was unable to provide a synthesis of an evolutionary economics despite his originality because his encyclopedic knowledge and extremely negative social criticism lead him to caustic and destructive social statements "rather than measured constructive and consol-idative statements" (p. 15). Also, since his most creative period came before Max Weber's and Vilfredo Pareto's most important and relevant work were available, he could not take advantage of their seminal insights. Finally, in what is one of the most interesting essays in the book, Perlman asserts that Veblen ignored the fact that "much persuasion is dependent upon understanding that the path to most people's hearts is not by dazzling them with the new, but by showing that what is new fits well with what to them is familiar" (p. 16). While Perlman's allegation that Veblen was stereotyped by 1898 is certainly debatable his claims about Veblen's lack of success in convincing his contemporaries about the truth of his views, while not the whole truth regarding their reception, are nevertheless insightful.

American Alan W. Dyer is an institutional economist who uses his knowledge of modern philosophy to elucidate economic problems and analyses. In the past his favorite philosopher has been Charles Sanders Peirce under whom Veblen worked informally at Johns Hopkins University. On this occasion, however, in "Thorstein Veblen and the Political Economy of the Ordinary: Hope and Despair" he turns to Stanley Cavell for a new reading of Veblen through ordinary language philosophy. He penetratingly comments in this vein that "Veblen identifies an inherent tendency to confuse economic need with commercial expediency in business culture, which transforms ordinary economic life into a ceaseless competition for pecuniary symbols of success" (p. 42). He then analyzes Veblen's ordinary language critique of neoclassical economics and ties it to what he says was Veblen's aspiration, namely, an ordinary language economics. However, he concludes that Veblen lost faith in the ordinary and, despite his achievement, Veblen's life and work ended in despair.

Ann Mayhew, until recently editor of the *Journal of Economic Issues*, makes three claims in her "Veblen and Theories of the Firm." Drawing on one of Veblen's own applications of his evolutionary approach in *the Theory of Business Enterprise* (1904), Mayhew argues:

(1) that analysis of organizations such as "the firm" require a more open approach than that found in most recent "evolutionary" theories of the firm;

(2) that it is in part a desire for "agency" that has perpetuated the anti-Veblenian and a nti-evolutionary aspects of these theories of the firm; and

(3) that new developments in economic sociology, cognitive anthropology and other social sciences may offer solutions to the problem of agency that are more truly Veblenian and evolutionary" (p. 54).

Once again the claim is made that economists may have more to learn from the other social sciences than from conventional economics.

Laure Bazzoli makes some interesting comparisons between Veblen and Commons, not always to Veblen's advantage, in "Institutional Economics and the Specificity of Social Evolution: About the Contribution of J. R. Commons." Such comparisons between the two are inevitable and, in this case, enlightening.

Bazzoli argues that both men view the common project for the institutional evolutionary theory as evolving around the issue of how to "build a theory of the genesis and evolution of modern institutions, that is, to understand the processes by which new forms of behavior and rules emerge and persist" (p. 65). Bazzoli concludes that

> Commons differentiated himself from Veblen in order to deal with this issue of the specificity of social evolution; although he adopted Veblen's general view of the logic of an evolutionary science, he nevertheless defended the metaphor of artificial selection, and not one of natural selection, as relevant for social sciences. Commons thereby developed a somewhat different conception of evolution and analysis of the process of institutional change, linked to an original epistemological vision of social sciences (p. 64).

Jackie and Ron Stanfield in "The Significance of Clarence Ayres and the Texas School" argue that Ayres (1891–1972) was the unofficial dean of the second generation of American old institutionalists, who fused Veblen's insights with John Dewey's instrumentalism. They accurately assert his influence on a third and fourth generation of institutional economists trained at the universities of Texas, Tennessee, Nebraska, North Texas State, Oklahoma, Denver and Colorado State, respectively. However, the Stanfields' analytical focus is not on the institutional affinities of the Ayresian influence, but on Ayres' view of the relationship between democracy and the economic process. This is best explained by the social phenomena of technological change and cultural lag, institutional adjustment through democratic participation and majority rule. In fact, "the application of the process of inquiry and peer review to the social value construct implies the merger of the social scientist and social reformer in the democratic process" (p. 89). The Stanfields assert that Ayres was the conduit for much of the theoretical flow from Dewey and Veblen to later generations but it was primarily as a philosopher and theorist of democracy.

Ugo Pagano in "Bounded Rationality, Institutionalism and the Diversity of Economic Institutions" argues that much of the New Institutional Economics has relied on some "mild form" of bounded rationality that Veblen's approach avoids. The Veblenian approach is preferable because of his emphasis on habit and his belief that "rationality" itself is influenced by the "conditions of production" of preferences of a past state of society" (p. 95). In short, preferences cannot be taken as given independently of a certain social context within which their formation takes place. The contrast between the New Institutionalism and the Old Institutionalism can be found in the individual who in the former paradigm is trying to economize on and beyond his own bounded rationality to achieve efficient institutions. In the latter the Veblenian individual's capacity to economize on bounded rationality is itself bounded. So if he or she can often be found trapped in inefficient habits and institutions; which is the way out of this impasse? According to Pagano, it is Veblen's view that while habits and preferences are largely endogenous in the sense of being strongly influenced by the history of society, the instincts of individuals are largely exogenous in the sense that they have been selected during long periods of natural and human history. Unfortunately, in an otherwise stimulating essay, Pagano repeats the erroneous view that Veblen's sanction of an evolutionary approach to economics is evidence of his "unilinearism."

Frank Hahn in "Is Economics an Evolutionary Science?" concludes that Veblen's "Why Economics is not an Evolutionary Science" was not about evolution at all but an argument in favor of abandoning equilibrium economics for a study of process. But Hahn advances two caveats which qualify his thesis. First, it is easier to analyze the nature of equilibria than of dynamic models. Secondly, it is not true that equilibrium means no "change" (p. 122). Hahn concludes that "what I believe an equilibrium in economics means is that no one has an incentive to deviate from his or her plan of action. In a sense this implies rational expectations and this in turn suggests that equilibrium states are unlikely" (p. 122). Veblen's dislike of equilibrium theory is thus given another rationale.

Probably the most direct criticism, indeed, repudiation of Veblen's essay on economics as an evolutionary science is by Hahn. He finds little ascertainable meaning in Veblen and asserts that what epistemological significance his essay may have is probably wrongheaded. He also claims accurately enough that Veblen's analysis is Lamarckian rather than Darwinian in that he focuses on social traits that are useful, can be inherited institutionally and bring about better instrumental adaption to change. On the whole, however, Hahn is unimpressed by Veblen's essay and he concludes that "evolutionary theory offers no shortcuts to an integrated social science nor advances in economics. It does, however, facilitate the clothing of many rather commonplace ideas in "scientific dress" (p. 123).

In the only remaining essay in the anthology that actually focuses on Veblen and his intellectual heritage Eyüp Özveren compares Karl Polanyi and Veblen as theorists of development studies. He argues that the two men "went further than their predecessors by venturing into the domain of institutional patterns, institutional tensions, institutional lags, and institutional adjustments and breakdowns in a systematic manner" (p. 155). In his essay, however, he does not attempt a paradigmatic contrast of the Polanyi/Veblen approaches. Rather he attempts to engage in a constructive synthesis. In so doing he uses their treatments of Germany and England, respectively, as a fulcrum for synthesis. He concludes that Veblen, like Polanyi, saw no conflict between the symbiotic co-existence of rapid economic development and centralized imperial growth.

The four pieces alluded to earlier which neither mention nor cite Veblen will, nevertheless, be of interest to economists whether or not they consider themselves to be heterodox. Co-editor Francisco Loucã in "Is Capitalism Doomed? A Nobel Discussion" focuses on three founders of modern mathematical economics and econometrics who were awarded the Nobel Prize – Ragnar Frisch, Jan Tinbergen, and Tjalling Koopmans. Loucã is primarily interested in discussing their analysis of the structure of capitalism and business cycle research. He sides with Frisch and Tinbergen in their disagreement with Koopmans over the causes and cures of economic oscillations in the context of the 1930s concluding that "economics should aim at producing the tools for economic intervention and monitoring economics is, according to this view, political economy" (p. 152).

Marco Crocco, in "The Future's Unknowability: Keynes' Probability, Probable Knowledge and the Decision to Innovate," states that:

> The aim of this paper is to show that Keynes' concept of probability can enrich the understanding of the process of innovation offered by the neoSchumpeterian approach. The latter has a peculiar understanding of the technical change process, which includes concepts such as knowledge base, cumulativeness, technological trajectory, and uncertainty. To deal with uncertainty, in particular, neoSchumpeterians introduce the concept of routines. What is suggested here is that the concepts of Probable Knowledge and Weight of Argument, draw from Keynes' theory of probability, when used together with the concept of routines, can clarify the rationality of the decision-making process in the introduction of the innovation (p. 173).

Keynes' *Treatise on Probability* thus contains an approach to predicting the outcome of technological innovation, for example, as well as an understanding of the probabilities underlying the more routine behavior of economic actors. Schumpeter's "creative waves of destruction" hypothesis can thus be made more rational and perhaps also subject to greater social control and constraint, or so Crocco's analysis would lead us to believe.

J. S. Metcalfe argues in his "Instituted Economic Processes, Increasing Returns and Endogenous Growth" that the case for the evolutionary viewpoint

> rests ultimately on two claims: that it can give an explanatory role to the enormous range of differences in behavior of individuals, firms and other organizations; and that this explanatory role hinges on the coordinating role of markets and other institutions (p. 197).

Perhaps the most Veblenian utterance Metcalfe makes without mentioning Veblen himself is that the foundation of economic growth is rooted in the knowledge of the economy we have which is itself a product of how firms, sectors, and economies grow; "Growth of knowledge and growth of the economy are simultaneous and interdependent processes" (p. 198). The advancement of economic science is thus directly dependent on the nature of economic change itself. Unlike many epistemologically naïve neoclassical economists, Metcalfe believes that neoclassical theory is itself a social byproduct with little scientific autonomy of its own. Its relevance and validity will thus depend mostly on successful adaptation to economic change and growth.

In conclusion, although the general level of scholarship and analyses is good, it is unclear why several of the essays were included in this anthology. They do not mention Veblen and there does not appear to be any direct efforts to link his work with them. The otherwise stimulating pieces by Jolink, Ozveren, Crocco and Metcalfe do deal with problems in which Veblen was interested, but there is little about them that requires a knowledge of Veblenian institutionalism. Furthermore, the co-editors make no effort to justify their inclusion.

On the whole, the book is a mixed bag viewed from the perspective of Veblen's disciples. Some of the essays are explicitly Veblenian in tone and analysis. Others simply use Veblen as a take-off point to develop their own hypotheses for analysis and later, perhaps, empirical verification. Still others mention him in passing, but pay little heed to any facet of his thought. Finally, three of the pieces do not mention him at all although they deal with problems and concepts which interested him; the Hahn essay focuses at times directly on Veblen but mostly to dismiss his essay as difficult to understand and of little value in any case. Of course, centennial "celebrations" of the relevance and importance of a particular thinker are not obliged to honor the thinker or sanction his doctrines so long as they stimulate critical analysis and reflection. In this sense, the anthology must be judged a success.

REFERENCES

Brown, D. (Ed.) (1998). *Thorstein Veblen in the Twenty-First Century: A Commemoration of the Theory of the Leisure Class*. Cheltenham, U.K.: Edward Elgar.

Fiorita, L. (Ed.) (1999). Centennial Celebration of *The Theory of the Leisure Class*. *History of Economic Ideas*, *7*, 81–180.

Loucã, F., & Pearlman, M. (Eds) (2000). *Is Economics An Evolutionary Science? The Legacy of Thorstein Veblen*. Cheltenham, U.K.: Edward Elgar.

Samuels, W. (Ed.) (1998). *The Founding of Institutional Economics: The Leisure Class and Sovereignty*. London and New York: Routledge.

Veblen, T. (1898). Why is Economics Not An Evolutionary Science? *Quarterly Journal of Economics*, *13*, 373–397.

THE VEBLENIAN EVOLUTIONARY LEGACY AFTER 100 YEARS

Geoffrey M. Hodgson

A review of Francisco Louçã and Mark Perlman (Eds.) (2000) *Is Economics an Evolutionary Science? The Legacy of Thorstein Veblen* (Cheltenham, U.K. and Northampton, MA: Edward Elgar), 234 pp., Hardback ISBN 1-84064 195-9, $90.00.

As the subtitle suggests, the title of this volume is a recasting of Thorstein Veblen's famous question 'Why is economics not an evolutionary science?' in his article published in the *Quarterly Journal of Economics*. This seminal 1898 article helped to inspire the creation of American institutional economics. The papers in the volume under review were presented at a 1998 meeting of the European Association for Evolutionary Political Economy held in Lisbon, in part to mark the centenary of Veblen's essay. As the editors explain in their introduction, they selected 13 essays from the very many presented at the conference, with the evolutionary themes of Veblen's essay uppermost in their mind. At first I shall outline the contents of these essays. Finally I shall add some evaluations of the book.

In the second chapter, Mark Perlman tries to explain why Veblen's ideas had a limited impact. He rightly observes that Veblen did not attempt to provide institutionalism with a systematic theoretical synthesis. He tries to probe some of the psychological and doctrinal reasons for this failure. In the following essay, Phillip O'Hara attempts to sketch out the kind of theoretical system that is implied by Veblen's work. Among other issues, he notes Veblen's insistence that economies are embedded in institutional structures, his adoption of Darwinian evolutionary principles, his development of an economic surplus approach, and his emphasis on socially embedded knowledge as a driver of economic growth.

In Chapter four, Alan Dyer restricts himself to a discussion of the nature and purpose of Veblen's use of language, particularly concerning such terms as property, wealth and economy. This is a more esoteric approach to Veblen, but one that is not without its insights. Moving from language to an aspect of what it attempts to signify, Anne Mayhew in Chapter five discusses Veblen's analysis of the firm. In part, this is a commentary on an article by Nicolai Foss (1998) on Veblen's theory of the firm, in a special issue of the *Cambridge Journal of Economics*. This was another symposium to mark the Veblenian centennial.

Subsequent chapters are not centred on Veblen alone. The ideas of John Commons on social evolution are the subject of Chapter six, by Laure Bazzoli. Comparing Commons with Veblen, Bazzoli argues that Commons's concept of 'artificial selection' is more able to deal with the reality of human volition than Veblen's non-teleological interpretation of Darwinism. In Chapter seven, James Stanfield and Jacqueline Stanfield consider the work of Clarence Ayres and the Texas school of institutional economics.

Some aspects of the new and the old institutional economics are compared by Ugo Pagano in Chapter eight. Pagano centres his analysis on the concept of bounded rationality and argues that old institutionalist approaches are more able to accommodate its several facets. Pagano makes particular reference to the works of Veblen and John Maurice Clark and shows that they had a more sophisticated appreciation of the theoretical issues involved in the analysis of human rationality than they are typically credited by modern theorists. In Chapter nine Frank Hahn asks: 'Is economics an evolutionary science?' He makes it clear at the outset that he does not believe that economics is a science. Neither does he find reading Veblen easy. This is representative Frank Hahn: witty, poignant, terse, dismissive, intelligent. His main point is that evolutionary theory, if it is applicable to economics, does not itself get us very far. This is partly because the meaning of concepts such as fitness and mutation are not obvious in such a context.

Some of the following papers are less evolutionary or Veblenian in their concerns. In Chapter ten Albert Jolink discusses the neglected contribution of Tjalling Koopmans to the socialist calculation debate. This connects neatly with the following paper. Francisco Louçã asks rather grandly in Chapter eleven whether capitalism is doomed. In fact, the main subject of his essay is an early and neglected 1935 exploration of non-linear dynamics by Ragnar Frisch. Louçã usefully brings this unpublished paper to light and shows how this too was placed in the context of the great debate between advocates of markets and devotees of planning. However, Frisch's simple two-agent model contributed very little to that contemporary debate and cannot give an adequate answer to the grand question posed in Louçã's title.

Chapter twelve returns to Veblen, with Karl Polanyi thrown in for good company. Therein Eyüp Özveren discusses the foundations of an institutionalist development economics. Özveren argues that the Veblen-Polanyi type of institutional economics is particularly persuasive in dealing with problems of country development. In contrast, the focus of Chapter thirteen is John Maynard Keynes, where Marco Crocco attaches some of Keynes's ideas on probability to the analyses of innovation and economic evolution in the tradition of Richard Nelson, Sidney Winter, Giovanni Dosi and others. This is a bold and interesting synthesis.

Finally, in Chapter fourteen, J. Stanley Metcalfe links the evolutionary themes of economic diversity and economic growth, discussing evidence of structural change, increasing returns and endogenous growth in the U.S. economy. The inspiration of the anti-equilibrium tradition of Allyn Young and Nicholas Kaldor is clearly evident. Veblen could have been mentioned too.

My overall impressions of this volume are as follows. First, like many volumes emanating from conferences, it suffers from some unevenness of quality. Some of the papers are not up to scratch and would have benefited from further work. However, there are some good essays in this collection. My personal favourites are the essays by Pagano, Crocco and Metcalfe. Each of these makes a significant contribution and they are highly recommended.

Second, while the editors have made some effort to select and organise the essays in order to provide some thematic coherence for the volume, they are not entirely successful. Not all the essays mention Veblen. The editors could have asked every author to comment on the Veblenian heritage, even if in some cases such a comment was brief. Admittedly, most of the essays take up some kind of 'evolutionary' theme. However, the term 'evolutionary' is so broad that it can (almost) cover everything nowadays. To give Hahn his due, his essay does provide an intelligent discussion – briefly mentioning Veblen – of the 'evolutionary' legacy.

Third, there are several underdeveloped insights concerning both Veblen's work and its evolutionary legacy. If we extract some of these insights then we have elements of an agenda for evolutionary economics in the twenty-first century. The remainder of this review is devoted to a brief discussion of these issues.

For example, both Hahn and Metcalfe touch on, but do not develop, one of the key questions of modern evolutionary theory. This is the extent to which Darwinian principles of variation, replication and selection apply to complex systems in general, and not simply Earthly organisms alone. This idea of 'universal Darwinism' has been developed by Donald Campbell (1965), Richard Dawkins (1983), Daniel Dennett (1995), David Hull, Henry Plotkin (1994), Lee Smolin, Gary Cziko and others. Without referencing this literature, Hahn hints at this issue and seems to acknowledge universal Darwinism as a possibility. He then suggests that such a broad-brush Darwinian theory might not itself explain very much.

This raises a second question, which is entirely undeveloped in this volume and elsewhere. The fact that universal Darwinism does not explain very much may not rule it out as an important theory. Indeed, we may require a multi-level theory, with broad Darwinian principles at some level and more detailed and particularistic theories at another. On reflection, even neoclassical economics works like this. In particular the concept of rationality tells us specifically very little about human behaviour. Nevertheless, within neoclassical economics, the concept of rationality acts as an organising framework to which more specific auxiliary hypotheses are added. I am convinced that evolutionary thinking in economics may also have to be organised with multiple levels of theory, consistent with each other but varying in their degree of generality or specificity (Hodgson, 2001).

A particular issue involved here arises when Metcalfe briefly discusses the concept of evolutionary fitness in his paper. He writes: 'Fitness is caused, not causal; it is the outcome, not the explanation of selection' (p. 200). I have three brief observations on this remark. First, philosophers of biology have had great difficulty in pinning down the concept of fitness, and some would see it as a potential rather than an outcome (Mills & Beatty, 1979). Second, if fitness is the outcome, then this leaves vacant the explanation of selection and the identification of selection criteria. Third, it may be that the answers to these questions can only be completed at a more specific level, involving the discussion of specific types of mechanism and structure. It is only in such a specific context that fitness can attain an adequate meaning. At the universal level we may have no more success in pinning down the concept of fitness than neoclassical economists have had in pinning down their general notion of rationality. (Pagano's essay in this volume is apposite here.) Accordingly, both Hahn and Metcalfe point to, but do not articulate, the question of the necessity and coexistence of different levels of theory.

Another underdeveloped question is posed in Louçã's paper. There is a dramatic contrast between the bold title of his paper ('is capitalism doomed?') and the relatively simple two-sector models that are its content. Again this raises unarticulated queries concerning the role and limits of models in theoretical and policy analysis. It was Joseph Schumpeter (1954, p. 1171) who criticised the 'Ricardian Vice' of 'piling a heavy load of practical conclusions upon a tenuous groundwork'. Those evolutionary modellers who are keen on describing everything evolutionary as 'Schumpeterian' – even if the ideas in question have little connection with those of Schumpeter himself – might take heed of Schumpeter's own words.

My final observation is that this book is only partly successful in addressing 'the legacy of Thorstein Veblen' one hundred years on. Veblen's own writing, despite its lack of system and structure, worked simultaneously on several levels. This book touches on several important Veblenian themes and Perlman notably tries to explain their subsequent neglect. But the volume does not fully come to grips with the Veblenian legacy. In my view it is the contribution of Veblen as a philosopher and social theorist that is widely misunderstood and that has suffered from the greatest unwarranted neglect. This volume does only a little to rectify this particular deficiency.

Nevertheless, despite its limitations, this interesting and stimulating volume will help to keep the explication of the Veblenian legacy on the agenda. It contains some excellent essays and offers much food for thought.

REFERENCES

Campbell, D. T. (1965). Variation, Selection and Retention in Sociocultural Evolution. In: H. R. Barringer, G. I. Blanksten & R. W. Mack (Eds), *Social Change in Developing Areas: A Reinterpretation of Evolutionary Theory* (pp. 19–49). Cambridge, MA: Schenkman. Reprinted in *General Systems, 14,* 1969, 69–85 and in G. M. Hodgson (Ed.) (1998), *The Foundations of Evolutionary Economics: 1890–1973,* 2 vols, International Library of Critical Writings in Economics. Cheltenham, Edward Elgar.

Dawkins, R. (1983). Universal Darwinism. In: D. S. Bendall (Ed.), *Evolution from Molecules to Man* (pp. 403–425). Cambridge: Cambridge University Press.

Dennett, D. C. (1995). *Darwin's Dangerous Idea: Evolution and the Meanings of Life.* London: Allen Lane.

Foss, N. J. (1998). The Competence-Based Approach: Veblenian Ideas in the Modern Theory of the Firm. *Cambridge Journal of Economics, 22*(4), July, 479–495.

Hodgson, G. M. (2001). *How Economics Forgot History: The Problem of Historical Specificity in Social Science.* London and New York: Routledge.

Mills, S., & Beatty, J. (1979). The Propensity Interpretation of Fitness. *Philosophy of Science, 46*(2), 263–286. Reprinted in E. Sober (Ed.) (1984), *Conceptual Issues in Evolutionary Biology: An Anthology* Cambridge, MA: MIT Press.

Plotkin, H. C. (1994). *Darwin Machines and the Nature of Knowledge: Concerning Adaptations, Instinct and the Evolution of Intelligence.* Harmondsworth: Penguin.

Schumpeter, J. A. (1954). *History of Economic Analysis.* New York: Oxford University Press.

JOAN ROBINSON REVISITED

Vivian C. Walsh

The Economics of Joan Robinson, edited by Maria Cristina Marcuzzo, Luigi L. Pasinetti, and Alessandro Roncaglia. New York, Routledge, 1996, hardcover pp. 370.

Joan Robinson, A Bio-Bibliography, James Ciccarelli and Julianne Ciccarelli. Westport, Connecticut, Greenwood Press, 1996, hardcover, pp. xix, 179.

Of the two volumes that are the concern of this article, the book edited by Marcuzzo, Pasinetti and Roncaglia (hereafter cited as MPR) offers no less than twenty six chapters on a wide range of aspects of Joan Robinson's work. The level of difficulty naturally varies from topic to topic; nevertheless, consistent with her life-long preference, the explicit use of mathematics has been kept to a minimum. This is a book which those seriously interested in Joan Robinson's work will not want to be without. The second of the two volumes, by James Ciccarelli and Julianne Ciccarelli (hereafter cited as C&C), is a slim volume, much lighter in tone. It should be informative and useful to anyone interested in a brief introduction to Robinson's life and work. Both volumes offer versions of the well-known bibliography assembled by Maria Cristina Marcuzzo. The version printed in MPR is the fifth version; on the other hand, C&C offer a version which they have annotated, as well as an annotated selected bibliography of works *about* Joan Robinson – both useful features to all but specialist Robinson scholars.

Research in the History of Economic Thought and Methodology, Volume 20-A, pages 165–193.
© 2002 Published by Elsevier Science Ltd.
ISBN: 0-7623-0847-8

I. THE HERITAGE OF MARSHALL

Joan Robinson's first book, which she was to disown in her later years, was written under the influence of those to whom she was close in the Cambridge of the late twenties and early thirties, notably Richard Kahn, John Maynard Keynes, and Piero Sraffa. In the first chapter of MPR, Christina Marcuzzo brings to vivid life the rather hot-house atmosphere in which this all took place, starting with Kahn lunching with Joan and Austin Robinson, reporting "an interesting concept, which was later christened by Austin Robinson 'marginal revenue'" (MPR, p. 18). A firm which faced a downward sloping marginal revenue curve would later be called by Joan an imperfect competitor. Marcuzzo notes that "[t]he starting point of *The Economics of Imperfect Competition* is Sraffa's proposal – later dismissed by him – "to re-write the theory of value, starting from the conception of the firm as a monopolist" (*Ibid.*, citing Robinson, 1969, p. 6). The role of Sraffa, isolated, 'feared and admired, rather than actually understood'" (Marcuzzo, 1998, p. 1) looms in the background. It is discussed in her recent paper (Marcuzzo, 1998).

What these young people up at Cambridge in the early 1930s had *in common*, was rebellion against the father figure of Alfred Marshall. He simply *was* orthodox economics to them. Or so they believed. But there is a paradox here which had profound implications for Joan Robinson's development. The young people were learning 'Marshall' from his successor, Arthur Cecil Pigou, and Pigou had solidified what was *worst* in Marshall into a cut and dried static theory. What was best – Marshall's vestiges of the original classics and his vivid sense of an economy moving through real-time – Pigou had simply eliminated. As we shall see, Joan kept coming back to some of Marshall's ideas all her life. I think the deepest reason why she rejected *Imperfect Competition* later it is that it is mostly *Pigou.*

In this atmosphere of Cambridge ferment, Joan wrote *The Economics of Imperfect Competition* (1933). Marcuzzo shows the role of the beginnings of more than 50 years of correspondence between Joan and Richard Kahn: "[t]he exchanges with Kahn were pressing and demanding, because Kahn checked every single passage, as he did with Keynes" (MPR, pp. 17–18). It is no exaggeration to describe this as "a lasting emotional and intellectual partnership" (MPR, pp. 17–18).

It is important to remember that in the context of the orthodox (or 'neo-classical') economics of its day, *Imperfect Competition* was progressive. It mounted a sustained critique of the *realism* of the orthodox theory of the distribution of income. Every economic agent was supposed to get a return equal to the money value of that agent's marginal contribution to output – it's 'marginal product'. She showed that this would not occur in the highly imperfect kinds of competition which alone could be found in the real world. There would, for example, be what she called monopsonistic exploitation of labor. But one does not have far to seek for reasons for her later dissatisfaction with this. To begin with, it leaves the marginal productivity theory intact – as a *theory* of what would happen in a perfectly competitive model. Later she would argue that the theory was incoherent *irrespective* of simple imperfections of competition. (But not, as Geoff Harcourt pointed out (MPR, p. 321), till *much* later!) And then the only concept of 'exploitation' which the book could identify paled beside the exploitation concepts to be derived from her later study of Marx. And, as already noted, there is the pervasive, static *Pigovian* character of the book.

One must never forget that her life-long, growing insistence that economic theory must encompass real time processes is not without echoes in Marshall: "The strength of Marshall's method, mirrored in much of Robinson's work, is that it highlights those partial and ultimately inconsistent equilibria which may be the nearest we can come to depicting certain aspects of real life ... There would appear to be a terrain from which Marshall is extremely difficult to dislodge" (Gram & Walsh, 1983, p. 520). Even in her last years she still respected some aspects of Marshall's economics – however much his nonconformist moralizing got her goat! Pigou she simply dismissed, blaming him for what she called her wrong turning: "Pigou emptied history out of Marshall and reduced the analysis to a two-dimensional scheme" (CEP, pp. 5, 54).[1]

It is unfortunate that this vital distinction between Marshall and Pigou does not surface in Marcuzzo's chapter (MPR, pp. 11–35). In their Introduction, however, she and the other editors do refer to "the critiques of Pigou's version of the Marshallian theory of value and the firm" (MPR, p. 2), which took place in Cambridge. And Marco Dardi, in Chapter 2, notes that "[t]o Marshall and Keynes alike, 'short-period' meant a situation of partial equilibrium, i.e. a state of things in which certain agents do what they believe to be their best in the given circumstances" (MPR, p. 30). This is pure Marshall, without a trace of Pigou, and in agreement with Joan's later appraisal, that Keynes "started from a Marshallian short-period" (CEP, pp. 4, 96).

A number of people have wondered why Keynes showed little interest in Joan's attack on perfect competition. The answer, surely, is that he never took what came to be the formal concept of perfect competition seriously. Even if by perfect competition we just mean price-taking behavior, then as Dardi points out "there is no possible relationship with Marshall's theory of competitive markets, as Keynes himself and others in Cambridge ... knew all too well" (MPR, pp. 31–32). A *real-world* 'competitive' market, which was what Marshall wrote about, was "a system of 'conditional' or 'provisional monopolies', admission to which costs time and resources because firms have to fight to conquer and defend their own market niches" (MPR, p. 32). As Dardi insists, this implies that in Marshall "each producer faces a downward sloping particular demand curve" (*Ibid.*).

Joan, alas, had learned what she mistakenly believed to be Marshallian economics from Pigou. And, as Brian Loasby has argued, Pigou had translated Marshall "into the language of static perfect competition . . . if any single action led to the overthrow of the Marshallian system, it was Pigou's establishment of the representative firm as the central instrument of analysis" (Loasby, 1991, p. 38). Dardi needed only to bring Pigou explicitly into his argument, and the picture would be complete in essentials.

In the final Chapter of Part I of MPR, Nicolo De Vecci considers Joseph Schumpeter's review of *Imperfect Competition*, and quotes Schumpeter's perceptive comment that "Marshall was bent on salvaging every bit of real life he could possibly leave in" (Schumpeter, 1954, p. 975, cited MPR, p. 40). De Vecci observes that Schumpeter "notes the static character of her theory and makes veiled hints about the doubt – which later he was to reinforce – about compatibility between the analytical procedure adopted by Joan Robinson and that of Marshall" (MPR, p. 37). Thus Joan's dehydration of Marshall is again discussed by De Vecci, without bringing in Pigou.

On the other hand De Vecci does endorse a claim concerning Joan's theoretical approach in *Imperfect Competition* which goes well *beyond* anything she could have picked up from Pigou. He claims that "she sets herself the objective of formulating an axiomatic theory" (MPR, 39) and sites Loasby, who had observed that "Joan Robinson's first book gave a powerful impulse towards the development of formalism which has been so characteristic of the last 50 years, and which she came to regard with such dismay" (Loasby, 1991, p. 41, cited in MPR, p. 48).

Surely a slight exaggeration? Cambridge as a whole, in Joan's generation, had ignored the general equilibrium theory developing in Europe from the work of Léon Walras and Vilfredo Pareto. Then when *neo*-Walrasian theory developed in America out of the axiomatic work of Kenneth Arrow and Gérard Debreu, the roots were in Europe, notably with the formalist school of mathematics, and not in the Cambridge of the 1930s. When Cambridge *did* challenge the Americans, it was over capital theory – and of course Joan was a major player.

The Ciccarellis, in their treatment of Joan's early work, stress the fact that *Imperfect Competition* was "what mainstream economists regard as her magnum opus" (C&C, p. 6). This is true, and hardly surprising: it is the last major work of Joan's which the neoclassical establishment can afford to tell students about, without risking their asking the awkward questions.

II. IN THE TRADITION OF KEYNES

The essential idea of Keynes' *General Theory of Employment, Interest and Money* (1936) is that a market economy can experience massive unemployment due to a vast deficiency of effective demand, and that there is no inherent mechanism which will necessarily act to bring the economy up to full employment if it is left to its own devices. It will be evident that, especially during the great depression, this was a highly explosive idea. Yet Keynes saw himself as conservative: after all, he was trying to save capitalism, and believed it could be done. But he was sure that it could *not* be done without radical surgery. Joan agreed with Keynes' diagnosis of what was wrong, and what (as a minimum) must be done to avert calamitous social cost. She drew more left-wing conclusions from all this, of course, than he did.

Unfortunately, the theoretical argument on which Keynes depended for his correct conclusions was deeply flawed. One can distinguish at least two major problems – which is not to deny that these problems are interconnected. Perhaps the most fundamental was that Keynes, who had no theory of the reproduction of capital, retained and used in his arguments concepts from neoclassical economics which required that aggregate 'capital' be a factor of production – indeed, required the whole marginal productivity theory of the distribution of income. The second problem concerned the construction of a satisfactory distinction between long and short periods. Keynes needed to make claims about the behavior of an economy over extended stretches of time – that drastic unemployment might not go away. Did this require a long-period argument? What are the limits of the short period? This question was "tackled jointly by Richard Kahn and Joan Robinson in the early 1930s" (MPR, p. 16).

From a short-period point of view, the level of output and employment is a matter of aggregate demand (the stock of capital goods is assumed fixed) and this is the terrain of the *General Theory*. But from the point of view of the long period, one needs to bring in the conditions which govern the level and nature of the reproduction of the various capital goods, changes in technique, and problems concerning how to measure the stock of capital goods. Joan often said that her life's work was the generalization of the General Theory – its expansion to cover the problems that arise in a long-period context.

Given the nature of Keynes' work, and the demons conjured up by some of its implications, it was inevitable that the orthodox economics profession, with an eye to the needs of their political masters, would seek (and find) aid and comfort in the unquestionably neoclassical underpinnings of the *General Theory*. Thus were born what Joan always referred to, in conversation, in lectures, and in learned journals, as the bastard Keynesians. It is a mistake to see them as one homogeneous group: Jan Kregel, in the first chapter of this part, does us a service by following the development of what he calls Keynes' "Bastard Progeny" (MPR, p. 53) through five generations – a genealogical tour de force which readers must experience in the original.

It is equally mistaken to see those who sought, like Joan, to free the essential idea of the *General Theory* from its neoclassical setting as a homogeneous group, often labeled post-Keynesians. They tended to diverge over a number of issues, notably over the respective roles to be assigned to long-period forces and to short-period uncertainty. These theorists, who began as legitimate descendants of Keynes (in Joan's eyes), but who drifted into some emphasis which she regarded as incorrect, are what Kregel calls the "prodigal sons" (MPR, pp. 64–65).

By 1937, as Kregel notes, only one year after the publication of the *General Theory*, work was being done which professed to be Keynesian, but whose policy conclusions were considerably watered down. Keynes, it was conceded, "might have some practical application in the 'short period', in the 'long run' the forces of competition would be fully operative and lead to the full utilization of resources." (MPR, p. 53). Bastard Keynesianism had already been born! The unemployed could stop having fantasies of revolt as their children got TB – everything would soon be fine. Kregel rightly insists that "[t]his is a *possible* interpretation of Keynes' theory" (*Ibid.*, emphasis added). Keynes, it must be realized, was Jeckyl and Hyde – he was partly true to himself, but also partly the first bastard Keynesian. Remarkably, however, as Kregel points out, Joan had seen this disastrous possible interpretation of the *General Theory* at once. It was one that "she had already identified while working through the proofs of the *General Theory* (see Robinson, 1937) and that was to become her major post-war preoccupation (see "The Generalization of the General Theory" reprinted in Robinson, 1952)" (*Ibid.*). This led naturally to her great work on the long-period theory of reproduction, *The Accumulation of Capital* (Robinson, 1956) and, ultimately, to the controversy concerning the nature of capital.

Pierangelo Garegnani considers a very early article (Robinson, 1936) in which he finds "a first attempt at what was to become Joan Robinson's central commitment in the rest of her life: to develop a long-period theory of aggregate activity and labour employment" (MPR, p. 67). Despite its deficiencies, including a hitherto unnoticed flaw in her argument which Garegnani exposes carefully, he believes that the article has "elements of considerable interest" (*Ibid.*). To begin with, the article shows "how natural it was for her, involved though she was with the ideas of the *General Theory*, to leave aside the [Keynesian] elements of expectations and uncertainty when approaching a theory of . . . the process of accumulation . . . [and] to base such a long-period theory on the method . . . [of] 'long-period' positions'" (MPR, p. 70). Secondly, "the article brings clearly into light the inconsistency between the premises of marginal theory and any conclusions about long-period labour unemployment" (*Ibid.*). Thirdly, "it brings into clear light how at the centre of the above incompatibility between long-period labour unemployment and marginal theory there lies the theory of distribution, and in particular the assumed long-period inverse relation between the interest rate and capital intensity" (MPR, p. 71). Thus her early article foreshadows how important the critique of the marginal theory of distribution, and its notion of capital, will prove to be, and points toward her revival of the classical, surplus theory, where capital is seen in a wholly different way. As Garegnani concludes, "the possibility of limits of aggregate demand to aggregate output in the long period, as well as in the short one, follows in an altogether natural way within the classical approach to distribution" (*Ibid.*).

Massimo Pivetti focuses on the development of Joan's ideas on the rate of interest "the subject at the very centre of Keynes' 'long struggle' to escape from traditional ways of thinking" (MPR, p. 75). Noting that in 1930 Keynes had still accepted the concept of a 'natural' rate of interest, Pivetti observes that belief in such a 'natural' rate determined by real forces implies "skepticism that monetary policy can *persistently* affect real interest rates" (*Ibid.*, emphasis in original). Here Keynes' marginal productivity theory of capital was a fatal albatross around his neck. The actions of savers, plus the marginal productivity of 'capital', would "ultimately make long-term real interest rates beyond the reach of policy" (*Ibid.*). Which, of course, was fatal to Keynes' need to be able to use monetary policy to stimulate investment and employment. It is thus hardly surprising that Keynes had changed his view on interest by the *General Theory* (1936).

So now we get Keynes' "new concept of interest as a conventional monetary phenomenon – 'determined from outside the system of production', as Sraffa was later to put it (1960, p. 33)" (MPR, p. 76). Pivetti stresses that this new concept of interest as a monetary phenomenon susceptible to policy determination by the authorities "was fully endorsed after his death by his chief pupils: Richard Kahn and, indeed, Joan Robinson" (MPR, p. 77). Keynes thus wanted to claim that the rate of interest depended on liquidity preference (the desire to hold money) and *not* upon the marginal productivity of capital. But, as already noted, he was unable to free himself from the whole marginal productivity theory of distribution. And with this virus infecting his system, how could he avoid its having an effect on his rate of interest?

Joan and Sraffa were later to demolish the marginal productivity theory, but she was not quite out of the wood concerning the interpretation of interest. She was open to the problems facing "anyone who maintains that the normal rate of profit is governed by the rate of capital accumulation, given the propensity to save. Indeed, with a normal profitability of capital determined in this way, the monetary authorities would be deprived of any substantial power [over the rate of interest]" (MPR, p. 78). As Pivetti points out, by 1979 "she explicitly criticizes as 'unnatural' the concept of the rate of interest as an independently determined monetary phenomenon that governs the rate of profit: "Over the long run", she writes, reversing Keynes' point of view, "the interest that rentiers can exact is dominated by the profits that entrepreneurs can earn, not the other way round" (1979, p. xxii)" (MPR, p. 79).

Giangiacomo Nardozzi develops further the theme of Joan's views on interest. He remarks that Keynes' theory of interest as a highly conventional phenomenon is "not among the topics most dealt with" (MPR, p. 81) by Richard Kahn or Joan Robinson. But then, as he notes, Keynes' point of view had been that of an active participant in the financial markets, while Joan "did not attach much importance to the financial aspects of the economy and to financial markets. She was mostly concerned with the aim of providing a long-period theory, that is, a growth theory, to complete Keynes' General Theory" (MPR, p. 84). For Nardozzi it is the rate of interest which would rule in a long-period position which Joan saw as strongly influenced by real forces, especially if we suppose (what is unlikely) that the long-period position were one of full employment. However, he adds that she "was ready to accept that real forces can also exert their influence on expectations even if the economy is far from full employment" (MPR, p. 85).

Nardozzi does not see Joan's writings on interest as giving any aid and comfort to today's apostles of laissez-faire. On the contrary, reading her "helps to point out ... a fundamental contradiction of present economic policy in Europe" (*Ibid.*) (He is writing at the "end of 1993" (MPR, p. 83). Policymakers in Europe, he points out, "did not seem to be conscious of the strength they were given by the recession in their confrontation with financial markets. Instead of taking advantage of recession and high rates of unemployment that deprived financial markets of arguments to resist a reduction in real interest rates, economic policymakers behave as if economies were already at full employment" (MPR, p. 86).

Questions of international economics are taken up by Annamaria Simonazzi, who notes that "[t]he relationship between the external equilibrium and the objective of a high level of employment is the leitmotiv in Joan Robinson's contributions to international economics" (MPR, p. 88). She was one of the first theorists to extend Keynes' ideas into the context of an open economy. Her famous papers on 'The Foreign Exchanges' and 'Beggar-My-Neighbor Remedies for Unemployment' (CEP, pp. 4, 212–240) "Were written while Keynes' *General Theory* was going through the press" (CEP, pp. 4, 174). As Harvey Gram and I noted, "Keynes read her drafts and she cut out anything which she could not persuade him was correct – these papers clearly represent the first impact of Keynesian thought in their field" (Gram & Walsh, 1983, p. 542).

Simonazzi describes with clarity and precision the reasons why Joan "subscribed to Keynes' plea for a policy of adjustable exchange rates designed to preserve national monetary independence and to avoid the need for deflation in the face of persistent external deficits" (MPR, p. 91). She then argues that the experience with the European Monetary System in the 1980s had many features in common with the interwar situation, so that "it is worth examining just how relevant Joan Robinson's analysis and proposals prompted by that experience may still be today" (MPR, p. 91). She shows how, under the neo-liberal dogma of price stability as the only legitimate policy goal, "the exchange rate has its role as an instrument for price stability" (*Ibid.*). She argues that the policies pursued "have resulted in a deflationary bias for the system as a whole and are largely responsible for the poor employment and growth record of Europe in the 1980s" (*Ibid.*). She notes that, "as Joan Robinson had already pointed out, when all countries are pursuing the same disinflationary policy, as in our case by pegging the exchange rate to the DM, individual attempts to reduce relative prices can lead only to a fall in the global demand" (MPR, p. 94. Compare Halevi & Fontaine, 1998).

It is no criticism of Simonazzi that her topic does not allow her to discuss the fact that "Joan Robinson made significant contributions to foreign trade theory at each stage of her work. She begins with the re-appraisal and critique of conventional neoclassical trade theory, in the light of Keynes, and ends with a post-Sraffian critique of the neoclassical interpretation of Ricardo's foreign trade theory" (Gram & Walsh, 1983, p. 541. See further, pp. 542–544).

The Ciccarellis briefly consider bastard Keynesianism, remarking that "[t]he Neoclassical tenet of equilibrium made for elegant mathematical models but shoddy economics in Robinson's view. Furthermore, the concept of general equilibrium was an intellectual affront to the Keynesian breakthrough. "The key insight of Keynes is that an unregulated economy contains no dynamic process that would tend, if left alone, to get it into a position of general equilibrium" (Gram & Walsh, 1983, p. 521). To argue otherwise was, in Robinson's opinion, a bastardization of Keynesian thought" (C&C, p. 14). Without a doubt, one of the most typical recurrent characteristics of bastard Keynesianism consisted in emptying the real time out of Keynes and then trying to capture him in snapshots of general equilibrium, in progressively more abstract and unreal models. Thus, as Gram and I noted, "an element of Marshall's thought survives in all of Robinson's later work; namely, the idea of a short-period equilibrium containing inherent contradictions, as distinct from the momentary multi-market equilibrium of Walras" (Gram & Walsh, 1983, p. 521).

III. FOLLOWING MARX, KALECKI AND SRAFFA

Despite the above title, Kalecki is discussed in Part III of MPR by only one author. Isolated references to his work are scattered through the rest of the book, but for some reflections on Kalecki's role in Joan's life and thought the reader must go to Chapter 26, by Geoffrey Harcourt. The Ciccarellis, on the other hand, despite the brevity of their Biographical Sketch, do offer a short account of Kalecki's role. They also include references to his influence in their annotations to the Marcuzzo bibliography, and in their useful select listing of works about Joan Robinson.

No one could be close to Joan without becoming aware that Kalecki had had a profound influence on her, which ripened as she grew old. He had played a major role in stimulating her interest in Marx: as Geoff Harcourt observes, "a sea change occurs in Joan Robinson's thought as Karl Marx comes over the horizon . . . with the beginning of her friendship with Michal Kalecki. This led to the making of her *Essay on Marxian Economics* [1942]" (MPR, p. 321).

Geoff Harcourt stresses that "though there was mutual and long-sustained interaction between these two great friends, causation did, most of the time, run more *from* Kalecki *to* Joan Robinson than the other way around. Increasingly, I believe, her own mode of thought and analysis were moulded by her absorption of Kalecki's approach, to the propagation of which she lent her very considerable powers of exposition" (MPR, p. 318, emphasis in original). And in turn she always stressed Kalecki's debt to Marx, something which set him apart from Keynes. In 1971 she wrote: "Kalecki's analytical system was based on Marx's schema of reproduction. He supplied the Marxists with a coherent solution to 'the problem of the realization of surplus value' – that is, the determination of effective demand" (CEP, pp. IV, 89). She ended "I learned far more, over 35 years, from the arguments with Kalecki that I lost than from those that I won" (CEP, pp. IV, 91).

As time went on she saw that Keynes' ideas were proving fatally easy for the neoclassical profession to absorb and neutralize because of his deep rooted neo-classical foundations. She was having to fight bastard Keynesians on every side. Kalecki, on the contrary, had completely escaped neoclassical theory and gone straight to Marx and Rosa Luxemburg. Keynes, mired in marginal productivity theory, had been in no position to generate a theory of the long-period repro-duction of capital, and he shied away from a treatment of demand deficiency based on an analysis of the division of national income between workers and capitalists. Kalecki, on the other hand, went straight to concepts of economic class. As she noted: "The workers spend what they get and the capitalists get what they spend. (The workers spend their wages individually; the capitalists receive *what they spend as a class*." (CEP, pp. IV, 89, emphasis added).

Joan sometimes felt that Kalecki did not do complete justice to Rosa Luxemburg (CEP, pp. IV, 91), although fully alert to what she believed to be Luxemburg's analytic errors. But it was Kalecki who had led her to Luxemburg's work, and from them both she saw the nature of the realization problem. Ever after she would regard the successful complete realization of the surplus in a dynamic real world economy as little less than a miracle. From this, of course, came some of her growing skepticism about long-period equilibria. But as Pierangelo Garegnani and others have repeatedly pointed out, the long-period positions toward which economies tend to gravitate in classical theory, are characterized by a uniform rate of profit *not* by a demand and supply equilibrium at full employment. Thus deficiency of effective demand can be fitted into classical long-period theory (Garegnani, [1978] 1983, pp. 21–69, [1979] 1983, pp. 72–78; MPR pp. 67–74).

The Ciccarellis quote Christina Marcuzzo's comment that Kalecki's analysis "provided not only a short period theory of distribution, according to which the share of wages in the value of output is determined by the degree of monopoly, but also laid the basis for a long run theory of distribution. According to the latter, the distributive shares are determined by the rate of investment and the propensity to consume of each class" (Marcuzzo, 1985, p. 24 cited from C&C, p. 18). As the Ciccarellis conclude, "[I]n *The Accumulation of Capital*, Robinson's thinking – as shaped by Marshall, Keynes, Marx, and Kalecki – came together to form a new school of economic thought . . . Robinson's book gave cohesion to a movement that had lacked a center, and economists who take exception to orthodox analysis have been grateful ever since" (C&C, p. 18).

The discussion of Marx in MPR Part 3 is undertaken by Mario Lippi, who declares he has a "preference for Joan Robinson as an interpreter of Marx" (MPR, p. 101). He argues that her "attentive and detailed reading takes us a long way from the image of Marx as an intermediate step between David Ricardo and Piero Sraffa that we get from some neo-Ricardian interpretations" (*Ibid.*). Lippi defends Joan's treatment of labor values, unlike Geoff Harcourt, who remarks later in the book that she "always had a blind spot about what the labour theory of value [LTV] really entailed . . . Basically, she insisted on seeing the LTV as a theory of relative prices rather than as a portmanteau term for Marx's explanation of the origin of profits in capitalism" (MPR, p. 322).

Thus it is fair to say that "Lippi represents the view that the labor theory is not necessary for Marxian analysis" (Commendatori, 2000, p. 116). This minimalist view, of course, has quite a long ancestry. It perhaps reached its peak in Steedman (1976). Commenting in a review on Steedman's claim that, on the plane of formal analysis, labor values add nothing, Joan characteristically observed that "[t]he present reviewer pointed this out in 1942" (CEP, pp. V, 276).

It should be observed here that Joan Robinson, like other important participants in the twentieth century revival of classical theory, had been somewhat infected by the logical positivism of the period (Walsh, 1996, pp. 256–262). In her conversation she frequently showed a reluctance to be led into what she regarded as speculative or value-laden issues. On the other hand, there *were* sound reasons for adopting a minimalist austerity in the period when the core concepts of a revived classical theory were being forged and tempered. (Walsh, 2000).

In the review of Steedman just cited, Joan remarked that "[p]rices of production correspond to Marshallian normal long-run prices, with a uniform rate of profit, but not to the Walrasian supply and demand prices which appear in modern textbooks" (CEP, pp. V, 275). Now Fernando Vianello discusses her views on normal prices in some of her early work, as she reacted to Sraffa (1960). He argues that she had "good reason to associate Marx's price of production (and, indeed, Smith's natural price), with Marshall's 'normal long-run supply price' " (MPR, p. 113). I think these prices were a genuinely classical residue which remained in Marshall as part of his concept of the long period (Walsh, 1992, pp. 26–27). Thus in reading Marshall she would have picked up some classical influence, later to flower.

Developing the theme of the influence on her of Piero Sraffa, Giorgio Gilibert offers a brief comparison of uses of a 'corn model' by Joan and by Sraffa, indicating how one can arrive at Sraffa's standard system by this route. He argues that Joan's well known ambivalence about the standard commodity was linked to her growing feeling that Sraffa's model was too pure for her dominant purpose of "throwing light on the real working of capitalism" (MPR, p. 128). It should be noted that uncertainty concerning the interpretation of the standard commodity has persisted until recently (See Kurz & Salvadori, 1995, pp. 116–121, 1998b, pp. 123–147).

IV. GROWTH, DEVELOPMENT, AND DYNAMICS

As Siro Lombardini observes, "[n]ew tools were provided by Joan Robinson's *The Accumulation of Capital* to analyze the factors accounting for growth"

(MPR, p. 137), He adds that "[t]o analyze how the thriftiness, capital and labour coefficients affect growth, we need to explore all possible equilibrium paths" (MPR, p. 139). In fact Joan considered an extensive taxonomy of cases, both in the *Accumulation* and in other works. As Harvey Gram and I suggested, "a Model of Accumulation" (Robinson, 1962, pp. 22–87) is particularly useful "because it specifies a list of six determinants of equilibrium which she regards as largely independent of each other; namely: (1) technical conditions, (2) investment policy, (3) thriftiness conditions, (4) competitive conditions, (5) the wage bargain, and (6) financial conditions" (Gram & Walsh, 1983, p. 532). Lombardini discusses a variety of evolutionary paths, limping golden ages, leaden ages, galloping platinum ages and creeping platinum ages. His account observes the important distinction between *classical* unemployment and Keynesian, or demand deficiency, unemployment.

Salvatore Biasco carries the investigation further, exploring "some insights into Joan Robinson's theory of economic growth by comparing specific features of various economies, each in a state of long-run equilibrium at different points on a given spectrum of techniques ... The range of techniques is assumed to permit re-switches in profitability [and the] focus is on the relative mechanization of golden age economies" (MPR, p. 149). This paper will appeal to readers who have worked on questions which concern the degree of mechanization in an economy. Such readers should note also the paper by Ferdinando Meacci which is to be found in part V (MPR, pp. 249–262).

Roberto Scazzieri supports the sensible view that Joan Robinson never believed in more than "the *logical* possibility of steady accumulation and expansion" (MPR, p. 178, emphasis in original) in a capitalist economy (compare Gram & Walsh, 1983, pp. 532–536). He notes that, despite her well known skepticism towards the steady state, she did not offer "an explicit, theoretical consideration of structural economic dynamics" (MPR, p. 174). He refers the reader to Luigi Pasinetti's celebrated work (Pasinetti, 1981). He is right, however, to claim as useful to the development of some subsequent models of structural dynamics her view that such investigations can be carried out "by considering the relationship between broad, overall movements of the economy ... rather than detailed transformations of the economic structure" (MPR, p. 183). In this he sees the influence of Keynes, and cites her belief in the possibility of showing with a highly simplified model "the main movements that may be expected to occur in reality, while ruling out innumerable detailed complications" (Robinson, 1965 [1956], pp. 63–64. Cited in MPR, p. 183). As he notes, this perspective is remarkably different from much more recent modeling, for example that of Pasinetti already referred to.

Scazzieri raises the question of the relationships between Joan's work and that of Adolph Lowe and the later John Hicks. On Lowe, he feels that her work on dynamics, in terms of a simplified model of the main movements "shifts economic theory away from the theoretical reconstruction of actual processes and turns it into an exercise in instrumental inference, which is, using Adolph Lowe's words, an attempt 'to discover the particular set of causes that are suitable for the realization of some postulated effect' (Lowe, 1965, p. 264)" (MPR, pp. 183–184). On the later work of John Hicks, however, he seems to see less possibility of fruitful interconnection with Joan: given her views, "the steady state cannot be a reference path in the study of transitions (or 'traverses')" (MPR, p. 181). For all this, however, some students of the work of Hicks and Lowe on traverse have pointed out interesting influences originating with Joan Robinson.

Thus, Joseph Halevi and Peter Kriesler have noted that in her *Accumulation* she "formulated the first (smooth) traverse entirely on the basis of the structural linkages between labour and capital equipment" (Halevi & Kriesler, 1992, pp. 229–230). They conclude that "[i]t would be difficult to deny that, on the analytical plane, Hicks' *Capital and Growth* (1965) has been profoundly influenced by the questions asked by Joan Robinson in her *Accumulation of Capital* and in her subsequent criticisms of neo-Classical theory" (*Ibid.*). Lowe then took the analysis of traverse further. In Lowe, "the macroeconomic goal is socially and institutionally determined, and it is used to gauge the consistency of atomistic behavior. This returns us to Joan Robinson's state of bliss [where all the labor force is absorbed into the economy] which both she and Lowe show cannot be reached by unguided individualistic behavior ... Without a visible hand, the invisible hand is likely to guide us on to the wrong path; this is perhaps the most important conclusion from the analysis of the traverse" (Halevi & Kriesler, 1992, p. 233).

Paulo Varri takes up the relationship between Joan's lifelong effort to provide an analysis of the long run compatible with Keynes, and the very similar work of Roy Harrod, who was well aware of the "internal contradictions of static analysis" (MPR, p. 188) and believed that the *General Theory* "from this point of view, was as open to criticism as was traditional theory" (*Ibid.*).

I remember Joan, in her later years, as kindly disposed towards Harrod, praising him for his early insistence on the absolute necessity for long-period analysis. And she increasingly acknowledged her intellectual debt to him in print. Harrod, alas, was much less generous to her, and Varri is hardly unjust in observing that his remarks on her (and other Cambridge economists) were "in the form of a defense of his own theory and against what he considered misrepresentations of his ideas" (MPR, p. 189). As Varri observes, she naturally agreed with Harrod's view "that long-run equilibrium (if it exists) is unstable" (MPR, 190). But she pounced on his disregard for the role of changes in income distribution, and as Varri notes, her comment on his conservative policy prescriptions, is "of course totally negative" (*Ibid.*). She had characteristically snapped that Harrod's proposals could not be taken "as more than a *jeu d'esprit*, but that does not detract from the interest and importance of his analysis upon its own plane" (Robinson, 1949, p. 85). For all their ideological differences, Joan was (as Varri rightly observes) as "ready to acknowledge her debt to Harrod" (MPR, p. 191) as she was "very proud to recognize that her model of steady accumulation is equivalent to Marx's schemes of expanded reproduction" (*Ibid.*). As he concludes, "Robinson and Harrod were at opposite extremes ideologically, but they shared a common scientific vision that derives directly from Keynes" (MPR, p. 193).

Joan's fascination with Harrod's theoretical ideas has been supported by Joseph Halevi: "Sir Roy Harrod's conception of an imminent disequilibrium between the warranted and the natural growth rates is a strong theory of the breakdown of capitalist investment since it envisages the possibility of a chronic depression. His approach encompasses and reconciles the two main strands of the Marxian debate over the future of capitalism" (Halevi, 1992, p. 266). Having discussed the demand deficiency and disproportionality strands of the issue, Halevi remarks that "Harrodian theory discusses the conditions leading up to a state of disequilibrium. Traverse analysis deals with the actual state of disequilibrium ... From a Marxian point of view the Traverse-based critique of Keynesianism is important because it is structurally grounded" (Halevi, 1992, p. 267). Despite Joan's interest in it, Harrod's method, as Halevi notes "while important for a Marxian theory of crisis, has been sidestepped in most post-Keynesian literature" (Halevi, 1992, p. 273). But, he concludes, "[t]he Hicks and Lowe structural Traverses show that Harrodian disequilibrium cannot be gotten over by means of some kind of flexibilities – whether in production coefficients or in the savings ratio" (Halevi, 1992, p. 287).

Amit Bhaduri, in the last paper of Part IV, lays stress on the relevance of the theory of capital for the analysis of economic growth. He insists that Joan Robinson's critique of neoclassical capital theory had an aspect "less emphasized in the literature, [which] concerns the *structure* of production" (MPR, p. 200, emphasis added). From early on, her "main criticism of neo-classical capital theory was ... that it did not have a coherent macroeconomic theory of the rate of profit" (*Ibid.*). By demonstrating that a higher value of capital per worker can be associated with a higher rate of profit, she destroyed logically "a central idea of neoclassical macroeconomics that the rate of profit is a sort of barometer of the relative scarcity of 'capital as a factor of production'. It is a proposition without any logical foundation outside a one-commodity world" (MPR, pp. 200–201). Bhaduri very properly adds that for "the full impact of this criticism" (MPR, p. 201) to be realized required the subsequent work of Piero Sraffa (1960) and Luigi Pasinetti (1966).

Bhaduri shows how her rejection of orthodox capital theory enabled her to "set up not only an alternative framework, but also a more flexible scheme of analysis" (MPR, pp. 202–203). Her analysis of accumulation was freed from the unreal assumptions of perfect competition, leaving profit share to be determined "by the bargaining power of the contending classes, paralleling Kalecki's idea of the 'degree of monopoly'" (MPR, p. 203). Elements of Harrod's treatment of technical progress, modified to avoid capital-theoretical problems, could be included. Meanwhile, "[i]n most of her writings, she relied on Marx's two departmental scheme for analyzing growth" (Ibid.). She "showed how the Marxist 'crisis of proportionality' was related to the 'crisis of realization', because the historically inherited proportions of sectoral capacities could be out of line with the market-clearing saving-investment flow equilibrium (Bhaduri and Robinson, 1980)" (MPR, p. 204). Above all, perhaps, she brought back into the debate on capital "the importance of the 'structure of capital', i.e. non-malleable capacities given in arbitrary historical proportions at any point of time" (MPR, p. 205).

Here Bhaduri highlights a vital part of what was so deeply significant to Joan about *historical time*. But as he concludes, for the neoclassicals "[i]t was too inconvenient a problem to face openly and still maintain that conventional neoclassical economics has a 'theory' of economic growth. The mainstream profession chose the soft option of pretending that her criticisms never existed!" (*Ibid.*).

V. CAPITAL THEORY AND TECHNICAL PROGRESS

Luigi Pasinetti, in a thoughtful paper, confronts one of the mysteries about Joan Robinson: her attitude towards 'reswitching'. He begins with what cannot be doubted: that for two decades she "relentlessly and consistently" (MPR, p. 209) wrote and spoke against the marginal productivity theory of capital. But he adds that in this critique she "consistently avoided making use of 'reswitching of techniques' arguments. Paradoxically, she anticipated the essence of 'reswitching', at the same time always taking an ambiguous attitude towards it" (*Ibid.*).

The reader will find an excellent summary and appraisal of the reswitching issue, from a present-day classical prospective, in Heinz Kurz and Neri Salvadori (1995). They define reswitching as a "situation in which a technique is cost-minimizing at two disconnected ranges of the rate of profit and not so in between these ranges" (Kurz & Salvadori, 1995, p. 447). As they remark, the implication of this is that "the direction of change of the 'input proportions' cannot be related unambiguously to changes of the so-called factor prices. The central element of the neoclassical explanation of distribution in terms of supply and demand is thus revealed as defective" (*Ibid.*). They show how this destroyed "the whole basis for the neoclassical view of substitution in production" (Kurz & Salvadori, 1995, pp. 447–448. See further, pp. 448–467).

It is thus no trivial issue why Joan was so ambivalent about reswitching. Passinetti's argument as to the explanation is subtle and carefully based on the documentation available when he wrote, and on oral tradition. Pending confirmation from the further study of the Joan Robinson and Sraffa papers, it carries conviction. But the interested reader must peruse it for herself. Pasinetti suggests that Joan had picked up the idea of reswitching from Sraffa, but on the occasions on which she initially presented it in print had treated it as a 'curiosum' – "an unusual, or abnormal, or 'perverse' case" (MPR, p. 215). He adds that: "All this must have infuriated Sraffa" (*Ibid.*) He argues that as a result "Joan Robinson had a bad conscience about the reswitching phenomenon. This is more than sufficient to explain her emotional aversion and hostility to it, especially when the discussions began to show the generality (not the abnormality) of the phenomenon" (*Ibid.*)

I fear it cannot be denied that Joan, and her vacillations over reswitching, gave aid and comfort to the neoclassics, while causing confusion among some of those who were well-meaning towards her. For example, even as late as 1996, the Ciccarellis treat the whole reswitching debate as if it were a special case "akin to the 'Giffen Paradox'" (C&C, p. 16). (Those interested in the fallacy involved in this analogy might see Garegnani, 1990, p. 72).

When the neoclassics were forced to admit defeat in the capital controversy (see Kurz & Salvadori, 1995, pp. 449–451 for sources), they fell back on several different lines of defense. Thus we have already seen the tactic of trivializing the issue, and the sad fact that Joan was of help with this. But the main expedients were two. First, there was a systematic avoidance of any mention of the whole controversy – at *all* levels, the American texts were (and are) silent on it. Meanwhile, secondly, Byzantine theoretical expedients were undertaken to restrict the class of models, which axiomatic neo-Walrasian theory would deal with, to what were called 'regular' economies. These were models where severe assumptions on available techniques prevented phenomena such as reswitching from arising: The dog had been strapped into a muzzle, so that it could not bite, and was being passed off as harmless!

Stefano Zamagni, commenting on Pasinetti's contribution just glanced at above, offers an interesting suggestion. He argues that the capital controversy "was analytically framed within a comparative statics framework" (MPR, p. 218), while for Joan Robinson, an insistence upon "the irrelevance of the comparative statics analytical framework for studying the process of capital accumulation going on in 'real-time'" (*Ibid.*) was a typical methodological theme of her entire work. She was not denying that the reswitching argument demonstrated the incoherence of neoclassical theory. But for her, neoclassical theory was *totally unreal anyhow*: it required "comparisons of equilibrium positions with different rates of profit and the same 'state of technical knowledge'. These are not found in nature and cannot be observed ... The benefit of the discussion is only to dispel illusions" (Robinson & Naqvi, 1967, p. 591). This gives one a glimpse of Joan which shows the error of those neoclassics who present her as mainly a carping critic. In fact, as one saw over and over in conversation, she would have much preferred just to forget about neoclassical theory and turn all her attention to the development of her own ideas. As Zamagni observes, "[t]he fact is that in a truly dynamic context – the context in which she was mainly interested – the methods of production are no longer given from the start. The methods that become available over time depend on the path taken by accumulation" (MPR, p. 221). The constructive side of Joan's thought is further emphasized by John Birner. Rounding out the discussion of reswitching, he draws attention to a number of ironies concerning the manner in which the capital controversy developed and various misunderstandings arose. He also stresses that "[t]he main purpose of Robinson's research programme was constructive, not critical" (MPR, p. 226).

Part V closes with three papers on technology. In the first of these, reswitching reappears as one of the phenomena exhibited formally in a paper by Neri Salvadori, concerning the treatment of technology by Joan Robinson, in her *Accumulation*, in terms of productivity curves. Arguably, neoclassics might have understood her better had this approach in terms of productivity curves not been neglected by her later, since as Salvadori argues this description of technology "is much more workable for economists with a neoclassical background and an interest in macroeconomics. This fact becomes especially relevant now that growth theory is again fashionable with endogenous growth" (MPR, p. 232). The argument should interest readers working in the areas of growth and choice of techniques.

The same is true of the two papers which follow. The next, by Ferdinand Meacci (which has already been referred to earlier) discusses "Joan Robinson's treatment of the transition to a higher degree of mechanization ... in the light of the distinction between *choice* and *change* of techniques. This distinction was first highlighted by Pasinetti (1981, Ch. IX)" (MPR, p. 249, emphasis in original). Finding ambiguities in her treatment of the transition to a higher degree of mechanization, he traces some of these to her failure to distinguish "between technical progress (as a reduction in coefficients) and technical change (as a change in coefficients)" (MPR, p. 259). In addition, he argues that "the neglect of the distinction between choice and change of techniques is also at the root of the question as to whether the transition to a higher degree of mechanization should be considered as an increase in the cost (and therefore as a 'social' relation) or as an increase in the volume (and therefore as a 'technical' relation) of investment per head in relation to output per head" (MPR, pp. 259–260). The final paper on technology, by Bruno Jossa, credits Joan Robinson with being "one of the very first economists to concern herself thoroughly and keenly with the economic theory of technical progress" (MPR, p. 263). Given the extensive nature of her contributions to this topic, which she addressed "time and again" (*Ibid.*), he confines himself to her treatment of the case of fixed coefficients (while recognizing that she had analyzed the case of variable coefficients "in a number of celebrated studies" (*Ibid.*).

VI. METHOD

It is necessary to notice here some rather deep methodological contrasts between the theoretical atmosphere in which Joan grew to maturity in Cambridge and the sharply different atmosphere in which her opponents had lived, some of them initially in Europe, but later in America. The Ciccarellis pertinently note "the obvious shift of the focus of economic theory from Cambridge University to Cambridge, Massachusetts" (C&C, p. 10). They cite Marjorie Turner on the "takeover of the mathematical economists from the conceptualists" (Turner, 1989, p. 74 cited C&C, p. 11). This is a case, however, where the Ciccarelli's brevity could be misleading. A young reader might get the impression that what happened was a home-grown American development. But, as E. Roy Weintraub has elegantly demonstrated, what actually took place began as a major resurgence of the Walrasian general equilibrium tradition by *European* theorists, particularly those associated with the Vienna colloquium of Karl Menger in the 1930s. Cambridge had always, under the influence of Marshall, simply ignored the Walrasian tradition, and especially mathematical models of general equilibrium. (Significantly, Sraffa as a European, was free from this insularity.) People directly or indirectly influenced by Menger's colloquium did seek refuge in America from Hitler's barbarism, and began to exert a powerful influence there by the 1940s. (On the remarkable group in Vienna, the interested reader should see Weintraub's much-needed treatment, especially in 1985, pp. 54–55, 62–107).

There is irony in the fact that at least two of the greatest mathematical economists who came to America, were in fact producing mathematical re-statements of *classical* reproduction theory – in Wassily Leontief's case actually inspired by Marx's reproduction schemas. 'General equilibrium' theorists they *may* have been in a sense, but not in the sense of *Walras* (see Walsh & Gram, 1980). It has been conventional in America to interpret John von Neumann as if he were a neo-Walrasian. But, as Kurz and Salvadori show clearly, "the conventional interpretation of [Neumann] is in serious trouble" (Kurz & Salvadori, 1995, p. 412). Among other things, the total neglect of the neo-Walrasian core problem of scarcity is "the characteristic feature of von Neumann's model" (Kurz & Salvadori, 1995, p. 413. See further, on Sraffa & Neumann, pp. 421–426; Kurz & Salvadori, 1998b, pp. 25–56).

As for Leontief, his work could hardly have been widely accepted in the America of the Cold War years had he *continually* insisted on its roots in the Marxian reproduction schemas – although, be it noted, these were "a source of inspiration avowed by Leontief" (Gilibert, 1998a, Vol. 2, p. 41). As it was, as Giorgio Gilibert has noted, "[h]is contribution was always played down from the theoretical point of view; indeed, it was normally strictly confined to the field of applied economics" (Gilibert, 1998a, Vol. 2, pp. 40–41). But Leontief's classical roots were ancient: as he himself noted, he was attempting to construct "a *Tableau Economique* of the United States" (Leontief, 1951, p. 9).

What the Americans chose to learn from the European mathematical economists, however, was not how to revive classical theory – as was indeed hardly to be expected in the political atmosphere of the 1950s and 1960s. What they rapidly absorbed, rather, was how to reformulate *neoclassical* theory in the elegant garb of axiomatic formalist mathematics, along with proofs of the (mathematical) existence of general equilibrium and of its (Pareto) optimality. The essential structure of the canonical models of Kenneth Arrow, Gérard Debreu and others, was then summarized with admirable clarity in Debreu (1959). With this selective absorption of imported European riches, the American profession became mathematically new rich. And, as is the universal tendency of new rich, they wanted to display their shiny new possessions. So it became the fashion to count nothing as economic theory unless it presented an axiom set, and proceeded to prove theorems in the formalist style. This stately minuet remained the dominant fashion for many years.

But Joan had grown up seeing *Marshall* (who believed in keeping mathematics in its place, and believed that place to be a humble one in economic theory) as her opponent – not a group of formalist mathematicians! Young readers today might regard Cambridge as ruled in the 1940s, 1950s and 1960s by Joan, together with the post Keynesians, and Sraffa. The Ciccarellis are therefore right to stress that Joan and the post Keynesians had powerful neoclassical enemies *at* Cambridge (C&C, pp. 10–11). *Marshallian* neoclassical orthodoxy lived on long enough for it to be the target at which the early contributions from Joan's side in the capital controversy were aimed. It was even believed for some years in the United States that the canonical Arrow-Debreu models, simply by not aggregating capital, 'escape' the Cambridge University critique. But this was realized by Joan and others to be a mistaken claim; as Kurz and Salvadori have remarked, "it was particularly Garegnani (most recently 1990a, 1993) who argued that, the fact that capital is resolved into a set of physical factors notwithstanding, the modern versions [of neo-classical theory] cannot evade the problem of capital" (Kurz & Salvadori, 1995, p. 466).

The Ciccarellis, however, could leave non-specialist readers with a couple of mistaken impressions: First, that a richly expanding mathematical literature in economic theory is peculiar to the American neoclassical tradition. It is easy to verify, however, that there is an extensive and rapidly growing literature of mathematically sophisticated present-day *classical* theory, mostly taking place *outside* America. See the sources cited in Kurz and Salvadori (1995, 1998), in Pasinetti (1981, 1993), in Baranzini and Harcourt (1993), in Bharadwaj and Schefold (1990), and in the papers presented to the Conference on 'Sraffa and Modern Economics', in Rome (1998).

The second mistaken impression which might be picked up by readers of the Ciccarellis is the idea that what they called "the shift of power in economics" (C&C, p. 11) from Europe to the United States remains intact today. In fact, the imperial sway of the canonical Arrow-Debreu models did not last much beyond the mid-1970s. Results had by then been published which can be seen with hindsight to have foreshadowed the end of the Augustan age. The story of the breakup of the original complete Arrow-Debreu models into a profoundly Balkanized and ever growing maze of particular game theoretical models is a complicated one, which cannot be retold here. (For some of the key issues, see Debreu, 1974; Mantel, 1974, 1976, 1977; Sonnenschein, 1972, 1973a, b). The initial reactions to this work were skeptical; now, however "even such erstwhile stalwarts of general equilibrium theory as Christopher Bliss compare that theory to theology (1993, p. 227)", (Rizvi, 1997, p. 271). He cites Bliss: "The near emptiness of general equilibrium theory is a theorem of the theory" (Bliss, 1993, p. 227).

The Ciccarellis nowhere inform their readers that the formalist mathematical splendors which characterized the high theory produced in America after World War II were part of an intellectual empire which had begun to break up by the mid-1970s. This could leave students of Joan Robinson with the mistaken belief that the once revered formal models of the 1950s and 1960s had put Keynes, and especially Joan's interpretation of him, permanently out of date rather than temporarily overshadowed by a passing fashion.

Turning now to the papers on methodology in MPR, Andrea Salanti observes that Joan Robinson "never engages herself in a comprehensive and dispassionate discussion of 'the scope and method' of economics with explicit reference to some well-established epistemological perspective" (MPR, p. 286). This was true also of her conversation. Over ten years, I do not recall any of our meetings during which she initiated, or showed enthusiasm for, philosophical discussion. Whereas she was tireless on the topics which gripped her. This was at least partly a reflection of her intense single-mindedness: she used to say that it was fatal to try to fight on two fronts. As Salanti remarks, when she does fall back on a methodological argument, she does so "in support of the particular piece of economic research she is pursuing" (*Ibid.*).

Her conversation in her later years (as well as some of her writings) showed a number of traces of what must have been the philosophical atmosphere she breathed when young. It dated from the mid-1930s, and was that peculiarly British mixture of Anglicized logical positivism with a good dash of Russell, and a nostalgic backward glance at Hume, which Freddy Ayer had made popular. The sad irony was that, while this was exactly the philosophy to make neoclassical economists happy, it was just confusing to Joan, given her goals. It made neoclassics happy because it told them that value judgments were 'meaningless' and therefore had no place in a science (and the neoclassics desperately wanted economics to be a 'science'). Breathing a sigh of relief, neoclassics could turn their backs on the gross inequalities of wealth and income and on the state of the poor and the unemployed. But all Joan's inherited instincts told her that there were desperately serious questions which had an inextricably moral aspect, and that these were just the sort of questions which classical political economy had developed in order to address.

Of course logical positivism (including the milder Anglican version) fell back under attack. One by one, each of the doctrines on which its once sharp fact/value dichotomy depended had to be abandoned. But the neoclassics did not go back to philosophy to find this out, so it's influence lived on until recently in economics. For the neoclassics, this ignorance was bliss – they could go on with business as usual. (On logical positivism and economic theory, see Walsh 1996, especially 176–184, 256–262, and 2000, pp. 6–10).

Salanti cites a passage (MPR, p. 286) where Joan showed a nodding acquaintance with early 'growth of knowledge' theory. And I do recall her mentioning Thomas Kuhn (1962). But neither his work nor that of the later growth of knowledge philosophers ever became a serious influence on her as far as I could see. Salanti concludes by describing Joan's struggle with methodological problems as "common sense in the service of (ethically) good reasons" (MPR, p. 296). Common sense, Salanti fears, "is not compelling enough to convince the majority in the economics profession" (*Ibid.*). Well, it certainly got no hearing in the days when the canonical Arrow-Debreu models, and their formalist mathematics, dominated the discourse of theoretical economics. As formalism has declined in philosophy, however, and as things said in natural languages become harder and harder to dismiss as necessarily second rate, common sense is notably strengthening (see Putnam, 1987, 1988, 1990, 1993; Walsh, 1996, 2000). How soon one can expect 'the majority in the economics profession' to become aware of these changes, of course, is quite another matter. Still, there are signs of change: Steven Pressman has recently commented on the "rising interest by economists in philosophical issues" (Pressman, 1997, p. 501).

Bertram Schefold, although known for the elegance of his formal work, is no defender of the more extreme pretensions of formalism. Rather, he defends "the historicist thesis according to which different economic models have to be used to capture the characteristics of different economic formations" (MPR, p. 300). He claims, I believe correctly, that Joan was sympathetic to this point of view. Under the evocative heading "Different Forms of Rationality" (MPR, p. 308), he notes that she had dealt with feudal society, although infrequently (for example, in Robinson, 1970). He observes that her treatment "is essentially a critique of Domar's contention that feudalism could be explained in neo-classical terms. It insists on the existence of a more specific rationality" (MPR, p. 308). Joan was aware that a revived classical theory could not just accept rationality concepts left over from neoclassicism. I recall trying to interest her in discussions of rationality in the early 1970s. I had been publishing some work critical of the axiomatic foundations of neoclassical rationality concepts (Walsh, 1967). Although she did not feel that individual rationality was much worth taking on, she did say that she thought concepts of *group* rationality might well be. But I soon came to agree with her that the first task was to concentrate on getting the core of classical theory as widely understood and accepted as possible. So Harvey and I dropped a formal treatment of rationality which had occupied the first few chapters of early versions of our joint work (Walsh & Gram, 1980) and in later versions plunged right in over head and ears in political economy from the start.

Now, however, I believe the time has come when those who have inherited the traditions of the classics (including Marx) should indeed investigate the proper concepts of rationality for the present-day versions of such theory. The idea of a hierarchy of needs has haunted classical theory for a very long time. Amartya Sen found his concept of needs and capabilities developed in Smith and Marx, noting that "productivity differences constituted only one of Marx's concerns. He also focused attention on the necessity to address our manifold diversities, including differences in needs" (Sen, 1992, p. 120). Bertram Schefold, in a recent work, has been one of those investigating the significance of the concept of needs for a treatment of rationality designed to be consistent with the discoveries of the surplus approach (Schefold, 1990, pp. 178–228, Walsh, 1995–1996, p. 557). Schefold's work on these issues leads one naturally to that of Pasinetti (1981, 1993). But I have discussed these matters elsewhere (Walsh, 1998, 2000).

One theme of Geoff Harcourt's paper, which concludes the volume, has already been referred to: Joan's treatment of Kalecki. In discussing Joan Robinson's changes of mind, he casts light on the ways in which those closest to her affected her changes – a demanding task for which he is ideally suited. As Gary Dymski has observed, Geoff "has become heterodox theory's genealogist; analytical, generous of spirit, and good humored, he has seemingly single handedly maintained lines of communication and dialogue among heterodox economists" (Dymski, 1998, p. 133). Dymski was writing about Geoff Harcourt's remarkable recent book (Harcourt, 1995), whose message Dymski summarizes as follows: "neoclassical theory must be opposed on the basis both of its empirical irrelevance and of its logical impossibility, and sustained opposition must be rooted equally in Keynes' ideas about uncertainty and Marx's ideas about economic conflict . . . no one 'camp' of Post-Keynesians is best: each taken on its own is incomplete" (*Ibid.*).

As Dymski puts it, "Robinson figures so centrally for Harcourt because of her paradigmatic role: at once an intimate of Kalecki and Sraffa – two of Marx's stoutest advocates among economic theorists – her running, spirited disagreements with neoclassical economists led her to want to take only as much from Marx as her purposes required. Harcourt makes clear his discomfort with her stance in this respect even while emphasizing his admiration for her grit" (Dymski, pp. 133–134). Well, as we have noted, the labor theory was a front which she would not defend for Marx. But she had picked up from logical positivism the idea that 'metaphysics' was nonsense, and had convinced herself that the labor theory was 'metaphysical'. I am quite sure that she felt that the labor theory was not helping Marx to be understood.

Geoff Harcourt's almost blow by blow description, in the final chapter of MPR, of the development of Joan's ideas must be sampled in the original. Seeing that he covers her life in 10 pages, it will cause no surprise that his account would be somewhat difficult reading for newcomers to her thought. The interested reader cannot do better than to supplement it with the volume whose review by Dymski we have been discussing (Harcourt, 1995). For all Geoff Harcourt's generosity to friend and foe alike, it must not be imagined that he balks at calling a spade a spade when this is necessary. Surveying the post-Keynesian movement as it has been developed (for example) he insists that "Joan *was* an original pioneer" (MPR, p. 317, emphasis in original), "despite an unhealthy American post-Keynesian attempt at hegemony" (*Ibid.*). And he notes that "though Joan Robinson and the neo-Ricardians have largely over-lapping 'visions' – Kalecki is not as acceptable to the neo- Ricardians as Keynes is – they were at loggerheads on method" (MPR, p. 319). The dispute, of course, concerned the classical method of long-period positions, about which Joan expresses doubts in her last years. But for the neo-Ricardians, (such as Garegnani), this involved "abandoning the one method – long-period positions – that allows general theoretical propositions to be derived" (*Ibid.*).

I shall offer reasons (as does Geoff) for believing her 'nihilism' at the end was not complete. But one must face the fact that she had said some things which, if taken literally, would imply the abandonment of the analytical method of Smith, Ricardo *and* Marx. Pierangelo Garegnani, John Eatwell, and others were not unjustified in objecting! (See Garegnani [1979] 1983, p. 76. Compare Eatwell & Milgate, 1983, pp. 1–17, Robinson [1979] 1983, pp. 70–71, Garegnani [1978] 1983, pp. 21–69, 72–78).

Meanwhile, as Geoff notes, the American post-Keynesians agreed with Joan in stressing that Keynes requires *uncertainty*, not just calculable risk as the bastard Keynesians assumed. But "with the exception of Jan Kregel and the partial exception of Hyman Minski, the agents in their stories are far too close to those of the neoclassical 'enemy' . . . and too far away from the class society of the classicals and the Marxists, in which conflict is ever present" (*Ibid.*).

Geoff Harcourt argues that her "final assessment of Sraffa's purposes and contributions is contained in two papers, 'Spring Cleaning' (1985) and 'Accumulation and Exploitation' (Bhaduri & Robinson, 1980), in which she and Bhaduri attempted to link up Sraffa and Kalecki's modes of analysis" (MPR, p. 325). Of the two pieces which he considers, Geoff is certainly right that the one co-authored with Bhaduri is "the more optimistic in tone" (*Ibid.*).

However, there is the evidence of a third piece published in 1980 (cited in MPR, p. 359, as [432]). This was her 'Introduction' to Walsh and Gram (1980). What is significant here is that the method of analysis used in the book (when addressing *classical* theory) was of course that of long-period positions. We called them classical 'general equilibria', but they were sharply distinguished from neo-Walrasian equilibria of supply and demand: the *classical* equilibrium condition was the equality of rates of profit across sectors. She had read and commented critically on several complete versions of this work, giving her formal approval to the one which went to press in the Fall of 1979. She was quite explicit in her evaluation of the classical tradition:

The art of constructing models ... is to make the most drastic simplifications that are possible without eliminating any element essential to the problem in hand. In this art, Ricardo was preeminent, but all the great classics, from Sir William Petty to Karl Marx, practiced it in some degree. The method came to them by instinct; now it has to be practiced systematically, in mathematical terms.

(Robinson, 1980).

But, after all, the practice of the classical method 'systematically, in mathematical terms' was *exactly* the program which was carried out by those who revived classical theory in the twentieth century. They thus laid the foundation for the enrichment of that theory which, as noted above, is now beginning (see Walsh, 2000).

NOTES

1. Joan Robinson. 1980. *Collected Economic Papers.* 1–5. Cambridge, MA, MIT Press.

ACKNOWLEDGMENTS

I have benefited from the advice of David Laibman, and from the advice and editorial assistance of Lisa Bendall-Walsh. The usual disclaimers apply.

REFERENCES

Bharadwaj, K., & Schefold, B. (Eds) (1990). *Essays on Piero Sraffa: Critical Perspectives on the Revival of Classical Theory.* London: Unwin Hyman.

Baranzini, M., & Harcourt, G. C. (Eds) (1993). *The Dynamics of the Wealth of Nations, Growth, Distribution and Structural Change. Essays in Honour of Luigi Pasinetti.* London: Macmillan.

Bliss, C. (1993). Oil Trade and General Equilibrium: A Review Article. *Journal of International and Comparative Economics, 2,* 227–242.

Commendatore, P. (2000). Maria Christina Marcuzzo. In: L. L. Pasinetti & A. Roncaglia (Eds), The Economics of Joan Robinson, *Review of Political Economy. 12*(1), 115.

Davis, J. B. (Ed.) (1997). *New Economics and its History: Annual Supplement to Volume 29. History of Political Economy.* Durham and London: Duke University Press.

Debreu, G. (1959). *The Theory of Value: An Axiomatic Analysis of Economic Equilibrium.* New York: Wiley.

Debreu, G. (1974). Excess Demand Functions. *Journal of Mathematical Economics. 11,* 15–23.

Dymski, G. (1998). Geoffrey C. Harcourt: Capitalism, Socialism and Post-Keynesianism. *Review of Radical Political Economics, 30*(1), 1998, 132–135.

Eatwell, J., & Milgate, M. (Eds) (1983). *Keynes's Economics and the Theory of Value and Distribution* (pp. 21–69). New York: Oxford University Press.

Eatwell, J., & Milgate, M. (1983). Introduction to Eatwell and Milgate (Eds), 1983.

Eatwell, J., Milgate M., & Newman, P. (Eds) (1987). *The New Palgrave: A Dictionary of Economics.* London: Macmillan.

Eatwell, J., Milgate M., & Newman, P. (1990). *Capital Theory*. London: Macmillan.

Eatwell, J., & Panico, C. (1987). Sraffa, Piero. In: J. Eatwell, M. Milgate & P. Newman (Eds), *The New Palgrave: A Dictionary of Economics*, IV (pp. 445–452). London: Macmillan.

Feiwel, G. R. (Ed.) (1985). *Issues in Contemporary Macroeconomics and Distribution* (pp. 157–165). London: Macmillan.

Garegnani, P. ([1978] 1983). Notes on consumption, investment and effective demand. In: J. Eatwell & M. Milgate (Eds) 1983, *Keynes's Economics and The Theory of Value and Distribution* (pp. 21–69). New York: Oxford University Press.

Garegnani, P. ([1979] 1983). A reply to Joan Robinson. In: J. Eatwell & M. Milgate, (Eds) 1983, *Keynes's Economics and The Theory of Value and Distribution* (pp. 72–78). New York: Oxford University Press.

Garegnani, P. (1990). Quantity of Capital. In: J. Eatwell, M. Milgate & P. Newman, *Capital Theory* (pp. 1–78). London: Macmillan.

Garegnani, P. (1993). Sraffa Lecture. Rome: mimeo.

Gilibert, G. (1998). Leontief, Wassily. In: H. D. Kurz & N. Salvadori (Eds), 1998a, 2 (pp. 60–65).

Gram, H. N., & Walsh, V. (1983). Joan Robinson's Economics in Retrospect. *Journal of Economic Literature, 21*(2), 518–550.

Halevi, J., Laibman, D., & Nell, E. J. (Eds) (1992). *Beyond the Steady State: A Revival of Growth Theory*. London: Macmillan.

Halevi, J., & Fontaine, J.-M. (Eds) (1998). *Restoring Demand in the World Economy, Trade, Finance and Technology*. Edward Elgar, Cheltenham.

Hamlin, A. (1997). Rationality, Allocation and Reproduction. *Economic Journal. 107*, 1592–1593.

Harcourt, G. C. (1995). *Capitalism, Socialism, and Post-Keynesianism*. Aldershot, England: Edward Elgar.

Hicks, J. R. (1965). *Capital and Growth*. Oxford: Clarendon Press.

Intriligator, M. D. (Ed.) (1997). *Frontiers of Quantitative Economics*. Amsterdam: North Holland.

Keynes, J. M. (1936). *The General Theory of Employment, Interest and Money*. In: D. Moggeridge (Ed.), *The Collected Writings of John Maynard Keynes*. Vol. VII. London: Macmillan, 1972.

Kuhn, T. S. (1960). *The Structure of Scientific Revolutions*. Chicago: University of Chicago Press.

Kurz, H. D., & Salvadori. N. (1995). *Theory of Production: A Long Period Analysis*. Cambridge: Cambridge University Press.

Kurz, H. D., & Salvadori. N. (1998a). *The Elgar Companion to Classical Economics*. Cheltenham: Edward Elgar.

Kurz, H. D., & Salvadori. N. (1998b). *Understanding Classical Economics; Studies in Long Period Theory*. Routledge: New York.

Leontief, W. (1951). *The Structure of American Economy* (2nd ed.). New York: Oxford University Press.

Loasby, B. J. (1991). Robinson's Wrong Turning. In: I. H. Rima (Ed.), *The Joan Robinson Legacy*. Armonk, New York: M. E. Sharpe.

Lowe, A. (1965). *On Economic Knowledge. Toward a Science of Political Economics*. New York: Harper and Row.

Mantel, R. (1974). On the Characterization of Aggregate Excess Demand *Journal of Economic Theory, 7*, 348–353.

Mantel, R. (1976). Homothetic Preferences and Community Excess Demand Functions. *Journal of Economic Theory, 12*, 197–201.

Mantel, R. (1977). Implications of Microeconomic Theory for Community Excess Demand Functions. In: M. D. Intriligator (Ed.), *Frontiers of Quantitative Economics*. Amsterdam: North Holland.

Marcuzzo, M. C. (1985). Joan Violet Robinson (1903–1983). Mimeographed working paper, Department of Economics, Universita Degli Studi: Modena, Italy.

Marcuzzo, M. C. (1998). Sraffa and Cambridge Economics, 1928–1931. Paper presented at the conference 'Sraffa and Modern Economics', Centro Studie Documentazione 'Piero Sraffa', Rome: 1998.

Moggridge, D. (Ed.) (1972). *The Collected Writings of John Maynard Keynes*. London: Macmillan.

Nussbaum, M., & Sen, A. (Eds) (1993). *The Quality of Life*. Oxford: Clarendon Press.

Pasinetti, L. L. (1966). Changes in the Rate of Profit and Switches of Techniques. *Quarterly Journal of Economics, 80*, 503–517.

Pasinetti, L. L. (1981). *Structural Change and Economic Growth: A Theoretical Essay on the Dynamics of the Wealth of Nations*. Cambridge: Cambridge University Press.

Pasinetti, L. L. (1993). *Structural Economic Dynamics: A Theory of the Economic Consequences of Human Learning*. Cambridge: Cambridge University Press.

Pressman, S. (1997). John B. Davis, Keynes's Philosophical Development. *Review of Political Economy, 9*(4), 501–505.

Putnam, H. (1987). *The Many Faces of Realism*. La Salle, IL: Open Court.

Putnam, H. (1988). *Representation and Reality*. Cambridge, MA: MIT Press.

Putnam, H. (1990). *Realism With a Human Face*. Cambridge, MA: Harvard University Press.

Putnam, H. (1993). Objectivity and the Science-Ethics Distinction. In: M. Nussbaum & A. Sen (Eds), *The Quality of Life* (pp. 143–164). Oxford: Clarendon Press.

Rima, I. H. (Ed.) (1991). *The Joan Robinson Legacy*. Armonk, New York: M. E. Sharpe.

Rizvi, S. A. T. (1997). Responses to Arbitrariness in Contemporary Economics. In: J. B. Davis (Ed.), *New Economics and its History: Annual Supplement to Volume 29. History of Political Economy* (pp. 273–88). Durham and London: Duke University Press.

Robinson, J. V. (1933). *The Economics of Imperfect Competition*. London: Macmillan (2nd ed.), 1969.

Robinson, J. V. (1936). The Long Period Theory of Employment. *Zeitschrift für Nationalökonomie, 7*, 74–93.

Robinson, J. V. (1937). *Essays in the Theory of Employment*. London: Macmillan.

Robinson, J. V. (1949). Mr. Harrod's Dynamics. *Economic Journal, 59*, 68–85.

Robinson, J. V. (1952). *The Rate of Interest and Other Essays*. London: Macmillan.

Robinson, J. V. (1956). *The Accumulation of Capital*. London: Macmillan.

Robinson, J. V. (1962). A Model of Accumulation. In: *Essays in the Theory of Economic Growth* (pp. 22–87). London: Macmillan.

Robinson, J. V. (1970). *Freedom and Necessity. An Introduction to the Study of Society*. London: Allen & Unwin.

Robinson, J. V. (1979). *The Generalization of the General Theory and Other Essays*. London: Macmillan.

Robinson, J. V. ([1979]). Garegnani on effective demand. In: J. Eatwell & M. Milgate (Eds) 1983, *Keynes's Economics and The Theory of Value and Distribution* (pp. 70–71). New York: Oxford University Press.

Robinson, J. V. (1980a). *Collected Economic Papers*, Vols. 1–5. Cambridge, MA: MIT Press.

Robinson, J. V. (1980b). 'Introduction' to Walsh and Gram. In: *Classical and NeoClassical Theories of General Equilbrium, Historical Origins and Mathematical Structure* (pp. xi–xvi). New York: Oxford University Press.

Robinson, J. V. (1985 [1980]) The Theory of Normal Prices and Reconstruction of Economic Theory (formerly called 'Spring Cleaning'). In: Feiwel, G. R. (Ed.) 1985, *Issues in Contemporary Macroeconomics and Distribution* (pp. 157–165). London: Macmillan.

Schefold, B. (1990). On Changes in the Composition of Output. In: K. Bharadwaj & B. Schefold (Eds) 1990, *Essays on Piero Sraffa: Critical Perspectives on the Revival of Classical Theory* (pp. 178–228). London: Unwin Hyman.

Schumpeter, J. A. (1954). *History of Economic analysis*. New York: Oxford University Press.

Sen, A. K. (1992). *Inequality Reexamined*. Cambridge, MA: Harvard University Press.

Sonnenschein, H. (1972). Market Excess Demand Functions. *Econometrica, 40*, 549–563.

Sonnenschein, H. (1973a). Do Walras' Identity and Continuity Characterize the Class of Community Excess Demand Functions?. *Journal of Economic Theory, 6*, 345–354.

Sonnenschein, H. (1973b). The Utility Hypothesis and Market Demand Theory. *Western Economic Journal, 11*, 404–410.

Sraffa, P. (1960). *The Production of Commodities by Means of Commodities: Prelude to a Critique of Economic Theory*. Cambridge: Cambridge University Press.

Steedman, I. (1976). *Marx After Sraffa*. London: New Left Books.

Turner, M. S. (1989). *Joan Robinson and the Americans*. Armonk, New York: M. E. Sharpe.

Walsh, V. (1967). On the Significance of Choice Sets with Incompatibilities. *Philosophy of Science, 34*, 243–250.

Walsh, V., & Gram, H. (1980). *Classical and Neoclassical Theories of General Equilibrium: Historical Origins and Mathematical Structure*. New York: Oxford University Press.

Walsh, V. (1992). The Classical Dynamics of Surplus and Accumulation. In: J. Halevi, D. Laibman & E. J. Nell (Eds) *Beyond the Steady State: A Revival of Growth Theory* (pp. 11–43). London: Macmillan.

Walsh, V. (1995–1996). Amartya Sen on Inequality, Capabilities and Needs. *Science and Society, 59*(4), 556–569.

Walsh, V. (1996). *Rationality, Allocation and Reproduction*. Oxford: Clarendon Press.

Walsh, V. (1998). Rationality in Reproduction Models. Paper presented to the Conference on Sraffa and Modern Economics. Centro Studie Documentazione 'Piero Sraffa', Rome.

Walsh, V. (2000). Smith After Sen. *Review of Political Economy, 12*(1), 5–25.

Weintraub, E. R. (1985). *General Equilibrium Analysis: Studies in Appraisal*. Cambridge: Cambridge University Press.

THREE RECENT BOOKS ON SRAFFA: A REVIEW ESSAY

David R. Andrews

Piero Sraffa: His Life, Thought and Cultural Heritage, by Alessandro Roncaglia, Routledge, London and New York 2000, ISBN 0-415-23480.

Piero Sraffa's Political Economy: A Centenary Estimate, edited by Terenzio Cozzi and Roberto Marchionatti, Routledge, London and New York 2001, ISBN 0-415-22424-1.

Critical Essays on Piero Sraffa's Legacy in Economics, edited by Heinz D. Kurz, Cambridge University Press, Cambridge 2000, ISBN 0-521-58089-7.

Over one hundred years after his birth, forty years since the publication of his last major work, and almost twenty years since his death, Piero Sraffa remains a deeply controversial figure. His stature has been widely recognized, for example, as "a great economist" (Samuelson in Kurz & Salvadori, 2000, p. 25), "one of the greatest economists of the twentieth century" (Cozzi & Marrchionatti, 2001, p. xv) and even as "one of the leading intellectual figures of the twentieth century" (Roncaglia, 2000, p. 1). But the significance of Sraffa's work is still the subject of contentious debate. His critical edition of Ricardo has been hailed as a model of objectivity and also as a mischievous distortion intended to promote his own favored theories. His book, *Production of Commodities by means of Commodities: Prelude to a Critique of Economic Theory* (1960), has inspired some to reject conventional economic theory and

Research in the History of Economic Thought and Methodology, Volume 20-A, pages 195–201.
Copyright © 2002 by Elsevier Science Ltd.
ISBN: 0-7623-0847-8

work toward a revival of classical political economy, but others have dismissed the book as already out of date when it was published. There does not appear to be any likelihood that the controversy around Sraffa will be resolved in the near future.

It is also becoming increasingly clear that Sraffa's economic work was produced within the context of an extraordinary personal life. His close friendships with John Maynard Keynes, Ludwig Wittgenstein and Antonio Gramsci have become well known. Less well known are his warm relations, not only with economists such as Friedrich Hayek and Lionel Robbins, but also with other notable figures, including Dag Hammerskjold and Ezra Pound.

The mathematical character of Sraffa's book has become familiar; the difficulties that remain concern the interpretation of the models, not the formal properties of the models themselves. Sraffa's work is difficult to interpret because Sraffa notoriously refused to provide the full context in which his work should be viewed. In this sense his writings present a clear example of Wittgenstein's argument that meaning depends crucially on context. Three recent books on Sraffa should make a great contribution to the literature on Sraffa because they do focus, albeit in very different ways, on the contexts in which Sraffa's work must be understood.

Piero Sraffa: His Life, Thought, and Cultural Heritage, by Alessandro Roncaglia, is the shortest and least ambitious of the three. It consists of three essays which draw heavily on Roncaglia's previous work: the first essay is an intellectual biography; the second provides an interpretation of Sraffa's book; and the third contrasts several different lines of research which have emerged out of Sraffa's work.

The biographical essay is clear and informative but covers ground that has been well trod before. It addresses Sraffa's early work on money and banking, his friendship with Gramsci, his 1925–1926 criticisms of Marshallian partial equilibrium theory, his role in the development of the theory of imperfect competition, his contribution to the *Economic Journal* symposium on the representative firm, his relationships with Wittgenstein and Keynes, his exchange with Hayek, his critical edition of Ricardo's writings, and concludes with very brief discussions of the influence of Sraffa's book as a critique of the marginalist approach and the attempt to revive the classical tradition. The essay does not endeavor to present any new insights, and others have covered the same material in more depth. It nonetheless serves as a useful brief introduction to Sraffa's work.

The second essay, on Sraffa's *Production of Commodities by means of Commodities* (1960), is also largely concerned with material that is already familiar to Sraffa scholars. In this case the material has been presented in much greater depth by Roncaglia himself, in his book *Sraffa and the Theory of Prices* (1978) and elsewhere. The essay addresses the significance of the absence of any assumption about returns to scale, the distinctive character of Sraffa's classical approach vis-à-vis the marginalist approach, methodological affinities between Sraffa and Wittgenstein, and the implications of Keynes's critique of Say's Law for the models of Sraffa's book. None of these points, however, is developed in great depth. Those familiar with the literature on Sraffa will not learn anything new.

The third essay is somewhat different in that its subject matter has not been addressed in any systematic or detailed way in the English language literature on Sraffa. Although it stresses the similarities among various interpreters of Sraffa, the main purpose of the essay is to highlight differences among various Sraffian "schools." This is a very useful exercise, and it is surprising that this has not been more fully addressed previously. While there is widespread agreement on the nature of Sraffa's critique of the marginalist theory, and widespread agreement that Sraffa's rediscovery of the classical approach is very important, there are substantial disagreements about the nature of the classical approach. This should dispel any lurking suspicions that the "Sraffians" are simply a monolithic bloc.

Roncaglia divides the Sraffians into three basic categories: the Ricardian approach associated with Luigi Pasinetti, the Marxian approach associated with Pierangelo Garegnani, and the Smithian approach associated with Paolo Sylos-Labini. The Ricardian approach focuses on building a comprehensive deductive model of the economy as a whole. The Marxian approach focuses on the core relationship between prices of production and the distribution of income between labor and capital. The Smithian approach focuses on market forms and the manner in which those are affected by the division of labor and the process of accumulation of capital. Here again, however, we find that neither the similarities between these approaches nor their differences are explored in more than a superficial manner.

The failure of Roncaglia's book to address crucial issues in depth must not be viewed as a serious flaw, as its purpose is to introduce readers to Sraffa's life and work. Previous books which have sought to introduce Sraffa and the Sraffians have tended to focus on the mathematics of Sraffa's book. While the mathematical structure of Sraffa's models may be quite interesting in itself, any approach to Sraffa that does not emphasize the interpretation of the models misses out on what is most important. For a very brief period in the 1960s, there was controversy over the mathematical properties of Sraffa's models, i.e. in the debate over the possibility of reswitching. But this controversy was settled quickly and decisively. What remains of interest is the theoretical significance of Sraffa's work.

Piero Sraffa's Political Economy: A Centenary Estimate, edited by Terenzio Cozzi and Roberto Marchionatti, is written for the student of Sraffa. The book contains essays written by a distinguished group of specialists concerned with Sraffa and his work. It is also the first book to appear in English which draws heavily on the unpublished papers of Sraffa in the Wren Library of Trinity College at the University of Cambridge. As such it represents a treasure of information that was previously unavailable except to those who have examined Sraffa's papers in Cambridge.

The book is divided into four sections. The first is concerned with Sraffa's biography and contains two essays, one by Angelo d'Orsi and the other by Nerio Naldi. D'Orsi's essay limns a fascinating picture of the extraordinary educational milieu in which Sraffa was educated, including the specific courses he took and the professors who taught and examined him. Naldi's piece explores the earliest phases of his education in economics. Rather than simply providing additional materials to issues that have been long discussed, these essays bring to light aspects of Sraffa's intellectual biography which have received little attention thus far, e.g. the intellectual trends, politics and preoccupations current among Sraffa's professors, and Sraffa's work in the labor office in Milan following his degree but preceding his academic career.

The second section considers Sraffa's contributions to debates in Cambridge in the 1920s and 1930s, when the ideas of Alfred Marshall were still pervasive. Marchionatti's essay addresses not only Sraffa's criticism of Marshall's theory, but the entire international context of debate over Marshall's theory and Sraffa's location within it. An essay by Maria Christina Marcuzzo presents new evidence concerning Sraffa's important influence on younger economists in Cambridge in the 1930s, such as Joan Robinson, Richard Kahn, etc., as well as his influence on older economists. Her argument supports the idea that although Sraffa was very important as a critic, his role in the positive development of theory was much more limited. The third essay in the section, by Duccio Cavalieri, addresses Sraffa's theoretical ideas in the late 1920s, a period that has been identified as a potentially crucial turning point in Sraffa's thought.

The third section examines continuity and change in Sraffa's thought from the 1930s to the publication of his 1960 book. The first two essays were written by Luigi Pasinetti and Giancarlo De Vivo. Pasinetti focuses on changes in Sraffa's view, while De Vivo focuses on continuity, but both emphasize the difficulties of drawing conclusions even from the mass of unpublished material Sraffa left behind. Andrea Salanti and Rudolfo Signorino compare the methodology of Sraffa's 1925 and 1926 articles with the methodology of his 1960 book and find important similarities. Annalisa Rosselli explores Sraffa's notes at the Wren for new insights on his edition of Ricardo. The section concludes with a slightly modified version of the second essay from Roncaglia's book discussed above.

The fourth section of the book deals with a variety of miscellaneous special topics. First a previously published essay by Ian Steedman extends the models of *Production of Commodities by means of Commodities* to the case of an open economy. Next, there is an examination of the help that Sraffa received from the mathematicians A. S. Besicovitch, Frank Ramsey, Alister Watson and David Champernowne, by Heinz D. Kurz and Neri Salvadori. This is followed by a discussion of Sraffa's writings on monetary analysis by Carlo Panico, an essay on the relationship between Sraffa and Keynes by Fabio Ranchetti, and an analysis of Sraffa's exchange with Hayek by Carlo Zappia.

Throughout the book, the essays are of high quality. One finds here great respect for Sraffa combined with an extremely cautious attitude toward the unpublished papers. The book also include comments from discussants on many of the papers.

As might be expected, the book lacks unity. The papers go in a number of different directions and one can only imagine how many more different directions Sraffa's papers might sustain. The most striking absence in the collection, as pointed out in a comment by Riccardo Bellofiore, is the absence of any systematic attempt to deal with Sraffa's unpublished writings on Marx, which are substantial.

Finally, *Critical Essays on Piero Sraffa's Legacy in Economics*, edited by Heinz D. Kurz, focuses on the challenge presented by Sraffa to mainstream economics. Sraffa's intent is made clear in the subtitle to his book: "Prelude to a Critique of Economic Theory." The precise nature of this intended critique, as well as its ongoing significance, are at the center of controversy over Sraffa's importance. Kurz's book is remarkable for having brought together prominent defenders of the mainstream against Sraffa's challenge and prominent supporters of Sraffa's challenge. Moreover, many of the essays included in the book have responses and rejoinders. Perhaps the greatest disappointment of the book is that there are several essays by Sraffians which do not have responses by defenders of the mainstream.

The book is divided into four parts. The first begins with a survey of Sraffa's contribution to economics by Heinz D. Kurz and Neri Salvadori. This is followed by a 1995 essay, "Revisionist Findings on Sraffa," by Paul A. Samuelson. Samuelson has shown through a series of writings that he takes Sraffa's challenge extremely seriously, but he nevertheless finds that the challenge is unsuccessful. The most interesting aspects of this essay are Samuelson's discussions of Sraffa's 1926 *Economic Journal* article on the laws of returns and the implications of Sraffa's analysis for the labor theory of value.

Samuelson finds a "fatal" error in Sraffa's article on the laws of returns, by producing a counter example to Sraffa's conclusion in which "each of n goods is produced by . . . a specialized land specific to itself" (p. 33); he appears, however, to be unaware that Sraffa claimed that this was a rare and uninteresting case. Samuelson goes to some trouble to show that "[n]o substantive deficiency of the labor theory of value is ameliorated by the standard commodity concept" (p. 36); but he never provides any evidence that Sraffa intended to defend the labor theory. Samuelson's essay is followed by comments by John Eatwell, Pierangelo Garegnani, and Bertram Schefold, and there is a reply to these comments by Samuelson.

The second part contains essays on a variety of subjects. It begins with a new essay by Samuelson, "Sraffa's Hits and Misses," which reaches essentially the same conclusion as the first: that the critique of marginalism is "doomed" (p. 115). Samuelson considers returns to scale, the basic-nonbasic distinction, the standard commodity, and the relation between the classical and neoclassical approaches. This is followed by a comment by Kurz and Salvadori and reactions by Samuelson. In both essays, Samuelson writes in his extraordinary rhetorical style and gives no ground, but the criticisms of his arguments are very powerful. There has clearly not been a meeting of minds and there is a great deal of provocative material for further controversy.

These two essays and the discussion around them constitute the central contribution of the book. Nevertheless, a number of the other essays are of considerable interest. The second section continues with an essay by Salvadori on the role of demand in Sraffa's work. Salvadori argues persuasively that Sraffa did not simply ignore demand, as various writers have suggested, but that utility theory is an inadequate basis for the theorization of demand. Unfortunately there is no response by a defender of the mainstream approach. This is followed by an essay by Samuel Hollander pursuing a theme which has generated much debate already, "Malthus and the Corn-profit Model," with a comment by Garegnani and a rejoinder by Hollander. The section concludes with a reconsideration of the debate of the early 1930s involving Sraffa, Keynes and Hayek, by Kurz. Kurz argues that Sraffa's criticism effectively demolished Hayek's argument. One regrets that there is no comment from a defender of Hayek.

The third section returns to the focus of debate in the 1960s, namely, capital theory. First there is an essay on the 1960s controversy itself from a mainstream perspective by Edwin Burmeister. Then comes an essay focused on the limitations of J. B. Clark's capital theory by Christian Bidard. The section closes with an essay by Lynn Mainwaring and Ian Steedman, "On the Probability of Re-switching and Capital Reversing in a Two-sector Sraffian Model," along with comments on the essay by Salvadori and Bidard and Lucette Carter.

The final section, with essays by Bertram Schefold and Garegnani, considers a highly controversial topic, i.e. the extent to which Sraffa's criticisms, developed in a long period context, apply to intertemporal equilibrium models. Both argue that Sraffa's criticisms do apply. Again, it is disappointing that there were no comments on these papers from defenders of the mainstream approach.

This is an outstanding collection, particularly due to the presence of the papers by Samuelson. Kurz deserves great credit. It is a rare accomplishment to bring together authors with such diametrically opposed positions on these issues. The book demonstrates convincingly that the debate over the significance of Sraffa's work is far from over. While it may appear that there is no more agreement among the participants in the debate today than there was in the 1960s, the volume also shows that reasoned debate on these issues is possible.

In summary, then, each of these three new books makes an important contribution to the literature on Sraffa, but these contributions are very different. Roncaglia's book is designed for the newcomer to Sraffa interested in a broad overview of his life and work. It marks a clear advance over previous introductions to Sraffa because it succeeds in introducing the reader, not only to the technical aspects of Sraffa's work, but also to its theoretical significance. The Cozzi and Marchionatti book is for the historically minded reader interested in a deeper understanding of Sraffa. By drawing on Sraffa's unpublished writings it brings to light much that has not been generally available for study by students of Sraffa. And the Kurz book is for those interested in the current status of Sraffa's challenge to economic theory. It provides a forum for the supporters of Sraffa's challenge and defenders of the mainstream to confront each other directly and to engage in sustained debate.

REFERENCES

Roncaglia, A. (1978). Sraffa and the Theory of Prices. John Wiley and Sons, New York.
Sraffa, P. (1926). The Laws of Returns under Competitive Conditions. Economic Journal, 36, 535–550.
Sraffa, P. (1960). Production of Commodities by means of Commodities: Prelude to a Critique of Economic Theory. Cambridge University Press, Cambridge.

A REVIEW ARTICLE: KARL MARX, RED OR GREEN

Murray Wolfson

John Bellamy Foster, Marx's Ecology: Materialism and Nature, pp x + 310, ISBN 1-58367-2 paper $18.00, ISBN: 1-58367-4 cloth, Monthly Review Press, New York, June 2000.

ABSTRACT

John Bellamy Foster argues on philosophical grounds that Marx's materialism was largely an environmental and anti-religious statement, rather than a class based economic analysis. This essay takes issue with his characterization of Marx, and points to the limitations of such a one sided view of human affairs.

For those who have not closely followed the more radical trends in the "Green" literature, this volume gives an insight into the line of argument current in these circles. Having evolved away from traditional Marxian viewpoints, Foster argues on philosophical grounds that the point of Marx's materialism was the primacy of nature. The evil of capitalism was its destruction of the "natural" unity of man with the soil, in favor of "huge farms" that destroyed the soil and displaced the population into pestilence filled cities. The solution to the problem, is communism, under which a society of "freely associated men" would restore the natural balance, employ scientific agricultural methods, and disperse industry between "town and country."

Research in the History of Economic Thought and Methodology, Volume 20-A, pages 203–210.

Perhaps this evolution should not come as a complete surprise after the criticism to which Marxian economic theory and its implementation has been subject. Nevertheless, one would expect an exposition of labor's interest in environmental issues, as part of its inherent conflict with capital over surplus value. But there is little or no such class-based or distributional argument in Foster's work. There is no agony over whether rapid economic growth will redound to the benefit of black workers who have been the "last hired and first fired." The history of all hitherto known societies, we are told, is the interaction of "man" with "nature" rather than *The Communist Manifesto*'s "history of class struggles." The point of communism, we learn, is to overcome "alienation". As such it is an extension of the once fashionable argument of the "alienation" of "man" from his "true essence" in Marx' juvenile, unpublished manuscripts such as *The Economic and Philosophic Manuscripts of 1844*, the anti-Semitic *On the Jewish Question* and the like. The thrust of this line of thought is to avoid the determinism in Marx, and present him as a humanist philosopher rather than a class based revolutionary.[1]

Nonetheless, Foster raises a number of interesting points and arguments that bear further discussion. This is so, even though the exposition is flawed by an excessive appeal to authority for legitimization. Let us not dwell on these technical matters any more than absolutely necessary, but focus on his overall approach. There are two questions that are much more worthy of discussion: first, is Foster's Green Marx[2] the real Marx? second, does Foster's argument itself make sense?

These issues are intertwined in the exposition which takes the form of a history of materialist philosophy, in which the author attempts to demonstrate a consistent line of thought from Marx's doctoral dissertation on Epicurus to his mature work. Marx preferred Epicurus' to Democritus' more deterministic form of atomistic materialism, by allowing the atoms to "swerve." At one blow, Epicurus reduced the gods to irrelevance in the space between atoms, and interpreted the "swerve" as an element of indeterminacy – and hence freedom – in the physical and social universe. Foster reads the swerve as a random variation which contradicts the determinism mistakenly attributed to Marx.

It is beyond my capacity to offer a definitive answer to the vexed question of the ontological status of stochastic processes. Does the well-studied and useful understanding of such processes in statistical methods reflect our ignorance of all the variables involved in the physical world and the inherent imprecision of measurement and limitations of observation? Or, does random variation reflect the nature of the material world "in itself?" Either way, exactly how one gets from this question to "freedom" from the garden variety laws of mechanics or statistical inference – not to speak of the hardly mentioned laws of value and distribution with which Marx struggled all of his adult life?

Before proceeding further, it is well for us to ask what is meant by materialism. Matter, John Locke told us, was "something I know not what," whence it played no part either in his epistemology or the empiricists to follow.[3] Foster quotes Bhaskar's three definitions of philosophical definitions:

(1) *ontological materialism,* asserting the unilateral dependence of social upon biological (and more generally physical) being and the emergence of the former from the latter;
(2) *epistemological materialism,* asserting the independent existence and trans-factual; that is, causal and lawlike activity of at least some of the objects of scientific thought;
(3) *practical materialism,* asserting the constitutive role of human transformative agency in the reproduction and transformation of social forms.[4]

Foster says Marx made most use of definition (3), but also employed the first two, principally in his discussions of science. He might have referred directly to the 1844 *Theses on Feuerbach* in which Marx referred to "practice" rather than "contemplative" materialism. It seems to me that this remark is an anticipatory way of asserting the primacy of the productive process in determining social institutions.[5] Yet Foster wants to claim all science for materialism, even though the point of natural science is empirical observation, rather than the *a priori* assertion of an order of causation from the biological to the social. To be sure, before they think it over, natural scientists deal in material relations and therefor either ignore the philosophical issues, or tend toward a materialist viewpoint. Usually they grow out of it, since materialism either is defined into meaninglessness or transcends observation Yet materialism, is not vacuous in Marx's hands. The significance of Marx's viewpoint, it seems to me, is the denial that ideas, mental constructs, can influence reality. Obviously this is the case in the physical world, but it does not follow that it is so for the history of human ideology and social relations.

Why was materialism so important to Marx? It is certainly true, as Foster says, that like other Young Hegelians, from the first Marx's philosophical expressions were directed against religion. Atheist though he was, Marx directed his criticism of the established church as a buttress of the fractionalized German polity that had yet to match the accomplishments of the French revolution. Indeed, Marx's famous description of religion as the "opiate of the masses" appears in his earliest largely unpublished Jacobin political writings of 1843, where he was arguing for capitalist democratic reforms in economic and political institutions.[6] But Marx was a quick study, especially when he realized that he didn't know very much about economics. His earliest attempts were embodied in the unpublished *Economic and Philosophic Manuscripts of 1844*, about which so much fuss has been made for its ideology of the alienation of man from his intrinsic nature by private property and the "dirty Jewish" nature of exchange, rather than the exploitation of labor as a class by specifically capitalist property relations. Even so, Marx did not get his economic theory of value and distribution right in his own mind, until *A Critique of Political Economy* (1859). Not coincidentally, the introduction to this work, is Marx's clearest statement of his materialist conception of history. Thenceforth, his economics moved away from the subjective, demand driven tendencies already evident in Mill and Say, toward the materialist labor theory of value and everything that Marx drew from it.

For the most part, Foster attempts to engross various scientists to his notion of materialism. But this certainly it is not the case for his discussion of Malthus. On the contrary, the charge against Malthus is that he is excessively materialist – mechanical Foster would say – in his method. Foster unleashes a diatribe against Malthus and the "parson naturalists" he personifies. Indeed, he is unwilling to view Malthus in historical perspective, but rebuts him even more ferociously than he would if he were a contemporary. Malthus, we learn, was unable to validate his arithmetic progression of food production because he did not originate the law of diminishing returns, and only incorporated it into later editions of his essay after learning of it. But from whom? The name of David Ricardo is conspicuous by its absence, despite the homage that Marx always paid to this arguably greatest of economists. Foster assails Malthus for his focus on rent, even though it was Ricardo who was responsible for the analysis that remains intact to this day. Nor is there any sign of Marx's lengthy discussion of rent in *Capital Vol 3 part V* Transformation of Surplus Value Into Ground Rent[7] where he attempted a formulation based on increasing as well as diminishing returns, and offered a theory of "absolute" as well as differential rent.

More substantively, the issue of population growth and food supply, is surely not a contrast between Malthus' arithmetic versus geometric progressions, but does entail their relative rates of growth. Ironically the dire predictions of the Club of Rome some years ago were Malthusian in their forecast of eventual starvation. All of these jeremiads are testimony to the extrapolation of trends rather than the sound economic analysis derived from Ricardo. It is certainly true that Ricardo did not stress the possibility of technical progress in food production, but it is also true that his marginal analysis of rent was an equilibrium condition elucidating the causal relations with the technology at hand rather than an extrapolation. Indeed, in their correspondence, Malthus suggested that the issue between them in many aspects of their work was the dynamics rather than the static analysis which Ricardo developed.

Foster cites Marx's attempt to refute Malthus in terms of the possibility that food supply can (and of course did) grow in geometric sequence. What is glaringly absent from this story is Marx's explanation of poverty in class terms as the exploitation of man by man, even as productivity increased dramatically. In fact, Marx was more nearly right in pointing to the social and institutional roots of starvation. In fact, he argued that "relative overpopulation" was a creature of the technological unemployment and cheapened food supply that gave rise to increased rates of surplus value. In fact, the contemporary studies of famine by Amartya Sen* show that the problem is not the limited food supply, but its distribution, that is at issue. Foster would do well to examine this matter in greater substantive detail if he hopes to draw current policy insights from these earlier debates.

Darwin's theory of evolution presents problems and opportunities for Foster, as it did for Marx. Certainly, the *Origin of the Species* advanced a dynamic evolutionary approach to science that dominated the second half of the nineteenth century. As such it was a model of the mutability of species as a result of cumulative random variations and natural selection. Foster details the storm of reaction to Darwin's revelations in an interesting and insightful manner. Foster is right to point out that Marx's thesis that social institutions were likewise subject to evolutionary processes. Indeed, as Jacques Barzun[8] (cite) and I[9] argued long ago, this developmental movement was stated in idealistic philosophical terms by Hegel[10] and motivated Marx and his early colleagues. The impact of this process was to undermine the creationist view of religion. Foster asserts that this made Darwin a "consistent materialist" even though he denied it.[11] Once again the issue of determinism in random processes makes itself felt in science.

To be sure Darwin could not forecast the next species to emerge, nor could he describe the genetic bio-chemical processes through which mutations occurred. That work has been taken up by analytical ecologists who speak of environmental niches that can be occupied, and genetic researchers in repeatable experiment and analysis since the discovery of the double helix. The same burden of demonstration was incumbent on Marx. He knew he had to demonstrate exactly how a capitalist economy worked, and how it was involved in various crises and exploitation of labor. He had to build on the work of his predecessors from Smith to Ricardo as well as the empirical results of the Royal

---

* *The Economics of Life and Death*, Scientific American, 1993.

Commissions into labor conditions in England. That point is completely over-looked in Foster's account, but it is to Marx's credit that Marx did not satisfy himself with philosophical discourse, but attempted an analytical model, the value and surplus value components of which were equilibrium in nature. If Marx failed, at least he knew what had to be done to validate his evolutionary viewpoint.

In so doing, despite his best efforts, Marx could not create a consistent materialist model. I pointed this out many years ago by referring to the definition of value as the "socially necessary labor-time required to reproduce a com-modity", where the term "socially necessary" was an euphemism for demand; likewise the definition of the subsistence of labor as "historically determined" rather than biological subsistence as posited by Malthus.[12] Thus subjective elements, already present in John Stuart Mill and J. B. Say, found their way in into his materialist value theory. If this were an important matter in his own time, it became a major division with the subjective theory of value initiated by Jevons (1870) and the Austrians shortly after the publication of *Capital I*. It is hard to imagine how Foster could have overlooked this core effort of Marx's lifetime work.

In the final analysis, Foster offers an epilogue which straddles the gap between the view that Marx was absolutely right on one hand, and on the other an attempt to escape the determinism in his theory. It is certainly understandable that he should do so. Although he blames the Soviet dictatorship on Stalin, the point is that the certainty of the Marxist determinism was in fact the rationale for treating the opponents of communism as either knaves or fools. In so doing, he cites Marxists such as Bukharin and Gramsci who offered a softer version of both economics and philosophy – who suffered from Stalin and Mussolini's oppression respectively. The questions that this argument comes back to is first, whether the humanist version of Marx was consistent with his labor theory of value and the model of the breakdown of capitalism, on one hand, and whether it was correct on the other. The second question, is whether Marx should be interpreted as a naturalist ecological advocate, more than an analyst of the inter-action of the labor process which reflected the human relationship with nature in the course of production. It is interesting that Foster does come around to discussing the materialist labor process in the epilogue, apparently unaware that the focus on production does mean that man transforms nature into something for his own purposes.

The ironic point in all this, is that Foster, in inveighing against religion with Darwinian tools, argues for evolutionary, historic, time dependent, dialectical processes. Yet programmatically nature appears as an absolute and fixed virtue. Clearly this is not the case either for Marx as a historical figure, or for physical or social reality itself. It appears, therefore, that human beings are capable of making choices about what they will produce, what resources they will use and what they might choose to use up. Clearly, there is no essential sanctified primeval natural resource, but an issue of what environments humans determine to keep and improve. What choices should be made for dealing with depletable resources such as petroleum? What natural features such as smallpox should be eradicated rather than preserved? Indeed, not far from Foster's base in Oregon, the great Douglas Firs were not the original timbers, but replaced the scrub oaks. Is it reasonable to argue that this forestry evolution made for a less beautiful and productive environment? That does not imply that all natural environments should be altered. Rather they should be preserved when they serve the human interest, and modified when they do not. It seems more reasonable for the "green" advocates, to avoid dogmatic disquisitions on the essential nature of man, and to expound the science of ecology in a scientific–deterministic biological and economic sense. That is the easy part. Then they should advocate their preferences for the kind of environment which they choose. This approach necessarily entails hard choices, incremental marginal decisions between alternatives and conflicts of interest. What else can one do?

NOTES

1. I have had the occasion to criticize this interpretation in "The Day Karl Marx Grew Up" (History of Political Economy) and "Three Stages in Marx's Thought" (History of Political Economy), and *Marx: Economist, Philosopher, Jew; Steps in the Development of a Doctrine,* Macmillan, London, 1982.

2. In his preface, Foster denies that his purpose is to paint Marx green, but then proceeds to do so nonetheless.

3. Presumably this is the basis for the author's frequent unargued denunciation of "positivists". He points out that Engels considered Hume and Kant to be "shamefaced materialists." (*Ludwig Feuerbach and the Outcome of Classical German Philosophy.* Lenin took a characteristically less charitable view in *Materialism and Empirio-Criticism.*

4. Foster p. 2; Roy Bhaskar "Materialism." In: Tom Bottomore (Ed.), *A Dictionary of Marxist Thought* (p. 324). Oxford: Blackwell, 1983.

5. See Wolfson, *A Reappraisal of Marxian Economics* (1966, Columbia University Press).

6. *Critique of Hegel's "Philosophy of Right"*, trans. A. Jolin and J. Omalley, London, Cambridge University Press, 1970.

7. *Capital* Vol. 3, Charles H. Kerr 1906, Part 6, Ch. 37–47 pp. 720–946. This discussion of ground rent deserves some further careful study and review by historians of economic thought.

8. J. Barzun, *Darwin, Marx, Wagner.* Doubleday, NY, 1958.

9. Wolfson, *ibid.*

10. G. W. F. Hegel, *The Phenomenology of Mind* (1807), trans. J. B. Baillie, 1910, (2nd ed.). Allen and Unwin.

11. Foster *op. Cit.* p. 202 c.f. p. 198. Darwin is presented as a somewhat timid and opportunist writer, who feared the uproar that would follow from his studies. Somewhat naively, Foster reads Darwin's polite thank you note to Marx for sending him a copy of *Capital I*, as a sign of approbation, even though Darwin remarks that he is not equipped to understand it.

12. Wolfson (*op. Cit*).

WALTER F. STETTNER, PUBLIC SECTOR ECONOMIST

Warren J. Samuels

A review of Walter F. Stettner, *Witness to a Changing World: A Personal History*, Huntington, West Virginia: University Editions, 1999.

Walter F. Stettner was born on June 28, 1914 in Trieste and died on May 11, 1998 while residing in Bethesda, Maryland, having become a naturalized U.S. citizen in 1944. His father had served in Franz Joseph's army under the Austro-Hungarian Empire and, when the empire broke up after World War I, had elected Czech citizenship for the family, since he had been born in Prague. Stettner was an intimate of many leading late-twentieth century economists, including *inter alia* Gottfried Haberler and Henry William Spiegel. He was an economist with a varied and important career in the international and national public sectors. He was involved in the early history of several of the most important international economic institutions of the post-World War II period. He also made several contributions to the study of the history of economic thought. This autobiographical memoir was privately published after his death.

Stettner received the Doctor of Jurisprudence from the University of Vienna in 1937. He was a student of Hans Mayer, Othmar Spann, and Ferdinand Degenfield-Schönburg.

His Jewish family had enjoyed a life of modest prosperity in a society stratified by nationality (ethnicity) and social status, laden with anti-semitism, and in which membership in the state religion was a condition of advancement in government, business, and academia. That life ended through financial reverses and, especially, the peril consequent to the ascendancy of Nazi Germany and

Research in the History of Economic Thought and Methodology, Volume 20-A, pages 211–216.
Copyright © 2002 by Elsevier Science Ltd.
ISBN: 0-7623-0847-8

its annexation of Austria (the Anschluss) in March 1938. Stettner managed to make it to the United States in December 1938, as did his sister. His mother and other members of his family died in the German extermination-camp system. His father reached Shanghai, where he died in 1944. Many who tried to escape Europe found themselves confronted by a catch-22 situation in which exit permits required entry visas and entry visas required exit permits, a predicament exacerbated if not fomented by decidedly unsympathetic and callous if not downright hostile immigration authorities in the United States and other countries.

In 1939 Stettner was awarded a refugee scholarship at Harvard University, where he studied economics with Alvin Hansen, John Williams, Haberler, Edward Chamberlin, Joseph Schumpeter, and others. He received the Ph.D. in economics in March 1944. His examiners were Hansen, whose assistant he had been, Seymour Harris, and Keith Butters.

Stettner had found that students in European schools were often expected to formulate answers specific to the orientation of particular teachers. At Harvard he enjoyed courses each cooperatively taught by two professors with radically different theoretical orientations. The feud between Mayer and Spann, for example, was now replaced by fiscal policy jointly taught by Hansen and Williams, and international economic relations by Haberler and Harris. This was, of course, during the first decade of Keynesian economics.

Stettner found Schumpeter's course on the history of economic thought disappointing. The great man's practice of interrupting his lecture every few minutes to make notations on slips of paper "made for a rather choppy presentation and taxed the concentration of the audience" (p. 121). While recognizing Schumpeter's "brilliance and imposing stature as an economist," both in and out of class, Stettner was "somewhat put off by his showmanship and intellectual arrogance" (p. 125; see also p. 122). Stettner's dissertation, "Nineteenth Century Public Debt Theories in Great Britain and Germany," was written under Hansen, not Schumpeter (p. 122). One revised chapter, on Sir James Steuart, was subsequently published in the *Quarterly Journal of Economics* and reprinted in collections edited by Harold M. Groves and by Mark Blaug. Another revised chapter, on Carl Dietzel, became a contribution to a festschrift honoring Hansen.

Stettner's first professional position as an economist was at the Board of Governors of the Federal Reserve System (1943–1948). He worked with Hansen (who had brought him to the position), Harvey Perloff, Evsey Domar, E. A. Goldenweisser, Haberler, Lloyd Metzler, Richard Musgrave, Howard Ellis, Alexander Gerschenkron, and others. There he worked on two major projects: postwar full employment and the establishment of an institutional system facilitating international trade and finance. The former led to the Employment

Act of 1946 and the latter to the Bretton Woods institutions, the International Monetary Fund and the International Bank for Reconstruction and Development. These latter, in particular, helped the world to avoid beggar-thy-neighbor policies that escalated adverse conditions.

He remembers a speech by John Maynard Keynes – the first in a biweekly seminar series – in which Keynes quipped, "Hansen and I, in our quest for disrespectability . . ." (p. 127).

Stettner's second position was with the European Cooperation Administration (ECA), later the Mutual Security Agency, established to administer the Marshall Plan of aid to Western Europe. Although Stettner only implies the point, the Marshall Plan – which came about almost three years after the defeat of Germany – had as one of its major objectives the creation of an obstacle to Soviet designs on European hegemony; this, he notes, was recognized as such by the Soviets (p. 149). Stettner worked for – and was for some time the Chief of – the Intra-European Trade Branch of ECA, which worked with the Organization of European Cooperation and the Bank for International Settlements to promote trade and achieve a multinational payments system, once again helping promote cooperative rather than mutually destructive international economic relations. He may or may not have known game theory then but he participated in the construction of institutions which ensconced and promoted cooperative rather than non-cooperative games.

He subsequently worked on three continents for various U.S. and OECD agencies and aid missions in Korea, Turkey, Argentina, Vietnam, Guyana, Laos, Costa Rica, and Pakistan, as well as with the Council of Economic Advisors and the Department of State. Much of his work was with or through the Agency for International Development (AID).

Stettner was involved at fairly high levels in both policy preparation and administration, including information acquisition and evaluation, and policy administration and negotiation (within U.S. agencies and with the governments of other donor countries and of aid-receiving countries). Throughout he represented U.S. global economic and military-security interests. His professional training and knowledge enabled him to acquire, interpret, and otherwise deal with complex economic and social materials. He was a beneficiary of splendid early, college and post-graduate education. His overall task was to utilize his specialized training and knowledge in the pursuit and administration of policies that were driven by political interests – not the putative a priori "optimal" policies of economic theory. His job sometimes required that he be a transmitter of information – technical know-how in production, physical distribution, and finance – to countries with negligible qualified personnel and often corrupt officials, often with rulers and elites more interested (as one would expect) in their own futures much more than those of non-elite populations – not least in South Vietnam. He also was involved in working out solutions to problems of stabilization and growth as well as of balance of payments and foreign exchange.

His professional career was at the heart of U.S. international economic policy during the Cold War – economic aid in pursuit of mutual security – and in the management of North-South economic relations – the latter eventually proving to be the more perennial sphere. For example, he writes that "The Alliance for progress was a new initiative for Latin America that President Kennedy had launched following the revolution in 1958 which brought Fidel Castro to power in Cuba, and threatened Latin America with an expansion of communist influence and political upheavals" (p. 310). Like the Marshall Plan the Alliance was driven less by humanitarian sentiments and more by strategic considerations.

His positions enabled him and his family to enjoy the benefits of world travel and to meet many interesting people; the writing of the memoir was clearly assisted by the use of his detailed travel diary (kept from age 14). One price was the danger he faced in several locations, especially at the collapse of U.S. activities in Laos in 1975 after the fall of South Vietnam, but also in Pakistan in 1979 after the Iranian Revolution.

Less dramatic but perhaps no less aggravating was dealing with self-serving and/or misanthropic agency bureaucrats and the insecurities due to temporary assignments and changing budgets.

Stettner's memoir provides many insights. One of the most dramatic and suggestive involves the post-independence situation of former colonies. Of Guyana Stettner writes that

> the independence achieved in 1966 had not changed the colonial structure of the Guyanese economy. Trade was primarily with the former mother country, Great Britain, ownership and exploitation of the country's natural resources were in foreign hands, and banking, insurance, and most commercial activities were controlled by foreign interests as well (p. 346).

Another insight involves the structure of domestic power. He contrasts the economy of Costa Rica as one of small farmers, democratic tradition, high literacy rate, and pro-poor social policies (e.g. minimum nutrition for poor children) with "the prevalence of large plantations in other former Spanish colonies in Central America." In Costa Rica, he found, the "government followed a deliberate policy of reducing the disparities between high- and low-income groups by enacting programs designed primarily to help the poor" (p. 401), rather than primarily give effect to and perpetuate elite interests. This was another game-theoretic situation that he observed.

In several countries Stettner found simple physical distribution to be a major problem: the inability of local farmers to market their products due to the absence of organizations and/or firms engaging in the collection, transportation, distribution of farm products; the hour-glass model is not a given. I encountered the same problem in a small rural village in Lithuania in August 2000. This problem is less dramatic but not less important than those of harnessing river waters for power and irrigation in the face of competing riparian states, sleeping sickness, and river blindness, not to mention Aids, in Africa (p. 407).

As for U.S. aid policy, Stettner recounts "the growing awareness [in 1974] that the aid programs and, in particular, the large capital investments had, by and large, benefited only a small segment of the population in the aid-receiving countries, while the preponderant majority had been largely unaffected." He tells also of Congressional efforts thereafter to change the program, so that "the emphasis henceforth be on programs of direct benefits to the poor majority, such as food production, nutrition, health, education and population planning" and that "wherever possible, the potential beneficiaries should be involved in the formulation of the program" (p. 411), i.e. the marshalling of local knowledge and beneficiary interests. Subsequently, U.S. policy along these lines was compromised by domestic conflict over financing birth control.

Stettner also writes of the growth of resentment by developing countries over perceived if not actual donor interference in their domestic affairs and of the 1975 effort to establish a New International Economic Order (NIEO) to help redress economic imbalance between North and South (p. 412). Issues of massive transfers of resources and, especially, debt forgiveness not surprisingly continue in 2000. Stettner clearly sympathizes with the plight of the would-be developing countries in the face of the unwillingness of the developed countries to provide effective massive amounts of economic assistance. But he candidly writes that

> Equally important . . . [is] the fact that, in many instances, the social and economic poli- cies followed by the developing countries, and their political regimes, were the major obstacles to more rapid development, rather than insufficient amounts of foreign aid or not enough concessions by the North (p. 452).

The questions of foreign economic aid and investment and the larger one of economic development in Africa, Asia, and Latin America are complex. The issues include differential economic political impacts on elites and non-elites; elite corruption; non-democratic if not authoritarian, mediaeval-like regimes; donor motivation along military and pseudo-colonial lines; exploitation of labor and resources by domestic and foreign interests; problems of surmounting disease, illiteracy, social traps, and hostile religion and culture; population growth; and so on. Economic policy manifests conflicts between the ideal and the practicable or workable, between competing diagnoses and lines of attack on problems, and between short run and long run perspectives. For example, foreign (and domestic) employers under various aid and foreign investment schemes may pay indigenous workers less than competing workers in developed countries – and be taken advantage of by global business for this very reason. Sweetheart deals between global corporations and non democratic regimes have been common. This may resemble exploitation by employers seeking cheap labor but the workers may well be earning more than other domestic labor in traditional jobs. The practicable alternative is continued lower-paid employment or unemployment. The history of the Western economies during the last three centuries is one of gradual, if uneven, improvement in real incomes coupled with pluralist political and social reforms, however gradual. The situation elsewhere is not likely to be different. The corporate system – "the market" to some – is not going away. Expectations now, however, are different; and the issues are further complicated by the increasingly recognized social and environmental costs of development.

Economics has had two modes of thought and analysis. In one, the economy, including the market, is examined as a pure abstract a-institutional conceptual system. In the other, the economy is examined in terms of the institutions – institutions that have histories – that form and operate through markets, insofar as there are markets. For the historian of economic thought, Stettner's memoir is important not so much for his interesting critical comments on Schumpeter but for the insight he implicitly brings to bear on the reception to be given to pure abstract a-institutional theories of population and of economic growth and development. The evidence recounted in the memoir, alas, is also testimony to the difficulties encountered in developing institution-rich theories. The conflict between Thomas Robert Malthus-David Ricardo and Richard Jones in the early 19th century over the theory of rent (in the light of population theory) has become a more vast and more complex conflict over theories of and approaches to economic growth and development – surely *the* great issue of economics as the study of the wealth of nations. Pure institution-free theories yield answers, but answers that beg important questions. There are the questions with which Walter Stettner, for all of his mainstream training, came to recognize.

ACKNOWLEDGMENTS

I am grateful to Cecile Spiegel and Rolf Glaeser for putting me in touch with Mrs. Jean Stettner and to Mrs. Stettner for a copy of the memoir and comments on an early draft of this review.

NIMITZ'S *MARX AND ENGELS:*
THEIR CONTRIBUTION TO THE
DEMOCRATIC BREAKTHROUGH

J. E. King

Review of August H. Nimitz Jr., *Marx and Engels: Their Contribution to the Democratic Breakthrough*, Albany, N.Y.: SUNY Press, 2000, pp. xiii, 377. $23.95 paper.

August H. Nimitz Jr. sets out, in this scholarly and comprehensive political biography, to challenge 'what has become an article of faith for much of the world at the end of the twentieth century – the supposed incompatibility between the projects of Marx and Engels and political democracy' (p. vii). The accusation that the founders of scientific socialism were enemies of democracy was not restricted to conservatives or bourgeois liberals. Here, for example, is the anarchist Mikhail Bakunin writing in 1872 on the political implications of Marx's thought:

> You can see quite well that behind all the democratic and socialistic phrases and promises in Marx's program for the State lies all that constitutes the true despotic and brutal nature of all states, regardless of their form of government. Moreover, in the final reckoning, the People's State of Marx and the aristocratic-monarchic state of Bismarck are completely identical in terms of their primary domestic and foreign objectives. In foreign affairs there is the same deployment of military force, that is to say, conquest. And in home affairs the same employment of armed force, the last argument of all threatened political leaders against the masses who, tired of always believing, hoping, submitting, and obeying, rise in revolt (Bakunin, 1872 [1973], pp. 319–320).

Research in the History of Economic Thought and Methodology, Volume 20-A, pages 217–222.
© 2002 Published by Elsevier Science Ltd.
ISBN: 0-7623-0847-8

While Bakunin's own political practice left a great deal to be desired, the case against Marxism-as-potential-tyranny has been endorsed repeatedly by the libertarian left no less than by the libertarian – and, of course, the authoritarian – right.

For Nimitz this is a grotesque parody of the truth:

> I make three related arguments. First – my most sweeping claim – Karl Marx and Frederick [*sic*] Engels were the leading protagonists in the democratic movement in the nineteenth century, the decisive breakthrough period in humanity's age-old struggle for democracy. Second, they played such a role because they were first and foremost political activists, and not simply 'thinkers', who constituted a revolutionary partnership. This much too ignored dimension of them is crucial in understanding why history knows of no other example of two who were more successful in promoting their own political perspective. Third, their active involvement in the revolutionary upheavals in 1848–1949 as communists allowed them to draw lessons and conclusions that enhanced their effectiveness in the fight for democracy. Implicit in the latter is the claim that it was exactly their success in advancing the fight for socialism that advanced the democratic struggle (p. vii).

In fact, as Nimitz himself admits (p. 298), he does no more than assert the first claim, and offers nothing by way of substantiation. It strikes me as quite literally incredible: were Marx and Engels really *the* 'leading protagonists' in the adoption of the secret ballot in the colony of Victoria in 1856, in the struggle for the 1867 Reform Act in Britain, or for the 1893 introduction of universal adult suffrage in New Zealand, to cite three important milestones in the history of nineteenth-century political democracy? Perhaps Nimitz should have used the indefinite rather than the definite article, but this would have weakened his argument quite considerably.

The great majority of his book is devoted to the second and third claims, which are much easier to defend. Nimitz does so with great energy, setting out the political activities and (to a lesser extent) the political ideas of Marx and Engels in over 300 pages of text, in a volume with very narrow margins and an uncomfortably small typeface. He provides much more detail on their 'party activities' than was available in the earlier sympathetic political biography by Nicolaievsky and Maenchen-Helfen (1973) and the related works by Draper (1977–1991) and Gilbert (1981). For the most part it is a well-written book, though the frequent references to 'the Marx-Engels team' eventually begin to grate, and there are a few curious expressions. Eyebrows may be raised at Nimitz's description of Engels as a 'high school dropout' (p. 10), for example, and of Paris as the 'capitol' of France (p. 74).

This is essentially a work of political history, and to a limited degree also of political theory, and it would be unfair to complain that it contains almost nothing on economics. What there is, however, is contentious, or underdeveloped, or both. I was surprised to read that, in the early 1870s, 'Engels took on tasks that freed Marx up to spend most of his time on the political economy research' (p. 250). If this was so, there was very little to show for it. 'Marx's return to the political economy project' (p. 296) did not lead to any significant progress on the neglected manuscripts that appeared only after his death as the second and third volumes of *Capital* and the three volumes of *Theories of Surplus Value*. Nimitz may be correct in disputing the verdict of Hobsbawm and others that Marx was demoralized in his last years. Perhaps his inactivity owed more to recurrent illness (Nelson, 1999) than to any subconscious recognition that his theoretical ambitions were fundamentally misconceived, as first alleged by Eugen von Bohm-Bawerk (1896 [1966]). Whatever the reasons, Marx's enthusiasm for the critique of political economy had evidently diminished by the last decade of his life, and this seems to have been true also of Engels. After an initial flurry of activity which led to the publication of *Capital*, volume II, only two years after Marx's death, Engels's editorial labours proceeded very slowly indeed (Howard & King, 1989, ch. 1).

Nimitz's only substantial discussion of Marxian political economy comes when he deals with *Value Price and Profit* (later published as *Wages, Price and Profit*, but not 'Profits', p. 189), a posthumously published pamphlet containing the text of a paper read by Marx in 1865 at the General Council of the International Working Men's Association. He was responding to the assertion of the Owenite, John Weston, that trade unions could not advance the material interests of the working class. Weston maintained that increases in money wages would not reduce profits but only increase the price level, leaving real wages unchanged. Marx denied this, invoking his theory of surplus value to argue that 'A general rise in the rate of wages would result in a fall of the general rate of profit, but, broadly speaking, not affect the prices of commodities' (cited, p. 190). Some of the issues raised by the Marx-Weston controversy have a remarkably modern ring. The causes of inflation, the role of class conflict in the distribution of income between capital and labour, the social and political determinants of hours of work – all these are important, and disputed, questions in twenty-first century political economy, and it would again be unreasonable to criticise Nimitz for failing to resolve them. He might, however, have noted that economists broadly sympathetic to Marx have sometimes reached conclusions on these matters diametrically opposed to his. Michal Kalecki, for example, inferred from the experience of the 'Blum experiment' in France under the Popular Front government in 1936 that a money wage increase would normally raise the price level and leave real wages unchanged – which was precisely what Weston had said (Kalecki, 1938).

Nimitz also ignores the crucial *political* dilemma that is posed for Marxists by the day-to-day activities of trade unions. If they can never succeed, if their work is (in Rosa Luxemburg's memorable phrase) 'the labour of Sisyphus', it is difficult to see why they should ever attract mass working-class support. If, however, unions are able to win significant and permanent improvements in wages and working conditions, they serve to make capitalism more palatable to workers than it would otherwise be, not (as Marx imagined) less palatable. Beginning with Engels himself, Marxists attempted to come to terms with the 'incorporation' of unions into the capitalist system, with its inescapable anti-revolutionary implications (see Hyman, 1971 for a useful guide to the literature). Nimitz seems to be unaware of the existence of the problem.

His resolutely uncritical attitude towards Marx (and Engels) leads him into even greater difficulties when it comes to establishing their democratic credentials. Nimitz defines democracy in conventional, liberal terms: 'the institution of "universal suffrage", the "responsibility of the state apparatus to the elected parliament", and the acquisition of civil liberties' (p. vii). The problem is, of course, that Marx's position on the second and third of these criteria was deeply ambivalent. As Steven Lukes has noted, the primary commitment of Marx and Engels was to the ideal of *direct* democracy, and their attitude to *bourgeois* democracy was 'complex and sensitive to its contradictory possibilities'. On the one hand, there seemed (especially to the later Engels) to be a real prospect of achieving socialism through the ballot box, at least in Britain, North America and some parts of Northern and Western Europe. On the other hand, bourgeois democracy was seen as just another form of capitalist class rule, which had to be overthrown by proletarian revolution. 'The implications of this view, which has been the dominant one ... among all Leninists and Trotskyists, are clear: an insurrectionary politics of the transition, an insensitivity to the differences between bourgeois forms of state, and a tendency to regard the suspension of bourgeois democratic freedoms in socialist societies as not incompatible with the socialist project' (Lukes, 1991, p. 134).

On this fundamental question Nimitz does not commit himself either way. I imagine that, forced to choose, he would side with Lenin, whose views on the 'dictatorship of the proletariat', on the principle of 'democratic centralism' and on the related need for rigorous party discipline, he clearly finds more congenial than social democratic 'Parliamentary cretinism'. Indeed, Nimitz attributes to Marx an essentially Leninist position on these issues when he comes to discuss his involvement in the Communist League (pp. 142–147) and the International Working Men's Association (chs 7–9). This takes us back to Bakunin's critique, that Marx and Engels were authoritarian elitists who treated the organisations they worked in as their own personal property, to be closed, reopened or (in the case of the IWMA) shifted across the Atlantic as and when they saw fit. Nimitz's description of these episodes is entirely consistent with the anarchist charge-sheet, and undermines his own interpretation of Marx and Engels as consistent and thoroughgoing democrats. The seeds of the Leninist conception of the vanguard party are clearly visible here. When, a generation on, Rosa Luxemburg and the young Leon Trotsky attacked Lenin's authoritarian stance, they could easily have applied the same criticisms to Marx – not to mention Kautsky and Plekhanov, whose views on this question were not vastly different from those of Lenin at the beginning of the twentieth century (Deutscher, 1954, pp. 89–90; Nettl, 1969, pp. 194–201).

There is one final, and closely related, question on which Nimitz lets Marx and Engels off far too lightly. As Lukes again observes, 'On the issue of democracy under socialism neither classical Marxism nor Marxism-Leninism has had much to say in detail (albeit for different reasons)' (Lukes, 1991, p. 134). Marx's refusal to provide blueprints for a socialist economy extended also, and even more damagingly, to the political organisation of the future classless society. Libertarian socialist and anarchist critics of Marx maintained, and continue to maintain, that direct democracy requires radical decentralisation of economic decision-making, with or without markets, and that vanguard parties of the Leninist type are innately hostile to genuine self-management (a classic text is Bookchin, 1969). For their part defenders of capitalism have always argued that economic freedom is a necessary (if not also a sufficient) condition for political freedom, so that the suppression of markets entails the suppression also of democratic rights. Nimitz never confronts these questions. Those who adhere to the 'article of faith' that he is attempting to undermine – the incompatibility of the socialist project with political democracy – will not find his book at all persuasive.

REFERENCES

Bakunin, M. (1872 [1973]). The International and Karl Marx. In: S. Dolgoff (Ed.), *Bakunin on Anarchy: Selected Works By the Founder of World Anarchism* (pp. 286–320). London: Allen and Unwin.

Bohm-Bawerk, E. von. (1896 [1966]). Karl Marx and the close of his system. In: P. M. Sweezy (Ed.), *Karl Marx and the Close of His System* (pp. 121–196). New York: Kelley.

Bookchin, M. (1969). Listen, Marxist! In: *Bookchin, Post-Scarcity Anarchism* (pp. 173–220). San Francisco: Ramparts Press, 1975.

Deutscher, I. (1954). *The Prophet Armed: Trotsky, 1879–1921*. Oxford: Oxford University Press.

Draper, H. (1977–1991). *Karl Marx's Theory of Revolution* (four vols). New York: Monthly Review Press.

Gilbert, A. (1981). *Marx's Politics: Communists and Citizens*. New Brunswick, N.J.: Rutgers University Press.

Howard, M. C., & King, J. E. (1989). *A History of Marxian Economics: Volume I, 1883–1929*. London: Macmillan and Princeton: Princeton University Press.

Hyman, R. (1971). *Marxism and the Sociology of Trade Unionism*. London: Pluto.

Kalecki, M. (1938). The lesson of the Blum experiment. *Economic Journal, 48,* 26–41.

Lukes, S. (1991). Democracy. In: T. Bottomore (Ed.), *A Dictionary of Marxist Thought* (2nd ed.) (pp. 133–134). Oxford: Blackwell.

Nelson, A. (1999). Marx and medicine. Part II: After the publication of *Das Kapital. Journal of Medical Biography, 7,* 100–110.

Nettl, J. P. (1969). *Rosa Luxemburg* (abridged ed.). Oxford: Oxford University Press.

Nicolaevsky, B., & Maenchen-Helfen, O. (1973). *Karl Marx: Man and Fighter*. London, Allen Lane.

PHILLIPS IN RETROSPECT

David Laidler

A Review Essay on A. W. H. Phillips, *Collected Works in Contemporary Perspective,* edited by Robert Leeson, Cambridge U.K.: Cambridge University Press, 2000, pp. 515 + xvii.

INTRODUCTION

Every economist has heard of Bill Phillips, most of them for the wrong reason. His 1958 empirical study (ch. 25 in this volume), which seemed to establish the existence of an inverse trade-off between wage-inflation and unemployment in the previous 90 years or so of United Kingdom data, was, in its author's own opinion, "quick and dirty" (Ann S. Schwier, p. 25), and "done in a weekend" (Bob Gregory to Leeson, p. 11).[1] Anyone who knows the rest of Phillips work will find Charles Holt's judgement that this famous paper was "without question ... his least solid piece of work" (p. 313) completely uncontroversial. Nor did the Phillips curve stand the test of time, though Fatemeh Shadman-Mehta does show here (ch. 34) that the inverse inflation unemployment trade-off such as Phillips found in the 1863–1913 data is still there when modern econometric techniques are deployed. Converted by others into a policy menu in the 1960s, the Phillips curve is now widely blamed (largely wrongly in my view, as I briefly argue in fn. 8, below) for the policies that led to the great inflation of the 1970s and 1980s. Its creator's other written contributions have largely faded from the sight of all but specialised readers, and there were not many of these others in the first place: barely enough to fill a slim book, even with all surviving unpublished and unfinished essays included.

Research in the History of Economic Thought and Methodology, Volume 20-A, pages 223–235.
Copyright © 2002 by Elsevier Science Ltd.
All rights of reproduction in any form reserved.
ISBN: 0-7623-0847-8

All this has long been a problem for those of us who still remember and unabashedly admire Phillips' work in macroeconomics and econometrics, and have wished to see it accurately remembered and his reputation restored.[2] With this book, Robert Leeson has taken a major step towards such a rehabilitation. He has collected together all of Phillips' written work in economics and econometrics – amounting to under 250 pages – and supplemented it with a series of commentaries and reminiscences by no fewer than 30 others, including himself. Everyone interested in macroeconomics should read the resulting volume, which would, however, be a great deal easier to use for scholarly purposes had its rather thin index had a few more entries, and been supplemented by a dated bibliography of Phillips' writings and a *curriculum vitae*.

PHILLIPS AND HIS RESEARCH AGENDA

Bill Phillips was an extraordinary human being: the same unimpeachable personal integrity that supported his heroism as a prisoner of war of the Japanese lay just below the surface of his academic work too. James Meade, who found him "unaffected, undemonstrative, true and lovable" as a friend, and recognised him as a "commonsensical and versatile genius" (p. 19) seems to me to have been astonishingly unperceptive in referring to him as "a rolling stone intellectually" (p. 18). On the contrary, Phillips' work in economics and econometrics was all-of-a-piece, and stemmed from his profound sense of the potential social importance of macro-stabilisation policy. If he seemed to lose interest in that topic in the mid-1960s, that might have been partly because he was disillusioned at the way in which his important contributions were being ignored, while the "quick and dirty" 1958 piece was attracting so much attention, but it was surely also because he could neither see any way of carrying his work further forward in a useful direction at that time, nor had any interest in playing intellectual games for their own sake.

Phillips was, as we shall see, working on problems that required the estimation of continuous-time dynamic models in an era when the state of the econometrician's art extended only (and only just) to systems of simultaneous equations in discrete time, and when most empirical work even in leading U.S. universities was still carried out with electric-mechanical calculators. It is small wonder that even a man of his quite extraordinary dedication should conclude by the mid-1960s that he had carried the task he had set for himself as far as was then feasible. His decision to move from London to Canberra in 1967 and begin serious work on the economics of China looks to me much more like the act of a profoundly honest man who wished to continue to earn his living by doing the most socially useful work of which he was capable, than an intellectual retreat on the part of someone with a short attention-span. Phillips had, after all, learned to speak and read Chinese while a prisoner of war, and not many China experts then or now combine this skill with capacities as an economist on Phillips' level. He might even have returned to his original line of enquiry as computing technology rapidly improved in the 1970s, but we cannot be sure. Though Bill Phillips lived until 1975, he never recovered from the crippling stroke that he suffered in 1969.

The key to understanding Phillips' research agenda lies in two biographical facts: just before the war, he had qualified as an electrical engineer; and just after it he took a degree in sociology at the London School of Economics.

As part of the latter program, he had to study some basic economics. He encountered the then rather new, but already almost standard, IS-LM interpretation of Keynesian economics. That model's intellectual dominance arose from its rendering technically tractable a key sub-set of the problems with which economists had struggled in the 1920s and 1930s. It had done so by reducing complicated dynamics to comparative statics, but the simplicity of IS-LM was deceptive, hiding all manner of difficulties, not least in the area of stock-flow interaction. For Phillips, there were obvious (because he was a genius) parallels between this model's configuration as well as the macro-stabilization issues its users wanted to address, and the continuous time dynamic systems and the control problems analysed by electrical engineers.

With some advice and encouragement from his fellow student and friend Walter Newlyn (see pp. 31–38), who would in due course make a distinguished career in the Economics Department at the University of Leeds, he set about designing a machine in which water flowed through transparent pipes and/or gathered in reservoirs, to demonstrate the macro-economy's properties. He described this machine, and the economic interpretation of its workings, in his first publication (ch. 10). There had been analyses along such lines before, complete with diagrams – see for example Foster and Catchings (1923) – but Phillips actually built his machine, and it worked too, give or take an unfortunate tendency to spring leaks, that had nothing to do with its basic design (see Elizabeth Johnson, p. 23). He thus constructed a working physical representation of what Alan Coddington (1976) would later call "hydraulic Keynesianism".

In those times, universities were still run by senior academics rather than professional administrators, and so it came about that, when Lionel Robbins' attention was drawn to Phillips' astonishing accomplishment in 1950, that recent recipient of a pass degree – the lowest non-failing grade that could be awarded – in sociology was appointed to the faculty of what was arguably already, and certainly soon to become, Britain's premier economics department. By 1958 Phillips had been appointed to the Tooke Chair, earlier held by Hayek, though his inaugural lecture (ch. 22) was not given until 1961. This was to be his last paper to appear in a journal (*Economica*, 1962), and his second last publication, but in the intervening decade he had helped to transform forever the way in which economists think about questions of stabilization policy.

Phillips' machine, though intended primarily as a teaching device, was also a pioneering analogue computer (see Doron Swade, ch. 14), which is why a working model now graces London's Science Museum, and it could not have been built if he had not had a crystal-clear understanding of the dynamics of stock-flow interaction in continuous time. Anyone who doubts that this in itself was a rare and notable achievement in 1950 need only recall that the debate among Patinkin (1956), Archibald and Lipsey (1958) and Clower and Burstein (1960) about stock flow interactions in and out of the steady state, which is the one still remembered as having finally tidied up the basics of this contentious topic, did not even begin till Patinkin's brief visit to LSE in 1957. But for Phillips, understanding the economic dynamics was but a means to a much more important end, namely the analysis of stabilization policy.

The first sentences of the three substantive articles (chs. 16, 17, 21) in which he extended the basic insights that had gone into constructing the machine, and developed their implications, make his intentions plain: "Recommendations for stabilising aggregate production and employment have usually been derived from the analysis of multiplier models, using the methods of comparative statics. This type of analysis does not provide a very firm basis for policy recommendations" (1954, p. 134). "In an earlier article I used a number of dynamic process models to illustrate the operation of certain types of stabilisation policy" (1957, p. 169). "The purpose of this article is to develop a simple aggregative model that may be used to study both the problem of reducing short-period fluctuations of an economy and the problem of attaining longer-term objectives relating to employment, the price level and growth" (1961, p. 195). These articles do not deal with questions of optimal control, as the title of Adrian Pagan's otherwise exemplary introduction to the first two of them misleadingly suggests, but with questions about how what we would now call policy reaction functions might be configured in order to ensure that their addition to the system would make it more, rather than less prone to fluctuate. It was only later, in the 1960s, that Phillips became explicitly concerned with optimal control, as Pagan (p. 131) does indeed make clear.

Be that as it may, the broad results of this work of Phillips are commonplace now, but to those exposed to them when they were first developed, who were used to analysing monetary and fiscal policy problems with IS-LM comparative statics, they were astounding. Phillips' summary of his conclusions for a general audience, presented in the first part of his 1961 inaugural lecture (ch. 22) may be paraphrased as follows: The implementation of stabilisation policy is subject to time delays and lags, and so is its influence on the economy; if that policy is to help, rather than make matters worse, the time form of its responses must be carefully calibrated to the dynamics of the economic system that is to be stabilised, because even quite small errors in such calibration can make all the difference between success and damaging failure; the policy tool least likely to do harm is one that can be implemented quickly and will have rapid effects on aggregate demand; and the most dangerous is one that has large effects that appear only after a long delay. So certain kinds of fiscal policy, for example "a general sales tax . . . adjusted by small amounts at frequent intervals . . . would do the job" (p. 217); but much more quantitative knowledge than was available in 1961 was required to make the world safe for activist monetary policy.[3]

Now Phillips was not the only one uttering such warnings about monetary policy at that time. The similarities between his and Friedman's (e.g. 1960) views are obvious. This is not entirely a co-incidence, for Phillips and Friedman met and had extensive discussions in 1952, during the latter's visit to the U.K., when, among other things, he had suggested to Friedman the adaptive expectations formula that would in due course appear in Philip Cagan's Ph.D. thesis, later published as his famous (1956) article on hyperinflation (see Cagan, p. 22). But there is an all-important difference between their approaches, nevertheless. Phillips did not share Friedman's belief in the inherent stability of the market economy, so where the latter sought to limit the harm that monetary policy could do by advocating a legislated constant money growth rule, Phillips canvassed the altogether more difficult alternative of seeking quantitative information sufficiently precise to enable it to do good by implementing well configured policy reaction functions.[4] Hence his interest in the problems of estimating the parameters of continuous time dynamic systems, not to mention his concern, in his final unfinished paper (ch. 52), with the influence of subjecting such systems to policy controls on the subsequent identifiability of those parameters.

THE PHILLIPS CURVE

Phillips' work on the infamous curve that still bears his name was nevertheless related to his overall agenda of macroeconomic research. Feedbacks from output to price level variations and hence to the stock of real balances were integral to the model presented in is 1954 paper on "Stabilisation in a Closed Economy" (ch. 16) which derived from his Ph.D. thesis, and their modelling there represented a considerable advance over the crude treatment they had received in his hydraulic machine. Indeed, figure 16–11 of this paper (p. 151) is an analytic version of the Phillips curve drawn in price inflation output space. This relationship is also given a lengthy theoretical discussion in the text, as William Baumol (pp. 285–286) points out. It is thus a myth that the Phillips curve was a purely empirical relationship, devoid of theoretical foundations.

The curve was presented in (1954) as an adjustment equation describing the out-of-equilibrium behaviour of the price level, not as a structural equation of the steady state system, and that is also how, with suitable substitutions of variables, its money-wage unemployment version would also be presented in (1958), albeit quite tersely. The idea of the curve came from Phillips' reading of Bent Hansen's (1951) *Theory of Inflation,* but, though this is not how Phillips ever put it, at least to my knowledge, it amounted to a formalization of the quite conventional price-output dynamics that underlay, for example, Patinkin's (1948) discussion of the real-balance effect. This perhaps explains the extreme hostility, noted by Lipsey (p. 237), displayed to the Phillips curve by such Cambridge Keynesians as Richard Kahn.

It seems to have been Henry Phelps-Brown who suggested to Phillips that available data on money wages and unemployment might throw some light on the empirical content of his adjustment mechanism, and recently published scatter diagrams in A. J. Brown's (1956) *Great Inflation,* with which Phillips was familiar (Brown, p. xiii), must have also pointed in this direction. There is nothing surprising, then, in Phillips, whose innate curiosity was legendary, having devoted a metaphorical weekend to looking into the possibility. But where Brown had simply drawn the scatters, Phillips fitted a curve, and superimposed it upon them: an apparently stable empirical relationship, capable of formulation as a simple inverse function, was thus called into being, and in an intellectual milieu at the LSE where, under the influence of Karl Popper, empirical testing was *de rigeur* among the younger faculty.[5] Lipsey (1961) followed up Phillips' study, and the subsequent history of the curve in mainstream economics needs no further elaboration here.[6]

It is, however, worth noting that Phillips followed up his own work in his own way. A subsequent paper dealt with Australian data, where, tantalisingly, real rather than money wages were the focus, and some preliminary work was clearly done on U.S. data too, for he referred to it in his inaugural lecture in 1961 (p. 222). Phillips himself never presented the curve as a policy menu, but he was clearly aware that it could be interpreted that way, and might treated as such by governments. That is why, when considering the implications of his work for the international monetary system towards the end of his inaugural lecture, he suggested that a "... limited degree of exchange rate flexibility would allow each country time to find by trial and error that compromise between its internal objectives which was consistent with its exchange rate policy" (1962, p. 223).

But as that same lecture also made clear, what interested Phillips about his curve was not what it revealed about an inflation-unemployment trade-off that might be exploitable for policy purposes, but what it revealed about the unemployment rate that would rule when the economy was in an inflation-free steady state. And as a number of contributors to this volume note, in discussing the factors determining this unemployment rate, and what might be done to reduce it should it turn out to be uncomfortably high, as he thought it probably was in the U.S., he came very close to anticipating many a much later discussion of the determinants of the "natural" unemployment rate and how to reduce it.

PHILLIPS' INFLUENCE

Though Phillips is nowadays mainly remembered as the author of the 1958 paper that he himself thought rather peripheral to his main line of enquiry, the ideas which he found really important had considerable and visible influence for a while. In the 1950s and 1960s, the computational burdens of implementing his agenda must have seemed insuperable, but, by the early 1970s, the technology available to academics had advanced sufficiently to permit his erstwhile colleague Rex Bergstrom, along with their student Clifford Wymer, to estimate what was clearly a development of Phillips' 1961 model of growth and cycles using United Kingdom data. This paper, the outcome of research largely carried out at LSE, was not published until 1976, but it was complete at least as early as 1974. It pioneered the application of continuous time estimation techniques to complete macroeconomic models, in which all the cross equation constraints implicit in the stock flow interactions that lay at their heart were observed and exploited; and the dynamics of various policy feedback rules could also be investigated by simulating the resulting system.

The empirical modelling of stock flow interactions that these techniques permitted turned out to be well suited to the then novel "monetary approach" to balance of payments analysis which was the focus of a research programme led by Harry Johnson at LSE and Alexander Swoboda in Geneva. A substantial literature soon developed out of the adoption of the Bergstrom-Wymer techniques by economists associated with this programme. It dealt with the analysis of monetary policy issues particularly, though not exclusively, as they arose in open economies, and among its highlights were papers by Jonson (1976), Jonson, Moses and Wymer (1976), not to mention Gandolfo's substantial (1981) monograph. For a while it seemed to some – this reviewer included – that this work would have a serious and permanent impact on mainstream macroeconomics.[7] This was not to be the case, and with hindsight I conjecture that this was for the following reasons.

To begin with the specific models spawned by this literature turned out to be extremely fragile in the face of new data, and relationships that had seemed stable when fitted down to the early 1970s, collapsed as new observations were generated and added to the sample.[8] Demand for money functions everywhere began to shift as a result of inflation-induced institutional change, and this was bound to undermine the stability of any empirical macro model in which a key factor driving expenditure flows was a discrepancy between stocks of money supplied and demanded. Closely related, the still unexplained productivity growth slowdown of the early 1970s shifted the steady state growth paths relative to which these models' endogenous variables fluctuated, and at the time it occurred, this slowdown was not even perceived for what it was, let alone successfully modelled. In any event, the gross empirical failure of an initially promising class of models was sufficient to ensure that any agency looking for policy guidance from them, as a number of central banks were doing in the 1970s, quickly lost interest in them.

Perhaps more important to the demise of this extension of Phillips' original research agenda, however, was the failure of his work, apart from that wretched (1958) curve, at any time to penetrate American thinking about macro-economics. In the early 1960s, when his ideas about stabilization policy were new, the major item on the policy agenda in the United States was the Kennedy-Johnson tax cut, which was supposed to be an exercise in demand management. A body of analysis that demonstrated the patent absurdity of using for such purposes measures that required 18 months or more to deploy was hardly going to be popular among their supporters, while their soon-to-be-called "monetarist" opponents had little interest in following up a body of work whose ultimate aim was nevertheless to render stabilization policy feasible and effective. Furthermore, as Lipsey (pp. 236–238) documents, many and various, and some-times quite extraordinary, misinterpretations of the Phillips curve are ubiquitous in the American literature of the 1960s, and it is hard to believe that the often distinguished economists who perpetrated them could have been familiar with the wider body of Phillips' work, or if they were, had taken the trouble to digest it.

And then, along came New-classical economics, an approach to macro-economic analysis that was quite antithetical to any work in the tradition to which Phillips' had sought to contribute. New-classical economics was, above all, about establishing the primacy in macroeconomics of maximising economic theory over empirical evidence, and with re-configuring on a new basis the monetarist case against stabilization policy. It was not about improving the empirical modelling that underlay such policy. The critical factor that its exponents stressed in making the case for their approach, and hence in attracting attention and followers, was the allegedly spectacular failure of an apparently well-established empirical relationship, namely, and ironically, the Phillips curve, which was demonstrably inconsistent with maximising premises, when it had, again allegedly, been made the basis for policy. And the potential audience for this case had already been rendered receptive by the fact that from the 1950s onwards maximising theory had demonstrated a considerable capacity for improving the component equations of standard macro-econometric models.[9]

What matters here is not whether the success of New-classical economics in the 1970s was deserved, but that it occurred, and more particularly that one of its key components, the "Lucas critique", quickly became close to conventional wisdom. It was essential to Phillips' approach to policy that the parameters of the system to be controlled remained independent of the rules being followed by those controlling it, but the Lucas critique had it that, in general, the properties of a macroeconomic system would be highly unlikely to remain invariant to the rules guiding stabilization policy. Hence, its widespread acceptance transformed Phillips' hitherto progressive research agenda into a theoretical dead-end.

In 1968, in his final and unfinished paper (ch. 52), Phillips himself came very close to developing the Lucas critique, as Robin Court (ch. 51) argues. Specifically, he showed that once a system was subject to control through a feedback rule, "observations during the period of control cannot be used to obtain improved estimates of parameters, which is a serious drawback" (p. 486). But this is not quite what Lucas later argued. Though Phillips' result was extremely damaging to his own agenda, its basis was purely *econometric*. It was not derived from the fundamentally *economic* premise, namely that maximising agents will gather information about any policy rule and then act upon it, which underlay Lucas's conclusions. This absence of any attention to maximising behaviour was not just a characteristic of Phillips' last paper, but of his whole *oeuvre*, and in this his *oeuvre* reflected the style of macro-economics of the 1950s.

There is nowadays a distinctly pejorative overtone to the phrase "hydraulic Keynesianism" which Phillips' work inspired. Had it been in use in the 1950s or 1960s, it would not have carried any such connotation, however. This is an accurate indicator of the extent to which New-classical ideas have changed the way all of us think about how macroeconomic theory should be done.

This observation should not be read as implying that I regard the triumph of New-classical macroeconomics as an unequivocal blessing. Those sound micro-foundations don't seem to impose many restrictions on aggregate behaviour once one takes aggregation over heterogeneous utility and production functions seriously, and I can't think of any reason why one should not do so, particularly in the light of the empirical difficulties that the New-classical agenda itself has encountered over the years. While we wait for further developments in macro-theory, moreover, we still need quantitative policy-relevant information on the workings of the economy, and much of what we have these days seems to be based on empirically established regularities of a type that Phillips would have felt at home with.

Phillips was developing the ideas and using the vocabulary of error-correction mechanisms in the early 1950s, and as Peter Phillips (ch. 36) and David Hendry and Graham Mizon (ch. 38) tell us, it was his teaching, along with that of Dennis Sargan that inspired the development of many of the techniques that are now routinely used to estimate the functions that we use to describe the above-mentioned regularities. Furthermore, the advent of inflation targeting in the 1990s has helped stimulate a now flourishing literature of the role of reaction functions that incorporate feedback rules in the conduct of monetary policy not to mention their stabilising properties. Phillips would easily have recognised the relationship of such work to his, and from time to time, some contributors to the modern literature explicitly acknowledge its existence, though perhaps not often enough.[10] In short, if those of his papers that Bill Phillips himself considered important have always been cited much less frequently than the 1958 *Economica* article, that does not mean that the ideas they developed have been less influential in the long run. The overarching scientific apparatus that he envisaged as the end product of his work would have been an estimated model with control mechanisms fully integrated into its structure, which would have been continuously re-estimated as new data accumulated. Such a model has proved impossible to build, but a number of the components that Phillips thought essential to its construction have turned out to be extremely useful, not to say durable, in their own right.

CONCLUDING COMMENT

Historians of economic thought know that citation counts are a very imperfect measure of an economist's influence. Imagine, for example, what Ricardo's might look like were he cited every time someone mentioned comparative advantage, or Walras' were he cited every time anyone mentioned general equilibrium, or indeed on a smaller scale, what Bill Phillips' own count might look like had he written up the adaptive expectations idea and published it in a journal, instead of simply passing it on to Friedman and Cagan. Even so, Phillips' personality mixed creativity and unselfish modesty in such an unusually high ratio that his contributions have long needed a little help to find their proper and important place in the history of our sometimes unpleasantly competitive subject. It is as fortunate as it is just that his work has found a capable and dedicated advocate in Robert Leeson. We are all in his debt for this volume.

NOTES

1. Unless otherwise explicitly indicated, author, chapter and page references in what follows refer to the volume under review.

2. Let me declare an interest here: though I was never close to Phillips, I attended his lectures on stabilization policy as a final year undergraduate in 1958–1959, had the privilege of being his very junior colleague in 1961–1962, and worked with one of his most able intellectual grandchildren, Peter Jonson, in the 1970s. This review is not, then, a disinterested commentary.

3. And because the world operates in continuous time, the quantitative information had to be obtained by methods that would yield the same numerical values for the parameters of the economic system regardless of the time intervals separating the observations used in the estimation process. Note that ordinary discrete time methods will not do this trick, as anyone who has contemplated the results of aggregating an equation with a lagged dependent variable fitted to, say, quarterly data, up to annual observations soon discovers. See Y. Mundlak (1961) for a contemporary discussion of this specific question.

4. The reader's attention is drawn to the considerable confusion created in modern discussions of these issues by the use of the words "rule" or "rule-guided" to characterise both approaches to policy, despite the fact that they are very different from one another. This confusion also underlies the classification by some historians of monetary economics of anyone who ever said that the rate of money growth should be held steady as a "pioneer monetarist". The point about Friedman's rule was that it was to be legally binding.

5. This activity was centered on the famous seminar on Methodology, Measurement and Testing. Its deliberations over Phillips paper are discussed here by Holt (pp. 310–311). De Marchi (Ed.) 1988 is the standard source on Popper's influence on empirical work in economics.

6. Complementary accounts of these subsequent developments are to be found in Laidler (1997) and Leeson (1997).

7. There were many close contacts between the Inflation Worshop at the University of Manchester that Michael Parkin and I were running at this time, and the LSE groups. And both of us, not to mention Wymer, were subsequently visitors to the Reserve Bank of Australia, into whose research agenda Peter Jonson introduced modelling of the Begstrom-Wymer type upon his return there from London in 1975.

8. Monetary instability, which had been latent in United States policies towards financing the Vietnam War and the War on Poverty, had been contained for a while by the workings of the Bretton Woods system, but it came into full view when that system broke down in the early 1970s under the stresses that those policies had created. That is how, in my view, the inflation of the 1970s and 1980s began. It had nothing to do with attempts to exploit the Phillips curve.

9. On all this, see Lucas and Sargent's (1978) polemic "The End of Keynesian Economics" To say that this article's presentation of the history of macroeconomics prior to the arrival of New-classical ideas is inaccurate would be to put it mildly, but what is important to note here is that it was nevertheless found persuasive by a large audience. The question of the article's accuracy must be taken up at another time. But see fn. 8 above on the role of the Phillips Curve in bringing about the inflation of the 1970s.

10. For example Levin, Wieland and Williams, economists at the Board of Governors of the Federal Reserve System, note that their (1999) paper on "Robustness of Simple Policy Rules under Model Uncertainty" is in "the long distinguished tradition dating to Phillips (1954)", but this is the only reference to Phillips' work in the entire volume.

REFERENCES

Archibald, G. C., & Lipsey, R. G. (1958). Money and Value Theory: a Critique of Lange and Patinkin. *Review of Economic Studies, 24* (Oct.), 1–22.

Bergstrom, A. R., & Wymer, C. R. (1976). A Model of Neoclassical Disequilibrium Growth and its Application to the United Kingdom. In: A. R. Bergstrom (Ed.), *Statistical Inference in Continuous Time Economic Models.* Amsterdam: North-Holland.

Brown, A. J. (1956). *The Great Inflation 1939–51.* London: Oxford University Press.

Cagan, P. (1956). The Monetary Dynamics of Hyperinflation. In: M. Friedman (Ed.), *Studies in the Quantity Theory of Money.* Chicago: Univ. of Chicago Press.

Clower, R. W., & Burstein, M.. L (1960). On the Invariance of Demand for Cash and Other Assets, *Review of Economic Studies, 28,* (Oct.), 32–36.

Coddington, A. (1976). Keynesian Economics: the Search for First Principles. *Journal of Economic Literature, 14* (Dec.), 1258–1273.

De Marchi, N. (Ed.) (1988). *The Popperian Legacy in Economics.* Cambridge U.K.: Cambridge Univ. Press.

Foster, W. T., & Catchings, W. (1923). *Money.* Boston: Houghton Mifflin.

Friedman, M. (1960). *A Program for Monetary Stability.* New York: Fordham Univ. Press.

Gandolfo, G. (1981). *Quantitative Analysis and Econometric Estimation of Continuous Time Dynamic Models.* Amsterdam: North Holland.

Hansen, B. (1951). *A Study in the Theory of Inflation.* London: Allen and Unwin.

Jonson, P. D. (1976). Money and Economic Activity in the Open Economy: the United Kingdom 1880–1970. *Journal of Political Economy, 84* (Nov.–Dec), 979–1012.

Jonson, P. D., Moses, E., & Wymer, C. R. (1976). A Minimal Model of the Australian Economy, Discussion Paper 7601. Sydney: Reserve Bank of Australia.

Laidler, D. (1997). The Emergence of the Phillips Curve as a Policy Menu. In: B. C. Eaton & R. D. Harris (Eds), *Essays in Trade, Technology and Economics in Honour of Richard G. Lipsey.* Cheltenham: Edward Elgar.

Leeson, R. (1997). The Political Economy of the Inflation-Unemployment Trade-Off. *History of Political Economy, 29* (Spring), 117–156.

Levin, A., Wieland, V., & Williams, J. C. (1999). Robustness of Simple Policy Rules under Model Uncertainty. In: J. B. Taylor (Ed.), *Monetary Policy Rules.* Chicago: Univ. of Chicago Press.

Lucas, R. E. Jr., & Sargent, T. J. (1978). After Keynesian Economics. In: Federal Reserve Bank of Boston, *After the Phillips Curve: Persistence of High Inflation and High Unemployment.* Conference Series No. 19, Boston, Massachusetts.

Mundlak, Y. (1961). Aggregation over Time in Distributed Lag Models. *International Economic Review, 2* (April) 154–163.

Patinkin, D. (1948). Price Flexibility and Full Employment. *American Economic Review, 48* (Sept.), 542–641.

Patinkin, D. (1956). *Money, Interest and Prices.* New York: Harper and Row.

A HAWK'S EYE VIEW OF ECONOMICS

Thomas Mayer

A Review Essay of Ross Emmett *Selected Essays by Frank Knight* Vol. 1, *What is Truth in Economics?* Chicago, University of Chicago Press, 1999.

INTRODUCTION

This first volume of a two volume set of essays of Frank Knight covers a broad range of topics. There are 14 essays plus Emmett's introduction. I discuss each of them separately to aid those who do not want to read all the essays, and do so under four rubrics, methodology, economic institutions and systems, microeconomics and capital theory and miscellaneous essays. I stress those essays that have most relevance to current debates, and that means largely those dealing with methodology, because here there has been less progress since Knight's time (1885–1972) than on most of his other topics. Given the depth of Knight's thoughts it is better to discuss a few of them in detail than to scatter one's shots, and it is also better to devote nearly all space to Knight's ideas than to discuss at length whether Emmett selected the right essays.

Page references, unless otherwise attributed, are to the Emmett book.

Research in the History of Economic Thought and Methodology, Volume 20-A, pages 237–249.
Copyright © 2002 by Elsevier Science Ltd.
All rights of reproduction in any form reserved.
ISBN: 0-7623-0847-8

1. METHODOLOGY

> Behind every fact is a theory and behind that an interest. There is no purely objective reason
> for believing anything ... and if our feelings tell us nothing about reality then we know
> and can know nothing about it, ... [T]esting observations is chiefly, and always ultimately
> a social activity. This fact makes all knowledge of the world of sense observation . . .. itself
> a social activity. ... Any simple antithesis between observation and inference is utterly
> untenable, if not downright foolish.
> ... [T]he general issue is whether any serious attempt to discuss any social phenomena in
> a really objective way can be more than a waste of effort or even less than a serious menace.

No, this is not by some trendy professor of English in 2001, but by Knight
(pp. 54, 377, 379–380, 176) writing between 1922 and 1940. Like post-
modernists he realized that the imposing temple of the social sciences is built
on sand, but unlike them he did not conclude that the god of reason is dead,
and that we are therefore free to believe anything we want. Instead, Knight
used it to attack only a narrow positivistic science that downgrades the traditional methods used to study ethics and the insights verstehen provides for
social scientists. Thus he wrote: "we must learn to think in terms of 'value
standards'. . .. It is the higher goal of conduct to test and try these values, to
define and improve them, ... There are no rules for judging values ... but it
is also most false to assert that one opinion is as good as another. . . ." (p. 55).
He also criticized the attempt to ban all metaphysical concepts in both the
natural and social sciences (see Hammond, 1991).

This is brought out best in the last essay in this book, "Truth in Economics",
a "review" of Terence Hutchison's *The Significance and Postulates of Economic
Theory*. I placed "review" in parentheses because, as Hutchison's (1940) reply
makes clear, Knight dealt only with a small part of the book, primarily the
introductory chapter, and used this as a peg for his criticism of positivism.
(Anyone with a serious interest in this essay should also read Hutchison's reply,
and Knight's (1940) rejoinder.) Hutchison had advocated some relatively
new positivistic ideas, and tried to give economics an empirical turn. Knight's
reaction was scathing, calling the book "dangerous and pernicious", superficial
and involving "dogmatic over-simplification." (p. 373). Like McCloskey (1985)
in our day, Knight objected to "science" with a capital S, and to the belief in
the unity of the sciences, though as Hammond (1991) points out, Knight held
up physics as an example for economics. But to Knight the social sciences are
not just natural sciences writ small. They have their own criteria of justification,
Since they deal not with inanimate objects but with subjects that have free
will, they cannot produce predictive laws like those of physics. But they also
possess a great advantage: our casual interaction with other people gives us

knowledge from which we can derive basic premises, a point encapsulated later by Fritz Machlup (1991) in the title of his paper: "If Atoms Could Talk. . . ." This provides the most useful source of knowledge for economists, and it is knowledge that is more certain than knowledge of physical reality.

Presumably one reason why Knight treated as so important the knowledge that we have of our fellow man from our personal experience is because he distrusted statistics:

> whose economic meaning and significance is uncertain and dubious. . . . In this field the Kelvin dictum ["where you cannot measure your knowledge is meager and unsatisfactory"] very largely means in practice "if you cannot measure, measure anyhow." . . . [I]n the field of human interests and relationships much of our most important knowledge is inherently nonquantitative (p. 397).

Knight – who rejected the distinction between analytic and synthetic statements and considered mathematics to be an empirical science – therefore argued that economics is like geometry a "concrete deductive science", though its "data are intuitive in a far higher or purer sense than is true of mathematics itself" (p. 386). To Knight prediction had little role in economic theory, and cannot be used to test it; there are no "facts" that are not steeped in theory (see Hammond, 1991).

Knight's methodology thus differs sharply from that of the second (Friedman and Stigler's) Chicago school with its positivistic base (see Hirsch & Hirsch, 1980). On the whole, I prefer the latter. But it does depart too far from Knight in its rejection of casual observation of human behavior and introspection. These tools provide us with much tacit knowledge that forms the background to our theory. Not only are they useful in the context of discovery, but also in the context of verification. Given the limitations of our theory, empirical methods and data, we should hesitate (though not be entirely unwilling) to accept results that are counter-intuitive, that is inconsistent with what we know about human behavior from casual observation and introspection. The less we have to rely on these the better, but beggars can't be choosers.

A serious problem for Knight's (and Robbins') methodology is that we want to go further than a very general version of the assumption of rational utility maximization will carry us. Some theories, e.g. Ricardian equivalence and efficient market theory, require very strong version of this assumption, and our general knowledge of human behavior and introspection does not necessarily tell us that it holds in such a strong form. But if assumptions are not a sufficiently accurate descriptions of reality, then conclusions validly drawn from them need not hold. And whether the assumptions are sufficiently accurate can only be determined by testing empirically the conclusions drawn from them (see

Hutchison, 1940; Mayer, 1995, Ch. 7, 2000), Put differently, granted that, by and large, people behave in a rational self-interested way, does anyone's introspection and observation of human behavior deny that occasionally economic agents act irrationally and with motives other than self-interest, unless the latter is defined broadly enough to be meaningless, and certainly not to be identified with income maximization? The Knightian response would be that economic theory is an idealization concerned only with the by and large, and that deciding whether a particular situation falls in that rubric is a matter for applied economics. That is unobjectionable, but it means that one cannot reject explanations of economic phenomena, such as irrational exuberance, out of hand because they are inconsistent with economic theory. Thus it limits the importance of economic theory and shifts the emphasis to applied economics, where the case for a soft version of positivism is stronger.

Knight developed his critique of positivism further in three other essays reprinted in this book. In "Statics and Dynamics: Some Queries Regarding Mechanical Analogy in Economics," (Ch. 7) Knight enlarged on his discussion of the superficiality of pretending to do economics as though it were physics; physicists and economists may use the same words but interpret them differently. It is not surprising that Knight with his sharp eye for confused language found the terms "statics" and "dynamics" vague and frequently misused. When Knight wrote this essay (1940) the former was frequently used as little more than a term of opprobrium and the latter as a term of approval.

The confusions that Knight criticized in 1940 have largely disappeared. We still use terms imported from physics, but few economists now treat them as analogies that lend credence to our theory. Even when stripped of its honorific association with physics the concept of equilibrium is a useful theoretical term that allows us to organize our thinking and to solve many problems better than we could in some other way. (Perhaps this is merely due to path dependency in economic research, but that does not maker it any less true.) Similarly, statics and dynamics are no longer vague concepts, but can be made specific. Yet Knight's essay still provides a useful warning that factors that can be taken as approximately fixed at one level of analysis become themselves variables in a longer time frame. Thus growth theorists may find useful Knight's catalogue of factors that come into play in the long run, and that cannot be properly viewed as equilibrium processes.

In his 1922 paper "Ethics and the Economic Interpretation" (Ch. 2) Knight discussed the limits of economic theory. One is that it cannot answer normative questions, a point that is nowadays generally thought of in connection with Robbins (1932). Another limitation is that economics is only one part of the positive study of the economy, since it deals only with the principles that govern conduct in the abstract, while we need history to tells us what actual conduct was in specific circumstances.

To Knight another major limitation of economic theory is that it treats wants as given. Wants should not be treated as fixed and known; their essence is growth and change. Sensible people do not desire satisfaction of their wants, but more and improved wants. "We strive to find out our real wants, more than to get what we want (p. 1). Wants are created and changed by the social system, and driven by the contrary desires both to be like others, and to differ from them. The satisfaction of real wants, that is of what is biologically necessary for life, accounts for only a small proportion of our expenditures." Thus "life is not fundamentally a striving for ends, for satisfactions, but rather for bases for further striving." (p. 43) To Knight happiness in the sense of having current wants satisfied is not what men strive for, since it depends more on spiritual than material resources. Thus almost 80 years ago Knight provided a solution for the now well-known puzzle that cross-country studies of happiness do not show the strong positive correlation with income that economists might expect.

Knight's message about the changeability of wants differs sharply from the conventional wisdom of economists. The issue is empirical. Presumably Knight argued on the basis of what we know from introspection and everyday observation. But do these really tell us that wants are highly changeable? Moreover. numerous demand functions that assume stable tastes have been successfully fitted since the time Knight wrote, which suggests that wants are stable. Knight would have to argue here either that: (a) the stable demand functions that have been reported are a biased sample of all demand functions because unstable ones are not reported; or (b) that the definition of stable as a high R^2, etc., is inadequate because it stresses short-run forecasting, or because it allows forecast errors that are too large; or else (c) that many demand functions show stability only because they hide changes in tastes behind other variables. A difficult issue here is that from a pragmatic viewpoint we need to ask not just whether wants are "stable" on some more or less arbitrary definition, but whether the assumption of stable wants allows us to be more productive than we would be if we do not assume stable wants. But "productive" generally cannot be defined without bringing in values.

In another essay, "The Limitations of Scientific Method in Economics", (Ch. 1), Knight argued for the importance of the role played by consciousness and human will, where scientific study is less helpful than is literature. Hence, he argued, while scientific methods have a limited role in finding "statistical laws", such as the causes of divorce, prediction and control are impossible in human affairs. All we can do in the science of economics is to draw from a few obviously correct premises implications that go well beyond what common sense tells us. In addition to scientific economics there is applied economics that both quantifies the theoretical factors in particular instances, and deals with factors specific to particular circumstances. But applied economics has very severe limitations since its data lack "the stability, classifiability and measurability requisite to scientific treatment" (p. 35).

Whether applied economics does have such serious limitation now that we have vastly more data, techniques and computational power is questionable. And so are discussions of whether economics is a "science" because at present we lack an adequate definition of "science." Besides, much of the support for calling economics a science may reflect not much more than the correct belief that economics will advance further if it adopts the scientific virtues of objectivity, intellectual openness, etc. But that is true also of literary criticism and art history. Moreover, one may question the extent to which these virtues are practiced in economics. A recent paper (McCullough & Vinod, 1999) showed that regression results are often highly dependent on the particular program used. If economists were really imbued with scientific values many of them would have rerun the regressions in their previously published papers. How many did?

In still another methodological essay, "Fact and Metaphysics in Economic Psychology," (Ch. 5) published in 1925, Knight focused specifically on the then popular doctrine of behaviorism, with its denial of consciousness as a theory of human behavior, and its insistence on looking only at observable physical facts. Knight's arguments are persuasive; for example, he rightly points out that if behaviorists really believed what they say they would not bother to try to convince anyone. In the process of rejecting behaviorism Knight argued for a Popperian recognition of the frailty of our knowledge, as well as for social constructionism. Knight deserves credit for having chosen the right side of the debate and supporting it with powerful arguments. But it is not clear why Emmett chose to reprint this essay, given the diminished status of behaviorism.

2. INSTITUTIONS AND ECONOMIC SYSTEMS

Knight is the progenitor of the Chicago School, which is known everywhere as a staunch supporter of capitalism. So one knows what to expect when Knight (in Ch. 3, "The Ethics of Competition") evaluated capitalism. But expectations can be wrong. Knight presented a scathing criticism. He listed the usual catalog of faults: market power, lack of information on product quality and markets, externalities and public goods, the need to control the money supply (and Knight argues, hence credit and the quality of bank loans), and an ethically arbitrary distribution of income along with a great degree of inequality (due to "the inheritance of wealth, culture, educational advantages, and economic opportunities"), that has "bad results for personality at both ends of the scale," (pp. 68–69), as well as a savings rate that is unlikely to be optimal. Knight adds to all this the social determination of wants, the market's corruption of tastes, imperfect factor mobility, and irrational attitudes toward risk among other irrationalities, since "human activity is largely impulsive" (p. 68).

Knight rejected any attempt to read an ethical message into marginal productivity theory, i.e. that owners of factors *ought* to be paid their marginal product. The capitalist ethics of payment according to marginal product is only one of several ethical systems, and only ethicists and not economists can tell us which system is preferable. Much of this essay is a rousing defence of the autonomy of ethics against attempts to treat it as a positive science. (This is, of course, a point that many consider to have been settled long ago by David Hune, but Knight does not refer to Hume.) Moreover, in a capitalist system not only marginal productivity, but also such factors as luck and inheritance, play a large role in the distribution of income.

Knight also looked at an alternative attempt to justify a capitalist ethic, that the competitive game with the striving that it engenders is ethically worthy. But he rejected this defence by contrasting an ethical system derived from competition with the Judeo-Christian ethic.

But unlike other critics of capitalism Knight did not urge its abandonment. Other systems may be worse. Though Knight does not discuss this in any detail (in these essays anyway), his position is clear. He is a Hobbsian pessimist. The problems in creating a just and efficient society are insuperable, so that a system can be both bad and yet the best.

Knight's antipathy to government intervention is brought out in his "review" of Sumner Slichter's (1931) elementary textbook, a book that advanced the "progressive" New Deal viewpoint ("The Newer Economics, and the Economics of Control," Chapter 8). As with Hutchison's book, this "review" deals with only a small part of the hook, and less than half of it focuses on Slichter's book; the major part is an insightful, though rambling, disquisition on the status of rationality and objectivity in the treatment of social problems. Here Knight showed himself as extraordinarily world-weary and cynical in explaining why Slichter's book is "a great textbook . . . written from the standpoint of control, which is the right standpoint, . . . [even though] it says practically nothing about the economics of control and a very large part of all the economics it contains is wrong" (p. 173). The solution of this paradox is that when calling it a "great textbook" Knight evaluated it by the market test: does it satisfy consumer demand? And Knight argued that both popular and academic demands are not for objective truth, but for what people want to hear. Hence what a rational supplier offers, is a "clarion call to action" or a denunciation of the opposition (p. 182).

Knight goes even further and argues that the market is correct in not wanting objectivity. Objectivity is bad because there can be no neutrality on moral issues, and all public-policy issues are basically moral issues. Moreover, inquiry into the foundations of accepted group values is obscene and sacrilegious; "objective inquiry is an attempt to uncover the nakedness of man's soul" (p. 184). Truthseekers should be kept away from leaders because they destroy the leaders' self-confidence.

Is this denunciation of objectivity as a goal just tongue-in-cheek? Perhaps it is, for Knight also wrote that: "I should begin by confessing a prejudice. It is the 'wish' that somewhere in the program of university education in economics there might be an emphasis on fact, truth and understanding. This is a sentiment merely, in conviction I have great doubts" (p. 179).

Knight then showed that Slichter's book does shun objectivity. For example, when Slichter talked about controlling the economy he did not say who is to do the controlling, but evaded this issue by frequently using the pronoun "we" without an antecedent. Similarly, Slichter seemed unaware of the contradiction in saying that we need to – and therefore should – control the economy, and his admission that this requires a greater ability to predict that we possess. Thus Knight convincingly exposed the rhetorical devices by which Slichter evaded the problematic aspects of economic controls. This essay should therefore be interesting to anyone concerned with economic rhetoric.

How persuasive is Knight's in saying that the market does not want objectivity and rationality, and that a textbook should therefore offer instead of reasoned analysis the cheap thrill of seeing ones ideological predilections confirmed? That in popular discussions objectivity is not in great demand seems obvious, and is not surprising. Given the trivial influence that my vote and preferences have on policy why should I bother with getting the facts right? In general, people want to act selfishly but also to feel that they are moral persons. They maximize utility by buying moral feeling in the cheapest market; that is, they continue to act selfishly in their personal dealings, and satisfy their wish to feel moral by taking morally "correct" positions on public issues. Perhaps it is this urge for seeming to do good rather than actually doing good that, in part, explains why in helping the poor so much money us spent to so little effect.

But one should not carry this argument too far. Rationality, and hence objectivity, do play a large role in our political thinking. We fail to notice this because we take it for granted. For example, Clinton haters have not accused him of stealing the U.S. gold stock. Similarly, while Knight is right that too much concern about objectivity could cause a policymaker to become "sickled o'er with the pale cast of thought" and hence ineffective, Knight's (tongue-in-cheek?) rejection of objectivity as generally worth striving for, goes much too far, because the striving for objectivity is a large component of intellectual honesty.

Chapter 6, "Historical and Theoretical Issues in the Problem of Modern Capitalism," may surprise those who think of Knight and the Chicago school as fervently anti-institutionalist. Knight not only translated Max Weber's *General Economic History*, but also wrote a highly critical review of the third volume of Werner Sombart's classic *Der Moderne Kapitalismus*. He did so, however, as an economic theorist highlighting major errors due to Sombart's ignorance of economics. In his review Knight stressed the role of cultural factors in economic development, and the need to explain economic development not as an isolated historical event, but through the lense of comparative history. He saw the essence of capitalist development in a shift of emphasis from the conquest of men to the conquest of nature, in the "invention of invention", in the evolution of the concept of property, and in the declining role of authority and tradition.

3. MICROECONOMICS AND CAPITAL THEORY

In "Some Fallacies in the Interpretation of Social Cost" (Ch. 4) Knight demonstrated the distinction between private and social costs, and showed how private ownership leads to the appropriate allocation of resources even when there are increasing costs in some industries and decreasing costs in others. He then dealt with Frank Graham's argument that a country that specializes in industries operating under conditions of decreasing returns loses from trading with a country that specializes in industries with increasing returns. Unlike the modern variant of this argument Graham presented a static case with no learning by doing, and Knight persuasively refuted his argument.

In another paper, "The Ricardian Theory of Production and Distribution," (Ch. 11) Knight listed seven fallacies of Ricardian economics: (1) the interpretation of value in terms of cost, and hence "pain"; (2) the identification of production with the creation of wealth; (3) the use of a labor theory of value; (4) an unclear conception of causality as a functional relation; (5) failure to think in terms of incremental changes; (6) unwillingness to use mathematical concepts, and (7) failure to treat the problem of distribution as a problem of imputation and evaluating. The first of these is a familiar point. The second rests on Knight's belief that income consists only of the flow of current consumption services and excludes increases in the capital stock. Knight also criticized the unwarranted Ricardian dichotomy between production and distribution theory – costs of production are, after all, what the factors of production receive. All in all, these criticisms are devastating.

Two essays from the 1930s represent Knight's side to the debate about capital theory. Knight was so successful that Henning in *The New Palgrave* (1987, p. 330) now calls Knight's position "the dominant doctrine", while Buchanan (1968, p. 426), though conceding that Knight's criticisms do not "entirely apply" to more subtle variants of Austrian capital theory, credits Knight with doing much to "undermine the more elementary versions." In the essays reprinted here (Chs 11 and 12) Knight cleared up many ambiguities in capital theory, and demonstrated that looking at capital as a collection of specific capital goods, whose stock denotes a particular degree of roundaboutness, as the Austrians did, creates insuperable difficulties. He also showed that interest-rate theory does not require measurement of the quantity of capital, and that there are serious difficulties in talking about demand and supply curves for capital, or more generally, in applying equilibrium analysis to capital theory.

4. MISCELLANEOUS ESSAYS

The book contains only one – but a remarkably powerful – essay on macroecomics, Knight's negative reaction to Keynes' *General Theory*. Not surpassingly his reaction was strongly negative: "the chief value of the book has seemed to lie in the hard labor involved in reading it, which enforces intense grappling with the problems" (p. 366). He criticized Keynes mainly on two grounds. First, Keynes does not say all that much that is new. He appeared to do so merely because he employs novel terms and concept in place of familiar ones that serve just as well, and because of his distorted account of classical theory. That theory starts out with a simplified case and then adds complications, such as speculation or monetary disturbances. By contrast, Keynes treats such qualifications as the general case, and criticized classical theory for lacking them.

Second, Keynes novel results are due only to his special assumptions. Thus, Keynes can reject Say's law only because he assumes fixed rather than flexible wages. Given Keynes' assumptions it is easy to revolutionize economic theory. But these assumptions cannot serve as the basis of equilibrium theory. So, instead of a book that revolutionizes economic theory, Keynes has provided only a relatively modest contribution to business-cycle theory.

Knight's focused much of his criticism on Keynes' inadequate treatment of the labor market, and his claim that underemployment can be an equilibrium. Although Keynes talks about unions having monopoly power to prevent wages from falling, he did not present a theory of monopoly pricing, and hence could not provide theoretical underpinnings for underemployment equilibrium. Classical theory, on the other hand, can explain massive, but temporary, unemployment as due to shocks. Indeed, Knight doubts that Keynes really meant that underemployment could be an equilibrium.

Knight's intuition here is unerring. Until the development of New Keynesian theory Keynesians could not explain adequately why labor markets do not clear, though that may be in part because they were reluctant to rely on such a "sociological" factor as a compelling concern with relative wages (a reluctance that is strange give how concerned academics themselves are about their relative salaries and status.) Within a year of the publication of the *General Theory* Knight had put his finger on its weakest point. What might explain Keynes' overstatement is his disjointed positions an academic economist, and as a practical man (adviser to the Treasury, journalist, speculator and political figure), appalled at the suffering of the unemployed. In the latter capacity someone might well call massive unemployment that lasts for a decade "permanent", while in the former capacity someone might then apply the label "equilibrium" to what seems permanent, And in either capacity one might object to calling it "temporary." Part of the problem is that economists after adopting the idea of equilibrium from physics unconsciously tended to give it a normative meaning.

Knight's review contains many other insights. Thus Knight criticized Keynes for making a great to-do about the identity of saving and investment, for ignoring the monetary (LM) side in his discussion of the multiplier, for advancing a simplistic theory of interest rates in which an increase in saving does not lower interest rates. Knight also took after Keynes' overoptimistic discussion of the policy implications that can be drawn from the *General Theory*.

All in all, Knight's review is a masterly performance. It makes one wonder why Keynesian theory was (and to a substantial extent still is) so widely used. And yet, despite the problems that Knight, and others since then, have pointed out, the *General Theory* has, both directly and indirectly, led to much progress. Would economics be further ahead if it had not been written? I don't know, but suspect that the answer is no.

In Knight's "Modern Thought: Is it Anti-intellectual and God and Professor Adler and Logic" (Ch. 10), Emmett has combined two articles not addressed to economists. Knight here defends modern thought against an attempt, particular by Mortimer Adler (the founder of the Chicago Great Books program) to replace it by neo-Thomism. While agreeing with his rejection of positivism Knight attacked various aspects of this philosophy, such as its emphasis on verbalism and its logical absolutism, and advocated instead an education that develops the critical intellect. That is what students need because "true philosophy is *good sense*" (p. 234) and there is no mark or test for that, there are only tests for error. This essay shows Knight's thinking on broader issues than do the other essays, and that is presumably why Emmett included it.

5. CONCLUSION

Modern economists, by and large, prefer technical sophistication and rigor to philosophical thinking. Knight's type of economics therefore seems dated But it is none the worse for that. These essays with their depth, broad range and sweep present a valuable supplement (or should one say antidote?) to current writings, I recommend them particularly to adherents of the second (Friedman-Stigler) and third (Lucas) Chicago schools. Emmett should be commended for collecting them. Two warning are, however, in order. First, the book is full of suggestive ideas that Knight does not work out, and may leave the reader wondering what – if anything – justifies them. Second, Knight is to my taste at least, an extraordinarily bad writer. His relentless pursuit of numerous tangents often obscures his main point. Many of his sentences resemble artillery shells that scatter both subsidiary clauses and related ideas like shrapnel in all directions.

ACKNOWLEDGMENT

I am indebted for helpful comments to Sherman Shapiro.

REFERENCES

Buchanan, J. (1968). In: F. Knight, *International Encyclopedia of the Social Sciences* (pp. 424–428). New York: Macmillan and Free Press.

Hammond, D. (1991). Frank Knight's Antipositivism. *History of Political Economy, 25*, Fall, 359–380.

Henning, K. H. (1987). Capital as a Factor of Production. In: J. Eatwell, M. Milgate & P. Newman (Eds). *The New Palgrave*, vol. 1. London: Macmillan.

Hirsch, A., & Hirsch, E. (1980). Heterodox Methodology and Two Chicago Economists. Reprinted in Warren Samuels, *The Methodology of Economic Thought*. New Brunswick, NJ: Transactions Books.

Hutchison, T. (1940). The Significance and Basic Postulates of Economic Theory: A Reply to Professor Knight. *Journal of Political Economy, 49*, October, 732–750.

Knight, F. (194?). Rejoinder. *Journal of Political Economy, 49*, October, 750–753.

Machlup, F. (1991). *Economic Semantics*. New Brunswick, NJ: Transaction Press.

Mayer, T. (1995). *Doing Economics*. Aldershot: Edward Elgar.

Mayer, T. (2000). The Domain of Hypotheses and the Realism of Assumptions. *Journal of Economic Methodology, 6*, November, 319–330.

McCloskey, D. (1985). *The Rhetoric of Economics*. Madison: University of Wisconsin Press.

McCullough, B. D., & Vinod, H. D. (1999). The Numerical Reliability of Econometric Software. *Journal of Economic Literature, 37*, June, 633–665.

Robbins, L. (1932). *An Essay on the Nature and Significance of Economic Science*. London: Macmillan.

Slichter, S. (1931). *Modern Economics*. New York: Henry Holt.

CAPTAINS OF INDUSTRY OR CAPTAINS OF SLEAZE? A REVIEW ARTICLE

Willie Henderson

The Representation of Business in English Literature **Arthur Pollard (Ed.) Readings 53 Institute of Economic Affairs, 2000 ISBN 0-255-36491-1.**

There has always been an interface between economics and literature ever since economics was the subject of written discourse but significance of it has not always been recognized. Economics, like many other emerging disciplines in the 18th and 19th century, was not locked away in Universities nor was it the discourse of a group of technically-motivated intellectuals. When writers developed an economic discourse prior to the 20th century, they had, by necessity to address themselves to a wider public (Alfred Marshall, even when engaged in the professionalization of the discipline, kept one eye on the public). Their ideas found their way into other discourses. Lyell's notion of geological formation and geological activity ('uniformitarianism') informed the development of plot and details of language in *The Mill on the Floss*. (Smith, 1994, p. 121).[1] By a similar process, Adam Smith's *Wealth of Nations* informed the development of economic themes in writers such as Maria Edgeworth, Jane Marcet and Harriet Martineau (Henderson, 1995). The difference between geology and economics however is that geology is a science. Economics must encompass ethical and moral issues. Value is central to economics but the question of values (aesthetic and moral) is central to the development of literature. Value in the technical sense is conjoined to values in the moral sense

Research in the History of Economic Thought and Methodology, Volume 20-A, pages 251–260.
© 2002 Published by Elsevier Science Ltd.
ISBN: 0-7623-0847-8

when we look at the substantive economic world. In the domain of human
action, whether it be economic or not, it could not be otherwise. 'Is this so?'
is a satisfactory question some of the time but in looking at socio-economic
conditions, so too are 'is this right? or 'is this good?' and, even, 'what else
could be so?'. Adam Smith knew this very well when he identified in *The
Theory of Moral Sentiments* a potential lack of agreement between economic
and moral hierarchies.

The whole notion of a 'rhetoric of economics' (whilst this can mean a number
of different things) carries within a concern for the instruments of persuasion
and embellishment that were central to the 'old rhetoric' i.e. an awareness of
tropes and figures or, of literary issues in communication. 'New rhetoric'
contributes an understanding that metaphor is an epistemological and thinking
issue as well as a 'mere' language issue. Given formal economics reliance on
a few simple metaphors and fictions, this is a good thing to learn. Furthermore
the application of ways of engaging in literary criticism, for example, whether
a text is 'monological' or 'dialogical' (Brown, 1994) can be used to undertake
a reading of a work such as Smith's *Wealth of Nations*. The concerns of those
engaged in the professional study of literature in English have also taken an
interdisciplinary turn as it were: there is interest in the way economic metaphors,
images and values are incorporated into fictional writing. And there is the notion
of congruity between 'money' and 'language' itself: both facilitate exchanges,
both can become debased and so on. Adam Smith, of course, recognized a link
between language, persuasion and exchange. Such issues have been brought
once again to the notice of economists by a literary movement called the 'new
economic criticism'. Those engaged in such literary projects (for example
Woodmansee & Osteen, 1999) see within economics a related interest that they
call 'critical economics' (a way of referring to a whole set of issues that gather
around the 'rhetoric of economics'). Either way, a new set of issues is emerging
around the cultural significance of economics.

The Representation of Business in English Literature does not make any
reference to 'the new economic criticism'. It does not have to. Representation
is a long-standing theme of literary criticism. Yet some of the issues raised
within the five historically organized surveys, could have had a finer critical
edge, for economics readers, had they done so. The 'new economic criticism'
would have provided a surer anchor for the project than that provided either
by John Blundell, the Director General of the IEA, or, even, by Arthur Pollard
in his introduction. Blundell's foreword justifies the publication of the volume
in terms of the IEA's mission 'to consider how the free economy is viewed,
why it is so viewed, and how such a view might be improved'. I suppose that
those engaged in the investigation of the portrayal of economic life and values

in literature in English can easily accommodate the first and second of these. The third feels uncomfortable in context, though this may be the value issue that is the IEA's underlying premise for its support of the volume. Perhaps we ought to remind ourselves that such a mission can be seen lurking behind the publication of Harriet Martineau's *Illustrations of Political Economy* (1832–1834) (Henderson, 1995). Blundell's approach to 'representation' of business and hence market values in literature is unsatisfactory both in the language that is used and it its relationship to the well-balanced articles that follow. He asks: 'why does the novelist, the writer of fiction, spit at the market, despise its institutions such as private property and the rule of law, and try to bite off the hand that feeds him?' This, somehow, misses the point. Reflect upon Smith's ironic comments in the *Wealth of Nations* concerning the motivation of landlords and merchants and on his skepticism concerning the individual pursuit of wealth. Both positive and negative representations of economic behaviours are built into a founding text.

Pollard's introduction makes it clear that writers, in the 19th century, in particular look at the dichotomy in values between 'men and money'. He points to Carlyle (though he could equally have pointed to Ruskin) in terms of the value split between 'matter and spirit' (Ruskin's 'soul'). Ruskin thought that the factory system produced both material goods and fragmented people. He also thought that a mechanistic representation of human motivation and values ('economic man') stripped the image of mankind of everything that makes us human. Both Carlyle and Ruskin's views, with respect to human capacities, could be seen as a development of Smith's analysis of the down-side of the division of labour, though this is not pointed out in the volume. Pollard points out the contempt for business – 'Making money is a dirty game' is ('almost') his summation of the representation of business. The idea of money as filth is, of course, culturally very old and very persistent. He also points out that Goldsmith's concerns about rural depopulation that he linked to the 'enclosure movement' prompted Crabbe's insights, developed in *The Village*, that rural living was rarely 'lovely but more often an abode of poverty, degradation and crime' (Pollard, 2000, p. 2). Whilst there is a predominant line, literature is not entirely one sided when it comes to looking at the causes and consequences of economic motivation. It is also necessary to keep two things in mind. First, the main thrust of the enclosure movement came after the writing of Goldsmith's poem. Second, Goldsmith was writing as political economy was starting to emerge: poetry engaging in the exploration of economic and social themes was still a possibility. Once political economy emerged as a distinct discourse, socially engaged poetry tended to give way to the workings of the Romantic imagination.

In his chapter on '18th century attitudes towards business' Speck traces out the links between themes in English literature and the development of the economy from the Glorious Revolution through to the late Hanoverians. His sub-headings are both appropriate and informative, for example: 'Reactions to the new Fiscal-Military State'; 'The Financial Revolution – Bribery and Corruption'; 'Defoe Champions Commerce'; 'Wealth and Greatness the Cause of Corruption'; 'Literary Condemnation of the Slave Trade'. The organization of Speck's contribution – general themes set out chronologically – is helpful for it provides an easy means of linking processes in the substantive economy to developments in the novel. This is in fact the system used within each article and is, no doubt, the result of the briefings given by the editor.

Adam Smith is quoted twice, only, but the use of Smith, on moral and economic hierarchies and on slavery, is to some effect. Smith's economic condemnation of slavery as inefficient, and Sterne's moral comments on slavery in *Tristram Shandy* and in his *Sermons*, sit nicely together in Speck's writing, illustrating how related, but different, representations can work towards the same end: the abolition of the slave trade. In later literature, the three great figures that are seen to provide novelistic themes are Marx, Darwin and Freud. Can any case be made for Smith?

Speck's interprets *Robinson Crusoe* as a 'paean of praise to business activity' though it is, also, a moral tale. Crusoe has to learn to be pious and prudent, failures in business are due to lack of moral capacities. Robinson Crusoe is a favorite target for those who dislike the way in which economic agency is represented in introductory economics texts. According to Sorensen, in a chapter in the *The New Economic Criticism*, Defoe's relationship with 'the expanding British empire around him' is difficult to specify – his own economic activities included spying and propaganda writing – for 'his writings exhibit multiple, contradictory positions' (Sorensen, 2000, p. 76). Sorensen sees aspects of Defoe's writing as incorporating problems over 'competing accounts of value . . . and evolving social relations' as society adjusts to new notions of capital and trade (Sorensen, 2000, p. 91). Robinson Crusoe also features in *The New Economic Criticism*, as a representation of '*Homo economicus*' though the representation moved from literature to economics (Browne & Quinn, 1999, p. 134).[2] Such slippages and continuations show the trade in images of economic life and behaviour to be a two-way process. The moral capacities expressed in the quote Speck provides from *The Compleat English Tradesman* are not dissimilar to the prudential passions listed by Smith in *The Theory of Moral Sentiments*. Defoe is clearly of huge importance, in this period, for the development of an understanding of the cultural significance of economic change and of the economic ideas, processes and behaviors that sustain it. Indeed the theme that cultural change is a dynamic that impacts on language, literature and economics so that the perception of issues shares common time-lines underlies the whole volume. The significance of this understanding can get lost in the details.

The nineteenth century is surveyed in two articles. This is not surprising. It is capitalistic economic development, through markets, increased specialization and the division of labour that helped support and sustain the market for the novel, providing an economic space for the profession and a set of institutional arrangements such as the net book agreement and, later, intellectual property rights. Walter Scott was, according to Carnall the first significant 'commercially successful author' (Carnall, 2000, p. 36). (What would Smollet, who was proud of the fact that he earned his living as a writer, have made of this generalisation?) It is no doubt such economic aspects that Blundell is thinking about when he criticizes the contempt that literature seems to have for the market. Blundell should reflect, perhaps, upon what Ruskin had to say about the market for innovative art – Ruskin was thinking about painting but it just as readily applies to creative writing. Innovative artistic work often does not find a market: it creates its own values and value and is not in a sense a response to market forces in the conventional way depicted in economics textbooks (Henderson, 2000). A century later, Galbraith made the same point. It is illustrated in the way in which artistic merit is judged: think of the fate of the innovative paintings of Vincent Van Gogh. The artist was ignored in his lifetime. William Blake, in a passage quoted by Carnall from *Prospectus* (1793) claims that 'poverty and obscurity' was the fate of artists and musicians. Blake himself looked for ways of 'cutting out the middle-man' and then there are Coleridge's direct efforts 'to secure subscribers for his radical periodical' (Carnall, 2000, pp. 42, 49). To some extent writers have also been entrepreneurs: Easson provides the example of Dickens' efforts 'to secure financial backing to launch a newspaper' (Easson, 2000, p. 67). The market for creative writing is not perfect, nor is a living income guaranteed. Even innovative writers, in to-day's world, require subsidies that come in the form of literary prizes or other forms of patronage.

Central to Carnall's survey are two psychological questions that have their justification in the speed of change in the early nineteenth century: 'How did this phenomenon affect the mental health and emotional condition of the people who lived through it? How did they perceive it?' (Carnall, 1999, p. 35). Carnall follows the questions through in terms of specific and significant authors, matching the author to an aspect of the questions as in the following examples: 'Walter Scott's Nostalgia for the Old Order'; 'Wordsworth's Denigration of Industrial Development'; 'Blake's Revolt Against Economic Expansion' and so on. Jane Austen's approach to the changes was, essentially, according to Carnall, 'to evade' them. Others, such as Southey, later Carlyle and Ruskin, struggle with the contrasts between abundance and poverty, between greed and deprivation. But even Southey in attacking the behaviour of those obsessed with Mammon, makes an 'emphatic concession to the business community' when discussing merchants as 'patrons' (Carnall, 2000, p. 48). One of Carnall's insights is the 'sheer invisibility of serious business activity in the literature of the early 19th century' (Carnall, 2000, p. 48).

Easson's article on the 'The High Victorian Period' has as its subtitle 'the worship of Mammon'. The literature of this period is vast and the survey is 'necessarily limited'. This contribution packs a lot in. It is perhaps as well to remember that although Dickens wrote social satire, George Bernard Shaw was of the opinion that Dickens was Marx by another name. 'Merdle' in *Little Dorrit*, a 'financier' and 'yet greater swindler' is based upon 'John Sadlier, the Irish banker and railway promoter, who committed suicide on Hampstead Heath in 1855' (Easson, 2000, p. 66). Whatever images we have of the theoretical construct of a 'fee economy' life as it is lived is messy and one of the functions of literature is to illustrate aspects of the messiness including social contradictions.

The writers of this period were themselves often associated with business (George Elliot was at one time '*de facto* editor of *The Westminster Review*') (Easson, 2000, p. 70) and had business people as friends. Charlotte Bronte owned shares and had 'a shrewd knowledge of the market'. The themes, of such significance to 'the new economic criticism' of writer-producer and of the relationship between artist and economy are well set out, even if briefly in Easson's contribution. There was familiarity with economic life based upon personal experience. Macauley according to Easson shows that 'commercial and financial processes could be the stuff of romance' (Easson, 2000, p. 67) whilst the bewildering behaviour of the cycles of boom and burst make a good basis for story lines.

Given the dramatic elements in the economy, the dynamism of Birmingham or Manchester and the contrasts between abundance and poverty, 'a strong literary convention of realism' was the means that many writers took 'to validate their work' (Easson, 2000, p. 71). Whilst there were other issues, 'the realities of the world of buying and selling, of goods against cash, are part of the world that these Victorians seek to recreate within their fiction' (Easson, 2000, p. 71). But the literary exercise is not representation as reproduction but representation as transformation. London's fog, itself a consequence of rapid economic expansion, is taken by Dickens as 'a metaphor for legal obfuscation, for pervasive disease' (Easson, 2000, p. 72). Indeed, Dickens can turn people into mechanistic objects, reconfiguring the mechanistic notions of economic behaviour or the power of the machine, though only a hint of this comes through in the volume. People in stories come to be identified not only through their work but by it. Easson sums up such themes thus: 'Trade takes your time and physically alters you' (Easson, 2000, p. 81). In the face of the economic function taking over the person, Ruskin talked of 'living a true life' in contrast to mechanistic conformity to market expectations, expressing himself in ways that are suggestive of the existentialist philosophy developed by Sartre in the twentieth century. In this context we should also recall that, according to Marx, the division of labour was also one of the tyrannies of capitalism.

Carlyle's notion of 'Captains of Industry' is, also, given some attention, though not enough. Such people are an idealized warrior caste, capable of mobilizing resources for agreed social ends and who tend to the needs of the workforce. But the force of Carlyle's writing is against the machine and mechanistic views of human motivation and society. The manifestation of such figures in the literature of the period is quickly sketched in: Rouncewell in *Bleak House*, John Thornton in Gaskell's *North and South*, and, even, Shaw's Undershaft. Carlyle is a much more sophisticated social analyst than Mrs. Gaskell and her representation, John Thornton, is a representation of a representation. Such issues are under-explored. Although Easson does not consider the links between Carlyle's notion and economic thought, it is worth stating that Alfred Marshall delivered, at the start of the new century a paper to his fellow economists, entitled 'The Social Consequences of Economic Chivalry'. Indeed, the notion of knightly motivation can be traced out from Spencer's romance via James Thomson's poetic image of the Knight of Trade and Industry (who challenges the inhabitants of the *Castle of Indolence*) to Carlyle and Ruskin (and others) and so to Marshall. This is a specific example of a wider phenomenon in which engaged poetry gives way to engaged social science. Cultural influences, even on ways of thinking about economic motivation, can, however, still run deep.[3]

There are two interesting articles on the 20th century. Simmons, who sees early 20th century notions of business and economy as one of 'Uniformity' and 'Drudgery' points to 'Modern literature as a literature of doubt' (Simmons, 2000, p. 101). Given the social and economic consequences of the First World War, and the wide-spread skepticism about the market as a result of the prolonged depression experienced in Britain and elsewhere, it is not surprising that the capitalist system itself was under question in literature. Even industrialists turned against the market. Democracy and the free market were under question in political life, more widely. Morris deals with the loss of faith in capitalism and the split in literature between the Left and Right. The representation shifts from representations of individuals (perhaps as metaphors for a wider set of values) to a fuller representation of or challenge to the system as a whole. Simmons chooses (mainly) to look at the early period in terms of the works of Wells, Hardy, Lawrence and Conrad. Wells challenges the 'clipped and limited lives' that the division of labour, and institutional arrangements, imply. Hardy worries about rural transformation and the incorporation of agriculture into the urbanized economy. Lawrence judges capitalism aesthetically, as did Ruskin in the previous century. Capitalism, Lawrence claimed in a famous and much quoted passage, condemned 'workers to ugliness, ugliness, ugliness' including environmental degradation and mean-spirited behaviour (quoted in Simmons, 2000, p. 119). Conrad exposes 'colonial expansion' as 'European greed masquerading as philanthropy' (Simmons, 2000, p. 128).

Morris has a more difficult task given the length and complexity of the mid to later 20th century. Capitalism is seen as debased, unemployment is a major social issue for George Orwell and H. G. Wells explored economic issues outside his work in creative writing – but literature itself was faced with a problem. Should writers focus, on 'the voice without' or on 'the voice within'? (Morris, 2000, p. 141). In Morris's view the world of the imagination split from the world of fact. Or is it, I wonder, that introspective authors mirror the representation of the utility-maximizing consumer, as subjective, introspective and individuated, that gradually emerged within formal economic writing from the 1930s onward. Are both responding to a wider social change as the emphasis on production gave way to the emphasis on consumption? Given the complexities of this period, Morris' overall conclusion is that: 'It is difficult to find positive and appreciative images of business in 20th century English literature' (Morris, 2000, p. 137). What's new? Here is an image of business behaviour from Adam Smith: 'People of the same trade seldom meet together, even for merriment and diversion, but the conversation ends in a conspiracy against the public, or in some contrivance to raise prices' (Smith, 1952 [1776] bk. 1, ch. 10, pt. 2). The world of human affairs is complex, historically located and messy, just like the market. Given Blundell's concern for positive images, how interesting, one may wonder, would a deliberately contrived 'appreciative' literature be? Harriet Martineau moved from provincial obscurity to exaggerated social prominence, in the 1830s, as a result of the publication of her monthly tales illustrating economic principles. If they are read at all to-day it is for their significance as economic popularization rather than for their literary merit.

CONCLUSION

Even if the formal ideas of 'the new economic criticism' are not well-understood, the fact that the IEA commissioned a publication entitled *The Representation of Business in English Literature* suggests that an examination of the interface between economic thought or circumstances, and literature, is becoming more widely acceptable. The IEA has taken, in context, a bold step, for the intellectual market for these ideas is not yet formed. It is still not clear what the target audience is, beyond English specialists, for this kind of exploration. The volume fulfills its brief: each essay is robust and interesting and contains useful insights and relevant critical comments. The project is, however, both too ambitious and not ambitious enough. It is too ambitious in that the amount of material surveyed and presented is too much for one short work, especially for a lay audience. It would be wrong to give the impression that the chapters are not sensitive to detail: they are but some significant detail – such as the ways in which Dickens' highly episodic writing is formed by the fact of the serial market – cannot be included. But, also, it is not ambitious enough in the sense that it is not critical enough. Representation, as such, is not critically addressed – the forward fails to take us anywhere useful, perhaps because of Blundell's use of Hayek's notion of intellectuals as a device for castigating writers. Pollard's introduction is fine so far as it goes, but it does not go so very far. Some discussion would have helped. Does not 'representation' assume that '[s]omething has to be present or to have been present in the first place in order to be presented again in a representation' i.e. something with which to correspond, whereas literature may be more about 'revelation'? (Miller, 1993, p. 159). It is on such topics that overt links with the new economic criticism may have been useful. Nonetheless, for anyone interested in looking at the cultural significance of business or economics this is an entertaining starting point.

NOTES

1. George Elliot as a young woman has read several works on geology but only gradually moved towards Lyell's ideas as faith gave way to loss of faith (Smith, 1994, pp. 124–127). Of Maria Edgeworth we know that *The Wealth of Nations* was given to her to read by her father shortly after she returned to Ireland, in 1782, from her schooling in England (Butler, 1992). Her comic novel, *Castle Rackrent*, published in 1800, inscribes Smithian economic ideas.

2. The image moved in other ways too. Martineau's *Life in the Wilds* (1832) could be seen as a Robinson Crusoe story reworked to illustrate simple themes from Adam Smith. Others, beyond teachers of introductory economics, have borrowed 'Crusoe'. In 1876, D. A. Wells published *Robinson Crusoe's Money, or, the Remarkable Fortunes and Misfortunes of a Remote Island Community*. P. Smith, New York. This includes satirical episodes and cartoons on the representation of money (see Shell, 1999).

3. The Edwardians created knighthoods for captains of industry, and so extended the domain of the economy of romance.

ACKNOWLEDGMENTS

I am grateful to Sebastian Mitchell, Colin Rickwood and Warren Samuels for comments on an earlier draft.

REFERENCES

Brown, V. (1994). *Adam Smith's Discourse: canonicity, commerce and conscience*. London: Routledge.

Browne, M. N., & Quinn, J. K. (1999). Dominant economic metaphors and the postmodern subversion of the subject. In: M Woodmansee & M. Osteen (Eds), *op. cit.* (pp. 131–149).

Butler, M. (1992). Introduction. In: M. Butler (Ed.), *Maria Edgeworth, Castle Rackrent and Ennui*. Harmondsworth: Penguin.

Carnall, G, (2000). Early Nineteenth Century: Birmingham – 'Something Direful in the Sound'. In: A. Pollard (Ed.), *op. cit.* (pp. 35–64).

Easson, A. (2000). The High Victorian Period (1850–1900): 'The worship of Mammon'. In: A. Pollard (Ed.), *op. cit.* (pp. 65–98).

Henderson, W. (2000). *John Ruskin's Political Economy*. London: Routledge.

Henderson, W. (1995). *Economics as Literature*. London: Routledge.

Martineau, H. (1832). *Life in the Wilds*. London: Charles Fox.

Miller, J. H. (1993). Is Literary Theory a Science? In: G. Levine, *Realism and Representation: Essays on the Problem of Realism in Relation to Science, Literature and Culture*. Maddison: University of Wisconsin Press.

Morris, J. (2000). Mid-Late Twentieth-Century: 'An Unprecedented Moral Quagmire'. In: A. Pollard (Ed.) *op. cit.* (pp. 137–182).

Pollard, A. (2000). Introduction. In: A. Pollard (Ed.), *The Representation of Business in English Literature* (pp. 1–7). London: IEA.

Shell, M. (1999). The issue of representation. In: M. Woodmansee & M. Osteen (Eds) *op. cit.* (pp. 53–74).

Smith. A. (1952 [1776]). *An Inquiry Into the Nature and Causes of the Wealth of Nations*. Chicago: Encyclopaedia Britannica.

Simmons, A. (2000). The Early Twentieth Century: Uniformity, Drudgery and Economics. In: A. Pollard (Ed.), *op. cit.* (pp. 99–135).

Smith, J. (1994). *Fact and Feeling: Baconian Science and the Nineteenth-Century Literary Imagination*. Madison: University of Wisconsin Press.

Speck, W. A. (2000). Eighteenth Century Attitudes Towards Business. In: A. Pollard (Ed.), *op. cit.* (pp. 9–34).

Woodmansee, M., & Osteen, M. (1999). *The New Economic Criticism: Studies at the intersection of literature and economics*. London: Routledge.

Sorensen, J. (1999). "I talk to everybody in their own way": Defoe's economies of identity. In: M. Woodmansee & M. Osteen (Eds), *op. cit.* (pp. 75–94).

Wells, D. A. (1876). *Robinson Crusoe's Money, or, the Remarkable Fortunes and Misfortunes of a Remote Island*. New York: P. Smith.

"THE BITTER ARGUMENT BETWEEN ECONOMISTS AND HUMAN BEINGS": THE RECEPTION OF MALTHUS'S *ESSAY ON POPULATION*

A. M. C. Waterman

A review essay on Andrew Pyle (Ed.). **1994.** *Population: Contemporary Responses to Thomas Malthus*. **Bristol: Thoemmes Press.**

I

"Do not forget Malthouses (sic) rascally metaphysics" wrote Robert Southey to John Rickman in 1803, "Break him on the wheel ... You ought to set your foot upon such a mischievous reptile and crush him" (Southey, 1965, I, p. 327). Such hatred and vituperation were typical. Late in the century Arnold Toynbee wrote of "the bitter argument between economists and human beings." Southey himself reviewed the *Essay* for the *Annual* in 1804 abetted by Samuel Taylor Coleridge, whose implacable malice towards his former Cambridge senior never abated till his death.

It was Southey's article that inaugurated what Donald Winch (1996, p. 418) has identified as "the schism, or fault line, separating economists from the self-appointed spokesmen for human beings." On the one side, Malthus and Ricardo, M'Culloch and Chalmers, the Philosophic Radicals and the Christian Political Economists, proposed explanations and offered diagnoses of the ills of society

Research in the History of Economic Thought and Methodology, Volume 20-A, pages 261–270.
© 2002 Published by Elsevier Science Ltd.
ISBN: 0-7623-0847-8

that rested upon the motive power of self-love in face of resource scarcity. On the other, the Lake Poets (Wordsworth, Coleridge, Southey) and most other literary Romantics howled in rage and execration at what they chose to regard as a libel on the human race and a blasphemous denial of the goodness of God. And in turn, the Philosophic Radicals' periodical, the *Westminster Review*, inflamed by James Mill's puritanical hatred of the Arts, retaliated with ritual abuse of the Lake Poets and their circle. The "bitter argument" was carried down to the third and fourth generations in the attitudes and assumptions of Hazlitt, Dickens, Kingsley, Carlyle, Ruskin, William Morris and their twentieth-century admirers (Winch, 1996; Levy, 2001). It is with us today in the mutual bafflement and failure to communicate that occurs whenever economists confront the partisans of "social justice" for example, or of Liberation Theology (Brennan & Waterman, 1994, pp. 3–4) and many other varieties of Christian social doctrine.

What strikes the historian as strange about all this is the abruptness with which the "schism" opened up in the early 1800s. There is no trace of any hostility towards economic thought in the eighteenth century, either in France or in Britain. In the one country, *économie politique* from Montchrétien to Turgot was a set of techniques for managing the state as a manorial fief of *le roi soleil* and his successors. In the other, economic theorizing – originally conducted for much the same reason – had become a branch of moral and political philosophy: a small part of the higher education of gentlemen in preparation for their duties as clergymen, magistrates and legislators. As late as the 1790s, Edmund Burke conjectured that *Wealth of Nations* was "probably the most important book ever written" (O'Brien, 1993, p. 144, n. 1) and affirmed that "the laws of commerce, which are the laws of nature [are] consequently the laws of God" (Burke, 1981–1997, IX, p. 125). All of a sudden the mood changed. Before Malthus's death a reputable journal could aver that Malthus and Ricardo had "tended to lead the public far away from the true path of inquiry," and to make of political economy "a hideous chain of paradoxes at apparent war with religion and humanity" (*Eclectic Review*, January, 1832, p. 9).

The reason for this sharp discontinuity is simple, but still not widely understood. *Scarcity*, which is now the central organising principle of economic analysis, entered into political economy for the first time in Robert Malthus's anonymous *Essay on Population* of 1798. Natural fecundity in a finite universe implies the existence and stability of an ecological general equilibrium: in which stationary populations of the fittest in each species exactly reproduce their numbers by consuming in total the whole of each period's net production (including each other). For human populations, Malthus thought in 1798, this means either "misery" or "vice." Contemporary European culture was entirely formed and governed by orthodox Christianity. Hence the first *Essay* was seen by all – including Malthus himself – as raising the perennial, theological "problem of evil" in a novel and threatening form. Why does a God who is all-powerful, all-wise and all-good create a world in which all or most human beings are condemned by the laws of Nature to live in privation at the margin of subsistence?

Of all who responded unfavourably to the new political economy of scarcity, poets and essayists of the rising Romantic Movement were by far the most outspoken. In part this is because many were disillusioned former Jacobins – horrified by the Terror and disgusted by Buonaparte – who had taken refuge in High-Tory Anglicanism and now saw themselves as defenders of orthodoxy. More fundamentally it was because Romanticism is precisely a "revolt against the finite" (Lovejoy, 1941, pp. 263–264); a refusal to admit that there are or ought to be any objective constraints upon human flourishing. Though rooted in a Christian understanding of humanity created in "the image and likeness of God" (Genesis 1: 26–27) defaced by the Original Sin but restored in Christ (I Corinthians 15: 22, etc.), Romanticism gradually assumed a secular, and therefore less defensible, character. It may still be seen in a degraded form in the popular desire to heal the disorders of society by waving a magic wand of legislation.

Now it might be questioned – and until recently would have been questioned – whether it is indeed the case that scarcity was not incorporated into modern economic thought before 1798. A widespread willingness to subsume Adam Smith, if not his predecessors, under the category of "classical political economy" was powerfully reinforced by Paul Samuelson's identification of a "Canonical Classical Model" (Samuelson, 1978). The hard core of that model is the "Ricardian" theory of rent; which – being based on diminishing returns in food production – formally incorporates scarcity into economic analysis. But it was pointed out by Samuel Hollander (1980, 1998) that diminishing returns, though detectible in *Wealth of Nations*, are not integrated into the Smith's analysis. And it has lately been argued that an "un-canonical, pre-classical" model may be constructed which includes Smith and virtually all his eighteenth-century contemporaries; but which differs sharply from the analysis of Malthus, Ricardo and their followers (Waterman, 2001a). For in the eighteenth-century model land is treated implicitly as a free good. The constraint upon growth is not land but capital. And capital may always be increased by "parsimony" regardless of the rate of profit (Waterman, 1999).

It would appear therefore that Malthus's polemic against Godwin, though constructed entirely from analytical materials well known to all his predecessors, is the ur-text of "classical political economy." For the notorious and much-derided "ratios" may be seen to imply diminishing returns (Stigler, 1952;

Waterman, 1992). And even if this is doubted, diminishing returns may readily be detected in other aspects of Malthus's argument (Hollander, 1997, pp. 13–35). The simultaneous discovery in 1815 of Ricardian rent by Malthus and three others only made explicit what was clearly implied by the argument of the first *Essay*. Hence the great divide between economists and human beings coincides with, and is caused by, the great divide in economic analysis (Waterman, 2001b). Ever since 1798 economists have looked at the world, and at the human societies that inhabit this world, in a way that is inherently offensive to Romantic sensibility, whether Christian or secular.

II

It might therefore be expected that the first few decades after the first *Essay* would afford a rich harvest of polemical literature, and such is the case. All students of classical political economy therefore have cause to be grateful to Thoemmes Press (among many other occasions of gratitude), for collating and printing a selection of some of the better-known specimens (Pyle, 1994). For the "bitter quarrel" was by no means one-sided. Several of the articles reprinted in Andrew Pyle's edition do indeed illustrate to perfection the detestation and loathing felt by Romantics for Malthusian political economy. But several others, including two from impeccably orthodox publications – the high-church *British Critic* and the Tory *Quarterly Review* – defend the arguments of the *Essay* from an explicitly Christian standpoint.

The collection begins with two of the five published reviews of the first *Essay*: [1] from the Rational Dissenters' flagship, *The Analytical Review*, and [2] from the almost equally pro-Jacobin *Monthly Review*. The *New Annual Register* (1798), the brief notice in *The Monthly Magazine* (1798, Sup. Vol. VI, p. 497) and the long-delayed review in the *British Critic* (1801, pp. 278–282) are not included. It is remarkable – and subversive of Southey's claim that Malthus had written "the political bible of the rich" ([9], p. 129) – that the *Analytical* and the *Monthly*, which had been derided by the *Anti-Jacobin Review* for their sympathy with the French Revolution (Waterman, 1991, pp. 18–21), should have accepted Malthus's *bona fides* as a "friend of mankind" ([Malthus, 1798], p. 3) and treated the anonymous *Essay* with respectful caution. The former was "glad to see a refutation of the new philosophy" ([1], p. 2); the latter praised the author's "fair discussion" of speculations that many would deem "fit . . . rather for ridicule than for refutation" ([2], p. 11). But neither [1] nor [2], nor also the *New Annual Register* and the *British Critic*, were convinced by the unsatisfactory theodicy of Malthus's last two chapters (see Waterman, 1991, pp. 97–112).

The collection continues with four substantial reviews of the second (1803) *Essay*: [3] and [4] being a two-part notice in the *Monthly Review*; [5] from the *Gentleman's Magazine*; another two-part article [6] and [7] from the *British Critic*; and [9], Southey's notorious attack in the *Annual Review* of 1804 alluded to above. It also includes an article by Arthur Young in his own periodical, the *Annals of Agriculture* (1804), which is largely a reply to some criticisms of his own work on land tenure in France and England in Book IV, chapter XI of the second *Essay* (Malthus, 1989, II, pp. 166–174) and might well have been omitted from this volume.

The *Monthly* praised Malthus for his willingness to explore the "truly momentous" consequences, "never before contemplated" of the "too obvious" principle of population; thus allowing us "to correct important errors in legislation . . . sanctioned by such high names as those of Montesquieu, Hume, Smith, Price and Robertson" ([3], p. 22); and to rank him as a political economist with the first three of these and with Turgot ([4], p. 62). The *Gentlemen's* noted Malthus's originality in perceiving – unlike any of his eighteenth-century predecessors – that the economic consequences of population pressures must appear long before all available land is cultivated ([5], p. 65). The *British Critic*, whilst apprehensively protestant about the revival of "monastic institutions for the female sex" (thirty-seven years later Edward Pusey received the vows of the first Anglican nun since the Dissolution of the Monasteries) was relieved at Malthus's abandonment of his heterodox "growth-of-mind" theodicy ([7], pp. 101, 102).

Southey's enraged invective in the *Annual* contains one important point. By including "moral restraint" in the 1803 *Essay* Malthus conceded to Godwin the possibility of "perfectibility" ([9], p. 125). That Malthus should have exposed himself to such criticism was chiefly the fault of his own greedy desire to kill two birds (*both* equality of property *and* perfectibility) with his one stone. But in the revolutionary circumstances of the 1790s perfectibility was an insignificant target. What was important to all but a handful of extreme Jacobins in England was the protection of private property rights. Both first and second *Essays* were welcomed for their demonstration that "the established administration of property" is a stable equilibrium to which society will always be conveyed by *self-love*, "the mainspring of the great machine" (Malthus, 1798, pp. 175, 207, 286, 370). Now in a world without property "the passion between the sexes" would operate with no economic sanction to restrain it. But with property rights and marriage it is rational to defer procreation: hence self-love reinforces the duty of moral restraint. Therefore by including "moral restraint" in the second *Essay* Malthus strengthened the argument for property (which mattered) by giving up the argument against perfectibility (which did not). Generations of later commentators who ought to have known better – Bagehot, Schumpeter, Gertrude Himmelfarb and George Stigler among others – have followed Southey in this fundamental misperception (Waterman, 1991, pp. 139–144).

The remainder of the material collected in this book refers to the recensions of 1806, 1807 and 1817. It consists of two appendices (1806 and 1817) in which Malthus replied to his critics [10], [16]; three unoriginal attacks by the Romantic essayist William Hazlitt [11], [12], [13] and an equally light-weight essay by Thomas De Quincy [18] who admired the Lake Poets for their art but despised them for their political economy; one of William Cobbett's *Rural Rides* [19]; two articles in the (Whig) *Edinburgh Review* that attacked Malthus's attackers [14], [15]; and J. B. Sumner's important notice in the (Tory) *Quarterly* [17].

It was actually De Quincy who uttered the most perceptive single comment ever made about Malthus's contribution to social theory, though not in the passage selected by Dr Pyle. Malthus (said De Quincy) "took an obvious and familiar truth, which until his own time had been a barren truism, and showed that it teemed with consequences" (Winch, 1996, p. 397). None of the three short pieces by Hazlitt reveal anything like this insight, but in the third ([13], p. 185) there is an important distinction between "the physical and necessary" limits set by Nature upon food production and the "arbitrary and artificial distribution of the produce according to the institutions of society." Now Malthus (1798, pp. 286–287) had argued that the existing institutions of society are necessary and inevitable; and that to "the established administration of property" (Godwin's own phrase) we owe "all that distinguishes the civilized, from the savage state." Nevertheless, better economists than Hazlitt continued to revert to the question, encouraged by J. S. Mill's ([1848] 1909, p. 21) specious distinction between "the laws of Production" (physical) and the "laws of Distribution" (political).

But at the heart of all the controversy was theology, as Francis Jeffrey clearly noted in the *Edinburgh*. Malthus's theories, "simple and obvious as they appear to be ... are rejected by a pretty large class of religious and respectable people, because they think, that the acknowledgement of a law of increase in the human race greater than any possible increase of the means of subsistence, is an impeachment of the power or benevolence of the Deity" ([15], p. 220). Malthus's own amateurish theodicy in the first *Essay* was a failure. He removed most of it from subsequent editions, and quietly retracted his heterodox rejection of human life as a state of trial for eternity. William Paley sketched a more satisfactory theodicy in *Natural Theology* (1802) but the definitive job was done by John Bird Sumner, whose *Treatise on the Records of the Creation* (1816) single-handedly converted many of the orthodox to Malthusian political economy (Waterman, 1991, ch. 4). Malthus's 1817 appendix acknowledged Mr. Sumner's "masterly developement and completion" of his own doctrines ([16], p. 242). And in turn, Sumner's review of the 1817 edition in the *Quarterly* congratulated Malthus on his "candour" in attending to the more cogent arguments of his critics and for "expunging those passages to which we had most pointedly objected" ([17], pp. 281–282, 251).

III

The editor recognizes in his Introduction that the first *Essay* was an anti-Jacobin response, not merely to hopes of human perfectibility but more fundamentally to Godwin's subversive doctrine that "the good things of the world are a common stock, upon which one man has as valid a title as another to draw what he wants" (Godwin, [1798] 1946, II, p. 423). But he is quite wrong to suggest that the *Essay* was part of a "reaction against the philosophy of the Enlightenment" (Pyle, 1994, p. xii). Apart from the fact that Malthus employed exactly the same social-theoretic vocabulary as Godwin and deliberately chose Godwin's own weapons to refute him, it is obvious that Malthus formed his analytical style on the model of David Hume's political essays (Waterman, 1991, pp. 28–42; on Malthus's reliance upon Hume; see also Winch, 1996, pp. 370–371). The center-piece of his polemic, the demolition of Godwin's "system of equality" in chapter X, is a "mental experiment" that closely resembles – both in style and in content – Hume's famous essay "Of the Balance of Trade" (Waterman, 1988). Malthus was and remained a typical, eighteenth-century Cambridge, Newtonian Anglican. It would be truer to regard him as the last major figure of the English Enlightenment before it was finally extinguished: not so much by political revolution as by Romantic frenzy.

It may be Dr Pyle's unwillingness to recognize the *intellectual* (as distinct from the *political*) context of the *Essay* that accounts for some of his selections and omissions. To be sure, "No selection policy will please all readers." Granted, his selection does indeed "provide some insight into the historical context of a classic work"; and it certainly "does not appear wildly arbitrary and eccentric" (p. xxv). The trouble is, rather, that it is too uncritically conventional, tamely accepting the widespread but wrong assumptions that Malthus's population theory can somehow be detached from political economy, and that "the moral and political philosophy" can be considered in abstraction from "the economics" which are its core (p. xxiv).

But in fact it is impossible to understand what Malthus was trying to do in 1798 without explicit economic theorising. Not only did he use ecological dynamics to construct a 'negative polemic' showing that Godwin's "system of equality" would revert to "the established administration of property." More importantly, he adumbrated a "positive polemic" to prove that at stationary equilibrium "the established administration of property" guarantees that the surplus is maximized. And upon that surplus depends "all that distinguishes the civilized, from the savage state" (see Waterman, 1991, pp. 37–50). Not only is private property inevitable, said Malthus to Godwin: it is also socially optimal.

None of the other authors selected for this volume had the faintest glimmering of such an argument, though Francis Jeffrey and J. B. Sumner could easily have assimilated it. Those who did see the point were Malthus's fellow-economists. Thomas Chalmers's first book (1808) can be regarded as a full scale "Contemporary Response" to the *Essay*. Seven years later Malthus, West, Torrens and Ricardo identified the analytical relation among the "ratios", diminishing returns, and the landlords' surplus. By 1817, Ricardo's arithmetical tables, by implying a quadratic production function for "corn" (Blaug, 1996, pp. 115–18), made it plain for all with eyes to see that rents would be maximized if the marginal return to labour-and-capital falls to that point at which accumulation and population-growth cease. Even one of the four 1815 essays would have improved both the balance and the scope of this collection. Arthur Young's apologia and Cobbett's "Ride" (not at all "a sustained anti-Malthusian argument" but an attack on some putative economic effects of the National Debt) could well have been omitted.

In view of the great service to intellectual historians performed in recent years by the Thoemmes Press it may seem churlish to object to the title of this book. But historians ought always to seek the truth, therefore it must be said that there was no such person as "Thomas Malthus." The author of *Population* was known to the public as "the Revd T. R. Malthus"; signed himself "T. Robt Malthus"; was addressed as "Robert" by close relations of his own and higher generations; and as "Bob" by his parents. To speak of "Thomas Malthus" is like speaking of "John Keynes". More is the pity that this egregious mistake has been repeated in a far more important publication by the same firm (Malthus, 1996).

REFERENCES

Anti-Jacobin Review
Blaug, M. (1996). *Economic Theory in Retrospect* (5th ed.). Cambridge: Cambridge University Press.
Brennan, H. G., & Waterman, A. M. C. (Eds) (1994). *Economics and Religion: Are They Distinct?* Boston: Kluwer.

Burke, E. (1981–1997). *The Writings and Speeches of Edmund Burke* (P. K. Langford et al., Eds). 9 vols. Oxford: Oxford University Press.

Chalmers, T. ([1808] 1995). *An Enquiry into the Nature and Stability of National Resources* (D. Gladstone, Ed.). London: Routledge/Thoemmes Press.

Eclectic Review.

Godwin, W. ([1798] 1946). *An Enquiry Concerning Political Justice and its Influence on Morals and Happiness* (3rd ed.), 2 vols. London: Robinson. (Photographic facsimile, F. E. L. Priestley (Ed.), with *variora*. Toronto: University of Toronto Press, 3 vols.)

Hollander, S. (1980). On Professor Samuelson's Canonical Classical Model of Political Economy. *Journal of Economic Literature, 18.*

Hollander, S. (1997). *The Economics of Thomas Robert Malthus.* Toronto: University of Toronto Press.

Hollander, S. (1998). The Canonical Classical Growth Model: Content, Adherence and Priority. *Journal of the History of Economic Thought, 20,* 253–277.

Levy, D. M. (2001). *How the Dismal Science Got Its Name: Classical Economics and the Ur-Text of Racial Politics.* Ann Arbor: University of Michigan Press.

Lovejoy, A. O. (1941). The Meaning of Romanticism in the History of Ideas. *Journal of the History of Ideas, 2,* 257–278.

[Malthus, T. R.] (1798). *An Essay on the Principle of Population as it Affects the Future Improvement of Society.* London: Johnson.

Malthus, T. R. (1989). *An Essay on the Principle of Population; or, A View of its past and present Effects on Human Happiness.* The version published in 1803, with the variora of 1806, 1807, 1817 and 1826. P. James (Ed.), 2 vols. Cambridge: Cambridge University Press.

Malthus, T. R. (1996). *Thomas Malthus: An Essay on Population. The Six Editions.* 11 vols. London: Routledge/Thoemmes Press.

Mill, J. S. ([1848] 1909). *Principles of Political Economy with some of their Applications to Social Philosophy* (W. J. Ashley, Ed.). London: Longmans, Green.

O'Brien, C. C. (1993). *The Great Melody.* London: Minerva.

Paley, W. ([1802] 1825). *Natural Theology.* In: *The Works of Edmund Paley, D. D.* (E. Paley, Ed.), 7 vols. London: Rivington.

Pyle, A. (Ed.) (1994). *Population: Contemporary Responses to Thomas Malthus.* Bristol: Thoemmes Press.

Samuelson, P. A. (1978). The Canonical Classical Model of Political Economy. *Journal of Economic Literature, 16,* 1415–1434.

Southey, R. (1965). *New Letters of Robert Southey* (K. Curry, Ed.). 2 vols. New York: Columbia University Press.

Stigler, G. (1952). The Ricardian Theory of Value and Distribution. *The Journal of Political Economy, 60,* 187–207.

Sumner, J. B. (1816). *A Treatise on the Records of the Creation; with Particular Reference to the Jewish History, and the Consistency of the Principle of Population with the Wisdom and Goodness of the Deity.* 2 vols. London: Hatchard.

Waterman, A. M. C. (1988). Hume, Malthus and the Stability of Equilibrium. *History of Political Economy, 20,* 85–94.

Waterman, A. M. C. (1991). *Revolution, Economics and Religion: Christian Political Economy 1798–1833.* Cambridge: Cambridge University Press.

Waterman, A. M. C. (1992). Analysis and Ideology in Malthus's 'Essay on Population'. *Australian Economic Papers, 31,* 203–217.

Waterman, A. M. C. (1999). Hollander on the 'Canonical Classical Growth Model': a Comment. *Journal of the History of Economic Thought, 21*, 311–313.

Waterman, A. M. C. (2001a). Notes Towards an Un-Canonical Pre-Classical Model of Political Œconomy. In: E. L. Forget & S. Peart (Eds), *Reflections on the Classical Canon in Economics: Essays in Honor of Samuel Hollander*. London: Routledge.

Waterman, A. M. C. (2001b). The Beginning of 'Boundaries': the Sudden Separation of Economics from Christian Theology. In: G. Erreygers (Ed.), *Economics and Interdisciplinary Exchange*. London: Routledge.

Winch, D. (1996). *Riches and Poverty: an Intellectual History of Political Economy in Britain, 1750–1834*. Cambridge: Cambridge University Press.

THEORIES OF DEVELOPMENT

Lawrence Busch

Peet, Richard with Elaine Harkwick. *Theories of Development*. New York: Guilford Press, 1999. 234pp. ISBN 1-57230-489-8. $24.00. Paper.

At least since the days when Adam Smith wrote his *Inquiry into The Nature and Causes of the Wealth of Nations*, economists have attempted to explain why wealth and poverty exist. Moreover, like Smith, they have put forth prescriptions designed to promote the former and reduce the latter. In contrast, the concept of development is a relatively new one, largely borne out of the devastation and decolonization after World War II.

Indeed, the postwar world was so radically altered that it demanded the creation of a range of new concepts. The split between the capitalist West and communist East required a "Cold War." Alfred Sauvy, a French demographer, making an analogy with the Third Estate of prerevolutionary France, coined the term "Third World," to distinguish the newly created nations in Africa and Asia from those of the First World nations of the West and the Second World nations of the East (Sauvy, 1952). The U.S. and other Western nations soon launched a "Green Revolution" to protect against Red Revolutions stimulated by the Soviet Bloc. Similarly, before 1949, the word "development" was usually applied only to film (Lummis, 1996). Only later was it applied as the cure for "underdevelopment."

Moreover, the full power and deep pockets of the American state were soon put behind the new concepts, especially in President Truman's Point Four program. With all the naïve zeal that only Americans seem to be able to muster, both diplomats and academics rushed to the new cause. Academics at large

Research in the History of Economic Thought and Methodology, Volume 20-A, pages 271–277.
Copyright © 2002 by Elsevier Science Ltd.
All rights of reproduction in any form reserved.
ISBN: 0-7623-0847-8

American research universities were soon mobilized to study the problems of development and to build educational institutions in what became known as developing nations. Infrastructural investment – roads, bridges, dams, irrigation systems and water supplies, schools, ports – were financed through what became known as "foreign assistance." Moreover, as colonial empires faded away, the various European colonial research institutes were transformed into development agencies. Furthermore, not to be outdone by the West, the Soviets created their development programs as well.

Indeed, it is fair to say that development as a concept was a child of the Cold War. Western social scientists (and especially economists) would show how capitalist development would resolve the problems of the Third World, eliminating poverty and squalor while demonstrating the fallacies of the communist alternative. More recently, with the collapse of the Soviet Union, development theory and practice took a new turn. Economists jumped at the opportunity to tackle the difficult task of transforming Russia, Eastern Europe, and the Central Asian "nations" into model free market economies. Textbooks in hand, they have provided all too simple answers: A central bank, a stock market, property laws, and a business school thrown in for good measure, would do the job. We now know, with the advantages of 20/20 hindsight, that these were very complex questions that spanned the economy, the polity and civil society. Russia's appauling decline from this "shock therapy" is all too obvious. Many other former Soviet bloc nations are hardly faring much better.

But with the Cold War and the threat of communism rapidly fading from memory, and a host of critics challenging both the concept of development and the assumptions behind it, the urgency of development is no longer what it once was. Today, U.S. foreign assistance is quite modest and focused on a handful of "strategic" countries. The current administration in Washington seems to have written off much of the world, including – until recently – Russia.

Thus, it is in this far less celebratory time that Richard Peet and Elaine Hartwick (henceforth PH) have put together an extraordinary volume that begins with that very same illusive and ineluctable question that Smith asked. But PH are content neither to limit their search to economics nor to accept the received views of development. Instead, they explore the literature across the social sciences and end each chapter with a critique. As geographers, they are concerned with spatial relations more than their colleagues in other social sciences. Nevertheless, they carefully synthesize and critique the diverse literature from across the social sciences. What they show is the complexity and diversity of the vast literature and practice as well as its parochial character.

PH present the panoply of development (and anti-development!) theories, devoting a chapter each to economic, sociological, Marxist, poststructuralist, feminist, and critical modernist theories – a range far beyond the mastery of most likely readers. The presentation is concise, clear, critical, and to the point.

Highly critical of mainstream economics, PH argue that it is far too limited in scope. They attempt "to demonstrate that the dominant notion of development as a certain kind of economic growth founded on capitalist efficiency results from *one* interpretation of *one* aspect of *one* people's history" (p. 13, emphasis in original). They correctly show that most classical economists from Smith to Bentham were concerned about increasing national wealth and distributing it in an equitable manner. However, this changed abruptly in the late nineteenth century as economists shifted to a mathematical concern for the efficient allocation of resources. Out of this emerged the neoclassical school, devoid of concern for either sociology or history. But PH see development economics as encompassing both neoclassical approaches and attempts to apply Keynesian growth models to the non-Western world. As they put it, "In general, Keynesian economic theory established the legitimacy of state intervention into market economies with the aim of achieving growth rates on the basis of social policy" (p. 40). Development theory, for them, is an elitist extension of Keynesian approaches to the Third World.

According to PH, among the key tenets of development economics have been: (1) recognition of the dualistic character of much development, (2) mobilization of domestic resources by increasing the savings rate, (3) mobilization of foreign resources, (4) an industrial strategy focusing on consumer goods, (5) an agricultural strategy enabling the rural poor to take advantage of new technologies, (6) a trade strategy including export promotion, (7) promotion of human resource development, (8) project appraisal to ensure that efficient use is made of capital, and (9) development planning and policy making.

The rise of conservative governments in the U.S. and the U.K. in the 1980s shifted the policy balance away from planning and toward "letting the market decide." One outcome of this approach was so-called "structural adjustment" programs, of which PH are particularly critical: "Structural adjustment more basically meant changing the structure of an economy so that it mirrored the competitive ideal derived from the Western experience" (p. 56).

In general, PH are quite pessimistic about development economists' ability to transcend their self-imposed, limited perspective – a perspective marked by methodological individualism (even when analyzing collective phenomena such as markets and firms), by a failure to recognize the constructed character of markets (not noticing that the market cannot *decide* anything), and by a firm belief that the social world can be mapped into mathematics (despite evidence to the contrary (viz. Ormerod, 1994)). Moreover, they suggest that the very reliance on mathematics serves to obfuscate issues and limit discussion to the cognoscenti, even while it enhances economists' policy-making role.

Neo-institutionalism, PH argue, merely extends the neoclassical model, but fails to break out of it. Indeed, even sympathetic observers wonder how production could occur if firms are merely the result of market failure (Dietrich, 1994). While PH credit neo-institutionalists with recognizing that the market is an institution, they critique what they share with neo-classicals – namely, that the operation of the market "magically transforms myriad selfish intentions into homogeneous socially beneficial tendencies" (p. 64). They suggest that this sleight of hand is accomplished by defining "beneficial" quite narrowly as the efficient use of resources to generate profits and material abundance.

But perhaps of greater interest is PH's examination of how development is treated in other disciplines. Mainstream sociologists, PH argue, take a broader view of development but still see a single path to the future. They see development as modernization, by which traditional people (who are uncreative and authoritarian) gradually become modern. Social psychologists pick up a similar theme arguing that through time people develop modern personalities. Indeed, psychologist David McClelland created short courses to help people develop a "need for achievement," ostensibly a modern approach to the world. Historians got into the act as well; notably, Walter Rostow, in his *Stages of Economic Growth: A Non-communist Manifesto* (1960), saw national development metaphorically as so many airplanes on a runway waiting in line to take off – all for the same destination. So well-accepted were his views that they became a key part of Kennedy's inaugural address. As PH put it, "Development meant assuming theoretical models of the West (rationalization), the institutions of the West (the market), the goals of the West (high mass consumption), and the culture of the West (worship of the commodity" (pp. 85–86).

What is remarkable about all these theories, even those ostensibly historical, is their nearly complete disregard for history. European plundering, colonization, slavery, and racism, as well as the artificial creation and rearrangement of national boundaries, and suppression of industrialization and education in the colonies simply disappear from these analyses. Moreover, nations which are entire subcontinents such as India, China, and Brazil are often lumped together with Djibouti and the Maldive Islands.

Contrasted with these positive views of development are a range of critical perspectives. Marx had a very different view of capitalism, one reflected in various Marxisms today. (Unlike the situation in economics, in most other social sciences, Marx still casts a large shadow.) While it stretches the imagination to call Marx a development theorist (PH do that), there is no doubt that he was concerned with issues germane to contemporary debates. Most Marxists, of whatever stripe or persuasion, agree that human nature is shaped by social and natural conditions. This process might be termed development. But if one does that, then one can no longer read contemporary understandings of capital and labor back into the past. For dependency theorists such as Celso Furtado and André Gunder Frank, both development and underdevelopment emerged from the very same processes: the surplus was transferred away from the Third World and towards the First. World Systems theorists, such as Immanuel Wallerstein, have emphasized unequal exchange. For them, nations of the center exploit those of the periphery through trade. In contrast, regulation theorists have emphasized the cultural habits and institutional rules that regulate the process of development. Borrowing from the Italian Marxist sociologist Antonio Gramsci, they introduced the concept of Fordism – the mass production of goods using relatively highly paid labor, leading to the creation of a large middle class. They argued that in the 1970s we witnessed a "crisis of Fordism" as a result of internationalization, the decline of the welfare state, and a crisis of demand. Fordism was replaced by "flexible accumulation." Production of goods shifted away from the West to where labor was cheap. Computer-enhanced manufacturing made it possible to tailor goods to rapidly changing markets. And, just-in-case warehousing of inputs into production was replaced by just-in-time manufacturing. Together, regulationists argue, these changes restructured the world economy, often in ways unexpected by mainstream theorists.

PH note that in more recent years, other schools of (anti-)development theory have emerged. Poststructuralists see development as merely a modern strategy of power and control. They argue that the Enlightenment turned into its very opposite by virtue of European domination and supremacy. They attack the central tenets of modern progress such as truth, accuracy, and reason. As such they see mainstream economics as merely another form of the false universalism preached by Enlightenment scholars and their progeny. Authors such as Michel Foucault have argued that what Europeans saw as universal was actually culturally specific. The emancipatory ideals of the Enlightenment were the basis for imposing a discipline and identity on everyone, such that they acted in accordance with the norms of modernity. "For poststructuralists, . . . the term 'development' was an invention, or social construction, and the concept had a discursive or a cultural (rather than a natural) history" (p. 143).

Equally critical are the postcolonial scholars. Raised in Western intellectual traditions, these indigenes of the European colonies found themselves at the epicenter of the contradictions of the development project. Franz Fanon, Albert Memmi, Camara Laye, and others like them demonstrated through accounts of their personal experience the "double consciousness" (Du Bois, 1999) of being at once Western and non-Western, at once a believer in values such as freedom, justice, and equality, while at the same time seeing their opposites imposed on their native lands.

Postmodernism, too, PH assure us, has had its impact on development theories. Like their poststructuralist counterparts, postmodernists have rejected holistic approaches, fearing replacing one hegemonic discourse with another equally hegemonic one. They have favored more fragmented, historically specific approaches, emphasizing the importance of language in legitimating development. Yet, as PH ironically note, there has never actually been a single, monolithic development discourse. From the beginning that discourse has been a cacaphony of disparate voices.

In recent years, feminists have also been vocal about development. Since the late 1970s, largely as a result of pressure from feminists, development projects have given at least nominal attention to the social position of women. Of particular importance has been the retheorizing of women's work, often missing from the mainstream development literature as it is usually not the subject of market transactions. From the vantage point of many feminists, women's work is a subsidy to other development activities. Three major viewpoints have emerged: Proponents of Women in Development (WID) accept the modernization approach but demand certain modifications. Proponents of Women and Development (WAD) argue that the development process has impoverished women. Supporters of Gender and Development (GAD) challenge the sexual division of labor, arguing that gender relations rather than the role of women need to be scruitinized. Finally, proponents of Women, Environment, and Development (WED) link the liberation of women to the liberation of nature.

In the concluding chapter, PH argue that, given the widespread poverty and hunger in the world today, the development project needs to be rethought rather than discarded. They argue that development has focused too much on material things and not sufficiently on democracy. They propose a "critical modernism" that allows us to learn to live with modernity by criticizing it and changing it. They argue poignantly for a radical democracy in which development would go beyond the production of goods to the transformation of power relations. They note that "A truly egalitarian society has to entail control over all life institutions by all their members as direct and equal participants" (p. 207).

This reader was somewhat frustrated by the rather truncated conclusion. If PH are right, then the only kind of development worth pursuing would be one in which democracy was extended far beyond what is now narrowly defined as Politics. It would encompass, among other things, challenges to the autocracy of the workplace, to the ways in which new technologies are often foisted upon the populace, to the notion that economic development trumps all other kinds.

But that is another volume – one that I heartily urge Peet and Hartwick to write.

REFERENCES

Dietrich, M. (1994). *Transaction Cost Economics and Beyond: Toward a New Economics of the Firm*. London: Routledge.

Du Bois, W. E. B. (1999 [1903]). *The Souls of Black Folk: Authoritative Text, Contexts, Criticism*. New York: W. W. Norton.

Lummis, C. D. (1996). *Radical Democracy*. Ithaca, NY: Cornell University Press.

Ormerod, P. (1994). *The Death of Economics*. London: Faber and Faber.

Rostow, W. W. (1960). *The Stages of Economic Growth: A Non-Communist Manifesto*. Cambridge: Cambridge University Press.

Sauvy, A. (1952). Trois Mondes, Une Planète. *L'Observateur*, *118*, 14.

RELIGION, ART, AND MONEY

John P. Tiemstra

A review of *About Religion: Economies of Faith in a Virtual Culture* by Mark C. Taylor. Chicago: University of Chicago Press, 1999. 300 pp. $19 (paper).

My students at Calvin College are familiar with the theological idea of God as creator out of nothing (*creatio ex nihilo,* in the traditional Latin), of all things seen and unseen. So when we come to talk about money, I make a little joke with them. Not only God can create out of nothing – Alan Greenspan also has that power, since he can create money out of nothing. The joke is that much more delicious since money can be used to buy almost anything else. If you can create money, you can create everything. And Mr. Greenspan does not appear very godlike. He looks like a bit of a nebbish, belying both his great power and his hip past as a jazz musician.

The media may seem at times to worship Greenspan, but many people find it more compelling to worship money itself. Jesus Christ himself was aware of this temptation when he said, "You can not serve both God and money." (Luke 16:13) Though money may seem to compel our worship, serious Christian commentators on economic and cultural matters, following the teaching of Jesus, try to steer our culture back toward the service of the biblical God, and away from the materialism (as it is called) of affluent, post-modern, post-Christian America.

To Mark Taylor, the idea of money as a god is no joke. Money is Aristotle's "universal equivalent," the Hegelian Absolute, the "unity of differences" that is the goal of all speculative philosophy, the "god among commodities" in the

Research in the History of Economic Thought and Methodology, Volume 20-A, pages 279–283.
Copyright © 2002 by Elsevier Science Ltd.
All rights of reproduction in any form reserved.
ISBN: 0-7623-0847-8

words of Marx. Money carries ultimate value, since it can be exchanged for everything, up to and including Christian salvation. The eucharist is to Taylor an exchange between God and people, its centerpiece not the communion, but the offertory. The wafer is a coin, minted at the bakery, exchanged to symbolize a trade of death for life. To venerate money, to seek it and serve it, is only natural.

Nor is the pursuit of money really "materialism," since money is increasingly immaterial. Once connected to full-bodied coin, it quickly became token coinage, paper currency, then pencil marks in a book, magnetized particles on a disk, and photons speeding down an optical fiber. Taylor thinks that the ultimate severance of the material from the virtual, finally ushering in the post-modern economy, occurred when President Nixon ended the connection between the dollar and gold in the "new economic policy" speech of August 15, 1971.

So for Taylor it is as much a mistake to pursue the Marxian agenda of materialism as it is to pursue an evangelical mission of returning to basic values. Both programs ignore the immateriality of the financial economy, the ephemeral quality of the information economy, and the virtual dream world sold to consumers on TV. Ignore reality – focus on symbols. The reality is that every-thing is a symbol. Salvation is not a matter of building things, or even remaking lives, but of manipulating symbols. Salvation is to be found in art. Art is Prof. Taylor's real religion.

This book, then, is mostly about art, visual and literary. There are extended discussions of the sculpture of Frank Serra and the prints of Andy Warhol, Melville's novella *The Confidence Man,* and the philosophy of Kant, Hegel, Kirkegaard, and Derrida. The book touches lightly on a host of other novelists, philosophers, and artists. Curiously, he does not mention the notorious artist J. S. G. Boggs, who draws pictures of U.S. currency and then exchanges this art for goods and services with knowing merchants. It must be too obvious. Historians of economic thought will find some interest in the discussion of the relationship of Marx's view of money to the philosophy of Hegel, but that takes up only a few pages. There is a disjointed quality to the book, as if the different chapters were essays written for different audiences and occasions. In fact, five of the ten chapters were previously published in journals or collective volumes.

Not only do the topics of different chapters range widely, but also do the methods. Some chapters (like the one on Serra) read like standard criticism, linear and carefully constructed. Others (like the opening one that focuses on Melville) consist largely of multi-lingual wordplay. It is impressive in its cleverness, but not really written to persuade the reader of the truth of any well-formed proposition. The book really belongs to the literature of "cultural studies" in the post-modern vein, both in the secondary sources it cites, and in the methods it uses. It is not theology or philosophy in the traditional analytical ("modern"?) sense of those terms.

The chapter on money, titled "Christianity and the Capitalism of Spirit," is firmly in the "cultural studies" tradition, and has little to do with Christianity as its adherents understand it. The point seems to be to deconstruct economic artifacts like money, and economic activities like investment, and reconstruct them with new meanings. Sometimes analogies are drawn with traditional Christian symbolism, but that's about as close as it comes. Philosophical arguments are embroidered with puns like "The Death of Go(l)d," a chapter subheading. The sources are Hegel, Marx, and Simmel. In contrast, Christian economic commentary tends to focus on ethical issues, uses analytical methods, and takes as its sources the Bible, the Church Fathers, the Reformers, and other Christian theological writers. Throughout the book it is clear that the author is committed to atheism, a strong belief that there is no personal God, so it is not surprising that he appropriates Christian symbols without much regard for their theological context.

The thing that I find most appealing about Mark Taylor's work is his understanding that the questions raised by the post-modern line of thinking are religious in nature (See Booth, 1997). The post-modernists have abandoned the idea that there is an infallible method that will lead us to truth, and that language corresponds definitively to some objective reality. But for all the games that Taylor plays with language, he still understands that art and language sometimes achieve a universal resonance, a beauty and coherence that goes beyond mere cleverness. He is not afraid to call this transcendence "God." Not Truth, not Objective Reality, it is not anything that mere mortals can adequately describe. But it is still beyond our human limitations, our situatedness, our perspectives, even though it is a human creation.

What should we economists take away from this connection of religion, art, and money? Taylor is not an economist, and he doesn't seem to address professional economists directly. Certainly he thinks that money has certain divine qualities. When it comes to social ethics, he says, "In a world where all reality is becoming virtual reality, effective economic strategies and political action must be calculated artfully" (p. 167). Remember, he's talking about real art, not just clever politics. Economists err on both sides of this truth. We insist that "money is a veil," having no importance of itself, but only cloaking the real workings of the economy. On the other side, we want to distinguish money sharply from other assets, and insist on the special role it has in facilitating economic activity. Maybe we could benefit from thinking more about money in a deconstructed way as a symbol, recognizing all the different meanings and functions it has in economy and society both.

Post-modernism has found its way into economics mostly through the "rhetoric in economics" approach to methodology that began with the work of McCloskey. It seems to have had little impact on the mainstream of the discipline, having mostly been embraced by institutionalists and other members of heterodox schools. The hope of the proponents of this work is that it will lead to a clearer understanding of the sources of disagreements among economists. In the process giving new legitimacy and standing to the heterodox schools, and perhaps thereby new vigor to the mainstream (see McCloskey, 1994, pp. 379–396; Tiemstra, 1998). It may also lead to greater self-confidence and renewed vigor in the institutionalist camp (Hoksbergen, 1994). In the work under review, Taylor stays away from most methodological issues. He only comments that theory is the search for unity in multiple data, and that therefore theory does not escape belief in God, because ultimately the One God is that unity (p. 76).

Many Christians find useful insights in post-modernism, but we would want to insist on a realist version of it (See Westphal, 2000; Wolterstorff, 1997; Schwehn, 1997). It is a mistake to confuse symbol with reality, and all of our theories and conversations about reality are socially constructed. Magritte's drawing of a pipe was not a pipe, and Boggs's drawings of money are not money, even though he uses them as if they are. But there is a reality that exists out there. God is real, and we are real, and there is a real creation of which we are a part. We will never be able to understand reality fully or completely or truthfully, but that is because of our limitations as human creatures, not because there is no truth to know. Deconstruction may even have its uses, though all too often its practice is based on anti-realist assumptions, as it seems to be in Taylor's case.

Christians will continue to insist that making money out to be divine, and making it an object of worship, is idolatry. It is not just mistaking creature for creator. Since money is an artifact of human society, it mistakes a creature of a creature for the creator God. A Christian post-modern realist would say that if you look for God in the economy, particularly in finance, you will not find God. Mark Taylor is right – the economy is virtual, not real. Money is an illusion. God is real. To find God, we have to look past the illusions. Christians may use a metaphor of debt and redemption to understand the idea of salvation, but it is necessary to do so only because of the limitations of our own intellect. If the post-modernists remind us that this is not true, that salvation is not an economic transaction, they are right, but we already knew that.

Most economists reading this book will find the technique of deconstruction difficult to understand, and off-putting. We were not trained to think or argue in this way, so it is frustrating to read. It may not be such a bad idea to read it anyway. Our colleagues in the humanities are being taught to think and argue this way, and if we are to communicate with them, it will help for us to understand their modes of thought (see Brownlee, 1997). The gulf between economics and the humanities, even between economics and other social sciences like sociology, has probably never been greater than it is now. If that gap is to be bridged, we will have to meet the other folks half way. Reading this book, with its strong interest in economic language, is one way that we economists can begin to make our contribution to the process.

REFERENCES

Booth, W. C. (1997). Deconstruction as a Religious Revival. In: D. Hoekema & B. Fong (Eds), *Christianity and Culture in the Crossfire* (pp. 131–154). Eerdmans, Grand Rapids.

Brownlee, P. P. (1997). 'I Was a Stranger and You Welcomed Me': Bridging Between Languages. In: D. Hoekema & B. Fong (Eds), *Christianity and Culture in the Crossfire* (pp. 171–178). Eerdmans, Grand Rapids.

Hoekema, D., & Fong, B. (Eds) (1997). *Christianity and Culture in the Crossfire.* Eerdmans, Grand Rapids.

Hoksbergen, R. (1994). Postmodernism and Institutionalism: Toward a Resolution of the Debate on Relativism. *Journal of Economic Issues, 28*(3), 679–713.

McCloskey, D. N. (1994). *Knowledge and Persuasion in Economics.* Cambridge University Press.

Schwehn, M. R. (1997). Christianity and Postmodernism: Uneasy Allies. In: D. Hoekema & B. Fong (Eds), *Christianity and Culture in the Crossfire* (pp. 155–168). Eerdmans, Grand Rapids.

Taylor, M. C. (1999). *About Religion: Economies of Faith in a Virtual Culture.* University of Chicago Press.

Tiemstra, J. (1998). Why Economists Disagree. *Challenge, 41*(3), 46–62.

Westphal, M. (2000). Postmodernism and the Gospel: Onto-theology, Metanarratives, and Perspectivism. *Perspectives* (Reformed Church Press), *15*(4), 6–10.

Wolterstorff, N. (1997). Suffering, Power, and Privileged Cognitive Access: The Revenge of the Particular. In: D. Hoekema & B. Fong (Eds), *Christianity and Culture in the Crossfire* (pp. 79–94). Eerdmans, Grand Rapids.

HARNESSING THE POWER OF FICTION, A REVIEW ESSAY

Ken Dennis

The Invention of Modern Science by Isabelle Stengers, translated by Daniel W. Smith, Minneapolis: University of Minnesota Press, 2000, 185 pp; index; $49.95 (Hardcover) $19.95 (Paperback)

ABSTRACT

Isabelle Stengers seeks the singularity of the modern sciences, and, in doing so, dares to relate science to politics. Modern science began in the laboratory where Galileo could call upon Nature to serve as faithful witness to his power of fiction (the power to imagine or speculate about the nature of reality). But the evolution of modern science compels us to acquire our knowledge beyond the confines of the laboratory, requiring new ways for science to relate to politics. But economics, considered as a science (and not as a field of policy), has yet to control the power of fiction.

This is a translation of the author's *L'Invention des sciences modernes* (Paris: La Découverte, 1993). Isabelle Stengers is a philosopher who has written widely in the history and philosophy of the sciences, and has authored, co-authored, and collaborated in a number of books, most notably those with Nobel prize-winning scientist Ilya Prigogine (1984, 1986, 1997).

In this book, Stengers sets out in search of the "singularity" of the modern sciences, the uniquely defining characteristics that distinguish them from other

Research in the History of Economic Thought and Methodology, Volume 20-A, pages 285–297.
ISBN: 0-7623-0847-8

human activities. In doing so, she "dares to associate scientific reason and politics," (p. 15). Noting Aristotle's definition of man as both rational and political animal, she contends that to understand modern science one must confront the problem of relating the legitimacy of knowledge with the legitimacy of power (p. 62), for the definition of science can never be neutral (p. 25). Whether it refers to Galileo's challenge to the Church, to Darwin's challenge to the creationist view of human origins, or to the many challenges we human beings create for the Earth's environment and atmosphere, "every [scientific] theory affirms a social power, a power to judge the value of human practices. No theory is imposed without social, economic, or political power being at play, somewhere" (p. 113). Thus, the challenge that Stengers sets for herself is a dual one: "to try to articulate what we understand by science and what we understand by politics" (p. 16).

As the argument unfolds, two items on her agenda begin to take on some prominence. One is to understand what constitutes scientific "evidence." Although she rarely uses this word,[1] it is implied in such legal turns of phrase as "bearing faithful witness to" and "calling into testimony" or by such metaphors as "making Nature speak." Bruno Latour has summarized Stengers' past work in these terms: "Isabelle Stengers has chosen to look for a touchstone distinguishing good science from bad not in epistemology but in ontology, not in the word but in the world," (from his Forward to Stengers, 1997, p. ix), but this preference for ontology over epistemology that he attributes to her is only partly true. Stengers is indeed concerned with the epistemological question: How can we recognize legitimate claims to scientific knowledge?, and it is only her method, which is both historical and empirical (rather than rational in the scholastic sense that applies to the literature on Popper and Lakatos), that sets her apart from many of her contemporaries.

A second major item on her agenda is to liberate the "field" sciences from a status that is typically judged inferior to the "privileged" status enjoyed by the "theoretico-experimental" sciences, but doing this without questioning the "primordial character" of the latter (p. 132), that is, without offending their representatives. Her diplomacy is based on two principles. One is to avow the "Leibnizian" constraint of respecting the "established sentiments," those widely held beliefs that "cannot be threatened without leading to panicked rigidity, indignation, or misunderstanding," sentiments such as surround notions like "objectivity, reality, rationality, truth, progress" (pp. 15–16). In short, she wants to give credit where credit is due (e.g. to Galileo's work) without thereby locking herself into fixed or rigid commitments (e.g. by acquiescing to the privileged status of the experimental method). "I have the weakness of preferring a more vulnerable approach to history, one that will allow us to speak of failure,"

(p. 34) she writes; so, while observing a respectful appreciation for past accomplishments, she will also retain the option to "begin again with other givens" (p. 80). In this she will be guided by another principle, Bruno Latour's "Irreduction," according to which one seeks to avoid the temptation to explain things by reducing them to a relation of "irreducible opposition" (p. 16). Thus, in relating science to politics, she wishes to steer clear of both the Scylla of "Science is only politics" and the Charybdis of "Science transcends political divisions" (p. 16). In her reading of the history of the sciences, she will adopt an attitude of "humor" (defined as "the capacity to recognize oneself as a product of the history whose construction one is trying to follow," p. 66), a humor that allows for the possibility of a "shared perplexity," a humor that is not to be confused with mere irony or mocking derision (p. 18).

The argumentation of this book is exceptionally intricate. Its scope is wide-ranging, its reach into the literature is deep. But a word of warning to potential readers: this is the sort of book that one must read twice in order to read once. Stengers' style of reasoning is extravagantly baroque in its convoluted twists and turns of disclaimer and qualification,[2] metaphors coming thick and fast, the burdening of ordinary words with special meanings at times almost willfully affected. And yet, even with these compositional or stylistic peculiarities, her text never fails to be provocative or fascinating.

To merely summarize the most elemental components of this book (without attempting any critical commentary) is daunting enough. And it is just that, a rather literal summary, that will be offered here, which (I hope) will not do too much violence to the subtlety of her argument. Following this summary, I will address the question as to the relevance that this work might have for the discipline of economics.

In seeking to identify the "singularity" of modern science, Stengers adopts an historical (one might even say evolutionary) approach. Believing, as she does, in the kind of genuine scientific progress that gives successful discoveries their longevity, she nevertheless views the process of discovery as contingent (p. 72), and hence "the impossibility of understanding the activity of the individual scientist independent of the historical tradition in which his engagement, and perhaps his singularity, is rooted" (p. 73).

Her understanding of the singularity of modern science is built around two major changes or "events" that "make history" by defining a "before and after" (p. 118), that is, changes that set precedents that other scientists will henceforth be incapable of ignoring (pp. 68–69). The first of these events is very precisely identified in Galileo's *Discourse* of 1637,[3] the dividing line between pre-modern (ancient and medieval, Aristotelian and Scholastic) science and modern science. But the second great division, which often seems to be portrayed as the evolution

from "experimental" to "field" sciences, is not so sharply defined, either tempo-
rally or by any one individual's accomplishment (though Darwin's contribution
is accorded some prominence).

To identify the emergence of modern science, Stengers views Galileo as
"creator of the mathematical description of [uniformly] accelerated motion of
heavy bodies" (p. 73) by his offering a mere "thought experiment" (p. 85) that
describes a type of motion "whose prototype is the descent of highly polished
balls down the length of a smooth inclined plane" (p. 73). What was the essential novelty here? Much of Stengers' discussion is couched in terms of
"invention" and "fiction." When she speaks of fiction, she has in mind not the
feigned truth of a literary work about imaginary events, but rather any product
of the human imagination. The word "hypothesis" might serve just as well here,
but Stengers rarely uses it,[4] preferring instead such phrases as "the speculative
powers of the imagination" (p. 136). As for invention, she speaks not only
of the invention of science but also the "invention of fact" (p. 50), noting
how the older "ideal of a pure fact" (p. 50) has given way to the belief
that facts are "invented" through the creative act of scientific explanation. The
"actualization" of such things as "atoms, the void, the force of gravity, nucleic
acid," etc. (p. 157), that is, "beings that science brings into existence" (p. 99),
puts in doubt the very distinction between discovering and inventing. Scientific
invention, then, attests to the power of fiction.

Thus, when Galileo asked his readers to imagine "an instantaneous speed
[i.e. velocity] in which a body traverses no space at all in no time whatsoever"
(p. 86), he was exercising the power of fiction, but in a novel way. Armed with
an experimental apparatus that would allow anyone, including his critics, to test
his claim, his "new use of reason" was not an "arbitrary definition" (as his
contemporary critics would say) but a "new way of arguing" that allowed
Galileo to withdraw himself as witness and to let Nature speak (p. 81), making
the laboratory the place where an "objective third party is invented, capable of
imposing on humans the putting in risk of their fictions" (p. 156). Galileo's
fiction, however, was not just like any other fiction, but one that sharpened the
distinction between the "legitimate representation" of reality and mere "opinion"
(p. 163).

But Stengers also stresses that Galileo's staging of a highly artificial event
was both scientific and political, for two reasons. First, he declined to explain
the "why" of uniformly accelerated motion (leaving that question to another
authority), limiting his "explanation" to a mathematical account of the "how"
of this type of motion (p. 82), thus deliberately limiting the scope of the scientific
enterprise. Second, by offering his experimental apparatus to put at risk (to
"test") his speculation, Galileo effectively defined his profession as "scientist"

by disqualifying all those who would not accept his challenge from being counted as "scientist" like himself (p. 91).

As a first (and provisional) attempt to identify the singularity of the modern sciences, Stengers writes: "Wherever a new use of reason is produced – and this is how I propose to identify the singularity of the modern sciences – it will imply and affirm the inability of reason alone to vanquish the power of fiction" (p. 80). This none too clear definition is re-stated variously throughout the ensuing text,[5] but essentially it signals the end of the phase of scientific evolution during which reason alone provided evidence, and the commencement of a new phase in which the "empirical" shares the stage with the "rational" as a source of evidence. Thus, by using reason (his mathematics) to call forth Nature as a faithful witness to establish that "his fiction [was] not a fiction like the others," Galileo effectively dismissed the prevailing scholastic use of reason to merely "save the phenomena" (p. 137), that is, to rationalize (in mere words) an existing textual authority.

Galileo's example created an "imperative of objectivity" by which other scientists were "constrained to speak of their invention as a discovery that others could have made" (p. 40), but the ultimate success of any discovery resides not in the "event" itself but in its "signification" (pp. 45, 67), that is, in the interest any new discovery generates by way of ensuing commentary and criticism, and most especially by the scope and diversity of the implications it brings to other scientific work. Moreover, the contrived artifices of the laboratory are always subject to limitations imposed by the very nature of their abstraction (p. 86), for "everything changes when one leaves the laboratory," even for Galileo. "Outside the laboratory, one finds friction, wind, . . . everything whose elimination allowed Galileo to establish his authority" (p. 128).

Before leaving the laboratory to re-define the singularity of the sciences for the present age, Stengers prepares the way by observing why her re-definition would be necessary even for the older "theoretico-experimental" sciences themselves. First, many laboratory activities conducted "in the name of science" (e.g. medical research) have come into public view with a scrutiny that raises issues of scientific ethics (p. 22). Second, the resources required to stage many of today's experiments and their far-reaching implications that lie beyond the laboratory (e.g. bio-engineering) are both so enormous that the older theoretico-experimental sciences can no longer be understood in terms of the bygone tradition of "paternalism" (p. 165), that is, without accounting for the ways these branches of science must now relate to politics (p. 106). Third, a very recent development, common to both the experimental and field sciences, illustrates how their singularity "is constantly being reinvented," namely, the techniques of computer simulation (p. 134). By blurring the distinction between real phenomena revealed through experimental contrivance and the new kinds of fiction created arbitrarily by computer model, the techniques of computer simulation re-introduce the problem Galileo seemed to have conquered centuries before: distinguishing between "the illegitimate power of fiction" and "the truth, irreducible to this fiction" (p. 147).

How, then, does Stengers propose to re-define the singularity of the modern sciences? Her much anticipated re-formulation will probably disappoint some readers, especially when it is judged alone, out of context. It is both vague, and yet just slightly reminiscent of the falsificationist doctrine that has been variously attributed (or attributable) to Popper (1959):

> This is thus the abstract definition of the singularity of the modern scientific practices I will propose: if it is no longer a question of vanquishing the power of fiction, *it is always a question of putting it to the test*, of subjecting the reasons we invent to a third party capable of putting them at risk. In other words, it is always a question of inventing practices that will render our opinions vulnerable in relation to something that is irreducible to another opinion (p. 134, her emphasis).

First of all, her insistence on the idea of "putting to the test" is not to be mistaken for a reformulation of the falsificationist doctrine of the "triple Popper" (as rationally re-constructed by Lakatos in 1970), nor of the "demarcationist" Popper whose analysis (she contends) ultimately failed to explain the "progressive" nature of science (pp. 28–29), though Stengers does approve of both Popper's "aesthetic of risk and audacity" (p. 28) and his notion of a "third world" of objective thought.[6] There can be no doubt as to Stengers' commitment to "objective truth" (p. 165), to "the power of truth, if it is truly true, to denounce fiction" (p. 148), nor as to her belief in the primary importance of taking risks, of exposing scientific claims to the possibility of being found wanting, as one of the hallmarks of the scientific enterprise (pp. 74, 112, 134, 142, 157). The question is: once the scientist leaves the confines of the laboratory and ventures into the field, how is this "putting to the test" to be achieved? In attempting to address this latter question, Stengers provides us with some clues, but only a suggestive and less than crystal clear idea, as to the full meaning of her revised definition.

What sets today's field sciences apart from older experimental sciences is the "irreducible uncertainty" (p. 145) they face in dealing with the historical problems of a contingent process (p. 132), that is, with concrete situations that "do not let themselves be staged in the laboratory, because they integrate an ill-defined number of interrelated problems" (p. 159). For example, evolutionary biologists lack the kind of explanatory power, the ability to stage their own questions, that would enable them to anticipate future events. They can only recount past events, hence their vulnerability to the creationist criticism of their claim to scientific status (p. 139). Yet, these "Darwinian narrators" use "as many sophisticated instruments as there are in a laboratory" to collect the various "indices" (empirical evidence) that guide them in reconstituting concrete situations (p. 140). The power being challenged here, Stengers insists, is not that of Galileo's Rome, but of the theoretico-experimental sciences (p. 141): "The science of evolution learns to affirm its singularity as a historical science" (p. 142), doing this, without the advantages of laboratory experiment, by multiplying its narratives and by relating these to other fields of scientific inquiry.

But the problem of integrating diverse kinds of knowledge is by no means limited to evolutionary biology. Controversies surrounding the greenhouse effect and the ozone hole provide obvious examples to illustrate the scope of the multi-disciplinary efforts needed to construct historical narratives, with their potentially far-reaching effects (pp. 143, 159). The essential change here is not the emergence of the new field sciences as such, nor is it the emerging need for some new "holistic" science to take their place (p. 132). The underlying reason for re-defining the singularity of the modern sciences lies in the changing nature of the traditional relationship in scientific inquiry between "subject" and "object" (p. 132).

In the traditional setting of the laboratory, the scientist as subject stands detached from the object of inquiry and exercises an initiating power to call upon that object to reveal something of its nature. But this relation no longer holds true throughout the totality of the sciences. And not just where human subjects interact with human objects does the notion of a scientific "witness" become ambiguous (p. 147). Consider again our planet Earth and its history as objects of study. Unlike the objects of laboratory experimentation, where science confronts reality in controlled isolation, "the Earth doesn't care about the questions we ask of it," Stengers notes wryly. "What we call a 'catastrophe' will be for it, a contingency, . . . one more contingent event in a long series" (p. 145).

This changing relationship between subject and object points to the continuing necessity for political engagement by the representatives of science, putting everyone "under the influence of a different way of doing politics" (p. 163). This new kind of politics, as depicted in Bruno Latour's "Parliament of Things" (p. 152), comprises a vast system of mediation through multiple networks of knowledge and communication, a public forum which, in Latour's own words (referring again to the ozone hole) "extends from my refrigerator to the Antarctic by way of chemistry, law, the State, the economy, and satellites" (p. 153, cited from Latour, 1993, p. 144).

Scientists, of course, are not alone in this "mobilization" of knowledge in the public sphere, being only one constituency in the production of public expertise (pp. 158–159). Concerned citizens also participate, pose questions, demand explanations (p. 160). Nor is the autonomy of science necessarily undermined by the political engagement of scientists. "Mobilized scientists will be happy and proud to see themselves called on as experts by a power that recognizes them as the sole legitimate representatives of a problem" (p. 129), that is, within their particular area of expertise. Thus, science remains both distinct from, and interactive with, politics. And in this dual role, one of the services that the modern sciences must provide is that of resisting the "intrusion of noncompetent people" (p. 161) into the political discourse.

What relevance does Stengers' account of modern science have for the field of economics? Although this discipline remains for the most part in the background of her text, it is included in the illustrative list of fields that make up a "proliferating population of academic undertakings, from the sciences of communication to administrative sciences, from economics to the pedagogical sciences, which seek in facts, measurements, logic, and statistical correlations the guarantee that they are indeed sciences" (p. 27).

In spite of her near silence on economics (at least, in the book under review), we might nevertheless attempt to apply Stengers' ideas to the case of economics, by posing the question: What was the "event" (if indeed there was one) that signalled the onset of economics as a science. Many, I suspect, would answer this question: Adam Smith, *The Wealth of Nations*, 1776.

Granted, Adam Smith did provide a visionary synthesis of the competitive market economy of his time, but his central policy message (the presumption in favor of competitive market solutions) now possesses more ceremonial value (as reflected in the orthodox text-book tradition) than instrumental value. The dominant orthodox mainstream of the economics profession, both academic and non-academic (and most especially those with a policy orientation), now seem to accept – even if only tacitly, by the default of a passive accommodation – the Schumpeterian doctrine that profitability reflects efficiency, and so what could possibly be wrong with the ever greater profits of Big Business?

And certainly economists cannot point to a body of empirical evidence to support the kinds of stable empirical regularities ("laws") that would confer upon their discipline the status of "hard science" in the traditional mould of physics and chemistry. Granted, many economists do make good instrumental use of empirical knowledge (of a contextually specific nature) for purposes that could be best described as a part of the ongoing practical administration of economic affairs. But this fact would hardly qualify as evidence to support the scientific character of economics. In Stengers' terms, economics would have to be included amongst those "would-be" sciences in which controversies have yet to be closed "in a stable manner" (p. 42).

No, if we are talking about the pretensions of economics as a science, and not as policy field, then the most conspicuous appeal that would be made today by the mainstream establishment of this discipline would be to its theoretical dimension of abstract reasoning – theorem and proof – and in that sense the relevant "event" for economics would be the appearance of Augustin Cournot's *Recherches* of 1838. Rather than Cournot being to Smith what Newton was to Galileo, we should say instead that Cournot was to Walras (or general equilibrium theory) what Galileo was to Newton (or classical physics).

The "event" of 1838 was not so much Cournot's famous model of duopoly, nor his introduction into economic theory of the first "function" (his simple demand function, $Q = D (P)$); it was instead his use of "unspecified functions such as $F (P)$," from which "he [was] able to deduce important general results from a few simple assumptions" (Baumol & Goldfeld, 1967, p. 163). As Baumol and Goldfeld note, this was "probably the first time this powerful device was utilized in economics." Cournot's "powerful device" relieved economists of that most embarrassing task of having to specify their functions precisely, thus paving the way for them to mathematize their subject matter and thereby to introduce the "power of fiction," a quasi-mathematical power, into economic discourse.

This power of fiction was "quasi-mathematical" because the fiction of mathematical economics does not originate in the use of mathematics *per se*, but arises instead from a sophistical appeal to incomprehensible phrases that are intended to impart an economic meaning to the mathematics. This is done by attributing imaginary, indeed even unimaginable, economic conditions to mere mathematical formulae, creating a willing suspension of critical disbelief by invoking the stock phrases now commonly associated with "perfect markets": perfect product homogeneity, perfect knowledge (or instantaneous transmission of information), and perfect competition requiring an indescribably (and hence unspecifiably) large number of market participants, that is, as large a number of market participants as will be "sufficient" (in some undisclosed sense) to render each of them completely powerless to influence "the" single uniform price that is alleged to arise (somehow – as if by magical incantation of the former phrases) in the process of arriving at a presumptive equilibrium outcome.[7] Economists cannot prove, but only assume, price uniformity emerges.

This single-price "theorem" for perfect markets is the logical crux that initially sanctioned a wholesale adoption of mathematical modelling. Jevons' purely literary formulation of the single-price theorem (his so-called "Law of Indifference," 1871, p. 91) was indirectly indebted to Cournot (1838, p. 55, n1), and remains to this day a *sine qua non* of microeconomic theory (see Mas-Colell et al., 1995, pp. 315, 411–412, 660ff.), even in the more recondite theories of information and uncertainty (see Hirshleifer & Riley, 1992, pp. 2–3, 7–8), having earlier convinced F. Y. Edgeworth that economics would truly be a "dismal science" without it (1881, p. 50), as well as John Hicks who worried that to abandon these contrivances would be to contemplate the "wreckage . . . of the greater part of general equilibrium theory" (Hicks, 1939, p. 84).

Why is this power of fiction so illegitimate? Not only because it tends to celebrate and re-enforce a doctrinal tradition (the sanctity of pure market solutions) that is no longer relevant to the world's material circumstances, but also because playing this chimerical mathematical game distorts priorities (e.g. in academic instruction at both undergraduate and graduate levels) and distracts intellectual effort away from real economic problems. It does not take an economist to recognize this. In her previously translated book, *Power and Invention: Situating Science* (1997), Stengers offers a throw-away line that sums up the situation very well. Discussing the possibilities for various disciplines to achieve the "envied status of a 'hard' science," she writes:

> . . . Thus, I have deliberately put into question the sciences that have tried to merit this title by mutilating their object (behaviorist psychology) or by forgetting it (mathematical economics), or rather, I refer their history to another register, where the dominant interests will be of an academic, economic, and political order (Stengers, 1997, pp. 87–88).

Intoxicated with the power of mathematical fiction, too many economic theorists have become so obsessed with sheer mathematical formality that they have forgotten what their subject is. How is this quasi-mathematical power of fiction to be combatted and ultimately brought under control? Certainly not by marshalling empirical evidence, since mathematical economists have already weathered that storm, immunizing their largely incomprehensible abstractions from any kind of reality-testing. So, the solution must be to "fight fire with fire" by directly challenging the mathematical economists on their most strongly defended ground: their claim to logical rigor. To put it simply, mathematical economists make logical claims that fail the test of logic, and showing this is the only way to liberate economics from this power of fiction.

To give credit where credit is due (as Stengers would wish), we can all agree that Cournot clarified the classical economists' confusion between demand (Cournot's function D) and quantity demanded (his variable Q) by positing his simple demand function, $Q = D(P)$, thereby contributing a valuable insight for the progress of economic analysis. However, his mathematical exercises also introduced mathematical reduction into formal economic logic.

Mathematical reduction is the attempt to reduce the non-mathematical to the mathematical. We can see how this works with Cournot's own simple demand function. The basic idea behind the demand *hypothesis* (i.e. that the quantity demanded by the buyers of a commodity is functionally related to the price of that commodity) can be parsed into semi-formal terms as: "For all x and y, if sellers ask a unit price of x units of money per unit of output, and if $y = f(x)$, then buyers demand y units of output." In predicate logic, this becomes: $(\forall x)(\forall y)(Px \cdot \{y = f(x)\} \rightarrow Qy)$. This formula shows how the economic content of the demand hypothesis ('$Px \rightarrow Qy$') is formally omitted by the reductionist method, leaving only the mathematical skeleton, $y = f(x)$, in formal symbols (see Dennis, 1996).

Now, defendants of reductionist mathematics might argue that the full parsing and formalizing of this simple hypothesis will serve no other purpose than to burden theory with an extra and unnecessary layer of formality, but this is to miss the point. Economic theory is built upon many premises or components: some are mathematical (as with the function 'f' above); some are behavioral (such as the market actions of buyers and sellers, 'Px' and 'Qy'); but many others are institutional in nature, such as the specification of a competitive market system with its property rights, laws of contract, patterns of communicating negotiations, etc., all of which are necessary to economic argumentation but which cannot be reduced to mathematics. The point, then, is that with their pure mathematics, economic theorists prove nothing but purely mathematical propositions, claiming all the while to be proving economic propositions (by illicitly reading economic meaning into purely mathematical formulae).

A further (and here a final) defense by orthodox reductionists might go something like this: If physicists can use mathematics in the reductionist mode – the Newtonian $F = ma$, the Galilean $s = (at^2)/2$, Einstein's $e = mc^2$ – then what could be wrong with economists doing essentially the same thing? This question calls for a very carefully qualified rebuttal.

Economists lacking expertise in other scientific disciplines have no authority to tell scientists in other scientific disciplines how to conduct their inquiries, and so it is with this reviewer. But, by the same token, just because physicists have a certain way of doing things does not mean that it is thereby appropriate for economists to do the same. Only by way of speculation do I offer these further thoughts. In sciences where the objects of study are elementary in their nature, with very few, perhaps only one, measurable dimension, the methods of mathematical reduction may work reasonably well, in contrast to sciences that deal with very complex entities such as human beings and their social, cultural, political and economic arrangements. Yet, even having said that, it is no great task to parse some of the mathematical formulae from other disciplines into a non-reductionist format. Consider that very icon of science, Einstein's $e = mc^2$. Of course, Einstein did not mean by 'mc^2' that we could mathematically multiply mass by the second power of the velocity of light, only that we could multiply the numerical term (numeric) of the measurement of mass by the numerical term (numeric) raised to the second power of the measurement of the velocity of light (Dennis, forthcoming). Thus, using '$z = xy^2$' for '$e = mc^2$' and taking k and s as givens, we might interpret Einstein's famous proposition regarding the equivalence of mass and energy (of which his formula is only the mathematical component) as follows:

> For all x and y, there exists exactly one z, such that if x is the numeric of the measurement of mass of particle k in measurement system s, and if y is the numeric of the measurement of the velocity of light in measurement system s, and if $z = xy^2$, then z is the numeric of the measurement of energy of particle k in measurement system s.

Using 'M', 'C' and 'E' as predicates, in formal symbols this might look like:

$$(\forall x)(\forall y)(\exists z)[\{x = (\text{IV})(Mvks)\} \cdot (y = (\text{IV})\ (Cvs))\} \cdot (z = xy^2) \rightarrow$$

$$\{z = (\text{IV})\ (Evks)\}].$$

Exposing the illegitimate use of the "power of fiction" in mathematical economics should compel economists to re-think their theories, and thereby to affirm Stengers' resolution "to begin again with other givens."

NOTES

1. I can recall seeing only one occurrence of the word "evidence" (p. 133) throughout her text.

2. The original French edition may well have posed for its translator a good many questions, but it seems that in responding to these he favored a literal rendering of Stengers' many labyrinthine clausal structures, rather than seeking a freer translation to capture the author's intentions in a more natural English idiom and cadence.

3. Stengers contributed the chapter on the "Galileo Affair" in the influential volume edited by Michel Serres (1989).

4. Again, as with "evidence," I can recall seeing the word "hypothesis" only once throughout her text (p. 105).

5. I.e. first as: "inventing ways to vanquish the power of fiction, and submitting the reasons that we invent to a third party capable of making the difference," (p. 126), again as "the invention of the means to create faithful witnesses," (p. 132); and finally as "invent[ing] an apparatus that is able to silence rivals, to institute a putting to the test," (p. 132).

6. Popper's "world 1" is the physical world, "world 2" the world of subjective thought, and "world 3" the world of objective thought (Popper, 1972).

7. Cournot introduced the kind of "thought experiment" soon to become routine in mathematical economics, by trying to mathematize the idea of hypothetically increasing the number of market participants towards a (mathematically conceived) limit, to produce a market outcome for "unlimited competition" or "concurrence indéfinie" (Cournot, 1838,

Chs. VII–VIII, pp. 88–111). At least Einstein's famous "thought experiments" asked us to imagine things that were imaginable (however improbable), and, to some extent, his "fictions" were sufficiently operational to be subjected to empirical test, quite unlike the imaginary fantasies attributed to "perfect markets."

REFERENCES

Baumol, W. J., & Goldfeld, S. M. (1968). *Precursors in Mathematical Economics: An Anthology.* London: London School of Economics and Political Science.

Cournot, A. (1838). *Recherches sur les Mathématiques de la Théorie des Richesses.* Paris: Hachette.

Dennis, K. (1996). A Logical Critique of Mathematical Formalism in Economics. *Journal of Economic Methodology, 3*(1), 151–169.

Dennis, K. (forthcoming). Nominalizing the Numeric: An Alternative to Mathematical Reduction in Economics. *Cambridge Journal of Economics.*

Edgeworth, F. Y. (1881). *Mathematical Psychics.* London: Kegan Paul.

Hicks, J. R. (1939). *Value and Capital.* Clarendon Press, Oxford.

Hirshleifer, J., & Riley, J. G. (1992). *The Analytics of Uncertainty and Information.* Cambridge: Cambridge University Press.

Jevons, W. S. (1871). *The Theory of Political Economy.* London: Macmillan.

Lakatos, I. (1970). Falsification and the Methodology of Research Programmes. In: I. Lakatos & A. Musgrave (Eds), *Criticism and the Growth of Knowledge.* Cambridge: Cambridge University Press.

Latour, B. (1993). *We Have Never Been Modern.* Trans. C. Porter. Cambridge, Mass.: Harvard University Press.

Mas-Colell, A., Whinston, M. D., & Green, J. R. (1995). *Microeconomic Theory.* New York: Oxford University Press.

Popper, K. (1959). *The Logic of Scientific Discovery.* New York: Basic Books.

Popper, K. (1972). *Objective Knowledge: An Evolutionary Approach.* Oxford: Clarendon Press.

Prigogine, I., & Stengers, I. (1984). *Order out of Chaos: Man's New Dialogue with Nature.* New York: Random House.

Prigogine, I., & Stengers, I. (1986). *La Nouvelle Alliance: Métamorphose de la Science.* Paris: Gallimard.

Prigogine, I., & Stengers, I. (1988). *Entre le temps et l'éternité.* Paris: Fayard.

Prigogine, I. (in collaboration with Stengers, I.) (1997). *The End of Certainty: Time, Chaos, and The New Laws of Nature.* New York: Free Press.

Serres, M. (Ed.) (1989). *Eléments d'histoire des sciences.* Paris: Bordas.

Stengers, I. (1997). *Power and Invention: Situating Science.* Trans. Paul Bains. Minneapolis: University of Minnesota Press.

THE RELEVANCE OF J. R. COMMONS' INSTITUTIONAL ECONOMICS: A PRAGMATIC METHODOLOGY FOR MAKING CAPITALISM MORE "REASONABLE".

Véronique Dutraive

A review of Laure Bazzoli, "*L'Economie politique de John R. Commons – Essai sur l'institutionnalisme en sciences sociales*" (*The Political Economy of John R. Commons: an essay on institutionalism in social sciences*). Paris: Editions L'Harmattan, 1999, pp. 234.

For the first time in France, a book has been devoted to the institutional economics of John R. Commons. We will begin by examining the status of American Institutionalist thought in France. Then we will develop two dominant themes in Bazzoli's interpretation of Commons' economics: first, the pragmatic methodology he defended for use in social science, and secondly, his normative view of "ethical" capitalism.

THE RECEPTION OF THE AMERICAN INSTITUTIONALIST SCHOOL IN FRANCE

Commons was one of the most important contributors to "Old Institutional Economics" (O.I.E.), but he was probably the least-known member of that

Research in the History of Economic Thought and Methodology, Volume 20-A, pages 299–307.
Copyright © 2002 by Elsevier Science Ltd.
All rights of reproduction in any form reserved.
ISBN: 0-7623-0847-8

school in France, where Old Institutional Economics itself was never very popular. This school of economic thought was later rediscovered by a group of French economists (Corei, 1995) who were very dissatisfied with the conception of "institutions" put forth by New Institutional Economics. Interest in O.I.E. has been growing ever since, as its analytical approach has much in common with the "French School of Regulation", represented by Boyer and Aglietta in the Eighties (see Samuels, 1995).

Among the historical members of the Institutionalist school, Mitchell was the better known by the economists, particularly because of his business cycle theory. Veblen, on the other hand, was more familiar to sociologists than economists. His *Theory of the Leisure Class* was given a favourable reception in France by the famous philosopher Raymond Aron, who wrote an introduction to the French translation of the book (Aron, 1978). In the Seventies, French theories of the role of mimicry and ostentation in consumption showed a definite similarity to Veblen's work (Baudriard, 1981). For economists, Veblen was known to have virtually inspired the thesis concerning cases in which demand increases with the price, due to the "snob effect". Most economists were not satisfied with this conception, since it implied that economic laws were not the sole explanation of human action. A few French economists recognized Veblen's contribution to economics (Pirou, 1946; Vinokur, 1969). His view of modern capitalism was widely disseminated and some of his papers were translated (Veblen, 1899, 1920, 1921). Veblen was also rediscovered as a precursor of modern evolutionary economics (Hodgson, 1994).

In contrast, not a single book was devoted to Commons' work. There were only a few comments about his contribution to American Institutional Economics (Perroux, 1941; Pirou, 1946). Jurists, who were interested in the idea of a legal-economic nexus, were more familiar with Commons than economists. Only two of his papers were translated in French, both of them in legal journals (Commons, 1935, 1938). In the field of economics, however, some dissertations on labour economics mentioned Commons and the Wisconsin school.

In this context, Bazzoli's book marks the first introduction to the work of Commons for French social scientists. The book is very useful in the context of growing interest in the role of institutions in economics. It presents an overview of old institutionalism and Commons' version of it. What Old Institutional Economics has to say is highly relevant in a period of enormous change in capitalist organization. Bazzoli's book is not only a thoroughly documented work about a past economist, it is also a plea to rediscover his institutional message for society and apply his institutional methodology in the social sciences and perhaps even the economics of our time.

THE PRAGMATIC FOUNDATION OF COMMONS' METHODOLOGY FOR SOCIAL SCIENCES

Bazzoli's text does not shun hagiography. She especially appreciates and defends Commons' approach. In particular, she responds to critics or those ignorant of Commons' concepts by noting that most of them failed to understand Commons' highly individual point of view. The main reason for this failure was the influence of Pragmatic philosophy on Commons' conception of economics. At the time, mainstream economic theory did not share the institutionalists' philosophical preconceptions. Consequently, the specific methodological features of Common's institutional economics were not taken seriously. Bazzoli spends much of the book discussing Pragmatism for two reasons: on the one hand, she thinks it is necessary to restore the consistency of Commons' methodology, which cannot be seriously considered using the traditional criteria of economics; on the other hand, Pragmatism is an American philosophy and is not very familiar to Europeans (except specialists in philosophy). In this regard, Bazzoli's book provides a clear introduction to this philosophical approach for non-specialists (economists and social scientists), in which Pragmatism is grasped as the general framework for the epistemological and methodological characteristics of institutional economic theories.

This orientation is noticeable from the first chapter, entitled *"Génèse et nature d'un projet institutionnaliste: quelques repères historiques"* (Genesis and Nature of the Institutionalist Project: a few historical references), in which Bazzoli tells the story of Commons' life. The chapter is not designed to paint a picture of the intellectual context of Commons' work in social sciences or economics, as many such biographies do. Rather, Bazzoli emphasizes the consistency between Common's practical life and professional experiences in economic and political organizations and his social theory. One of the lessons of Pragmatism is the importance of experimentation in science. As Commons explains in his autobiography, it was his experience in economic and professional life that led him to develop his economic theory (Commons, 1934). Pragmatism also teaches that scientific work, like most human activities, is directed towards solving problems. At the same time, the solution of practical problems is a criterion of the social validation of theories. Commons always viewed economic knowledge as a tool to "improve capitalism", i.e. to inform public decision-makers in the area of economics. In fact, Commons was not only an economics professor, but he was involved in economic activities and public commissions. Mitchell wrote that it was impossible to separate Commons' activities as an economist from his commitments as a citizen (Mitchell, 1969). In particular, he took part in the first experiments in the field of social legislation in the U.S. Commons himself speaks of "pragmatism in action" to describe the connections among his research, teaching and public consulting activities.

The second chapter deals more specifically with pragmatic principles and their implications for social science, especially Commons' Institutional Economics. The chapter is entitled *"De nouveaux fondements à l'économie politique: la philosophie pragmatique, méthode et éthique"* (New Foundations for Political Economy: pragmatic philosophy, methodology and ethics). The first point that Pragmatism has in common with Institutional Economics is that both are held to be original products of American intellectual thought. Pragmatism was developed not only by philosophers but also by jurists and scientists, out of a controversy with European philosophy. On the one hand, pragmatism maintained that continental philosophy showed too much interest in the role of consciousness in human action and underestimated the role of experience. On the other hand, it considered English philosophy too empirical, in the sense that it stressed the significance of private sense experience as our means of understanding the world. In opposition to both, Pragmatism called for the use of the scientific method and public testing to guarantee the validity of ideas and theories. In particular, scientific activity was viewed as collective action. In modern times, it has become increasingly difficult to identify individual creativity in research because science is a collective process, but the social dimension of research activity extends to each mental process. Pragmatism insisted on the social dimension of cognition (Samuels, 1990) and on the role of learning and habits in human action. Pragmatism was also inspired by the notion of evolution, professing that there is no Truth as such, but rather evolving, changing reality.

Among the original authors of Pragmatism, the most important were Peirce, James and Dewey, and in Bazzoli's view, Commons was mainly inspired by Peirce. The first feature of pragmatism is that it transcends the dualism characteristic of most of the epistemological ideas in science and economics (mind/action, induction/deduction, fact/theory, and fact/value). The refusal to separate mind and action leads to a connection between mental processes and experimentation. Experimentation is not an individual affair, however; it is always a collective occurrence. The ontological unit of reality is not the individual but the interaction between individuals and their environment or the "transaction", as Dewey called it. The term "transaction" is also used in law to describe the process of reaching an agreement out of a conflict. We know that for Commons the "transaction" is the unit of activity in his Institutional Economics. It expresses the social dimension of all human choices and actions. The other traditional dualities are versions of Descartes' categories. For example, Peirce gives the name of "abduction" to a method designed to go beyond the opposition between induction and deduction, based on the fact that theory and empirical reality are always involved in a process of interrelation. From this standpoint, theory is a procedure for developing operating knowledge and theories change with the ever-changing reality. Consequently, the goal of social science is not to find laws but changing "part-whole relationships". The pragmatic conception of scientific activity advocates "realism" over both "empiricism", which can be anti-theoretical, and "rationalism", which can be too formal. Commons agreed with this view and chose the "institution" as the methodological unit of investigation in social science. His "methodological institutionalism" is designed to get beyond the problems associated with "individualism" and "holism". Individualism takes an insufficiently social view of the individual, by eliminating the social context within which preferences are formed and choice made. It is typical of most economic analysis, which favors a logical interpretation of reality. Holism takes an excessively social view of the individual, by eliminating the power of human agency to shape the social world. It is typical of sociological analysis and prefers empirical data. Commons chose the wider concept of "institution" to investigate reality, without the limitations of individualism or holism. The concept of "institution" covers at once the formal rules and regular features emerging from interaction and the constraints and products of human behavior. The "cognitive" dimension of rules is what connects the learning process to anticipation, routine and habit to strategic deliberation, the past to the future, and permanence to flexibility. The "political" dimension of rules is what achieves compromise out of conflict, public welfare out of private interests. Taking institutional factors (the "cognitive" and "political" functions of rules) into account makes it possible to tie individual to collective action in "going concerns", without the over-simplification of either individualism or holism. Moreover, according to Commons, economic activities could not be separated from their social context. He subscribed to the "embeddedness" thesis. Institutional rules were precisely the unit of analysis capable of linking economic, legal and ethical areas into a general theory of social phenomena.

As we can see, the Institutionalism as a methodology is a *via media* between all the various types of conceptual dichotomies used in social science. This *via media* is also perceptible in the practical goal sought by Commons as the outcome of theoretical economic analysis: a reasonable balance between labor and capital interests in capitalist economy.

Bazzoli deals with the economic analysis arising from Common's Institutional Economics in the last two chapters of the book, Chapter 3 *"Une économie institutionnaliste et évolutionniste de l'action collective"* (An Institutionalist and Evolutionary Economics of Collective Action) and Chapter 4, *"Plaidoyer pour un capitalisme raisonnable: analyse et pratique*" (In defense of reasonable capitalism: analysis and practice).

INSTITUTIONAL FACTORS IN ECONOMICS AND THE RULES FOR "REASONABLE" CAPITALISM

Commons was not interested in formal economics. In the wake of Weber, he wanted to develop a comprehensive theory of the evolution of capitalism. He was opposed to economic conceptions that upheld the natural harmony of interests or spontaneous order. He saw the market as the product of institutional processes in the history of capitalism. He maintained that, in a context of scarcity, there was no natural harmony but rather conflict, and that the continuity of human society and joining of individual action to collective action were based on voluntary regulation. The market process is seen not as an abstract, a-historical, "compositive" coordinating principle but as an ever-changing, institutional configuration of more or less formal rules of economic behavior. Although freedom does not automatically lead to social harmony, the specific activity of defining the rules is a crucial part of social order (Commons called it "rationing transactions"). Commons attributes a very important role to the judiciary process because, as the society becomes more complex, the informal rules of custom become less effective in resolving conflicts. Consequently, in modern society, social rules are increasingly formal and law plays a greater part in social ordering.

Economic dynamics can be analyzed as an evolutionary process of institutional change. Change is an emerging property of human actions and interactions. According to the theory of the Austrian School, institutions emerge by imitating efficient new practices. In Commons' opinion, on the contrary, the authorities are the ones who artificially select emerging practices. This phenomenon exists at each stage of the social order: in organizations as well as in the legal or political process. Commons called it the "artificial selection" of new rules. The more equitably the power of choice is shared, the more the selection will reflect a social compromise. The selection process may, however, reflect only the values or purposes of the authorities, and there is no guarantee of efficiency.

Commons thought that American capitalism could be improved. In his view, the 20th century economy is characterized by the importance of collective action, particularly by business enterprises (which Commons called economic "going concerns"). Commons pointed out the problems arising from the divergence of interests within an enterprise. In keeping with Veblen, Commons asserts the duality of "institutions" within the capitalist firm. Economic organization is based on the confrontation of two value and accounting systems: first, the social system of "use value", and secondly, the individual system of "exchange value" which is accentuated by scarcity and restricted production. Credit and monetary affairs play a major role in the workings of modern capitalism and increase the predominance of "exchange value". Commons called the economic system of the early 20th century "Banker Capitalism". Finance takes control of corporate governance over management, i.e. the power to combine the different functions of the firm: on the one hand, the rules of business or the market functions of fixing prices and quantities; on the other hand, the rules of labor or the functions of fixing wages and the employment level. Credit also allows a gap between production and consumption, resulting in over-production or under-production phases in business cycles. The institution of credit underscores the cyclical aspect of business, as banks lend money easily in periods of growth and restrict loans during periods of recession. It also sustains and amplifies anticipation within the cycle.

From this angle, the major problem of modern capitalism lies in the conflict between labor and capital, which reveals the paradox between individual and collective values in society. In reality, the control of the firm exercised by finance is opposed to the interests of labor. Finance encourages restricting wages and adjusting to recession by laying off employees. The paradox, as J. M. Clark has said, is that employment is considered a variable cost by individual enterprises but unemployment is a fixed cost for society. According to Commons, this dilemma could be solved by institutional reforms giving rise to "reasonable capitalism". In his optimistic opinion, the reconciliation of shareholder, manager and employee interests is not incompatible with the capitalist system. Peaceful resolution of social conflicts contributes to efficiency because it enhances "good will" and, consequently, greater productivity. Commons advocates a more democratic system of decision-making in firms that would take labor interests into account. The idea is to find a system that would induce decision-makers not to adjust employment to fluctuations of the economic situation. In the "Wisconsin plan" for the American Association for Labor Legislation, he proposed concrete measures to encourage employers to assume legal responsibility towards their employees. He suggested that the social consequences of economic decisions be considered part of company costs, and that reserves should be specifically set aside to deal with any unfavorable circumstances that might arise. Moreover, Commons thought that the federal government must play an essential role in organizing the collective negotiation of rules. For many situations, however, he recommended setting up intermediary institutions between individuals and the state or between the market and the state. In addition to legislative, executive and judiciary powers, Commons

envisaged the power of independent commissions bringing together representatives of various economic interests. The goal of such commissions would be
to investigate, prevent and solve problems in a pragmatic perspective.

Bazzoli's book testifies to the relevance of Institutional Economic theory
today, particularly that of Commons. From a methodological standpoint, the
rediscovery of institutionalism is closely correlated to the disfavor into which
both strict individualism and naïve holism have fallen in social sciences. It
also can be linked to disfavor (in France) with the trend towards excessive
mathematization and formalization in the academic approach to economics. On
the other hand, after a rather peaceful period of labor and capital relations during
the "Glorious Thirty Years" or "Fordist capitalism", the conflict between
labor and capital has again come to the fore. The so-called new economy is
characterized by the globalization of production and of financial markets, by
great technical changes, by government disengagement, unstable growth, etc.
The dominant role played by shareholders in the strategic decisions of firms
also contributes to the precarious situation of employees. The institutionalist
demand for new rules to increase democratic practices in firms and social control
over economic power seem to be particularly relevant.

REFERENCES

Aron, R. (1978). "Avez-vous lu Veblen?" Introduction to Veblen T. *La Théorie de la Classe des loisirs*. Gallimard.
Baudriard, J. (1981). *For a Critique of the Political Economy of the Sign*. St. Louis: Telos Press.
Bazzoli, L. (2000). *L'économie politique de J. R. Commons. Essai sur l'institutionnalisme en sciences sociales*. L'Harmattan (Ed.).
Commons, J. R. (1934). *Myself*. The Macmillan Company.
Commons, J. R. (1935). Le problème de la corrélation du droit, de l'économie et de la morale. In: F. Geny, *Les sources du droit- en l'honneur*. Vol. 2. Recueil Sirey.
Commons, J. R. (1938). La valeur raisonnable dans l'économie politique américaine. In: *Recueil d'Études en l'Honneur d'E. Lambert*. Librairie génerale du droit et de la jurisprudence.
Corei, T. (1995). *L'Economie Institutionnaliste- les fondateurs*. Economica.
Hodgson, G. (1994). Precursors of Modern Evolutionary Economics. In: R. England (Ed.), *Evolutionary Concepts in Contemporary Economics*. Michigan University Press.
Mitchell, W. C. (1969). *Types of Economics Theory from mercantilism to Institutionalism*, Vol. 2. New York: A. M. Kelley Publishers.
Perroux, F. (1941). *Cours d'Economie Politique*, Vol. 4. *mimeo*, Lyon.
Pirou, G. (1946). *Les nouveaux courants de la théorie économique aux Etats-Unis*, 3 vols. Paris: Domat-Montchrétien.
Samuels, W. J. (1990). Institutional Economics and the Theory of Cognition. *Cambridge Journal of Economics*, *14* (June, 1990), 219–227.
Samuels, W. J. (1995). Present State of Institutional Economics. *Cambridge Journal of Economics*, *19* (August, 1995), 569–590.
Veblen, T. (1899). *La Théorie de la Classe des loisirs*. Gallimard (1978).

Veblen, T. (1920). La Nature du capital. In: *Les Ingénieurs et le Capitalisme*. Coll. L'esprit des lois. Gordon et Breach (1971).

Veblen, T. (1921). Les ingénieurs et le système des prix. In: *Les Ingénieurs et le Capitalisme*. Coll. L'esprit des lois. Gordon et Breach (1971).

Vinokur, A. (1969). *T. Veblen et la tradition dissidente dans la pensée économique américaine.* Paris, Pichon et Durand-Auzias.

(RE)DEFINING CULTURE

Anne Mayhew

A review essay on Ellis Cashmore and Chris Rojek, (Eds.), with a forward by Douglas Kellner, 1999. *Dictionary of Cultural Theorists*. London, Edward Arnold Ltd., and co-published in the United States by Oxford University Press.

By early in the 20th century, social theorists of most academic disciplines had abandoned racial, linearly evolutionary, and purely geographic explanations of observed variation among humans across time and space.[1] The explanatory gap left by this abandonment engendered a concept of culture that incorporated human conceptions of themselves and the social and physical world they inhabit, their notions of propriety and impropriety in behavior toward others, as well as the mental and physical tools used in manipulation of both physical and social worlds. However, because explanations of difference and of similarity across time, and especially across space, necessarily intersect with political, social and economic treatment of "others," the development of this crucial concept has been hotly contested, often in battles that appeared to have little to do with the academic idea of culture. Consider, for example, the often-repeated criticism of the Soviet Union in the early years of the Cold War: "Communism will not work; you cannot change human nature." This political slogan essentially asserted the universality, or non-cultural nature of some forms of human behavior in the economic arena. More recently, the belief that market economies might emerge quickly and painlessly in the transition economies of Central and Eastern Europe reflected the same view. Within the United States, "culture wars" involving protest against the introduction of works of literature and art from outside the Western canon have enmeshed educational institutions

Research in the History of Economic Thought and Methodology, Volume 20-A, pages 309–313.
Copyright © 2002 by Elsevier Science Ltd.
All rights of reproduction in any form reserved.
ISBN: 0-7623-0847-8

in questions of superiority/inferiority of diverse cultural traditions. The appropriateness of political asylum for women threatened with clitorectomy and other genital mutilation has brought the question of cultural superiority and rights in different form into public debate.

Within academic disciplines, concepts of culture have also provoked fierce debate, though for the most part they are not quite the same debates that have most engaged the public. Social scientists have long accepted the idea that much or most of human behavior is accounted for by culture; the issue that has engaged them is whether culture should be conceptualized as determinative or as manipulable. During the first half of the 20th century while the idea of culture was being incorporated into social explanation, this question did not seem crucial. By mid-century, in the face of global migration and global communication, anthropologists and sociologists became intent on freeing themselves and their tools from any taint of determinism (Mayhew, 1987). In their zeal to do so, they not only found determinism where there probably was none and they also came close to abandonment of the core concept itself. If culture was not in any sense determinative, and totally a matter of human choice, as observation of the widespread adoption of American culture made it appear, then humans might be thought of as universally uniform and the need for an explanatory concept such as culture had been disappeared. To imperialistic economists who saw their own discipline as potential provider of a universally applicable model of human choice of institutions as well as of commodities, of family structure as much as of vegetables, abandonment of a deterministic model of culture appeared to offer new opportunities for the "queen of the social sciences."

The opportunities for economic imperialism were short lived as new concepts of culture that merged deterministic properties with the possibility of *encultured* choice began to appear (Mayhew, 2001). The new and improved concepts retained the notion that because all humans are encultured from birth, and because cultures do vary for reasons of history as well as geography, people differ across time and space. However, because the new concepts emphasized culture as mental systems of understanding employed by both learning and encultured individuals, variation within the lifetime of single individuals could also be explained.

The struggle for a new and more workable conception of culture has not engaged the attention of many economists. Those working within the tradition of the Original Institutional Economics (OIE) were interested, as were some who worked on issues involving the transition economies (Koslowski, 1992). However, most economists have not used a concept of culture in their work and the brouhaha created by the "return of culture" has been of little importance.

For this reason few economists are likely to consult the *Dictionary of Cultural Theorists*. However, for those who might pick it up expecting a useful volume a few words of warning may be worthwhile.

In their dictionary, Cashmore and Rojek, both Professors of Sociology in the United Kingdom, offer just over 200 brief essays written by 62 contributors. Almost a quarter of the theorists included are classified by the editors as "philosophers." Another quarter are variously classified as literary theorists, social theorists, cultural theorists, essayists, critics of various sorts and so on. Among social scientists as traditionally defined, Sociology is the best represented discipline by far, with 37 entries. What is surprising is that Economics has almost as many entries as Anthropology and more than Political Science/Political Theory or History.

What is even more surprising are the economists who have been chosen for inclusion: Walter Bagehot, Andre Gunder Frank, John Kenneth Galbraith, John Maynard Keynes, Thorstein Veblen, Richard Tawney (as economic historian), Ernst Schumacher, Alfred Marshall, David Ricardo, W. W. Rostow, and Joseph A. Schumpeter. Karl Marx is included, but as a philosopher; Max Weber is classified as a sociologist. To this reviewer this seems an odd group of economists to identify as "cultural theorists."

Confusion over what makes a "cultural theorist," and confusion about why David Ricardo, W. W. Rostow, Susan Sontag, Francis Fukuyama (to name just a few) should be so classified, is only partly cleared up by the Introduction. The intent of the editors was, they tell us, to create a primer, one that would help students faced with "textbooks written by people in cultural studies departments [that] give the impression that sociology doesn't exist, and vice versa" (p. 1). According to Cashmore and Rojek, modern cultural theory has emerged from abandonment of "the project of modernity." The loss of confidence in "modernity," loosely defined as a "secular, scientific understanding of natural and human reality," has, say the editors led to a "decline in the concept of society and a rise in the concept of culture" (p. 5).

The most interesting part of the book comes in Cashmore and Rojek's explanation of what they mean by this statement. Society to them means a "grid" of relationships between more or less fixed groups or classes. The very meaning of what would have appeared (at least to those trained in a British Marxian tradition) as fixed categories of class and gender has been undermined by "the dominant ethos today . . . of living with capitalism and accepting difference" (p. 5). Ironically, Ms. Thatcher's statement that "there is no such thing as society" appears to have been accepted by new intellectuals of Britain such as Cashmore and Rojek. What replaces society with its assumed stable groupings is "culture" as a set of tools for making sense of the world and for making that sense change. In this new understanding,

> 'We' are all living through texts, all reading, all transforming our experiences into texts that we can relate to other texts. In this way, 'we' make sense of experiences: nothing has meaning in itself; we give it meaning. This opens up the possibility of many meanings and many voices (p. 7).

In short, post-modernism abandons the idea of society as a group of more or less cohesive collective groups, and replaces that idea with individuals who shift and reshift allegiance as they interpret the changing world around them. Cultural theory is theory of how this happens. Further, the kind of cultural theory that the editors of this volume are interested in is theory that people should understand the consequences of cultural theory for everyday life. And that, say the editors is

> ... why we have included entries, for example, on the French existentialist philosopher Sartre, the critic and novelist Sontag, the architect Le Corbusier and the critic, dramatist and film-maker Debord, with the work of professional academic theorists like Gadamer, Bourdieu and Chomsky, policy-makers such as Fukuyama and scholars whose influence has reached the highest political levels, Galbraith and Etzioni being obvious examples (p. 12).

Even though I have tried to follow this and to make sense of the choice of theorists, I confess that another explanation works as well for me: it is possible that this is a collection of brief essays written about people whose names get mentioned by faculty struggling to develop a coherent theory of society in a global world where the "isms" of the last part of the twentieth century have lost what people thought to be their explanatory power. This seems a better explanation of the presence of Ricardo than does his cultural explanation of everyday life.

What I suspect is happening is that Ricardo's name is invoked in discussions of free trade, a concept that in modern, if not Ricardian form, does have presence in everyday life Hence Ricardo becomes for purposes of this dictionary a "cultural theorist." I fault the editors for many of their choices, inclusions as well as omissions. Why should David Landes, who in both *The Unbound Prometheus* (1969) and *The Wealth and Poverty of Nations* (1998) has stressed the importance of culture for understanding economic growth, not have been included? Why should Marshall Sahlins who has written extensively of the importance of culture in, among other works, *Culture and Practical Reason* (1976) have been omitted? I suspect that the answer is that these people are writing about the concept of culture as it was, not about the concept of culture that is emerging as replacement for the idea of society.

The result it seems to me is a muddle. Those who offer courses in "cultural studies" in departments and colleges of education, and in some of the traditional areas of the humanities are seeking to replace a post-Marxian notion of society in which human relations were explained as class relations (with complex interactions of gender and race with class) with "culture" as the whole set of ideas, words, names that are used in popular political and social debate. In the meantime, social scientists who work in the traditions established in the first half of the 20th century, are using a modified notion of culture that incorporates both enculturation as determinative of patterns of human thought and response, as well as learning and choice.

The two concepts of culture overlap at times, but belong to two as yet unmerged realms of discourse. This is too bad. The discourse to which *The Dictionary of Culture* is devoted would be much richer had the editors showed more awareness of the debate among social scientists over culture. Further, the strong reaction against "society" might have been prevented had their been greater understanding that the very classes and other groups in the social grid were themselves parts of changing cultures. In other words, Cashmore and Rojek show a lack of awareness of the power of a fully developed notion of culture. For all that *The Dictionary of Culture* probably can serve a useful purpose for undergraduate students. For a more sophisticated audience the entries are too brief and sketchy to be of value. For historians of economic thought the *Dictionary* offers little beyond the opportunity to think once more on how divergent from other traditions the path of economic thought has been in the 20th century.

NOTE

1. See George R. Stocking, Jr. (1968) for the best single account of this transformation in Western thought.

REFERENCES

Koslowski, R. (1992). Institutions, East European Reform, and Economic Theory. *Journal of Economic Issues, 26*, 673–707.

Landes, D. (1969). *The Unbound Prometheus*. London: Cambridge University Press.

Landes, D. (1998). *The Wealth and Poverty of Nations*. New York: W. W. Norton.

Mayhew, A. (1987). Culture: Core Concept Under Attack. *Journal of Economic Issues, 21*, 587–603.

Mayhew, A. (2001). Human Agency, Cumulative Causation, and the State. *Journal of Economic Issues, 35*, 239–250.

Sahlins, M. (1976). *Culture and Practical Reason*. Chicago, IL: University of Chicago Press.

Stocking, Jr., G. W. (1968). *Race, Culture and Evolution*. New York: The Free Press.

FREE TRADE VS. FREE TRADE OFFS

William D. Grampp

> They show that though they are without exception adherents of free trade, they are not
> adherents of free trade without exception.
>
> – Gladstone on certain contemporaries.

A review essay on Johannes Overbeek. *Free Trade versus Protectionism, A Source Book of Essays and Readings.* **Cheltenham: Elgar, 1999.**

Free Trade versus Protectionism is, according to its subtitle, "a source book of essays and readings". That is misleading. It is more of a discourse on trade policy with supporting evidence from what has been said on the subject by eminent men of the past and present. The work is a substantial affair and should not be taken for a book of readings. It is much more.

The "author-editor" is Johannes Overbeek, and he is well suited for the enterprise. He is from an eminent trading nation, The Netherlands, he was educated in Geneva, is now in the economics department of the College of the Virgin Islands, and is at home in France as well as the Caribbean. The cosmopolitan quality of his book is not surprising. There are selections by Austrian, German, Swedish, Argentinian, and Dutch writers as well as American and British. Some are well remembered, some possibly too well. The editor allows Reed Smoot and Willis Hawley to defend their never-to-be-forgotten tariff of 1930, and he gives a few pages to Mussolini to state the philosophic foundations of fascism.

However, the distinctive feature of the book is not its eclecticism but the editorial commentary, the "essays". The selections, some 35 of them, are divided into seven periods, from the mid-17th century to the late 20th, and are grouped according to whether they advocate free trade or protection, the latter interpreted

Research in the History of Economic Thought and Methodology, Volume 20-A, pages 315–325.
Copyright © 2002 by Elsevier Science Ltd.
All rights of reproduction in any form reserved.
ISBN: 0-7623-0847-8

to include trade restrictions of many kinds and the former to include free trade of a distinctly qualified sort. For each period the editor: (a) describes its salient historical features, (b) gives a precis of the ideas of the writer from whose work an extract follows, and (c) sketches a short biography of him.

The sketch can be interesting or informative or sometimes neither and just distracting. We read that Adam Heinrich Muller of the German Historical School was "an assistant and advisor" to Prince Metternich, a fact that will set teeth on edge in the liberal community. Friederich List when young was not the nationalist he came to be but was a dissident in the parliament of Württemberg, so much so that he was given the choice of prison or exile. He came to the U.S., became an arch protectionist, an enthusiast of the ideas of Hamilton, and in time returned to Germany where he was made U.S. Consul in Leipzig by Andrew Jackson. F. W. Taussig, *primo inter pares* among American free traders, was an advisor to Woodrow Wilson at the peace conference following the first world war and commented that the dignitaries there assembled were as benighted as the journalists who reported their doings and the businessmen who importuned them, all being agreed that the policy is best which increases exports and decreases imports.

The editorial introduction to each writer is followed by an extract from his work except for a few writers whose ideas the editor summarizes in his own words, possibly because in the original they resisted abridgment. Men who write about economics are not men of a few words. An exception is Hume. "Of the Balance of Trade" explains in 18 pages the specie-flow mechanism and gold points, and describes the operation of the quantity theory of money in domestic and international trade.[1] Another exception is Francis Bacon; his essays on economic subjects rival those of Hume in concision and clarity though not in substance. The verbosity of others invites speculation. Is the market for economic writing inefficient? Or are the returns from verbosity higher than those from brevity? Surely we would know more if what we were told was said in fewer words. Do we prefer not to know more? Or do we know as much as we can manage?

The editor's portion of the book includes his judgment of what in the extracts and summaries is valid and what is not. Thus, "Mun drew the (wrong) conclusion that a nation can get rich only if it exports (earns) more than it imports (spends)." Or, "Muller helped Metternich in his work of oppression and intrigue."

Hans Overbeek is not an impartial Jove; he is a lively partisan of free trade. However, there is no evidence of his misrepresenting the writers with whom he differs, or does he scrimp the space he allots them. They actually have more than the free traders. His book recalls the American edition of Say's *Treatise of Political Economy*.[2] It is celebrated, not altogether correctly, for its advocacy of the market, but Say did make exceptions. His editor, Clement C. Biddle, a dedicated free trader, reproves, even scolds, him for them.[3] Hans Overbeek does not scold his authors but does tell them and the reader where they went wrong. Example: Gunnar Myrdal and Raul Prebisch, we are warned, used out-of-date and unrepresentative prices to uphold their claim that free trade redistributes the income of the world in favor of the "center" (the developed countries) and away from the "periphery" (the undeveloped). Again: Robert Reich (Clinton's first Secretary of Labor) said the U.S., if it is to maintain its position, should promote the new and capital intensive industries such as aero-space. They actually use less capital per worker than older industries like automobiles, we are informed.

The opening readings are on mercantilism and are interpreted in the familiar way, as a policy that repudiates the postulates of the market. Those postulates, I would state briefly, possibly too briefly, are that men are self-interested, that they look after their interest in a sensible way, and that doing what they do is ethically proper either because it is their right or because it is efficient. The first two postulates are claims of fact and the last a claim of value.

The first mercantilist to speak is Thomas Mun.[4] That he could have repudiated the market is a droll thought. The directors of the East India Company, of which he was one, would have been surprised to hear him say they were not self-interested, did not act sensibly, and that what they are (unsuccessfully) trying to do was immoral. "Hear, hear, Brother Thomas!" they would have said and have shown him the door. English mercantilism did not repudiate the market in principle, and few if any of the mercantilists subscribed to all of the measures that one or another of them proposed. Had all been enacted and enforced, the market would have been repudiated in practice. How to explain them – as remedies for market failure, as rent seeking, or mistaken notions – is a long story, and this is not the place to tell it. What can be said is that if all of the measures that one or another of the mercantilists found objectionable had been bundled into a portmanteau prohibition, the result would have been a market to make a libertarian chortle.

This cannot be said about mercantilists on the Continent such as Phillip von Hornick. There, economic policy was and still is influenced more than it has been in England by philosophic idealism, the belief that the group or body politic is an entity separate from and superior to the people who comprise it and that it is directed by forces of an unalterable nature whether of supernatural or material origin. The postulates of idealism cannot be stated as plainly as those of the market, and they have been interpreted in different, although not contradictory, ways. One is that they imply autarky. Something near to it was prescribed by von Hornick and by most of the other Germans who have a presence in the book.

Their ideas are likely to be dismissed as absurd. Von Hornick said high priced goods add more to the nation's income than low priced goods.[5] Absurd, surely, except if autarky brings about an increase in the productivity of resources, hence in the value of what they produce (cotton farmers become silk farmers). What is absurd is the likelihood of autarky having such an effect. Adolph Wagner, a Socialist of the Chair and member of the Prussian Diet, said metallic money should be prohibited and only paper allowed. Not so absurd if one reads on and learns Wagner believed foreign trade should be prohibited.[6]

In America in the 18th century, arguments of a different sort were made about trade policy. A few advocated free trade. Most did not. They often began by professing the principle, then moved to an explanation of why it could not be followed; the main reason given was that other nations did not follow it, the minor was that America was too young, too new, too small, and weak.[7] The longest and most cogently (if unconvincingly) argued statement was made by Hamilton in his *Report on Manufactures* (1791) with additional argument in his reports on public credit (1790) and on the constitutionality of a national bank (1790). He proposed numerous measures to hasten economic development, and in addition to a protective tariff they included the control of exports, subsidies and other monetary incentives to manufacturing and to agriculture also, non-monetary inducements, the control of the quality of certain products, and a Board of Industry to preside over the whole. In the constitutional convention of 1787, there were proposals to grant the federal government broad and detailed authority over the economy, one made by the delegates from New York state who included Hamilton. None of the proposals was adopted. Nor were most of the proposals of the *Report*. The Congress in 1789 had passed a tariff law (the first law of any kind in American history) and while its purpose may have been protection, its principal, although not only, effect was revenue. What is best remembered of the *Report* is the argument for protecting infant industries, and it is so closely associated with Hamilton that one would think he invented it. He didn't. He had a grander thing in mind, and it was the protection of the Infant Economy. Not so, the Congress, and it passed by most of his ideas. They did not vanish however. Some returned after the second world war, not in Congressional action, to be sure, but in a new field of study, development economics. It was meant for what then were called "backward" countries, later called "undeveloped," then "less developed," and now "developing". The subject itself (after having had a verbal effect at least) seems to have returned to the theory of international trade from which it emerged.

About the term "infant industries," the editor says it may have been used first by J. A. Chaptal in *De l'industrie francaise* (1819) and cites a reference to him in *A History of Economic Doctrines* by Gide and Rist (who once were household names to historians of economics). Chaptal writes of *manufactures naissantes* which in the English edition of Gide and Rist is translated "infant industries".[8] Should it be? The indispensable *Harrap's Standard French and English Dictionary* – the last, as well as first, word for all who have toddled beyond French 101 – defines *manufactures* not as "industries" but simply as "manufactures" and translates *industries* (French) as "industries" (English). If *manufactures* are not "industries," Chaptal could not have been the first to use the term "infant industries" since he did not use it at all He did write of "infant manufactures," but then Hamilton did also, some 30 years earlier, and may not have been the first to do so. He could have been the first to advocate the protection of pre-natal industries. In extolling the merits of the woollen industry in Connecticut, he said, "to cherish and bring to maturity this precious embryo must engage the most ardent wishes . . .".[9]

Needless to say, this has nothing to do with the idea the words describe. Its origin may be in the mists of time since it is a device for restricting competition, and restricting competition is something that must have been on the mind of each of the buyers and sellers at the first market in history.

Smith refers to the protection of new industries, and Hamilton may have gotten the idea from him.[10] He was a close reader of *The Wealth of Nations* and is known to have written an extensive commentary on it. (He was also familiar with Hume.) He did not come to Smith's conclusion which was that protection, while it will increase the amount of capital in the protected industry, will reduce the amount of capital elsewhere by a greater amount, hence will reduce the wealth of the nation.

The net effect of protection on capital and income is usually glossed over. The advocates of protection, in order to make their case persuasive, could claim the protected industries will in time become more efficient than those that do not need protection, hence the protected in time will add more (or as much) to the national wealth as they initially take away. While that is what could be said, it has not been until recently and for long was left to the Impartial Spectator to discover for himself. While doing so, the thought may have occurred to him that firms which are protected by a tariff might also want to be protected from the entry of new firms that would be attracted to the industry by its rate of return. If new firms were to enter, the return would eventually fall to what it is in the unprotected areas of the economy. Smith warned against monopolies coming into being under the shelter of protection.

The infant industry argument assumes the government can forecast the future better than individuals can. The assumption was noticed and disputed by Nicolaas Pierson, "the foremost Dutch economist of the 19th century," the author-editor states and accords him the longest selection in the book (Hamilton's is the second).[11] Pierson said protection raised domestic prices, reduced exports, and fostered vested interests. He observed that extensive suffrage, like that in the U.S., France, and Germany, promoted restrictions on trade.

The idea reappears in a shrewd analysis by the late Mancur Olson and in the comments on it.[12] The latter explains why a policy like free trade which benefits the many is less likely to bring into being a "collective action organization" (an effective lobby) than is a policy which benefits the few or the fewer. The explanation is that the benefit to each of the many, if not combined with an additional reason to act ("a selective incentive" or private benefit), is less than the cost to each of the many of engaging in the action. "The free traders win the arguments, and the protectionists win the elections," Frank Knight said many years ago. The new political economy explains why.

Yet there is no reason for the free traders to despair. The cost to a collective action group of restricting trade increases, according to Professor Olsen, as international trade becomes more extensive. There is no world government on which the group can prevail: it must importune scores of separate governments. Unless (the Impartial Spectator could dryly observe) the scores are brought together by an international organization or by the few and mighty under the rubric of Managed Trade. Just such a prospect disturbs the free traders of the present, among them Jagdish Bhagwati who says managed trade is one of the great impediments to the removing of trade barriers, the others being regional trade blocs, "aggressive multilateralism," and fictions about fair trade. Anent the last is his surprising statement that "an objective of a free trade system should be fairness".[13]

Can a tariff to protect a young industry ever be justified "on mere principles of political economy," to use the phrase of John Stuart Mill? He said, Yes, as many have. Pierson said No, as few have. A principal point on which they differed is no longer in the argument, that being the assumption of superior foresight by the government. Its absence is a victory, however small, for Pierson. The new version claims to rest on "principles of political economy." Gerald M. Meier gives an account.[14]

A young industry merits protection if in time it will yield a "technological externality" (which seems to be a positive externality of a real, not monetary, kind). This is one of three necessary conditions for protection. Another is that the long-run rate of return must be expected to be above the average rate for all industry (actually, all unprotected industry) by an amount equal to the opportunity cost of protection. The third condition is that the period of time during which the industry is to be protected must be specified when the protection is initiated.

The characteristics of the capital market have a place in the new argument but are not one of its conditions. If a young industry was not expected to yield a positive externality but was expected to reduce its costs in time (a positive "internality"), it would not need protection because it would attract private capital. So it would also if it did yield a positive externality. But the amount of capital it would attract would be less than optimal. A subsidy would ensure the optimal amount. So the argument runs.

These considerations, along with others, appear in what Paul Krugman calls "the rethinking of trade theory".[15] The principle of comparative advantage, the bedrock and capstone of standard theory, is modified or replaced, as circumstances dictate, by increasing returns, imperfect competition, and positive externalities. The three figure in "strategic trade policy," and it maintains that tariffs and subsidies can, under certain circumstances, increase the aggregate welfare of a nation even though they reduce the amount of international trade. No longer is more trade always better than less. Now, less may be more. Krugman subscribes to the principles on which the argument rests, which is not surprising since he has contributed substantially to the development of them, but, he states, the empirical difficulties of applying are so great "that free trade is nevertheless the right policy".

The new argument for protecting infant industries incorporates more "principles of political economy" than the old but also makes factual assumptions that (like those made by strategic trade policy) are more difficult to demonstrate. It calls for calculating rates of return throughout the economy, adjusting them for externalities, estimating the opportunity costs of protection and the time needed to recover them. There is, moreover, a puzzling relation among the principles. If a protected firm yields a positive externality, why should the time it is protected be limited? Cannot the externality conceivably be large enough to compensate for the opportunity cost of protection? If it can be, then the measured rate of return should not be greater but equal to that of the unprotected firms; and if the value of the externality is greater than the cost of protection, the firm's measured return should be less than that of the unprotected firms. Then there is a question of how to determine an externality. The answer in economic theory is that the marginal unit of labor or capital measured in real terms must be greater than that measured in monetary terms. The editor, alas, does not make the distinction between real and monetary externalities.[16] If he does not, can one expect it to be made by the Solons who enact trade policy and who may be as benighted as those described by Taussig?

Taussig, although he professed the principle of free trade, made exceptions to it and in doing so was one of a body of distinguished economists (Conservatives of the Chair) who have done so. He said the protection of new industries from foreign competition was permissible and to that exception he added another which is that a tariff is permissible if the demand for the country's imports is elastic and the demand for its exports is inelastic. The tariff would improve the terms of trade, hence would redistribute world income in the country's favor. (If all trading partners used such a tariff, there conceivably could be a redistribution of world income in favor of some but the aggregate income itself would be less because there is a cost to enacting and enforcing the tariff.)

Lionel Robbins, another worthy of the last century, said the infant industry argument was valid and if such industries did not abuse their protection he would favor it and provide it by a subsidy instead of a tariff. He added that the gains were likely to be very slender.[17]

Keynes had notions about trade policy although they are rarely recalled. They did not constitute a grand design as his macro-economics came to do and barely touched on such matters as prosaic as an infant industry. They were a collection of particulars which were meant to serve discriminating ends, some great, some not, and all of them important to him. In 1931 he was averse to Britain's continuing its historic policy of (more or less) free trade. He said it could lead to war. Some illustrious forebears, such as Ricardo and Cobden, had said the opposite, namely, that trade can make war prohibitively expensive or a practical impossibility because no country can produce for itself all it needs to wage a war. (Cobden's pacifism led him to free trade, and Ricardo's free trade led him to pacifism.) Another of Keynes' notions was that foreign trade disturbs "the age-long traditions attendant on husbandry". Still another was that it could interfere with a country's undertaking its "own favorite experiments toward the ideal social republic".[18]

"Half frivolous," Robbins said of the notions. He and Keynes in 1930 were on a committee to advise the Prime Minister about economic policy. Keynes advised that trade be restricted in order to increase employment and support the pound. Robbins was for nothing of the kind and deplored the impugning of free trade. He was being "difficult," according to Roy Harrod, the first biographer of Keynes.[19]

After the second world war, there again were economists who professed the principle and made exceptions to it. J. R. Hicks said free trade must be qualified in order to maintain full employment, stable exchanges, and to guard a country from being exploited by its trading partners.[20] He advised the backward countries to use the tariff to hasten their development. Gottfried Haberler affirmed the principle and said "marginal deviations from it" were not objectionable. "Drastic deviations" were objectionable except when made by backward countries.[21]

In deviating from the principle in one way or another, these distinguished men did not deviate from their distinguished predecessors. Of the Classical triumvirate, Mill favored protection (as did Hume before him).[22] Ricardo and

Smith did not but did favor other restrictions. Ricardo did not propose to abolish the Corn Laws but to modify them in order that manufacturing, which was not subject to as much taxation as agriculture, would not attract excessive capital.[23] Cobden and the Manchester School wanted none of that and called for the complete and immediate repeal of the laws; yet Cobden himself objected to Russia's selling securities in the London market in order to buy war materials.[24] About the Corn Laws, Smith made the same proposal Ricardo made later and a number of others Ricardo did not make, among them a duty on the export of domestic wool in order to protect the manufacture of woolen goods (the mirror image of a duty on the import of woolen goods or analogous to a subsidy in place of a protective tariff). Smith approved of the Navigation Laws (praised them, actually) because they contributed to defense.[25] Mill was not given to saber-rattling as Smith was, yet did not expressly deny that military considerations can justify restricting trade. What he did deny was that British shipping still needed protection.[26] Smith was opposed to unrestricted trade in military goods (and favored subsidizing the domestic production of some). He did urge removing the tariff on many manufactured goods, but said retaining it might induce the exporting countries to reduce their tariff on British goods. If there was to be a reduction, it should be gradual, he said. The Manchester School, one recalls, declared, "Not one shilling's duty, not one day's delay".

The principle of free trade may not seem to be impaired by some of these exceptions. Nevertheless they had an economic effect, directly by way of altering the allocation of resources and indirectly by the aid and comfort they gave to those who opposed free trade in principle. On the several occasions when Parliament considered a major change in the Corn Laws, their supporters invoked the name of Smith and cited the fact that he had favored a permanent duty on grain and had advised that if a duty was to be eliminated the elimination should be gradual, not swift. The Navigation Laws, though they may have enabled, or in fact did enable, Britain to rule the seas, also yielded rents for shipowners and operators. In the debate over them in the 19th century, those who wished to retain them cited Smith.

The 19th century has been called the age of free trade. It was really an aberration, according to Walton Hamilton, the American economist, lawyer, and, unlike the other Hamilton, a phrase maker. Gladstone knew more about it, as he should have, since among all of those in public life who professed to believe in free trade he was pre-eminent. He knew, or believed he knew, the choice could not be free trade or protection but had to be something of both.

The same can be said about domestic policy. While the market was its polestar, the measures that comprised it moved in various directions, and only one was due north. The discrepancy between principle and practice in the affairs of government – the difference between what is said and what is done – is so familiar it is commonplace. What is not familiar is the discrepancy in what economists have written about policy. A merit of the work of Professor Overbeek is that it places the discrepancy before the readers, leaving us to make of it what we can.

NOTES

1. David Hume, *Writings on Economics*, (Ed.) Eugene Rotwein (Edinburg, 1955). The specie-flow mechanism is described in two paragraphs, p. 63; gold points in a foot-note, p. 64; and the quantity theory of money, p. 68 and passim. A portion of the essay is in Overbeek, pp. 18–25.
2. Overbeek, pp. 63–74.
3. Jean-Baptiste Say, *A Treatise on Political Economy, etc.*, trans. C. R. Prinsep, New American Edition, (Ed.) Clement C. Biddle (Philadelphia, 1846). Say remarks, "there are some extremely rare cases, where interference between the owner and his property is even beneficial," and Biddle replies "if no one knows so well as the proprietor, how to make the best use of his property, as our author has just remarked, what advantage can result . . . from the interference?" Biddle's note follows a milder but still censorious note by the translator (pp. 130–131). Say, having died 14 years earlier, was at the mercy of his disciples.
4. *Discourse on England's Treasure by Forraign Trade*, Overbeek, pp. 6–12.
5. Philipp Wilhelm von Hornick, *Austria Over All if She Only Will* (1664), *ibid.*, pp. 13–17.
6. Adolph Wagner, "Agrarian State versus Manufacturing State," (1901), *ibid.* pp. 235–254.
7. An example is the letter of James Madison to Cabell (1828) in *The Debates in the Several State Conventions on the Adoption of the Federal Constitution, etc.*, (Ed.) Jonathan Elliot, 2d ed. (Washington, 1836), IV, 349–51.
8. Charles Gide and Charles Rist, *Histoire des Doctrines Économiques*, (7th ed. Paris, 1947), p. 308n. For the English, see Overbeek, p. 215.
9. Alexander Hamilton, "Report on Manufactures," *Works*, (Ed.) H. C. Lodge (New York, 1904), IV, 184, 187.
10. Adam Smith, *The Wealth of Nations* (Indianapolis, 1981), I, 458.
11. Nicolaas Pierson, *The Principles of Economics* (1912) in Overbeek, pp. 103–134.
12. The extract is compiled from several works of Mancur Olson including *The Logic of Collective Action* (1965) and is accompanied by an extended commentary. Overbeek, pp. 489–502.
13. The extract is taken from three works of Jagdish Bhagwati including *Protectionism* (1988), *ibid.*, pp. 511–515.
14. Gerald M. Meier, "Infant Industry," *The New Palgrave, etc.*, (Eds.) Eatwell, Milgate, and Newman (London, 1987), II, 829.
15. Paul Krugman, "Is Free Trade Passé?" (1987), in Overbeek, pp. 535–550.
16. The examples on p. 531 are some of them real and some monetary externalities.
17. Lionel Robbins, *Economic Planning and International Order* (1937), in Overbeek, pp. 371–372.

18. J. M. Keynes, "Proposals for a Revenue Tariff," (1931), *ibid.*, pp. 414–425.

19. R. F. Harrod, *The Life of John Maynard Keynes* (New York, 1951), pp. 426–427.

20. J. R. Hicks, "Free Trade and Modern Economics" (1951) in Overbeek, pp. 465–485.

21. Gottfried Haberler, *International Trade and Economic Development, ibid.*, pp. 452–460.

22. John Stuart Mill, *Principles of Political Economy, etc.* (London, 1891), p. 593. Hume, *op. cit.*, p. 76.

23. David Ricardo, "On Protection to Agriculture," *Works*, (Ed.) Piero Sraffa (Cambridge, 1951), IV, 244.

24. *Speeches on Questions of Public Policy by Richard Cobden*, (Ed.) John Bright and James E. Thorold Rogers (London, 1870), II, 418.

25. Smith, *op. cit.*, I, 464–465.

26. Mill, *op. cit.*, p. 592.

CLASSICAL LONG-PERIOD THEORY

Vivian C. Walsh

A review essay on Heinz Kurz and Neri Salvadori, (Eds.), *Understanding "Classical" Economics. Studies in Long-Period Theory*, Vol. 16 of Routledge Studies in the History of Economics. London and New York: Routledge, 1998, pp. viii, 283. £45.00. ISBN 0-415-15871-0.

INTRODUCTION

Readers of current scholarly work on classical theory and its revival should need no introduction to Heinz Kurz and Neri Salvadori after the massive works which they have already written or edited in this field. In the present volume they have collected thirteen papers by one or both of them (eleven of which were previously published) with, on occasion, the collaboration of Carlo Panico, Christian Gehrke, or Ian Steedman.

They stressed right away in their introduction their conviction "that there is a thing that may, for good reasons, be called 'classical' economics, which is distinct from other kinds of economics, in particular 'neoclassical' economics" (*Understanding 'Classical' Economics*, hereafter referred to as "KS, 1998a", p. 1). They recognize the "heterogeneity and multilayeredness of the writings of authors in the two groups" (*Ibid*). Clearly, especially in the early development of classical theory, an author might combine strikingly classical concepts with occasional vestiges of mercantilism, while a leading early neoclassic like Marshall might retain classical features, so they are wise to abstain from a classification in terms of authors. They stress that they are "concerned rather with classifying various analytical approaches ... what we have in mind is

Research in the History of Economic Thought and Methodology, Volume 20-A, pages 327–342.
Copyright © 2002 by Elsevier Science Ltd.
All rights of reproduction in any form reserved.
ISBN: 0-7623-0847-8

a particular rational reconstruction of 'classical' economics which, in our view, is useful" (*Ibid*). (Compare KS, 1998b, p. xiii). As they observed on another occasion, classical political economy should be seen as "[c]onstituting a fertile research programme rather than a fully developed and immutable doctrine" (KS, 1998b, pp. 1, 163).

This is surely true. Classical political economy has gone through several distinguishable phases: the early agricultural phase, from Petty to Quesnay, the mature understanding of surplus throughout industry and its dual a uniform intersectorial profit rate, and the revival of classical theory in the 20th century in a mathematical and austere form. Arguably, the minimalism characteristic of classical theory's revival in the 20th century now has achieved its analytic purpose, and can be seen to be in a process of enrichment in a manner which may signal the arrival of a new phase (see Walsh, 2000, and the sources cited there).

Indeed, KS emphasize that their interest in classical theory is "not purely and not even predominantly historical" (KS, 1998a, p. 1). It results rather from their considering classical theory "as containing the key to a better explanation of important economic phenomena. Our concern with classical economics is therefore first and foremost a concern with its analytic potentialities *which in our view have not yet been fully explored*" (*Ibid*., emphasis in original). This exploration, as I have argued elsewhere, can be seen to be ushering in a newly enriched classicism (Walsh, 2000).

They begin by identifying "a first characteristic feature of classical economics: its *long-period* method" (KS, 1998a, p. 2). They note that "a version of their method was also shared by all major marginalist authors until the late 1920s" (*Ibid*). The crucial question, however, is whether the long-period analysis once regarded as an important part of traditional neoclassical theory was in fact consistent with its assumptions, which differ in significant ways from the assumptions underlying classical theory. As KS observe, "whilst traditional classical theory can be formulated in a consistent way, traditional neoclassical theory faces insurmountable difficulties in this regard." (*Ibid*). Compare (KS, 1995, pp. 443–448). As has recently been remarked by Ian Steedman, commenting on these matters, "it is now widely recognized that each version of such traditional long-period marginalist theory of value and distribution encountered insoluble problems" (Steedman, 1998, 1, p. 121).

This would appear to be one respect in which a rather clear distinction can be drawn between classical and neoclassical theories. Of course, in a world haunted by desperate issues of long-period global sustainability and destruction, some neoclassical economists are (like Moliere's amusing character) doing classical economics without being aware of it.

KS rightly draw attention to "[t]he appeal exerted by the long-period method", which "can be inferred from the fact that all early major marginalist authors . . . fundamentally adopted it" (KS, 1998a, p. 6). They also do justice to the sometimes neglected fact that the problems of a neoclassical long-period theory were "well understood by some major protagonists of the demand and supply approach as early as the late 1920s" (KS, 1998a, p. 13). Thus the early neo-classical use of the method of long-period positions was abandoned essentially as a result of *internal* criticism. The result was "the development of the notions of *intertemporal* and *temporary equilibrium*" (*Ibid*). They sketch the develop-ment of these concepts up to the canonical Arrow-Debreu models in which the concept of intertemporal general equilibrium reached its high water mark, sending the reader for details to their earlier work (KS, 1995, pp. 455–467).

Readers of previous works by KS will have been made well aware of the large and escalating number of economic theorists who contributed to the revival of classical theory during the 20th century. KS had nevertheless singled out Piero Sraffa (1960) and John von Neumann ([1937] 1945) as their "two main intellectual sources" (KS, 1995, p. 379) for that work, which they described as "essentially a 'cross-breed' of the analysis of Sraffa and von Neumann" (*Ibid*). This description also fits the blend of present day classicism to be found in the book under review. KS, it will be seen, are faithful and stalwart champions of the classical interpretation of John von Neumann's growth model, which is the subject of the second chapter.

JOHN VON NEUMANN'S GROWN MODEL AND THE CLASSICAL TRADITION

This view of Neumann's celebrated paper ([1937] 1945) goes back to David Champernowne (1945), and has been adopted by a steadily growing number of theorists as classicism revived. Harvey Gram and I used essentially the same Sraffa-Neumann blend as KS and others have done, in our joint work (Walsh & Gram, 1980), and it may be worth noting that Oskar Morgenstern (who read an early version of part of our book) "helped us to see the pivotal role of John von Neumann in the development of modern classical theory" (Walsh & Gram, 1980, p. viii). We had also been influenced by work of Morgenstern and his collaborators, and noted that "[a]n important generalization of Neumann's model of an expanding economy appeared in a paper of John G. Kemeny, Oskar Morgenstern, and Gerald L. Thompson in 1956" (Walsh & Gram, 1980, p. 4. See further Morgenstern & Thompson, 1976).

Despite their clearly stated judgment that the conventional interpretation of Neumann's work as neoclassical " does not stand up to examination" (KS,

p. 26), KS offer a careful and scrupulous examination of the neoclassical interpretation of Neumann's expanding economy model in their second chapter,
before confronting this with the historical and analytical evidence for the
classical interpretation.

It is important to note that KS are not concerned with whether or not Neumann
was familiar with the classical tradition "in all probability he was not and did
not care whether his analysis was 'classical', 'neoclassical' or anything else.
What matters is the similarity of the structure of their respective approaches.
Interestingly, though, von Neumann may well have come across pieces of
economic analysis of classical derivation while he was a Privatdozent at the
University of Berlin from 1927 to 1929" (ibid.).

KS do their best to show how Neumann's model might excusably have been
confused with the early neo-Walrasian work which was emerging in the period
of his expanding economy paper. After all, in 1936 Neumann gave a paper in
Karl Menger's mathematical colloquium at the University of Vienna, where the
early neo-Walrasian contributors were previously presented. And then Neumann
used inequalities rather than equations, as had the Viennese economists'. But
Neumann "had read his paper for the first time in the winter of 1932 at the
Mathematical Seminar of Princeton University" (KS, pp. 27–28), a year before
the Viennese economists' papers. The story is a fascinating one, which the
reader must sample in the original-KS trace highly plausible roots for some
of the most important concepts developed by Neumann (and also by Sraffa)
right back to the earliest beginnings of the revival of classical theory in the
20th century. In the work of Georg von Charasoff, for example, they find
the concept of "what von Neumann more than two decades later was to call
'the remarkable duality (symmetry) of the monetary variables ... and the
technical variables ...' (von Neumann, 1945, p. 1)" (KS, p. 36).

Especially notable is the case of the tragic figure Robert Remak, "a colleague
of von Neumann's while a Privatdozent at the Berlin Institute of Mathematics"
(KS, p. 40). As KS note, in work by neoclassical historians of general equilibrium theory, "in which von Neumann's model generally features prominently,
Robert Remak is hardly paid any attention at all" (KS, p. 41). Was Neumann's
paper a response to Remak's? Remak had given a paper at a meeting of the
Berlin Mathematical Society and, as KS note "his ideas were discussed at the
Institute of Mathematics in Berlin" (KS, p. 45). We cannot know, since Remak
died at Auschwitz.

It is interesting, however, that (as KS observe) in Remak's paper "scarce
natural resources, such as land, play no significant role. He rather focuses attention on systems of production that are in a self-replacing state ... [i]nterestingly,
the total neglect of the problem of scarcity is also a characteristic feature of

von Neumann's model. If his concern had been with generalizing the 'Walras-Cassel model', as is maintained by the conventional interpretation, this neglect would be totally incomprehensible" (KS, p. 45).

KS stress that " in every respect von Neumann's model is more general than Remak's" (KS, p. 46). But, as KS show in detail, the core concepts are common to both. As they conclude, "von Neumann's approach has been anticipated in all relevant aspects by authors whose contributions can be strictly located within the classical tradition" (KS, p. 47).

One classical concept found in Neumann will be singled out for special notice here: the "Rule of Free Goods." Arguably, the position of KS on this is perhaps their most original analytical point in the chapter. KS distinguish between the application of the Rule of Free Goods to factors of production, and its application to produced commodities. A factor of production, which was in excess supply, would have a zero price. But Neumann assumed that all natural resources were non-scarce – he simply sets aside the problem of primary, non-produced resources becoming scarce (See KS, p. 50, note 22). For Neumann, the Rule of Free Goods arises, not because a given factor endowment is in excess supply, but because of the presence of joint production. He "generalized the Rule of Free Goods to products. This is because unlike the Viennese economists (and Walras), who assumed single production, he allowed joint production: with single production no produced commodity can be a free good, other than in the ultra-short period." (KS, p. 37). KS observe that the application of the Rule of Free Goods to products can be found in the original classics: "Adam Smith pointed out that with joint production the proportions in which the products can be produced need not coincide with those in which the are wanted" (KS, pp. 37–38).

Thus the method of inequalities, as used by Neumann, did not offer support to interpreting him as a neoclassic. As KS dryly observe, inequalities had been used, "[o]nly a few years after the appearance of the third edition of Ricardo's Principles" by "a group around William Whewell at the University of Cambridge" (KS, p. 39). They offer pertinent sources of this flowering of Cambridge Mathematics which had apparently been stimulated by the canonically classical economics of Ricardo, roughly a hundred years before the better known debate in Vienna with its neo-Walrasian preoccupations.

ADAM SMITH ON FOREIGN TRADE

Heinz Kurz (the sole author of this chapter) begins by remarking that Adam Smith "is commonly given little credit as a trade theorist" (KS, p. 57). Kurz adds significantly that "[t]he main criticism offered against him is that he failed to elaborate the principal of comparative costs and based his explanation of the benefits from trade on absolute cost differences only" (Ibid). Kurz is right that intellectual historians and theorists of the neoclassical period would dismiss Smith's analysis of trade (or anyone else's) if it was not based on comparative costs. What these neoclassics did not grasp was that, if basing foreign trade theory on absolute cost differences trivialized it, then the first to fall would be David Ricardo.

True, Ricardo had about one and a half pages devoted to a comparative costs example, clearly meant as a reductio ad absurdum argument (see Walsh, 1979, and the sources cited there). But all the rest of the massive output on foreign trade to be found throughout his work is about how importing a cheap necessary (foreign), from countries which had an absolute advantage in producing it, will raise the rate of profits and increase capital accumulation in Britain, which had an absolute advantage in manufactures. Importing wine, in which Britain has an absolute disadvantage, but which was a luxury and thus not consumed by the working-class, would do nothing to raise the rate of profits or stimulate accumulation of capital. True to their classical character, Ricardo and Smith cared most about the accumulation of capital, with would increase the sustenance for productive workers.

Thus Kurz is right on target when he writes of Smith (what is also true of Ricardo) that "Smith's great merit is . . . that his investigation is not restricted to static gains from trade arising from the reallocation of given resources, but is also concerned with the gains from trade in terms of economic development" (KS, p. 57). The main purpose of Kurz's paper, however, is to defend Smith's trade theory from another issue over which it "has generally met with fierce criticism: his 'vent for surplus' argument" (ibid.). In doing so Kurz makes a fruitful use of the concept of joint production, noting that "Smith refers to joint production rather than to single production, as is implicitly assumed in all contributions dealing with his trade theory" (KS, p. 58, emphasis in original).

Where outputs are jointly produced, they may well not emerge in just the proportions needed in the producing country. With foreign trade, however, the "surplus" (in the sense of unwanted) output can be sent abroad in exchange for imports. Where it is based on joint production, Smith's argument, as Kurz argues, "appears to be perfectly sensible" (KS, p. 63).

"ENDOGENOUS" GROWTH MODELS AND THE "CLASSICAL" TRADITION

In their fourth chapter, KS propose the somewhat extreme claim that the so-called new growth theory (NGT), with its "endogenous" growth models, "can be said to involve a return to modes of thought and the method of analysis characteristic of the classical authors." (KS, p. 67, emphasis in original). This claim is primarily based on arguing that the conditions of production of human capital (or knowledge) play the same analytical role in NGT as did the assumption of a given real wage in the original classics. As KS summarize their point: "To put it in a nutshell, the 'secret' of the endogeneity of growth in the classical authors consisted of the assumption of a 'technology' producing labor. We shall see . . . that essentially the same secret is at the heart of the NGT." (KS, p. 74).

However, as has recently been observed by Harvey Gram, it needs to be emphasized that "the neoclassical approach regards the steady state as a good approximation to any actual growth path because it is a supply and demand equilibrium, whereas, the classical prospective regards the long-period position as an attractor continually making itself felt in actual short-period positions with no presumption that supply and demand equilibrium is maintained" (Gram, 1998, p. 142, emphasis in original). When may two equilibria, which look similar in the formalism, actually not have the same significance? This issue, highly pertinent to the putative "similarity" between NGT and the classics, was explored by Gram in a different context years ago in an earlier work (Gram, 1976, pp. 891–903).

KS are quite explicit about the existence of profoundly neoclassical tendencies in NGT. As they rightly insist, it is "anachronistic to attempt to develop a theory of growth that focuses on product innovations, new 'industrial designs', etc., in terms of a model which preserves several of the disquieting features of the neoclassical growth theory of the 1950s and 1960s, including the setting aside of the diversity of behavior and the heterogeneity of goods, particularly capital goods" (KS, p. 86). They point out that the NGT shares with earlier neoclassical work "a homogeneous capital jelly" (ibid.), and justly conclude that "[t]here is no need and indeed no justification for continuing to dwell on such fairy tales" (ibid.).

THE NON-SUBSTITUTION THEOREM: MAKING GOOD A LACUNA

This formal paper deals with a limiting case: namely whether the theorem applies at a wage rate equal to zero. The interest of KS in this arises from their use of it in their work on the NGT. KS concede dryly "that there is no particular economic motivation to study this situation" (KS, p. 90). However, as they point out, it is startling that a limiting case of a theorem which has been studied so extensively and is generally accepted in the scientific community has not been analyzed. The paper contains an improved proof, not published earlier by them.

SRAFFA, MARSHALL AND THE PROBLEM OF RETURNS

This chapter, by Carlo Panico and Neri Salvadori, aims to point out "the existence of some links between Sraffa's 1920s critique and *Production of Commodities*" (KS, p. 103). Many theorists (including a number sincerely friendly towards Sraffa's project of reviving classical theory) have been puzzled by why he felt it necessary to treat the level and composition of output as given in 1960, especially since changes "either in the *scale of production* or in the *proportions* with which the 'factors of production' are employed ... were instead at the centre of the stage in his 1920s critique of Marshall's supply functions". (KS, p. 103, emphasis in original).

Panico and Salvadori note that their study belongs to a tradition which regards it as necessary to see Sraffa's work in the 1960s against the background of what he did in the 1920s – without in any way denying the ultimately classical derivation of his theory. They draw attention to the fact that "[t]he 'central propositions' of *Production of Commodities* were ... elaborated shortly after writing the article published in December 1926 in the *Economic Journal*" (KS, p. 104), and cite the passage in which Sraffa acknowledged this (Sraffa, 1960, p. vi). So in fact little time had elapsed between Sraffa's "early" work and his arriving at the "central propositions" of the 1960 book.

Panico and Salvadori present a detailed case, which must be considered in its entirety by the interested reader, for the following striking claim: "that some important aspects of the development of Production of Commodities find their origin in the Marshallian tradition as well as in the 'classical' one" (KS, p. 116). They stress that "the acceptance of a Marshallian derivation of some developments of Production of Commodities does not deny the links of Sraffa's work with the classical authors that the literature has clearly emphasized" (ibid.).

The Marshallian method of partial equilibrium had resulted in a tangle of confusions concerning the relations between costs and quantity produced, and Sraffa had been an important force in bringing these issues to light in the 1920s. Naturally, he would not want these confusions to cloud the presentation of the core concepts of classical theory which are the subject of his book. As Panico and Salvadori stress, Sraffa's method of given quantities can be seen as an effort to avoid these problems and also "to prevent the reader from misinterpreting his position by stating that certain kinds of returns, and not others, actually prevail in the economy or in some industries" (KS, pp. 116–117). They cite a letter by Sraffa to Keynes of June 6, 1926: "This conclusion has been misunderstood and taken to imply that in actual life constant returns prevail . . . of course in reality the connection between costs and quantity produced is obvious. It simply cannot be considered by means of the system of partial equilibria for single commodities in a regime of competition devised by Marshall" (Sraffa, 1926b, cited KS, p. 117).

Panico and Salvadori end by stressing that "[f]urther work and evidence are necessary" (KS, p. 117) to verify their conclusions; now that the Sraffa papers are being edited by Heinz Kurz, we may clearly look forward to such developments.

THE "STANDARD COMMODITY" AND RICARDO'S SEARCH FOR AN "INVARIABLE MEASURE OF VALUE"

As KS note, even forty years after Sraffa (1960), there is still not a commonly accepted view of the meaning of the Standard Commodity, or of its relationship to Ricardo's search for an invariable measure of value. Another controversial issue concerns the relationship between the Standard commodity and the labor theory of value, but this question is set aside by KS, to be "dealt with in a separate study" (KS, p. 143, note 1).

KS point out that Ricardo's views as to the function and characteristic features of the measure of value which he sought "underwent considerable change" (KS, p. 124). Which, if any, of these conceptualizations may be related to Sraffa's Standard Commodity? To address this question, they begin with a recapitulation of Ricardo's changing views. They show that, right up to his last illness, in 1823, "Ricardo's main concern was still with intertemporal and interspatial comparisons" (KS, p. 128). But, of course, as they point out clearly, '[a]s a matter of fact there is no *general* theoretical solution to the problem of intertemporal and interspatial comparisons" (KS, p. 133, emphasis in origianl). It is therefore understandable that "in his Introduction, Sraffa focused his attention on those aspects of Ricardo's search for an invariable measure of value which concerned the theory of value and distribution with a given technological environment, whereas the intertemporal and interspatial aspects of Ricardo's problem is neglected" (ibid.).

They then offer a detailed analysis of the role of the Standard commodity in Sraffa (1960). Sraffa had argued that "the perfect composite commodity of this type . . . is one which consists of the same commodities (combined in the same proportions) as does the aggregate of its own means of production – in other words, such that both products and means of production are quantities of the self-same composite commodity" (Sraffa, 1960, p. 19). KS follows Sraffa closely, construing the Standard commodity as a strictly technical construction, whose role is to be "that of a special numeraire" (KS, p. 144, note 11), and stressing that Sraffa had emphasized explicitly that the Standard commodity was "a purely auxiliary construction" (Sraffa, 1960, p. 31), and therefore cannot alter the system's mathematical properties (see Sraffa, 1960, p. 23; KS, p. 145, note 11).

Having analyzed a number of results which can be shown conveniently using the Standard commodity as numeraire, KS observed that "these results can also be obtained by using the Perron-Frobenius theorem. In fact Sraffa's demonstration of the existence and uniqueness of the Standard commodity can be considered a (not fully complete) proof of this theorem. Yet Sraffa does even better, simultaneously providing an economic rationale of the analytical tools he uses" (KS, p. 137). They conclude that "Sraffa, for perfectly good reasons it seems, saw only a single analytical purpose of the Standard commodity, i.e. to simplify the analysis of the effects of changes in the division of the product between profits and wages on prices" (KS, p. 143).

MORISHIMA ON RICARDO

Here KS offer a critical account of Morishima (1989), emphasizing parts of the work which "are either based on a misreading of Ricardo or major interpreters of Ricardo, or appear to be misconceived from a theoretical point of view" (KS, pp. 171–172). They observe that Morishima concentrates on Ricardo's Principles, "setting aside most of Ricardo's correspondence, his other published and non-published works and his parliamentary speeches" (KS, p. 148). Ignoring, that is, most of the Works and Correspondence, edited by Sraffa and M. H. Dobb (1951 ssq.), together with "almost all the secondary literature on Ricardo" (KS, p. 149). The book is thus "largely Professor Morishima in the garb of Ricardo" (ibid.).

KS are quick to stress, however, that the book has "enriched the debate about the interpretation of the classical economists ... [and] ... contributed in important ways to the time-honoured question of how different schools of economic thought relate to one another." (KS, p. 150). They emphasize "how much they owe to the works of Professor Morishima for their own training as economists" (ibid.).

They begin with issues concerning the production period, and show in detail why maintaining (as Morishima does) that Ricardo "envisaged the entire manufacturing sector as characterized by instantaneous production appears to be in stark contrast to Ricardo's own writings" (KS, p. 152). Turning to the theory of rent, they note that, for Morishima, Pasinetti's formulation of Ricardo's rent theory "is fundamentally flawed" (ibid.). A specialist literature has grown up around the writings on rent of Sraffa and Pasinetti, and devotees of this area will want to read for themselves KS's vindication of Pasinetti's argument, and their grounds for claiming that Morishima's criticism of Pasinetti's formulation "has to be rejected" (KS, p. 158).

An important part of KS's critique focuses on Morishima's "inadequate treatment of fixed capital" (ibid.). In the third edition of his Principles, Ricardo had changed his mind, now claiming "that the substitution of machinery for human labour, is often very injurious to the interests of the class of labourers" (Works, 1, p. 388). Morishima, however, dissents from Ricardo's argument, leading KS to argue that "[w]hat Professor Morishima's procedure amounts to is assuming away the existence of *any* kind of fixed capital" (KS, p. 168, emphasis in original). But Ricardo was assuming an increase in fixed capital, and, as KS argue, "[t]his increase in the fixed capital intensity, given total capital, is the very cause of the displacement of workers analyzed by Ricardo" (KS, p. 169).

PEACH ON RICARDO

In this review of Terry Peach (1993), Heinz Kurz echoes the theme which we have just left: the importance of Ricardo's Chapter "On Machinery", added to the third edition of his Principles. Among certain important themes in Ricardo's writings which Kurz argues are either neglected "or dealt with only to the extent to which Peach sees them as contributing to [his] objectives" (KS, p. 177), Kurz notes that, "[w]hile the origins and substance of Ricardo's version of the 'law of markets' are given detailed consideration (pp. 131–142) there is, somewhat surprisingly, no discussion of his new view of machinery, published in the third edition of the Principles, and its compatibility, or otherwise, with the 'law of markets' " [ibid.].

As Kurz observes, Peach examines "three different interpretations of Ricardo's pre-Essay theory of profits: the versions proposed by Sraffa, Samuel Hollander, and the 'new' one by Peach himself" (KS, pp. 177–178). As for the "corn model" interpretation, Peach treats this as an incidence of "Sraffa having reconstituted Ricardo in its own image" (Peach, 1993, p. 38). Kurz comments that, "[s]ince no conclusive evidence is put forward in support of this, one can only wonder what is the foundation, and status, of Peach's accusation" (KS, p. 178). In Peach's discussion of Ricardo's later writings, Hollander comes under heavy fire, as does Morishima. Kurz treats each stage of Peach's argument in careful detail, and finally sums up his findings with characteristic generosity of spirit "Peach's book is instructive, interesting, provocative and often correct. It is strong on certain aspects of the intellectual evolution of Ricardo, pungent on the interpretations of Ricardo put forward by Hollander and Morishima, and weak on Sraffa, especially as regards the latter's book . . . It goes without saying that Peach's study is a must for all interested in Ricardo's and Ricardian economics" (KS, p. 184).

KARL MARX ON PHYSIOCRACY

Christian Gehrke and Heinz Kurz, in this chapter, tell us that their concern is "first and foremost with what *Marx thought* the physiocrats had done . . . What matters is the productive use Marx made of the physiocratic doctrines *as he understood them*" (KS, p. 187, emphasis in original). They argue, with justification, that "physiocratic ideas stood godfather to crucial elements of Marx's own system of economic thought" (KS, p. 188). They are careful to specify the physiocratic sources which Marx actually used, insofar as it is possible today to identify these (see Appendix A, KS, pp. 207–211).

Gehrke and Kurz point out that "Marx saw elements of two different, but not necessarily contradictory theories in the physiocratic writings: a material-based and a labour-based determination of value" (KS, p. 191). And they observe that, "[w]hile Marx was critical of [the material based] approach to the problem of value, interestingly his criticism was moderate" (KS, p. 193). Marx had argued that, in agriculture, the generation of surplus can be directly seen, whereas in manufacture it cannot. As Gehrke and Kurz remarke, "[t]his reasoning would only be correct if agriculture . . . were totally independent of the manufacturing sector as a supplier of capital goods or necessaries" (KS, p. 191). Marx, of course, was aware of the physiocrat's mistake. But they argue that nevertheless he saw it as a great contribution that the physiocrats "engaged in these kinds of abstraction, that they *thought* of agriculture as a branch in which the self-same commodity and only it figure both as input and output." (KS, p. 192, emphasis in original).

They observe that, for Marx, it is in Turgot that the physiocratic system is most fully developed. Today, of course, we would regard Turgot as representing a more mature stage in the development of classical theory, and distinct from the physiocrats – influenced more, probably, by his friendship with Adam Smith. (Walsh & Gram, 1980, pp. 40–44, Kurz & Salvadori, 1995, pp. 39, 40). But the subject of the present chapter, as noted above, is Physiocracy as Marx saw it.

Gehrke and Kurz devote a section (and their Appendix B) to Marx's appreciation of the *Tableau Économique*, for which he was "full of praise . . . even after he had carefully studied it in 1862–1863" (KS, p. 196). They point out that Marx had rightly claimed that "the *Tableau* had been unduly neglected by the British political economists, so that an important achievement of economic analysis has been lost sight of for almost an entire century" (ibid.). They do justice, however, to one British classic who had essayed a reproduction structure, noting that "prior to Marx, Robert Torrens had displayed a clear understanding of the duality relationship, and there is evidence that Marx had benefited from Torrens's work" (KS, p. 219, Note 22, compare Kurz & Salvadori, 1995, pp. 381–384).

When classical theory began to revive at the beginning of the 20th-century, however, explicit reproduction structures formed the core of the theory, so that the Tableau, as adapted by Marx to show the generation of surplus throughout industry, now had its rightful place. (Kurz & Salvadori, 1995, pp. 384–407).

NO RESWITCHING? NO SWITCHING!

As Neri Salvadori and Ian Steedman observe in this chapter, it has often been pointed out "that reswitching cannot occur between techniques both of which have 'equal organic composition of capital' " (KS, p. 266). And that "[i]t has even been proved . . . that capital aggregation is assured, and an aggregate production function can be built up, if the labour shares in all sectors are equal, i.e. if all relevant techniques have the 'equal organic composition' property" (ibid.). Their object is to reinforce a more striking claim, which they believe has not received sufficient recognition, that in this situation "techniques cannot switch *even once*" (ibid., emphasis in original). They supplement their formal argument with a diagrammatic explanation. They consider three apparent counter examples, showing that these fail to be genuine. They finally generalize a result to cover joint production. Their argument has implications for the relationship between Paul Samuelson's "surrogate production function" and the labor theory of value. Samuelson's "surrogate" had been known to rely on "equal organic composition." Salvadori and Steedman, however, argue that is dependent also on assuming that "*no* two techniques had *any* process in common" (KS, p. 230, emphasis in original). Arguing that this extreme case is not an exception to their "main result" (ibid.), they conclude that "the surrogate construction is even more special than has often been thought" (ibid.).

ON CRITICS AND PROTECTIVE BELTS

Kurz and Salvadori begin with some reflections on the Cambridge capital controversy, prefaced by an urbane defense of pluralism in economics, arguing that there is no reason "to presume that any of the rival theories available at a given moment of time could provide a full answer to the question under consideration" (KS, p. 236). Such a sensible position has been somewhat rare in recent years. A broadly similar spirit seems, however, to have characterized much of the work of Amartya Sen. (For recent viewpoints, see Sen, 1999; Walsh, 2000).

Kurz and Salvadori hasten to point out that their defense of pluralism "does not mean that anything goes" (KS, p. 237). There are criteria which any theory ought to satisfy; in particular, "an important requirement is that the theory be logically coherent" (ibid.). They lay out the failings of neoclassical long-period analysis in this regard, which should be useful to today's graduate students, who are not taught about such matters. (KS, pp. 243–254).

"PRODUCTIVITY CURVES" IN THE ACCUMULATION OF CAPITAL

In the final chapter, Neri Salvadori offers an analytical treatment of the "productivity curves" which Joan Robinson had used in her Accumulation of Capital (1956), and also in a paper she wrote with K. A. Naqvi (1967). Salvadori remarks that Joan Robinson's later lack of interest in these productivity curves "certainly did not invite" (KS, p. 259) their consideration by others. He adds that: "This is a pity for at least one reason: the description of technology in terms of productivity curves is much more workable for economists with a neoclassical background and interest in macroeconomics" (ibid.).

Among other things, he explores the bearing of this apparatus on Robinson's use of the concept of a "pseudo-production function." Extensive references to the relevant literature are supplied.

SOME CONCLUSIONS

Reviewers characteristically have issues which they wish authors had addressed. Authors, reasonably, have their own agendas – as have editors. Readers, on the whole, should find themselves well provided for by the collection of papers offered in this volume. Some important issues concerning classical theory, of course, are not among those discussed. It has, for example, been argued that "[t]he best hope for developing the potentialities of modern classical theory lies in using its degrees of freedom to forge connections with other disciplines. Only then can it confront neoclassical orthodoxy with a robust alternative approach to the analysis of capital accumulation, structural change, and socio-economic development" (Gram, 1999, p. 144). Likewise, it has been suggested that one can "distinguish two phases in the revival of classical theory during the 20th century. The first phase was severely minimalist, and looked back to David

Ricardo for inspiration, re-interpreting his work in terms of present day concepts and formal methods. The second phase, on the other hand, seeks an enriched present-day classicism, and is appropriately inspired by the work of Adam Smith" (Walsh, 2000. p. 5).

But it must never be forgotten that this minimalism "reflected the most critical need for the successful revival of classical theory: the most precise possible mathematical development of the structure of the theory" (Walsh, 1998, p. 4). That one can now contemplate and detect the emergence of a number of enrichments of classical theory is in no small measure due to the detailed, extensive and rigorous work on the formal structure of classical economics undertaken by Kurz and Salvadori over the last twenty-five years, some of which is now collected in the present volume.

ACKNOWLEDGMENTS

I am indebted to Harvey Gram for valuable advice and to Lisa Bendall-Walsh for editorial assistance. The usual disclaimers apply.

REFERENCES

Champernowne, D. G. (1945). A note on J. von Neumann's article on "A Model of economic equilibrium". *Review of Economic Studies, 13*, 10–18.

Gram, H. N. (1999). H. D. Kurz and N. Salvadori. *Understanding "Classical" Economics. Studies in Long-Period Theory. The European Journal of the History of Economic Thought, 6*(1), 141–144.

Gram, H. N. (1976). 'Two-Sector Models in the Theory of Capital and Growth'. *American Economic Review, 66*(5), 891–903.

Kemeny, J. G., Morgenstern, O., & Thompson, G. L. (1956). A Generalization of the von Neumann Model of an Expanding Economy, *Econometrica, 24*, 115–135.

Kurz, H. D., & Salvadori, N. (Eds) (1998a). *Understanding "Classical" Economics. Studies in Long-Period Theory*. New York: Routledge.

Kurz, H. D., & Salvadori, N. (Eds) (1998b). *The Elgar Companion to Classical Economics*. Edward Elgar: Cheltenham, 2 vols.

Kurz, H. D., & Salvadori, N. (Eds) (1995). *Theory of Production: A Long-Period Analysis*. Cambridge, Cambridge University Press.

Morgenstern, O., & Thompson, G. L. (1976). *Mathematical Theory of Expanding and Contracting Economies*. Lexington, MA: D. C. Heath.

Morishima, M. (1989). *Ricardo's Economics: A General Theory of Distribution and Growth*. Cambridge, Cambridge University Press.

Neumann, J. von ([1937] 1945). A Model of General Economic Equilibrium. *Review of Economic Studies, 13*, 1–9. English translation of Neumann [1937].

Peach, T. (1993). *Interpreting Ricardo*. Cambridge, Cambridge University Press.

Ricardo, D. (1951ssq.). *The Works and Correspondence of David Ricardo*. P. Sraffa (Ed., with the collaboration of M. H. Dobb), referred to as *Works*. Cambridge, Cambridge University Press.

Robinson, J. V. (1956). *The Accumulation of Capital*. London: Macmillan.

Robinson, J. V., & Naqvi, K. A. (1967). The badly behaved Production Function. *Quarterly Journal of Economics. 81*, 579–591.

Roncaglia, A. (1978). *Sraffa and the Theory of Prices*. Chichester, Wiley.

Sen, A. K. (1999). *Development as Freedom*. New York: Knopf.

Sraffa, P. (1960). *The Production of Commodities by Means of Commodities: Prelude to a Critique of Economic Theory*. Cambridge, Cambridge University Press.

Sraffa, P. (1926a). The Laws of Returns Under Competitive Conditions. *Economic Journal, 36*, 535–550.

Sraffa, P. (1926b). Letter to Keynes, dated 6 June, 1926, in Keynes Papers, Cambridge King's College Library. Partly printed in Roncaglia, 1978, 12.

Steedman, J. (1998b). Classical Economics and Marginalism. In: H. D. Kurz & N. Salvadori (Eds), *The Elgar Companion to Classical Economics* (Vol. 1, pp. 117–122). Edward Elgar: Cheltenham.

Walsh, V. C. (2000). Smith After Sen. *Review of Political Economy, 12*(1), 5–25.

Walsh, V. C. (1998). Rationality in Reproduction Models. Conference on Sraffa and Modern Economics, Centro Studie Documentazione 'Piero Sraffa', Rome, Italy.

Walsh, V. C. (1979). Ricardian Foreign Trade Theory in the Light of the Classical Revival. *Eastern Economic Journal, 5*(3), 421–427.

Walsh, V. C., & Gram, H. N. (1980). *Classical and Neoclassical Theories of General Equilibrium: Historical Origins and Mathematical Structure*. New York: Oxford University Press.

THE LIMITS OF MALTHUS'S DEMOGRAPHIC VISION

Geoffrey Gilbert

A review essay on Robert Woods, *The Demography of Victorian England and Wales*, New York: Cambridge University Press, 2000, pp. xxv, 447. $69.95.

The economist, demographer, and clergyman T. R. Malthus died in 1834, three years before Victoria's accession to the British throne. He thus missed the opportunity of being counted among the Victorians, eminent or otherwise. Yet throughout the nineteenth century, Malthusian ideas retained their vitality, especially in Britain; during the long reign of Queen Victoria (1837–1901) it was almost impossible to address a major population-related issue without reference to Malthus.[1] That even today demographers are writing the population history of the nineteenth century within a recognizably Malthusian framework is confirmed by Robert Woods's recently published book, *The Demography of Victorian England and Wales*. Woods, a self-described "geographer" who holds a chair in that subject at the University of Liverpool, has studied English-Welsh population patterns for the better part of two decades. He is the author of a succinct *Population History of Britain in the Nineteenth Century* (1995) and many related articles. His latest book displays technical virtuosity, mastery of a wide range of source materials, and a firm grounding in previous scholarship in the field. Its appearance marks a suitable occasion for some wider reflections on the population vision of the Reverend Malthus.

In his *Essay on the Principle of Population* (1798), Malthus warned of the potential for excessive population growth at all times and in all places.

Research in the History of Economic Thought and Methodology, Volume 20-A, pages 343–350.
Copyright © 2002 by Elsevier Science Ltd.
All rights of reproduction in any form reserved.
ISBN: 0-7623-0847-8

Population tended to increase "geometrically" – it doubled every twenty-five years in the United States, for example (Malthus, 1993, p. 16) – while food supplies could not be made to grow any faster than "arithmetically." Thus population always pressed against, and was restrained by, the available stock of resources. Two types of checks kept the lid on human numbers. War, famine, and disease raised the mortality rate; they were "positive" checks. Delay or avoidance of marriage, abortion, and contraception lowered fertility; these were "preventive" checks. A particular preventive check was brought forward in the second (1803) and later editions of the essay: *moral restraint*. What Malthus meant by this term was the postponement of marriage until the parties were in a position to support their children, and chastity in the meantime. Absent chastity, restraint was still the desirable conduct, but in such case it could only be called "prudential," not "moral."

If we build the checks described above into a simple Malthusian model,[2] we can see how an imbalance between population and resources gets righted. Brisk population growth, for example, causes higher food prices and lower real wages, which lead in turn to higher mortality (positive check), lower nuptiality and fertility (preventive check), and eventually a return to demographic equilibrium. The feedback loops keep the model simple and self-regulating. Adding exogenous factors like migration, foreign trade in food, outbreaks of contagious disease, and a changing rural-urban residential pattern makes the model more "complete" but its diagrammatic representation, unavoidably, more complex. E. A. Wrigley and R. S. Schofield present several versions of the diagram in their *Population History of England, 1541–1871* (1981), the authoritative work in its field. Woods reproduces them in his new book (p. 12).[3]

This model, like any other, brings some key logical relationships into focus and suggests some areas for empirical research. By itself, however, it does little justice to the insight and vision of Malthus as a social thinker. In the first place, Malthus resisted making simple cause-and-effect assertions; he continually qualified his general statements, often in footnotes, often in ways that appeared to cut the ground from under the principle at issue. No feedback-loop diagram can accommodate such tergiversation! Moreover, as early as the first edition of the *Essay*, Malthus demonstrated an awareness of wide cultural, historical, and class differences in the way the population checks were felt. Not for him a one-size-fits-all model of how populations were constrained. He noted, for instance, the contrast between a demographic system like that in China, where population was stabilized by high birth and death rates, and the kind seen in Britain, where stability was maintained through *low* birth and death rates. (Today's terminology would be: "high-pressure" vs. "low-pressure" systems.) And political moralist that he was,[4] Malthus made it clear, in a way no systems diagram could, that he strongly preferred the preventive to the positive checks. In the 1803 edition, he noted – and endorsed – the increased practice of prudential restraint that had occurred in Europe since earlier times. He hoped to see the trend continue, as "the happiness of society will evidently be promoted by it" (Malthus, 1989, II, p. 198).[5]

Conceding, then, the gulf between a Malthusian *model* and Malthus the sophisticated (for his time) demographic, economic and moral *thinker*, let us ask how well the simple model outlined above performs as an aid to understanding British demographic experience. For example, consider the relationship posited by Malthus between real wages and fertility. In 1798, Malthus suggested an almost immediate impact on marriage and fertility from a change in the real wage rate (p. 19). Wrigley and Schofield report data that substantiate this causal link in the model but, in a highly controversial finding, see a "sluggish" 40-year lag from wage change to measured change in fertility (p. 434). A careful reexamination of the data by J. A. Goldstone (1986, pp. 6–9) has shortened the lag to about 15 to 20 years. Yet whoever is right, the postulated lag applies only from the late sixteenth to the early nineteenth century. After that, the empirical connection between wages and nuptiality disappears. Another causal link to be examined runs from food prices to real wages. Does the negative correlation featured in the model hold true through the nineteenth century? Wrigley and Schofield find that it does, but also that real wages are *more strongly* determined by what is happening elsewhere in the economy, namely, in the secondary and tertiary sectors rather than in agriculture (p. 476).

A cornerstone of any "Malthusian" population model must be the predictable effect of faster- or slower-than-usual population growth on food prices. This, after all, is at the core of the Malthusian analysis of 1798: in periods when population grows too fast, food supplies cannot respond quickly or proportionately, and economic logic requires that food prices spike upward. Wrigley and Schofield find the expected correlation between population and food prices during the late sixteenth and seventeenth centuries, but by the nineteenth century, *no correlation at all* (pp. 468–470, 474–477). Taking this result together with the previous ones, it becomes all too clear that the entire Malthusian "preventive-check cycle," in Wrigley and Schofield's phrase, has collapsed by the nineteenth century. That still leaves, of course, the "positive-check cycle," a separate feedback loop involving higher mortality as real wage rates decline in response to faster-than-average population growth. The problem here is a serious lack of empirical support at *any* stage of modern English history, from the sixteenth century through the nineteenth (pp. 412–417, 472). This particular feedback loop apparently fed back only in pre-modern times!

What can one say about the near-total failure of the Malthusian model to comport with the demographic facts in Britain during the century in which Malthus spent most of his adult life? The simplest observation to be made – and not a trivial one – is that the Malthusian feedback approach has high explanatory value when applied to Britain's pre-industrial economy and little or no explanatory value when applied to the industrialized economy that followed. Professor Wrigley has expressed this view on several occasions.[6] It is neither praise nor blame to define the range of application of a social theory. Few if any social science models are expected to have universal applicability, and there is no reason this one should be the exception. Why Malthus's demographic vision fails when directed *forward* in time rather than backward is an intriguing question. Wrigley, Schofield, Woods, and many others have been assembling and interpreting the key statistical series – nuptiality, fertility, and mortality – that provide some basis, along with Malthus's own writings, for answering that question.

Nuptiality indexes the proportion of a population married. Its long-term trend is determined primarily by average age at marriage and the incidence of celibacy. A fall in either variable will raise nuptiality, while a rise in either will lower it. In a non-contraceptive population, changes in nuptiality translate directly to changes in fertility, as postulated in the basic Malthusian model. Malthus's strong advocacy of moral, or at least prudential, restraint from the 1803 edition onward may thus be seen as a position in favor of restrained nuptiality and fertility, and modest population growth. Only in this way could the best balance be struck between population and resources. Slowing the "hare" of population would give the "tortoise" of food production a chance to catch up.[7]

As noted above, Malthus believed Europeans to have become much more prudent in his day than formerly. In one passage he speaks of the "decided change" that has occurred in the practice of "prudential restraint"; in another he states his opinion that "in modern Europe, a much larger proportion of women pass a considerable part of their lives in the exercise of this virtue than in past times" (Malthus, 1989, II, p. 198; I, p. 304). In the fifth edition of his *Essay* (1817), noting that the term preventive check implies "a delay of the marriage union from prudential considerations," he concludes that "it may be considered . . . as the most powerful of the checks which in modern Europe keep down the population to the level of the means of subsistence" (I, p. 305). England is of course subsumed under "Europe" in all these passages. Malthus considered his countrymen at least as prudent as the generality of "Europeans." Here is the very specific demographic assertion he makes about them in the Appendix to the fourth edition of the *Essay* (1806):

The marriages in this country now are later than they were before the revolution.... Two or three years in the average age of marriage, by lengthening each generation, and tending, in a small degree, both to diminish the prolificness of marriages, and the number of born living to be married, may make a considerable difference in the rate of increase" (Malthus, 1989, II, p. 221).

But the premise is dead wrong. Long-term variations in the mean age of English and Welsh women at marriage, from 1576 to 1931, are charted in Fig. 3.5 (p. 82) of Woods's book. One of the graph's most striking features is the sustained *drop* in age at marriage from before the revolution (of 1688) to the early nineteenth century.[8] The size of the drop – roughly four years – may seem rather modest, but demographically speaking, it is huge. If we correct the premise of the passage and retain the logic of what follows (though reversed), we can see, in part, why English fertility climbed higher and higher from the mid-1600s to the second decade of the 1800s. Younger marriages are indeed more "prolific" – if there is no resort to birth control.

With his (mistaken) belief that his countrymen were becoming more prudent in regard to nuptiality, how could Malthus account for the "extraordinary" popu-lation increase disclosed in the census results of 1801? Higher marital fertility would have been a logical answer, but it was not his. Rather, his explanation lay in falling mortality.[9] Thus he wrote in 1803, "It would appear . . . that the more rapid increase of population, supposed to have taken place since the year 1780, has arisen more from the diminution of deaths than the increase of the births" (I, p. 258). In surveying the general progress of society over the long run, he found that "taking Europe throughout, fewer famines, and fewer diseases arising from want have prevailed in the last century than in those which preceded it" (II, p. 202). No doubt there *were* fewer famines, and the incidence of disease *did* decrease, and in fact, mortality rates *did* fall, but modern demographers now have access to, and have digested, enough historical data to be confident in attributing most of the rise in English population in this period to higher fertility rather than lower mortality.[10]

Much of Woods's book consists in a minutely detailed examination of the geographic and gender differences in the various components of fertility and mortality as played out in Victorian times. This is an approach that Malthus would certainly have sympathized with. He was, for instance, much interested in the different mortality rates reported in cities versus rural areas of Britain – an issue to which Woods devotes an illuminating chapter. Malthus's cataloguing bent with regard to the population checks is impressively mirrored in tables like that on pp. 314–315, which lists the "nosologies" (disease classifications) used in official government reports from 1851 to 1910. But constantly in the background of all the issues and details of the book is a powerful pair of demographic trends which extend well past the close of Victoria's reign: falling fertility and mortality rates.

These trends, of course, take center stage in any discussion of the *demographic transition*, which is the familiar theoretical notion of the movement a society can make over time – all western industrialized nations have done so – from a high birth-and-death-rate equilibrium to a low birth-and-death-rate equilibrium of population. In theory, the transition is initiated by a drop in mortality, followed at some distance by a drop in fertility. As the transition occurs, population climbs rapidly. Woods reviews what has long befuddled historical demographers – the peculiarity of British population beginning its sustained rise in the early nineteenth century with an increase in nuptiality and fertility, rather than a textbook drop in mortality. (We have seen how Malthus erred on these trends.) But regardless of its anomalous beginnings, England's demographic transition soon conformed to the textbook pattern: fertility declined from about 1820 onward, and life expectancy began a steady upward march around 1800 that continues to this day. Could Malthus have anticipated all of this? Any of this?

Taking mortality first, we know that the *Essay on Population* was conceived in a setting of controversy, with Malthus determined to undermine the claims of Condorcet and Godwin that man was "perfectible." Those authors had made extravagant predictions of fundamental improvements in the human frame, including longer lifespans. Malthus disputed this at great length. Thus, we may take as basic to his mindset an early and deeply ingrained skepticism about the possibility of long-term, substantial improvements in life expectancy. It is true he wrote about the elimination of the plague from English cities, the introduction of smallpox inoculation, and the public health measures that had improved people's chances of avoiding premature death, but beyond these known, limited advances he was loath to speculate.

With regard to fertility, Malthus's demographic vision was severely blinkered by presuppositions about marital fertility which, while not unique to him, surely mark his thinking as "Victorian" in the most common, strait-laced sense of the term. He regarded the "prolificness" of marriage as variable according to age at marriage and subject to infant/child mortality rates that were, in turn, related to disease incidence and the debilitating effects of poverty. He did *not* acknowledge or foresee any impact on marital fertility from the deliberate control of conception by married couples. He rejected birth control as morally unacceptable, for reasons that need not detain us here.[11] And he never ventured, at least in print, into a full discussion of the social and economic impacts that might have flowed from the widespread practice of birth control within marriage. A few writers of his time (notably Francis Place) did enter that hypothetical realm, but only the most farsighted could have imagined the stunning decline in marital fertility so graphically depicted in Woods's Fig. 4.17, which documents, on a district-by-district basis for England and Wales, the successive drops in marital fertility from 1861 to 1911.

One hastens to add that *for his time* Malthus's understanding of the determinants of marital fertility was broadly correct. Not until the final decades of the nineteenth century do the figures for English marital fertility chart the precipitous decline that signals widespread, conscious efforts to control family size. Just how that control was achieved remains unclear. As Woods notes, we still know surprisingly little about the contraceptive strategies employed by couples before the twentieth century (see Chap. 4). One thing is beyond dispute: the longest-reigning English monarch in history was a stranger to all such strategies. Queen Victoria was a mother within a year of her marriage and bore a total of nine children in seventeen years.

NOTES

1. The range of popular and scholarly reaction to Malthus in the nineteenth century may be sampled in Gilbert, 1998.

2. In the spirit of Malthus, 1798, Chapter II, especially p. 19.

3. Oddly, no proofreader caught the amusing typo in Fig. 1.3 which turned "exogenous influences" into "erogenous influences."

4. I borrow the term from Donald Winch, who has presented Malthus in this light on many occasions, most notably in *Malthus* (1987).

5. J. Hajnal has credited Malthus with anticipating his own research findings, in 1965, to the effect that a "European marriage pattern" of late marriage and high proportions never marrying set Europe apart from the rest of the world for centuries (Hajnal, 1965, p. 130).

6. For example, in his article, "Malthus's Model of a Pre-Industrial Economy" (Wrigley, 1983, p. 112), Wrigley states: "As it happened, it was Malthus's fate to frame an analysis of the relationship between population, economy and society during the last generation to which it was applicable."

7. For a long list of the non-economic advantages also to be anticipated from the practice of moral restraint, see Malthus, 1989, II, 96–103.

8. See also Wrigley and Schofield 1981, p. 423. Woods's Fig. 3.5 also makes it clear that over the same period from the revolution to the early nineteenth century, the proportion of English-Welsh women marrying rose substantially, though nearly all of that shift occurred before 1700.

9. The dilemma for Malthus of first trying to explain slow British population growth (1798) and then (1803) trying to explain the rapid growth revealed by the 1801 census is nicely depicted in Hollander 1997, Chap. 16.

10. Lee and Schofield 1981, p. 31.

11. The whole issue of Malthus's position on birth control is explored in Gilbert, 1993.

REFERENCES

Gilbert, G. (1993). Why did Malthus oppose birth control? *Research in the History of Economic Thought and Methodology*, *11*, 1–15.

Gilbert, G. (Ed.) (1998). *Malthus: Critical Responses*. 4 vols. London and New York: Routledge.

Goldstone, J. A. (1986). The demographic revolution in England: a re-examination. *Population Studies*, *40*, 5–33.

Hajnal, H. J. (1965). European marriage patterns in perspective. In: D. V. Glass & D. E. C. Eversley (Eds), *Population in History* (pp. 101–143). London: Edward Arnold.

Hollander, S. (1997). *The Economics of Thomas Robert Malthus*. Toronto: University of Toronto Press.

Lee, R. D., & Schofield, R. S. (1981). British population in the eighteenth century. In: R. D. Floud & D. McCloskey (Eds), *The Economic History of Britain since 1700*, 2 vols (Vol. 1, pp. 17–35). Cambridge: Cambridge University Press.

Malthus, T. R. (1989). *An Essay on the Principle of Population* (1803). 2 vols. P. James (Ed.). Cambridge: Cambridge University Press.

Malthus, T. R. (1993). *An Essay on the Principle of Population* (1798). G. Gilbert (Ed.). Oxford and New York: Oxford University Press. Reissued, 1999.

Winch, D. (1987). *Malthus*. Oxford and New York: Oxford University Press.

Woods, R. (1995). *The Population History of Britain in the Nineteenth Century*, Cambridge: Cambridge University Press.

Wrigley, E. A. (1983). Malthus's Model of a Pre-Industrial Economy. In: J. Dupaquier et al. (Eds), *Malthus Past and Present* (pp. 111–124). New York: Academic Press.

Wrigley, E. A., & Schofield, R. S. (1981). *The Population History of England, 1541–1871*. Cambridge, Mass.: Harvard University Press.

NEW BOOKS RECEIVED

Agamben, Giorgio. *Means without Ends: Notes on Politics*. Minneapolis, MN: University of Minnesota Press, 2000. Pp. 160. $44.95, cloth; $17.95, paper.

Archer, Margaret; Roy Bhaskar, Andrew Collier, Tony Lawson, and Alan Norrie, (Eds), *Critical Realism: Essential Readings*. New York: Routledge, 2000. Pp. xxiv, 756. $23.99.

Aune, James Arnt. *Selling the Free Market: The Rhetoric of Economic Correctness*. New York: Guilford Press, 2001. Pp. xiv, 215. $23.95.

Berlin, Isaiah. *Three Critics of the Enlightenment: Vico, Hamann, Herder*. (Ed.), Henry Hardy. Princeton, NJ: Princeton University Press, 2000. Pp. xiii, 382. Cloth, $45.00; paper, $16.95.

Berlin, Isaiah. *Personal Impressions*. Expanded edition. (Ed.), Henry Hardy. Princeton, NJ: Princeton University Press, 2001. Paper, $16.95.

Billington, Tom. *Separating, Losing and Excluding Children: Narratives of Difference*. New York: Routledge, 2000. Pp. x, 131. Paper.

Boggs, Carl. *The End of Politics: Corporate Power and the Decline of the Public Sphere*. New York: Guilford Press, 2000. Pp. x, 309. $23.95.

Brazelton, W. Robert. *Designing U.S. Economic Policy: An Analytical Biography of Leon H. Keyserling*. New York: Palgrave, 2001. Pp. ix, 181. $65.00.

Bulgakov, Sergei. *Philosophy of Economy: The World as Household*. New Haven, CT: Yale University Press, 2000. Pp. vii, 347. $35.00.

Burk, Kathleen. *Troublemaker: The Life and history of A. J. P. Taylor*. New Haven, CT: Yale University Press, 2000. Pp. xiv, 491. $35.00.

Coats, A. W. Bob, ed. *The Development of Economics in Western Europe since 1945*. New York: Routledge, 2000. Pp. iv, 262. $65.00.

Cullenberg, Stephen; Jack Amariglio, and David F. Ruccio, (Eds), *Postmodernism, Economics and Knowledge*. New York: Routledge, 2001. Pp. xv, 495. $23.99, paper.

Dugger, William M., and Howard J. Sherman. *Reclaiming Evolution: A Dialogue Between Marxism and Institutionalism on Social Change*. New York: Routledge, 2000. Pp. ix, 211. Cloth, $85.00; paper, $25.99.

Earl, Peter E., and Stephen F. Frowen (Eds) *Economics as an Art of Thought: Essays in Memory of G.L.S. Shackle.* New York: Routledge, 2000. Pp. xxvi, 425. $65.00.

Ebenstein, Alan. *Friedrich Hayek: A Biography.* New York: Palgrave, 2001. Pp. xiii, 403.

Edgell, Stephen. *Veblen in Perspective: His Life and Thought.* Armonk, NY: M. E. Sharpe, 2001. Pp. xiii, 207. Cloth, $56.95; paper, $22.95.

Eltis, Walter. *The Classical Theory of Economic Growth.* (2nd ed.). New York: Palgrave, 2001. Pp. xlvii, 373 Cloth, $79.95; paper, $24.95.

Ferguson, Niall. *The Cash Nexus: Money and Power in the Modern World, 1700–2000.* New York: Basic Books, 2001. Pp. xix, 552. $30.00.

Fleischacker, Samuel. *A Third Concept of Liberty: Judgment and Freedom in Kant and Adam Smith.* Princeton, NJ: Princeton University Press, 1999. Pp. xiv, 336. Paper, $19.95.

Fletcher, Gordon. *Understanding Dennis Robertson: The Man and His Work.* Northampton. MA: Edward Elgar, 2000. Pp. xiii, 433. $120.00.

Forget, Evelyn L., and Sandra Peart (Eds), *Reflections on the Classical Canon in Economics: Essays in Honor of Samuel Hollander.* New York: Routledge, 2001. Pp. xx, 524.

Griliches, Zvi. *R&D, Education and Productivity: A Retrospective.* Cambridge, MA: Harvard University Press, 2001. Pp. 127. $39.95.

Guehenno, Jean-Marie. *The End of the Nation-State.* Minneapolis, MN: University of Minnesota Press, 2000. Pp. xiii, 144. $16.95, paper.

Hamburger, Joseph. *John Stuart Mill on Liberty and Control.* Princeton, NJ: Princeton University Press, 1999. Pp. xx, 239. $37.50.

Hands, D. Wade. *Reflection without Rules: Economic Methodology and Contemporary Science Theory.* New York: Cambridge University Press, 2001. Pp. xi, 480. Cloth, $95.00; paper, $34.95.

Haslam, Jonathan. *The Vices of Integrity: E. H. Carr, 1892-1982.* New York: Verso, 1999. Pp. xiv, 306.

Hill, Roland. *Lord Acton.* New Haven, Ct: Yale University Press, 2000. Pp. xxiv, 548. $39.95.

Houck, Davis W. *Rhetoric as Currency: Hoover, Roosevelt, and the Great Depression.* College Station, TX: Texas A&M University Press, 2001. Pp. x, 219. $39.95.

Hudson, Ray. *Producing Places.* New York: Guilford Press, 2001. Pp. xiii, 385. Paper.

Jay, Peter. *The Wealth of Man.* New York: Public Affairs, 2000. Pp. xxiii, 373. $30.00.

Jensen, Michael C. *A Theory of the Firm: Governance, Residual Claims, and Organizational Forms.* Cambridge, MA: Harvard University Press, 2000. Pp. ix, 311. $45.00.

Keaney, Michael. *Economist with a Public Purpose: Essays in Honour of John Kenneth Galbraith.* New York: Routledge, 2001. Pp. xi, 274. $100.00.

Keuzenkamp, Hugo A. *Probability, Econometrics and Truth: The Methodology of Econometrics.* New York: Cambridge University Press, 2000. Pp. ix, 312. $69.95.

Kirzner, Israel M. *The Driving Force of the Market: Essays in Austrian Economics.* New York: Routledge, 2000. Pp. xli, 295. $100.00.

Klausen, Jytte. *War and Welfare: Europe and the United States, 1945 to the Present.* New York: Palgrave, 2001. Pp. v, 341.

Kornai, Janos; Stephan Haggard, and Robert R. Kaufman (Eds), *Reforming the State: Fiscal and Welfare Reform in Post-Socialist Countries.* New York: Cambridge University Press, 2001. Pp. xv, 284. Cloth, $69.95; paper, $24.95.

Kyvig, David. E. (Ed.) *Unintended Consequences of Constitutional Amendment.* Athens, GA: University of Georgia Press, 2000. Pp. 260. Paper.

Laurent, John; and John Nightingale (Eds), *Darwinism and Evolutionary Economics.* Northampton, MA: Edward Elgar, 2001. Pp. xii, 254. $90.00.

Leeson, Robert. (Ed.) *A. W. H. Phillips: Collected Works in Contemporary Perspective.* New York: Cambridge University Press, 2000. Pp. xvii, 515. $95.00.

Levin, Miriam R. (Ed.) *Cultures of Control.* Amsterdam, The Netherlands: Harwood Academic Publishers, 2000. Pp. xix, 274. $24.00.

Lehne, Richard. *Government and Business.* New York: Seven Bridges Press, Chatham House Publishers, 2001. Pp. xvi, 320.

Lindblom, Charles E. *The Market System: What It Is, How It Works, and What To Make of It.* New Haven, CT: Yale University Press, 2001. Pp. 296.

Macfarlane, Alan. *The Riddle of the Modern World.* New York: Palgrave, 2000. Pp. xiii, 326. $65.00.

Mandeville, Bernard. *Free Thoughts on Religion, The Church, and National Happiness.* Irwin Primer (Ed.). New Brunswick, NJ: Transaction, 2001. Pp. xxxix, 234. $49.95.

Mantzavinos, C. *Individuals, Institutions, and Markets.* New York: Cambridge University Press, 2001. Pp. xviii, 313. $54.95.

Martinich, A. P. *Hobbes: A Biography.* New York: Cambridge University Press, 2000. Pp. xvi, 390. $22.95.

McCloskey, Deirdre. *Measurement and Meaning in Economics.* Stephen Thomas Ziliak (Ed.). Northampton, MA: Edward Elgar, 2001. Pp. xxviii, 371. $100.00.

McLure, Michael. *Pareto, Economics and Society: The Mechanical Analogy.* New York: Routledge, 2001. Pp. xvii, 221. $59.00.

McDonald, Forrest. *States' Rights and the Union: Imperium in Imperio, 1776–1876.* Lawrence, KS: University Press of Kansas, 2000. Pp. viii, 296. $29.95.

McNally, David. *Bodies of Meaning.* Albany, NY: SUNY Press, 2000. Pp. ix, 277. $23.95, paper.

Menand, Louis. *The Metaphysical Club.* New York: Farrar, Straus and Giroux, 2001. Pp. xii, 546. $27.00.

Miller, George. *On Fairness and Efficiency: The Privatisation of the Public Income Over the Past Millenium,* Bristol, U.K.: Policy Press, 2000. Pp. x, 470.

Murphy, Antoin E., and Renee Prendergast (Eds), *Contributions to the History of Economic Thought: Essays in Honour of R.D.C.* Black. New York: Routledge. Pp. xvii, 349. $110.00.

Negishi, Takashi. *Economic Thought from Smith to Keynes.* Collected Essays, Vol. III. Northampton, MA: Edward Elgar, 2000. Pp. xvii, 289. $100.00.

Nelson, Robert H. *Economics as Religion: From Samuelson to Chicago and Beyond.* University Park, PA: Pennsylvania State University Press, 2001. Pp. xxvi, 378. $35.00.

Overheck, Johannes; (Ed.) *Free Trade versus Protectionism: A Source Book of Essays and Readings.* Northampton, MA: Edward Elgar, 1999. Pp. ix, 646.

Peck, Jamie. *Workfare States.* New York: Guilford Press, 2001. Pp. xviii, 413. Paper.

Poitras, Geoffrey. *The Early History of Financial Economics, 1478-1776: From Commercial Arithmetic to Life Annuities and Joint Stocks.* Northampton, MA: Edward Elgar, 2000. Pp. x, 522. $120.00.

Prak, Maarten (Ed.) *Early Modern Capitalism: Economic and Social Change in Europe, 1400-1800.* New York: Routledge, 2001. Pp. xv, 236.

Reynolds, Larry J., and Gordon Hutner (Eds), *National Imaginaries, American Identities.* Princeton, NJ: Princeton University Press, 2000. Pp. xiv, 245. Paper, $17.95.

Rima, Ingrid Hahne. *Development of Economic Analysis.* 6th edition. New York: Routledge, 2001. Pp. xiv, 585. $125.00, cloth; $39.99, paper.

Roemer, John E. *Equality of Opportunity.* Cambridge, MA: Harvard University Press, 2000. Pp. vii, 120. $18.95, paper.

Roncaglia, Alessandro. *Piero Sraffa: His Life, Thought and Cultural Heritage.* New York: Routledge, 2000. Pp. 129. $40.00.

Rothschild, Emma. *Economic Sentiments: Adam Smith, Condorcet, and the Enlightenment.* Cambridge, MA: Harvard University Press, 2001. Pp. ix, 353. $45.00.

Rubenstein, Ariel. *Economics and Language*. New York: Cambridge University Press, 2000. Pp. viii, 128. $42.95, cloth; $15.95, paper.

Schaer, Roland; Gregory Claeys, and Lyman Tower Sargent (Eds), *Utopia: The Search for the Ideal Society in the Western World*. New York: New York Public Library and Oxford University Press, 2000. Pp. xii, 386. $49.95, cloth; $27.50, paper.

Schleifer, Ronald. *Analogical Thinking*. Ann Arbor, MI: University of Michigan Press, 2000. Pp. xiv, 222. $49.50.

Sciabarra, Chris Matthew. *Total Freedom: Toward a Dialectical Libertarianism*. University Park, PA: Pennsylvania State University Press, 2000. Pp. xi, 467. Cloth, $65.00; paper, $24.50.

Shionoya, Yuichi (Ed.) *The German Historical School: The Historical and Ethical Approach to Economics*. New York: Routledge, 2001. Pp. xi, 224.

Singer, Peter. *A Darwinian Left: Politics, Evolution and Cooperation*. New Haven, CT: Yale University Press, 2000. Pp. ix, 70. $9.95.

Skousen, Mark. *The Making of Modern Economics: The Lives and Ideas of the Great Thinkers*. Armonk, NY: M. E. Sharpe, 2001. Pp. xv, 485. Cloth, $74.95; paper, $29.95.

Slesnick, Daniel T. *Consumption and Social Welfare: Living Standards and their Distribution in the United States*. New York: Cambridge University Press, 2001. Pp. vi, 236. $54.95.

Stengers, Isabelle. *The Invention of Modern Science*. Minneapolis, MN: University of Minnesota Press, 2000. Pp. vii, 185. $19.95, paper.

Sutton, John. *Marshall's Tendencies. What Can Economists Know?* Cambridge, MA: MIT Press, 2000. Pp. xvi, 122. $22.95.

Tilman, Rick. *Ideology and Utopia in the Social Philosophy of the Libertarian Economists*. Westport, CT: Greenwood Press, 2001. Pp. xxi, 196.

Toninelli, Pier Angelo. *The Rise and Fall of State-Owned Enterprise in the Western World*. New York: Cambridge University Press, 2000. Pp. xv, 320. $49.95.

Wells, Tom. *Wild Man: The Life and Times of Daniel Ellsberg*. New York: Palgrave, 2001. Pp. xi, 692.

Whatmore, Richard. *Republicanism and the French Revolution: An Intellectual History of Jean-Baptiste Say's Political Economy*. New York: Oxford University Press, 2000. Pp. xiv, 248. $70.00.

Woods, Robert. *The Demography of Victorian England and Wales*. New York: Cambridge University Press, 2000. Pp. xxv, 447. $69.95.